Electronic Performance Support

Electronic Performance Support

Using Digital Technology to Enhance
Human Ability

Edited by
PHILIP BARKER
and
PAUL VAN SCHAIK

 Routledge
Taylor & Francis Group

LONDON AND NEW YORK

First published 2013 by Gower Publishing

2 Park Square, Milton Park, Abingdon, Oxon OX14 4RN
711 Third Avenue, New York, NY 10017, USA

Routledge is an imprint of the Taylor & Francis Group, an informa business

First issued in paperback 2016

British Library Cataloguing in Publication Data
Electronic performance support : using digital technology
   to enhance human ability.
   1. Digital electronics--Social aspects. 2. Performance
   technology. 3. Educational technology. 4. Employees--
   Effect of technological innovations on.
   I. Barker, Philip. II. Schaik, Paul van.
   303.4'834-dc22

ISBN 978-0-566-08884-1 (hbk)
ISBN 978-1-138-25627-9 (pbk)

Library of Congress Control Number: 2009941772

Contents

List of Figures

List of Tables

Acknowledgements

Invariably, most publishing projects involve a substantial number of people, each of whom contributes his/her particular specialist skills and knowledge in order to accomplish the tasks that need to be undertaken. Bearing this in mind, the authors are indebted to all those people who have so willingly offered us their help during the preparation of this book. We would therefore like to thank everyone who has, in any way, been involved in helping us to complete this work.

We would particularly like to thank our colleague Bruce Ingraham who put us in touch with the commissioning editor from Gower Publishing who subsequently put the wheels of the project into motion. Of course, the book would never have been finished without the authors whose contributions have been included. Thank you all for the wonderful efforts you have each made.

Our main contact with Gower Publishing has been through two people: Jonathan Norman and Fiona Martin. Thank you both for your guidance, help, enthusiasm and, above all, the very professional approach that you have adopted throughout the project. Of course, many other staff at Gower Publishing have also contributed to the successful completion of our book. Again, we would like to thank you all – in particular, Gillian Steadman and Charlotte Parkins We think you have done a tremendous job in relation to converting our submitted manuscripts into the completed chapters that make up our book.

While writing this book, many companies and organisations have helped us with technical advice and suggestions. We are particularly appreciative of the help you have so willingly offered to us. My personal thanks (PGB) go to *Garmin International*, *Hewlett Packard* and *Seagate* for permission to use images from their websites for the purposes of illustration. Also, on behalf of the contributing authors, the editors would like to thank all those people and organisations who have given us permission to use their copyrighted material within our book.

Naturally, we are indebted to Professor Tom Reeves of the University of Georgia in the USA who wrote the Foreword to the book. Many thanks for doing such a splendid job.

Finally, both of the editors would like to express their thanks and appreciation to Teesside University (UK) for providing us with time and resources to enable us to produce this book. Philip Barker would also like to express his appreciation to the UK's Higher Education Academy for the provision of a grant (under its National Teaching Fellowship Scheme) to enable some of the research work involved in preparing the book to be undertaken.

Philip Barker and Paul van Schaik
Teesside University, UK.

List of Contributors

The Editors

Philip Barker is the Eyetech Professor of Applied Computing within the School of Computing at Teesside University in the UK. He has published numerous books, research papers and conference publications. He was appointed as a National Teaching Fellow by the UK's Higher Education Academy in 2005 for his outstanding contributions to the development of electronic learning. He has travelled the world giving lectures, workshops and keynote presentations on his research specialisms. These fall broadly into the general area of human-computer interaction and include performance support, digital knowledge management and electronic learning using mobile and hybrid learning technologies.
P.G.Barker@tees.ac.uk
School of Computing, Teesside University, UK.

Paul van Schaik is a Professor of Psychology at Teesside University and a National Teaching Fellow, with a special interest in human-computer interaction. His research focuses on interaction experience ('user experience') including technology acceptance, web-site usability, electronic performance support and the psychology of decision making. His work has been published in leading human-computer interaction journals.
p.van-schaik@tees.ac.uk
School of Social Sciences and Law, Psychology Subject Group, Teesside University, UK.

The Contributors

Ashok Banerji studied for his Ph.D. in the School of Computing and Mathematics at Teesside University in the UK. As a member of the Interactive Systems Research Group, he was the first of a line of postgraduate students to conduct research in the area of electronic performance support systems at Teesside. Since achieving his Ph.D. he has had a distinguished career both in industry and in academia. He has just finished writing the manuscript of a new book entitled Fundamentals of Multimedia that is to be published in 2009. Ashok undertakes research and consultancy projects in the area of electronic performance support systems and teaches online courses at Jones International University.
a.banerji@ieee.org
Faculty: School of Education, Jones International University, Colorado, USA.
Industry: Director, Monisha Electronic Education Trust, Calcutta, India.

Nigel Beacham is a Research Fellow within the School of Education at the University of Aberdeen. After completing his Ph.D. studies into electronic performance support systems with the Interactive Systems Research Group at Teeside University, he worked as a Research Fellow at Loughborough University (in the UK) and subsequently moved to Aberdeen University. His research interests fall broadly into the areas of performance support, electronic learning and assistive technologies for learners with additional support needs. He is particularly interested in exploring the role of computer and information technology in inclusive education and practice. His research has also resulted in the development of a number of commercial support tools within education. He has published numerous papers about his research within international peer-reviewed journals and at conferences and he is a referee for a number of international journals.

N.Beacham@abdn.ac.uk
University of Aberdeen, School of Education, UK.

Oladeji Famakinwa is a Research Assistant working with the Interactive Systems Research Group at Teeside University – from where he recently obtained his M.Sc. award for research into performance support systems. As well as working on an electronic performance support systems project that is funded by the Higher Education Funding Council for England, Oladeji is also registered as a Ph.D. student with the School of Computing. His Ph.D. programme is funded both by the University of Teesside and by a National Teaching Fellowship award made to one of his supervisors (PGB). His research covers the area of electronic performance support in relation to accessing information in both digital and conventional formats. In his spare time, Oladeji is an avid photographer.

O.Famakinwa@tees.ac.uk
School of Computing, Teesside University, UK.

Eran Gal is the e-Learning and Instructional Technologies Manager at Pelephone, a large telecommunications firm in Israel. He has over 10 years of experience as an instructional designer and training manager in large corporations – mainly in implementing technology-based cross-organisational learning solutions. Since 2007 he has been leading a large-scale implementation project of an advanced electronic performance support systems platform, supporting approximately 4,000 users nationwide. He is a doctoral student in the School of Education, Knowledge Technology Lab at the Tel Aviv University. The research is focused on the effectiveness of performance support technology in corporate settings.

eranga@pelephone.co.il
Faculty: School of Education, Tel Aviv University (http://muse.tau.ac.il).
Industry: Pelephone, Israel (www.pelephone.co.il).

Steve Green is the Section Head for Digital Media and the Web within the School of Computing at Teeside University in the UK. He has been actively involved in special-needs and e-learning research since starting a professional research interest in autism and computer-assisted learning in the early 1980s. Currently he researches in areas associated with personal learning environments and open-access systems. He is the Technical Director of a cultural studies e-journal and electronic archive, as well as being a member of the Digital Futures Research Institute and the Pedagogy Research Forum at Teeside University.

S.J.Green@tees.ac.uk
School of Computing, Teesside University, UK.

Barry Ip is Senior Lecturer at Swansea Metropolitan University. His research interests include the design of computer and video games, and the use of learning technology in higher education. He also has a keen interest in a variety of business, health, and research-related topics, having published in the areas of succession planning, customer and market segmentation, quality control, health-services research and research techniques. He is currently working on projects relating to narrative structures in interactive games, assessment procedures for computer games degrees and a longitudinal study into game quality.
Barry.Ip@smu.ac.uk
Swansea Metropolitan University, School of Digital Media, UK.

Christopher G. Jennings is a doctoral student in Computing Science at Simon Fraser University, British Columbia, Canada. His research has focused on computer support of creativity and design, with an emphasis on methods that enable and encourage the consideration of alternatives. He has also contributed to the study of string algorithms, most notably with the 'FJS' ('Franek, Jennings, Smyth') pattern matching algorithm.
cjennings@acm.org
School of Computing Science, Simon Fraser University, Burnaby, BC, Canada.

Arthur E. Kirkpatrick is an Associate Professor of Computing Science at Simon Fraser University, British Columbia, Canada. His research has focused on improving expert performance, through cognitive support as described in Chapter 13 of this book, and also through development of interaction techniques specifically for expert use. For example, the Pokespace technique is designed to distract experts less and allow them to attend more to their domain problem. Arthur is also interested in improving undergraduate computing education.
ted@sfu.ca
School of Computing Science, Simon Fraser University, Burnaby, BC, Canada.

Peyvand Mohseni recently completed her master's degree in Computing Science at Simon Fraser University, British Columbia, Canada. For her masters thesis, she developed the *Treesta* system, a facility to support the performance of the process of statistical analysis. She would like to continue developing systems that improve the performance of people in their everyday lives.
peyvandm@sfu.ca
School of Computing Science, Simon Fraser University, Burnaby, BC, Canada.

Elaine Pearson is a Principal Lecturer in the School of Computing at Teeside University in the UK. She was awarded her Ph.D. at this University for studies into disability and special-needs computing. Her current research interests centre on accessibility issues in relation to promoting and enhancing inclusivity practice.
e.pearson@tees.ac.uk
School of Computing, Teesside University, UK.

Jean Roberts is based in the School of Public Health and Clinical Sciences in the University of Central Lancashire, UK. She is internationally known for 'spreading the word' with regard to health informatics and for her involvement in relation to defining the scope of the discipline. She has worked in and for the NHS, in consultancy and commercial organisations and has an involvement in academic research and teaching in a number of universities. Her research interests include the information implications of the convergence of health, social care and lifestyle management; the inclusion of citizens into their own health management; and the maturing of the professional brand of Health Informatics across the domain of health care.

JRoberts1@uclan.ac.uk
University of Central Lancashire, School of Public Health and Clinical Sciences, UK.

Dick Slettenhaar is based in the Enschede area of the Netherlands. He is an Assistant Professor at ELAN, the Institute for Teacher Education, Science Communication & School Practices at the University of Twente. His current research focus is continual professional development in blended settings. Based on his involvement in the development of and research on realistic mathematics education, his expertise is in evoking and steering learning processes.

H.K.Slettenhaar@utwente.nl
University of Twente, Faculty of Engineering, The Netherlands.

Sjoerd de Vries is Assistant Professor at the University of Twente in the Netherlands. His research interests are the design and implementation of networked communication. His projects focus on knowledge networks, communities of practice and virtual projects. Sjoerd is also co-founder of Konict, a communication consultancy and service provider in networked communication applications. As a Senior Communication Consultant, he is involved in national and international consultancy, and research and development projects. More information can be found at *http://www.rinc.nl* and *http://www.konict.nl*.

S.A.deVries@gw.utwente.nl
University of Twente, Faculty of Behavioural Sciences, The Netherlands.

Foreword

Life, especially our work life, is becoming increasingly complex in the 21st Century. At first glance, this seems counterintuitive given that our performance of work is increasingly supported by ever more sophisticated technology. But new evidence appears on a daily basis that despite ubiquitous powerful technologies such as networked computers, global positioning systems, and cell phones, human failures in decision-making and performance continue to have disastrous consequences. As this book goes to press, the world teeters on the brink of economic depression, ecological devastation, and/or global pandemic, all of which can be traced back to fundamental failures in human performance. On a smaller, local scale, the daily news highlights a plane crash with no survivors 'due to a combination of pilot error and technical faults,' fatal automotive accidents traced to people text-messaging while driving, and deaths from secondary infections stemming from the failure of hospital personnel to disinfect their hands, despite widespread availability of sterilization technologies.

With these and other global and local catastrophes in mind, this book, *Electronic Performance Support: Using Technology to Enhance Human Ability*, reminds everyone involved in education, training, human performance engineering, and related fields of the enormous importance of their efforts. Philip Barker, Paul van Schaik, and the other contributors to this volume provide invaluable insight and guidance that will inform experts as well as novices in all fields related to learning and performance. The extraordinary expertise shared in this book is especially valuable because of the degree to which the authors emphasize the psychological aspects of performance support. The fundamental limitations of human memory, perception, cognition, conation, and psychomotor skills and how they can be reduced through electronic performance support is one of the most important pursuits of this still young century, and this book points the way in a clear and inspiring manner.

Of course, Barker, van Schaik, and their collaborators do not underestimate the importance of technology and its ever increasing impact on our lives. They remind us of Alex Broers' contention that 'Technology will determine the future of the human race.' Moreover, they directly address the obvious corollary question: 'How should we use technology to build performance-support tools to help humankind solve the problems it will face in the future?' The global as well as local challenges we face today are more urgent than most people seem willing to acknowledge, and there is no time to waste putting the ideas expressed in this book into action. Ironically, the more complex technology becomes, the more performance support may be needed. I sincerely hope that the authors' optimism about the power of electronic performance support to enhance learning, problem-solving, and decision-making spreads widely so that the gaps between our potential knowledge and existing knowledge as well as our necessary performance and actual performance are closed. It's not too late... yet.

Thomas C. Reeves

Prelude

Every 'encounter' is a learning event.
Sometimes we learn something new.
Sometimes we change our beliefs about what we think we know.
Oftentimes we realise how little we really know.

Learning is fundamental to everything that we do.
It is as ubiquitous as the air that surrounds us.
It is a powerful agent for change.
It offers a mechanism for personal and social empowerment.

Learning is also important because:
If we know something, we can always know it better,
If we understand something, we can always understand it better,
If we can do something, we can always do it better.

Technology, thoughtfully used, can improve people's quality of life.
Using technology we can raise the limits of what people can achieve.
We can use it to enhance the capability of experts and novices alike.
This is the fundamental rationale underlying 'performance support'.

Electronic technology provides us with many new horizons.
Each new generation extends the capability of what went before.
Digital technologies provide many possibilities for performance support.
This book offers some underlying theory that underpins our ideas.
It also acts as a showcase for some of the things that we can now achieve.

Philip Barker

Foundations

1 *Introduction*

PHILIP BARKER

This initial chapter of the book is intended to provide an introduction to the basic nature of performance support systems (in general) and electronic performance support systems (in particular). The chapter begins by introducing and describing the ideas underlying the use of the term 'system'. It then identifies human-activity systems as being an important issue in relation to the material covered in subsequent chapters of this book. All humans have innate limitations; some of the major causes of these limitations are discussed and some of the consequences of these are illustrated using a selection of anecdotal evidence. Human behaviour and performance in any given task domain is critically dependent on the knowledge and skills that individuals possess. Because much of the work that is undertaken in the area of performance support relates to skill improvement, the chapter discusses the basic nature of skills and skilled performance – and how this may be improved through the use of different types of supportive intervention and/or performance aid. Consideration is then given to the importance of knowledge in relation to skilled performance.

Systems Orientation

In my introductory lectures on the subject of human-computer interaction (HCI), I tell my students that 'everything is a system'. Indeed, according to many theorists, '*the Universe consists of a set of interacting systems*'. So, what exactly is a system? According to Ackoff (1972: p. 84), a system is a '*set of interrelated elements*'. In his definition, however, Jenkins (1972: p. 60) emphasises the role of people when he states that a system is a '*complex grouping of human beings and machines*'. Checkland's view (1972: p. 52; 2001) is that a system is '*a structured set of objects and/or attributes together with the relationships between them*'. Systems and their properties are examined in greater detail as part of the '*soft systems methodology*' described by Checkland and Poulter (2006: p. 7).

Bearing in mind what has been said above, we[1] consider a system to be some part of a physical or abstract universe that has been 'set aside' for the purpose of study. Items that make up the identified system are delineated from items that are not within it by means of the system's boundary. Everything that is not within the system itself is said to

---

1   I often use the term 'we' in my writing to refer to myself and my readers, as a group of people, who are sharing the content of the book. I also use this pronoun to refer to: either (a) myself and my co-editor or (b) to myself and the other contributing authors. In situations where ambiguity may arise, I will make clear my usage.

constitute the environment in which the system exists. Thus, in Figure 1.1, items A, B and C each form part of the system 'X' while objects P, Q and R are not within the system. These latter objects form part of the environment in which the system exists. The line that surrounds the three objects A, B and C is the system boundary.

The environment of a system is important because it can influence both the properties and the behaviour of a system. Similarly, the system itself can have an effect on its environment. The extent to which a system and its environment influence each other will depend upon the 'permeability' of the boundary. That is, how easily energy, material or information can pass through it. Depending upon the relative ease with which this can happen, systems can be broadly classified into two basic types: open and closed.

Any given system can usually be visualised in terms of the various sub-systems from which it is composed and the ways in which these interact with each other. In Figure 1.1, for example, the objects labelled A, B and C could be regarded as the three sub-systems that make up the system X. In a motor-car, three of the important sub-systems are: the electrical sub-system, the steering sub-system and the propulsion sub-system. Similarly, in a human being, three examples of sub-systems would be: the digestive system, the respiratory system and the cognitive system.

Different systems (and sub-systems within a given system) will normally interact with each other by means of the sets of inputs and outputs associated with them. In Figure 1.2, the three systems X, Y and Z influence each other's behaviour by means of the input and output channels that interconnect them. One of the outputs from system X appears as an input to system Y; X can therefore influence the behaviour of Y. Both X and Y can influence the behaviour of system Z. System Z can influence X but cannot influence Y nor can Y directly influence the behaviour of system X.

In a human-computer system, for example, the human component can influence the computer by using its keyboard and its mouse – sometimes speech interaction is also possible. Similarly, the computer component can influence its human user by means of

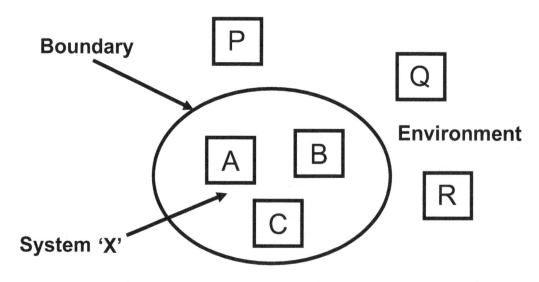

Figure 1.1   A system, its boundary and its environment

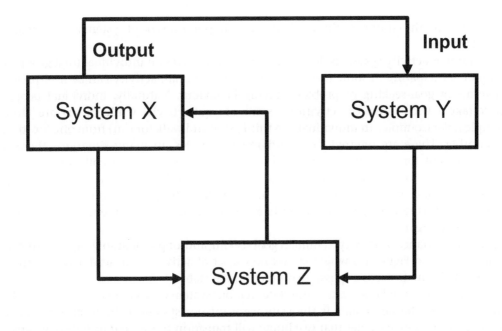

Figure 1.2   System interaction through input/output channels

its visual display unit and the various audio effects that it can produce. Special forms of tactile interaction are also possible.

At any given instant in time, a system will exist in a particular state. A system could change its state (and hence its behaviour) as a result of interaction with other systems or as a result of internal events that take place within its internal sub-systems. For example, a computer could influence its user's state of knowledge as a result of material displayed on its screen. Similarly, the type of action a computer performs could be influenced by what a user types at his/her keyboard.

Systems are an important concept which we will use quite extensively in subsequent parts of this book. We will be particularly concerned with the design and development of Electronic Performance Support Systems. Such systems – often referred to by the acronym 'EPSS' – are computer-based systems that are intended to improve the performance of human beings within some particular task domain. An EPSS is an example of a human-activity system. The origin and nature of human-activity systems are briefly discussed in the following section.

Human-Activity Systems

Bearing in mind that 'everything is a system', there is obviously a very large number of systems in existence. It is therefore very important to have a mechanism by which systems can be classified into different types. Again, Peter Checkland comes to our aid (1972; 2001). He proposed a taxonomy containing five basic types of system: natural systems, designed physical systems, designed abstract systems, human-activity systems and transcendental systems. The latter category refers to systems that are beyond our current state of knowledge – systems that do not currently exist but will exist in the future. Within the context of this book, the most important type of system is the human-activity system.

A human-activity system is defined as one that involves an individual (or a group of people) participating in some form of activity. Most human activity can be interpreted in terms of goal-seeking or problem-solving behaviour. Naturally, individual people undertake a wide range of activities – some are quite trivial while others are more complex. For example, an individual can think, sing and walk (or run) from one location to another. These are referred to as individual activities. In many situations there is a requirement for a group of people to undertake an activity in a collaborative way – thereby functioning as a team. Typical examples of collaborative activity involving a team of people are: a game of football, an army defending (or invading) a country, a surgical team conducting an operation in a hospital and a management team within a company or organisation.

The importance of activity in human goal seeking and/or problem solving is illustrated schematically in Figure 1.3 which shows how a set of activities can lead a system from some initial state towards a (possibly different) final state.

In Figure 1.3, the *initial state* is the state that our system exists in before we undertake any activities. The *target state* is the state we want our system to be in after we have undertaken a set of activities that (we hope) will transform the system into its new target state. Three sets of activities are depicted in Figure 1.3. The first of these (Activity Set 1) leads to a target state that we are trying to achieve. The second activity chain leads to a final state that is not the target that we are trying to achieve while the third activity set has no effect in moving the system out of its initial state.

As was mentioned above, there are many different types of activity. There is a need therefore to have a method of classifying these. One useful approach, from the perspective of this book, is to divide activities into two broad categories: *aided* and *unaided*. These terms are defined and described below.

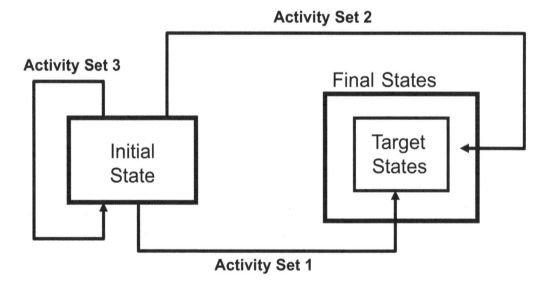

Figure 1.3   System state transitions achieved through activity chains

UNAIDED ACTIVITY

An unaided activity is one which does not require the use of any other form of tool or support aid to facilitate its completion. Nowadays, there are not many activities that we conduct in an unaided way. Some simple examples are: thinking, speaking, walking and reading. The last of these is an interesting one for two reasons. First, an additional system component is needed – namely, something to read (such as a book or newspaper); second, unaided reading assumes that the person who is doing the reading has 'good' eyesight. As people age, their near-vision capability decreases and some form of optical aid is needed to facilitate the reading process – such as spectacles or a magnifying glass. In this situation the reading process has now become an aided activity.

AIDED ACTIVITY

Bearing in mind what has been said above, we can now define an aided activity as one that requires the use of some form of aid, tool or machine in order to complete it satisfactorily. Most of the activities that we now undertake are aided activities. For example, cleaning ones teeth requires the use of a toothbrush – be this of the simple variety or an 'electric' one. Writing a letter or an essay requires us to use a pen, a pencil or a computer-based word-processing system. Similarly, it would be totally impossible to make a telephone call without the use of a mobile phone or a conventional telephone handset.

The concept of aided activity is fundamental to subsequent sections of this book. It is important because we shall be concerned with the design of aids (tools and machines) that will help a human operative to improve his/her performance within some activity that he/she has to undertake. However, before such aids can be designed, it is important to understand the nature of the factors that influence and/or inhibit optimal performance within a given task activity. Some of the limitations that we need to consider are briefly introduced in the following section.

Human Limitations

For a variety of different reasons, and to various extents, human beings are constrained by a range of different kinds of limitation. Some of these are innate or 'inherent' while others are 'acquired'. This section discusses the basic nature of human shortcomings and the sources from which they originate. A number of generic shortcomings are identified as a basis for the development of some of the performance aids that are identified and described in later parts of the book.

INHERENT LIMITATIONS

An *inherent limitation* is one that originates either from some natural cause or arises as a result of a disability that a person may be born with. For example, the distance that an individual can reach with his/her arm (a roughly spherical or cardiod 'touch space' of about three feet in diameter) is a natural innate limitation. Of course, the extent of a person's reach will depend upon the length of that individual's arm when it is fully extended. Naturally, the exact shape of the touch space will vary from one person to another – thereby allowing a range of reach possibilities. An individual's reach limit could be extended by the design of appropriate 'reaching tools'.

Another important source of inherent limitation is that derived from the numerous types of disability from which people may suffer from birth. Thus, people who are born blind, for example, have a very distinct visual limitation compared with those that are born with 'normal' vision.

ACQUIRED LIMITATIONS

Limitations arising from disability can also be 'acquired' as a result of some form of accident or as a result of the natural aging processes. For example, a person who is involved in an accident that subsequently necessitates the amputation of a limb will suffer from quite severe limitations in comparison to what he/she was capable of before the accident. In this type of situation, support aids can be designed to compensate for the loss of the limb but these may require the acquisition of new skills.

THE AGING PROCESS

As people grow older, significant changes can take place in their bodies. These changes will, quite naturally, influence what they are able to do and achieve in later life. Therefore, as people with perfectly 'normal' health profiles grow older, they will begin to develop age-related (acquired) disabilities. Two of the most obvious changes that people notice as they grow older are the deficiencies that arise in their visual and aural systems. Of course, these degradations can be compensated for and corrected by means of appropriately designed 'performance interventions' – spectacles and hearing aids, respectively.

DISABILITY

There is a tremendous range of both physical and mental disability[2] that can afflict the human species. Needless to say, a considerable amount of research has been undertaken in relation to the design and fabrication of performance support aids that allow different types of disability to be overcome or, at least, coped with. With many types of disability, the use of an appropriate performance intervention can restore the victim of disability to 'near normal' health again. In lots of other situations, such interventions may not restore full 'normality' but can be used successfully in order to improve the sufferer's ability to cope with his/her predicament.

HUMAN LIMITATIONS – SOME EXAMPLES

In order to demonstrate the existence of innate limitations, four simple examples will be used. These will illustrate the natural limits that are placed upon our ability to do things – and how these limits can be overcome through appropriate aids and tools.

---

2   The word 'disability' is used here in a generic way to reflect any sort of human shortcoming such as impairments and handicaps of various sorts.

Example 1: Ambulation

As a person who enjoys walking and running, I have often pondered about people's limits in terms of the distance and speed with which the unaided human species can ambulate from one location to another. Of course, there will be innate limits on both the maximum speed and distance that can be covered. In order to overcome these physical barriers to movement, performance aids are often used; a scooter, a bicycle, a car, a ship, a train and an aeroplane are typical examples of the 'aids' that we employ in order to move ourselves around. For people who are disabled, various kinds of disability aid can be used to support their ambulation processes – such as crutches, artificial limbs, wheelchairs and mobility scooters.

Example 2: Sound production

The range of sounds that the human voice can produce is very impressive. However, the number of different sounds each individual can achieve varies considerably from one person to another. Despite what it can do, the human voice is very restricted in terms of the range, quality and intensity of the sounds that it can produce. Therefore, in order to extend the repertoire of human sonic ability, a wide range of musical instruments have evolved. These have been based on different physical principles for sound generation – for example, percussion and string or wind vibration. The range of sounds that can be produced by human effort can also be augmented through the use of computer-generated digital music and sound effects.

Example 3: Simple arithmetic

The human mind is quite a remarkable 'machine' in terms of what it can do – particularly in terms of its ability to reason things out – in both inductive and deductive ways. It is also quite good at doing simple arithmetical computations – provided the numbers involved are not too complex. For example, by the time they leave school, most people can add together a list of simple numbers (such as, 23+13+16+17) or multiply two numbers together without the need for pencil and paper. However, if the numbers become more complicated, the computational limitations of the human mind soon become apparent. Consider, for example, adding together a string of numbers such as 23.582+13.738+16.949+17.697, or multiplying 389 by 986. These computations are too difficult for most people to do 'in their head'. Consequently, an electronic calculator or a procedure involving the use of pencil and paper would be needed.

Example 4: Remembering things

As well as its computational ability, the human brain is also quite good at remembering things and making associations between different events and the various phenomena to which it is exposed via our sense organs. However, it has severe limitations both with respect to how much it can remember and to the level of detail that can be recalled. For example, there are very few people who could recall, without the aid of a diary, what they were doing on their tenth birthday – or, for that matter, any of their other birthdays. Sadly, human memory shortcomings are a major limitation in relation to human behaviour – especially in situations where 'remembering things' is of prime importance.

Major sources of natural human limitation

We have already mentioned some of the human species' natural limitations earlier in this section. These were specific examples that apply to most people. It is important to consider the 'deep-rooted', underlying causes of the limitations from which we suffer. Obviously, there will be a number of sources that are either singularly, or in-combination, responsible for our shortcomings. Some of the most often cited sources of our limitations are listed in Table 1.1.

Table 1.1   Common sources of human performance shortcomings

Perceptual Limitations	Lack of Motivation
Attentional Limitations	Laziness
Processing-speed Limitations	Clumsiness
Memory Shortcomings	Carelessness
Problem-solving Limitations	Reaction-time Limitations
Decision-making Limitations	System Overload
Language Limitations	Distractions
Physical Limitations	Physical Disability
Lack of Knowledge	Mental Disability
Lack of Skills	

Cognitive limitations arise from our inability to perform cognitive processes – such as mental arithmetic and decoding material that we read from books or on the Internet. Many of the errors or mistakes that a human being makes can often arise from either memory or perceptual causes. That is, an inability to remember something or to be able to understand the meaning of an event or issue. In addition, there can be limitations which arise from cognitive and/or physical problems. Physical limitations arise as a result of limits that our bodies place on the activities we undertake – for example, how far we can run or walk and how quickly we can write or type at a keyboard.

Sometimes, a plain lack of knowledge can be the cause of a poor performance in the things that we do – or would like to do. For example, when driving a car, not knowing which route to take when going from one place to another can result in getting lost – unless the vehicle being driven is fitted with a 'sat-nav' facility. Similarly, a lack of requisite skills can also be a source of poor performance which thereby imposes limitations on what we can achieve or undertake. For example, a person who cannot swim could not participate in water-sports such as water polo or scuba diving. Motivation is another important factor that influences and places limits on what an individual can achieve.

Many human limitations can often be overcome by means of an appropriately designed performance support intervention – like the satellite-navigation system that was mentioned above. We shall discuss the nature of these performance interventions in subsequent parts of this book.

Anecdotal Evidence

In order to illustrate some of the 'unusual' behaviour that can be caused by the human shortcomings identified in the previous sections, one of us (PGB) sat down and thought about a number of different events that happened to him during a recent period of time (the summer of 2007). Some of these are briefly described below; each event is a consequence of some of the human limitations that were listed in the previous section.

LOST CABLES

I recently made a business trip to Taiwan. When my travel requires absence from home for more than a day or two, I usually take with me a number of 'power sources'. Normally, I take a battery charger for my *iPod*, one for my digital camera and yet another for my mobile phone. Some days into my visit (and now in my third hotel), I needed to charge my *iPod*. I looked in my baggage for the cables but I could not find them. I then wondered whether or not I had actually packed these cables before leaving home. Maybe I had put them ready to be packed and then, for some reason, forgot to put them into my suitcase? When I got back home from my trip, I searched everywhere in my house for the missing cables – but I was unable to find them. Where could they be? I then sat quietly and reflected on my trip; suddenly, with a 'flash of inspiration', I remembered what I had done. I had taken the cables out of my suitcase and put them in one of the drawers of the dressing table at the first hotel that I stayed in. When I left that hotel, I forgot to retrieve the cables from the drawer and pack them into my baggage. I immediately e-mailed my host and explained what had happened; he rang the hotel. The hotel staff found my cables in the location that I described in my e-mail and they were eventually returned to me.

LOST RAILCARD

Within the UK it is possible to get reductions in the cost of personal rail travel provided one is in possession of a railcard. Some time ago I lost mine. I remember using it to make a travel booking but subsequently could not find it anywhere. I therefore had to buy a new one – some three months before my old one was due to expire. Not only was I irritated by the fact I could not remember where I put it, I was also upset by the extra financial burden I had to bear. Several weeks after this event, I had to replace the toner cartridge for my laser printer. As I was withdrawing the expended cartridge, I found my lost railcard sitting inside the printer on top of the paper contained within the input tray. How on earth did it get there? Well, I can only think that I placed the railcard on the paper tray (see Figure 1.4) and then, forgetting that it was there, printed out a document. As the paper fed into the printer, so my railcard went with it! Of course, I had forgotten where I had 'temporarily' placed the card and so did not think of looking inside my printer. Mystery solved!

AN EARLY BIRTHDAY CARD

One morning in mid-August I received a telephone call from my sister. I had recently sent her a birthday card and was about to arrange to have some flowers sent to her. She

Figure 1.4   The wrong place to put a railcard

thanked me for the card and commented on how nice it was. She then explained that it was just a little early – in fact, two months early! So, I thanked her for reminding me and told her that this year she would get two birthday cards from me – I would send another in October (along with the flowers that I was just about to send but then rescheduled). How did this happen? On reflection, I realised that I had confused my (now deceased) mother's birth date with that of my sister. This event shows just how easily one can get confused. Of course, had I checked in my diary, this would not have happened. I was 'negligent' and paid the price – an incorrectly sent birthday card.

A LOST SOCK

I belong to a rambling club and do quite a lot of walking over rough terrain. I usually wear two pairs of socks with my walking boots: a thin pair next to my skin and a thick pair on top. Every weekend, we hire a coach to take us to the location where we are going to walk. I usually put my walking socks on while travelling on the coach. One day I took two thin socks and two thick socks out of my bag. I successfully fitted my thin socks but found that I was short of a thick sock. I got on my hands and knees and crawled around the area where I was sitting in order to search for my missing sock – but could not find it anywhere. A friend said that he had a pair of socks I could borrow. So, I proceeded to take off the thick sock from my left foot – only then to find that I had (inadvertently) fitted two thick socks to my left foot! Why was this? I guess I was distracted and lost my concentration. I was so busy talking to people as I was putting on my socks, I failed to notice that I had put two thick socks on one foot.

DUPLICATE PURCHASES

Like many other people, I have quite a sizable collection of music CDs. Naturally, because of my memory limitation, I am always at a loss with respect to being able to recall the details of any particular CD that I own. Of course, I have a good idea of which composers are in my collection and I have a general 'feel' for the material that I have from each composer and artist. Despite this, on numerous occasions I have made CD purchases in music shops only to find when I get home that the purchase I made is already present in my collection. Consequently, I then have to take my purchase back to the CD shop and exchange it for something else. Incidentally, I have exactly the same problem with my large collection of paperback books that I use for light reading, entertainment and relaxation!

KNOWING WHERE TO GO

Quite often, when I travel to a new city or town that I have not previously visited, I am 'at a loss' in knowing where things are and how things are done. Although the meta-knowledge that I have gained from previous similar situations and experiences is useful, I lack the detailed local knowledge needed to handle my new situation. As I spend time exploring the city, I gradually acquire the knowledge that I need in order to locate things (such as the local supermarket) and how to get things done (for example, travelling from one part of the city to another). This knowledge, once acquired, will usually 'stay with me' for the duration of my visit – and can normally be recalled on subsequent visits. However, the amount I retain and the ease of recall invariably depends upon how often I visit the city and the frequency between the visits that I make.

KNOWING WHAT TO DO

For many years I have been a very keen photographer. I recently purchased a new digital camera. This camera had considerably more functions than any of the previous ones I have owned. Of course, the problem was there were so many potentially useful facilities (and so many buttons to press) that I did not know what to do in order to take, and subsequently manipulate, my photographs. Indeed, it took me quite a while both to figure out how everything worked and to gain the skills needed in order to take respectable photographs. Of course, my meta-knowledge of digital cameras was a useful starting point. However, learning 'what to do' required some investment of time in terms of reading both the paper-based and electronic manuals that accompanied my new camera. Of course, some considerable practice was needed before my skills developed.

On the Nature of Skills

In any human activity, success (or failure) depends very much on the amount of knowledge that an individual (or team) has and the level of skills that he/she/ (or it) possesses (Barker, 1990: p. 130). Much of our research into performance support is concerned with helping people to develop and/or improve the skills that they have. It is therefore important to understand the basic purpose and nature of a skill.

Essentially, a skill is a physical or mental ability (or dexterity) that a person has and which enables some task or goal to be achieved. More precisely, a skill (or set of skills) is essentially a collection of one or more executable procedures that an operative uses in order to successfully complete a task or job in an effective and/or efficient way, thereby producing some desired outcome or artefact. Skills are often associated with some particular domain of expertise. Table 1.2 lists some examples of different skill domains.

Table 1.2   Examples of types of skill domain

Mathematical
Scientific
Engineering
Management
Musical
Artistic
Dancing
Writing
Communication

Skills are used to achieve particular goals as a result of executing the different tasks involved in a given 'doing' activity – as depicted schematically in Figure 1.5. In this diagram, the collection of skills that is needed in order to achieve some desired outcome is referred to as a skill set.

Normally, the procedure that we would use in order to convert an intent (to achieve something) into a sought-after result would usually be as follows: (1) identify the doing activity that is required to achieve the desired goal; (2) identify the skill set needed in order to execute the tasks involved; (3) acquire the necessary skills; (4) practise the

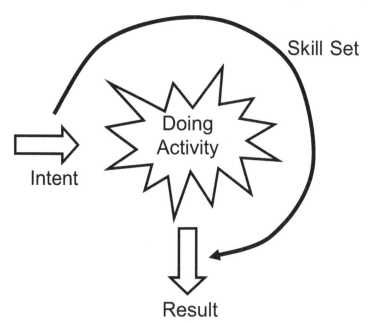

Figure 1.5   Using skill sets to realise 'doing' activities

skills in order to achieve the required levels of competence; (5) use the skills within the doing activity; and (6) create the outcome, result or product. However, in many cases, the procedure may not be followed because of the 'paradox of the active user' (Carroll, 1987): first, users may not be willing to spend the time required to acquire the necessary skills (assimilation failure) and, second, they may employ previously acquired skills that do not apply to the current situation (accommodation failure). Thus the paradox of the active user provides a justification for the importance of performance support discussed later in this chapter and in the following chapters of this book. The procedures involved in developing the skills needed to become a skilful domain expert have been captured in the MAPARI model of skill acquisition (Barker, 1994). This model is considered in detail later in Chapter 4.

The skills that any given individual has can be classified into two basic types: innate and acquired. An innate skill is one which someone possesses as a natural consequence of his/her existence. Examples of innate skills include: the ability to observe one's environment using visual techniques; the recognition of pleasant and unpleasant aromas using one's sense of smell; the sensing of different acoustic stimuli; tactile sensing; and the generation of sonic utterances of various sorts. Acquired skills are ones that are developed through the processes of learning and training; they can usually be 'fine-tuned' and enhanced as a result of practice. For example, people can learn how to sing and then have their voices trained so as to produce acceptable sounds. Similarly, an individual could learn how to play a musical instrument and then practise with it in order to achieve a required level of accomplishment. The relationship between practice and increased speed of skilled performance is embodied in a famous law called the 'Power Law of Practice' (Card, Moran and Newell, 1983). We shall discuss this topic in more detail later in the book.

Two very important examples of acquired skills are reading and writing. These are quite complex activities that can themselves involve a variety of skill sets. For example, if we consider reading, the skills needed will depend upon the type of reading process involved – silent reading, reading aloud, reading to understand, and so on. Within the context of silent reading (for understanding), the level of skill that a person shows will depend very much upon the cognitive complexity of the material being read and the amount of experience and tuition that a person has had. The level of skill that a person shows will usually be reflected in the speed with which the material can be read, the accuracy of reading (at both the lexical and cognitive levels) and the ease with which the reader can extract the meaning that is embedded in the material being processed. Of course, reading aloud involves extra skills – for example, the vocalisation of the material as it is being read without making any mistakes (either in the reading process or in the pronunciation). Newsreaders have particularly high levels of skill when reading aloud. Skill levels and performance is considered further in the following section.

The skills that a person has will invariably influence his/her approach to problem solving and, therefore, the nature of the activity chains that he/she designs in order to solve a problem or achieve a sought-after goal. One possible relationship between problem-solving activity and the skill sets that a human may possess is depicted schematically in Figure 1.6.

In Figure 1.6, we are attempting to show that humans (and hence, human behaviour) are influenced by internal mental processes such as creative thinking and reflective thought. These can generate ideas that can be used within a problem-solving context. Of course, human behaviour is also strongly influenced by the wide variety of internal

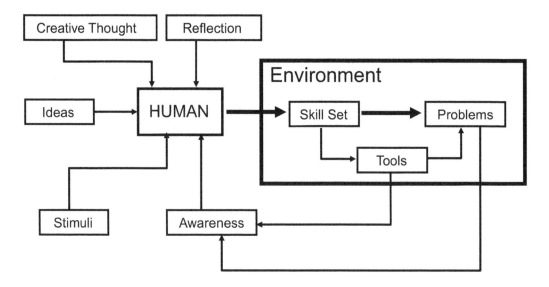

Figure 1.6   Skill sets and problem-solving activity

and external stimuli to which individuals may be exposed; these originate from a wide variety of different sources. Depending upon their origin, these stimuli could act as a powerful source of motivation – or, contrariwise – of demotivation. People's motivation to solve any particular problem will depend critically on their having an awareness that a particular problem exists – and also, an awareness of the tools that are available for solving it. Self-realisation is also a powerful motivational force – the realisation that one has (or does not have) the necessary skills that are needed to solve a particular problem.

Figure 1.6 also shows how a skill set can be used within the context of problem-solving activity. In this context, the term is used to denote a particular collection of skills that an individual or a group of people use in order to solve problems (a 'doing activity') within a particular type of problem-solving environment. Notice that the skill set shown in Figure 1.6 could involve the use of appropriate devices and/or tools and/or machines as aids to help in the problem-solving activity. We have discussed the concept of aided activity earlier in this chapter. It is important to emphasise the fact that the nature of the skill sets needed in any given situation will depend critically upon the types of problem being solved and the kinds of environment within which these problems exist. The environment that hosts a given problem can be classified according to its complexity and the demands that it places on problem solvers. Three typical examples of categories of environment are: *challenging* (for example, flying an aeroplane), *mundane* (for example, washing dishes) and *creative* (for example, painting a picture or creating a sculpture).

From the perspective of designing performance support facilities, the relationship between devices, tools and machines and human skills is an interesting one – this is depicted schematically in Figure 1.7.

This diagram is intended to convey four important facts. First, individuals are endowed with various sets of skills. Second, humans have the ability to design and create various kinds of tools and machines. Third, human skill sets will be strongly influenced by the nature of the tools/machines available within different kinds of application domain. Fourth, human design and fabrication skills will also strongly influence the nature of the

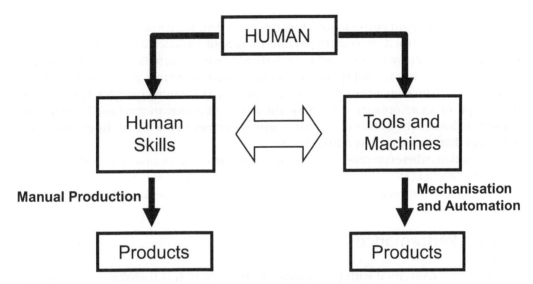

Figure 1.7   Relationship between tools and human skills

tools and machines that can be produced. We have previously considered the difference between aided and unaided activity. Of course, tools and machines are a vital component of any sort of aided activity environment. Depending upon the application environment, the products referred to in Figure 1.7 could be a motor-car, a poem, a book, an action or just a transient thought. It is important to remember that many products (such as a motor-car or an aeroplane) could not be produced without suitable tools or machines. Similarly, we must remember that there are no tools available to create some types of product.

When people use tools and/or machines to augment their ability to solve problems, it is important to realise that there will invariably be some form of interface between the tool/machine/device and its user – as illustrated schematically in Figure 1.8.

CR = Control Requirement
CE = Control Execution

FS = Feedback Status
FD = Feedback Information Display

Figure 1.8   The basic function of a human-machine interface

There are two main purposes for a user interface: first, to enable a user of a device, tool or machine to control it; second, to provide a source of feedback information relating to the status of the artefact being used for a particular activity. Interfaces vary considerably in their characteristics, quality and capability. Some interfaces are quite simple (for example, the handle on a teacup or a mug) while others are more complex (for example, the cockpit of an aeroplane). Invariably, the nature of a human-machine interface will strongly influence the nature of the skills needed in order to use it and the quality of the outcomes that can be achieved from its use.

In situations where computers play an important part of the tool/machine architecture (as will be the case in EPSS – as discussed in this book), the design of human-computer interfaces will be an important issue to consider. We shall return to this issue later – in Chapter 3.

What is Performance?

This section is concerned with performance-related issues. It is therefore important that we clearly establish exactly what we mean by the term 'performance' – and the related concepts of 'performance improvement' and 'performance support'. First, let us consider the meaning of the term 'system performance'.

We can think of the performance of a system as reflecting how well its behaviour matches some required desired outcome. Even though they are very relative things, and are very context sensitive issues, most people understand the notions of good and bad. For example, having seen a play, we may describe the performance of the actress who portrayed a particular character as 'good'. Similarly, after having experienced an orchestral concert we may say that the orchestra's rendering of the music that it played was very 'bad'. On the other hand, we could take a 'middle-of-the-road' judgement and describe something as 'acceptable'. Figure 1.9 shows a diagram that allows us to classify certain cost-speed relationships (for a particular type of machine) into one or other of the three categories of *good*, *bad* or *acceptable*.

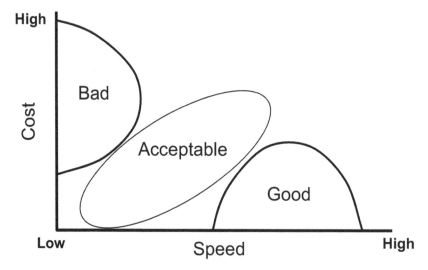

Figure 1.9   Classification of system performance

In most cases, a level of performance is measured against some standard that needs to be achieved. Bearing this in mind, it is possible to identify three broad levels of performance in relation to the standard: *satisfactory* (the standard has been achieved), *below standard* (the standard has not been achieved and some improvement is necessary in order to achieve it) and *above standard* (an individual's performance lies above that required by the standard).

In many cases, the standards or merits by which we judge things are quite arbitrary. Coming to an agreement about things, that is, reaching a consensus view about our performance assessment metrics is therefore very important if we are truly to understand what we mean by 'good' or 'bad' performance. Obviously, in order to pass judgment on things we need to have a judgemental framework or a set of judgement values that enable us to classify something as good, bad or acceptable. The use of a judgemental framework is illustrated in some recent work that we undertook relating to the assessment of the relative quality of a series of World Wide Web sites (Barker, 2006). Each of the evaluators involved had to rate the performance of a set of ten websites by ranking them into order – best first, worst last. A quantification algorithm was then used to assess the group's overall view about the sites that had been examined.

A judgemental framework can be regarded as a multi-dimensional space in which each dimension represents an attribute (of a performance/product) for which a good/bad decision has to be made. The summation of the outcomes for each decision then allows us to come to an overall conclusion about how we feel about something's goodness, badness or acceptability. Of course, the decisions that we make do not have to be simple yes or no choices; a rating can be given – say on a scale of 0–10 or 0–100. Thus, the performance of a student who gains 100 per cent in an examination could be described as good while that of one who achieves 0 per cent could be deemed to be bad. Similarly, a student achieving 50 per cent could be classified as acceptable. In many cases the attributes do not represent a single underlying dimension (or 'factor'), but each dimension represents one of two or more underlying dimensions of quality. The scores on the attributes are then added for each underlying dimension to produce a 'quality profile' pertaining to these (Tabachnick and Fidell, 2007).

Naturally, once we have made a decision on the merits of something, we should be able to use our judgemental framework to explain why something is good or bad. If something is not good (or not good enough), we should also be able to use our judgemental framework in order to explain why this is the case and how the situation may be improved upon. Hence, the appropriate use of a judgemental framework can be used as a basis for a performance improvement mechanism. In general, we define 'performance improvement' within a system as a change in its behaviour in order to achieve a more desirable state. Using the 'examination performance' example that was introduced above, if a student (who wants to learn about information technology, say) has done badly in his/her computer programming examination, an analysis of the relevant judgemental framework (examination question paper and student's answer script) should enable us to recommend various activities that will lead to a performance improvement in this subject.

Performance improvement is an important requirement of performance support systems. It is therefore essential that we are able to measure the improvements that have been gained as a result of introducing a particular performance support intervention. If it is necessary, we should also be able to justify the gains that have been achieved in terms of cost benefit or an improved 'quality of life' for those involved in using the intervention. For example, suppose we have a machine or process that produces a particular product at a given rate – but which fails to meet the required demand for the product. Of course, improving the performance of the machine in order to produce more items per unit time would be beneficial in terms of meeting the demand for the product. It could also lead to a financial gain in terms of greater sales and a possible increase in customers' satisfaction in terms of product availability.

In the above example, we have introduced three basic ways of measuring the performance of a system: increased output, an increase in financial income and an improvement in customers' satisfaction with the product or service. These measures of system performance are often referred to as performance indicators. When designing and creating performance support tools it is also important that we simultaneously identify appropriate performance measures that will enable us to assess the merits of the tools that we provide – in terms of the increases in performance that can be achieved. This is especially true in the case of a complex, multi-parameter electronic performance support system of the type depicted in Figure 1.10.

In the example shown in Figure 1.10, the inputs to the EPSS will represent various constraints and variabilities (such as different levels of human performance capability) that the system will need to accommodate. Relevant control parameters will normally be available in order to 'fine-tune' the performance of the EPSS facility so that its overall output is optimal for the prevailing set of input variables.

This section has explained the meaning of the term 'performance' and how 'performance indicators' can be used to measure the quality of a system's performance – and, hopefully, then improve the way in which it performs (if it is possible to do so). It is also important to consider why we need to monitor and improve performance. This issue is discussed in the following section.

Why Improve Performance?

This section addresses the question of why we may want to improve the performance of a system. We start with a personal reflection on this issue (PGB). On the top of my

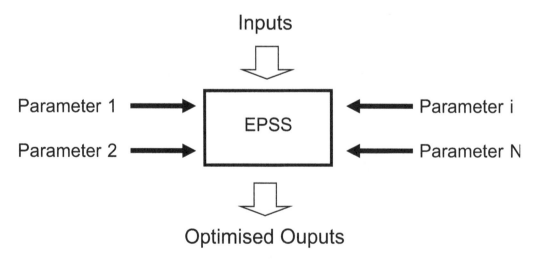

Figure 1.10 Multi-parameter EPSS facility

computer display screen I have a banner that reads: 'Continuous Improvement Through Positive Incremental Change'. I keep this here as a reminder, both to myself and others who see it, about the need to always achieve the best possible solution that we can when solving any particular problem that confronts us. If a problem can be solved, there will invariably be quite a wide range of solutions – but it may not always be easy to find the best one. Quite naturally, I take a pride in what I do and I always want to achieve the best possible results that I can – within the constraint limitations that are imposed upon me. I am therefore always looking for better, more efficient and more effective ways of doing things – because that's just the way I am! In this context, I am sure that there are lots (and lots and lots...) of other people just like me.

In a broader context, let us now consider some performance improvement issues relating to the more general area of consumer products and services. Here, of course, it is important to remember that, when buying something, most people will want to achieve 'value for money' in terms of the purchases they make – be these 'hard' physical commodities (such as refrigerators or motor-cars) or 'softer' services (such as the provision of Internet access or a telephone service). Bearing this in mind, we have to realise that most people would like to have the best motor-car possible for the given financial outlay that they can afford to make. As well as 'best products', people also want to receive the best quality services within the price range they can afford. In a competitive world, products and services which do not strive to become the best available (within their price range) are unlikely to survive. In this context, 'survival' is taken to mean a growth in sales and high levels of satisfaction in a product's consumer population. Achieving this usually means ongoing improvement in a product (or service) in order to meet the changing demands of its marketplace.

Bearing in mind what was said above, it is important that organisations (and the people that they employ) are mindful of the need for continual ongoing performance improvement. This point is admirably made by Gloria Gery in her seminal book on improving workplace performance (Gery, 1991). The case for this has also been made by William Bezanson (2002) in his book and in our own research (Banerji, 1995; Barker, 1995; Beacham, 1998; Flinders, 2000; Famakinwa, 2004; van Schaik, Barker and Famakinwa, 2006, 2007; van Schaik, Pearson and Barker, 2002).

From the perspective of human performance, it is well known that a person's skill at performing a task usually improves with practice. Ackerman (2007) has examined this issue in the context of understanding the nature of skilled performance in both physical and cognitive tasks. This increase in performance with practice is summarised in the 'Power Law of Practice' that was described earlier in this chapter (Card, Moran and Newell, 1983). Unfortunately, due to natural and innate human limitations, a person's performance does not improve indefinitely; there comes a point at which further practice does not produce any further substantial improvement in performance – see Figure 1.11 (Barker, van Schaik and Famakinwa, 2007).

So, when a person's skill level plateaus out (as shown in Figure 1.11), how can his/her performance then be improved? The answer, of course, lies in the study of performance support. Indeed, one of the fundamental motivations for studying this topic is the need to discover appropriate interventions that will shift the skill bands shown in Figure 1.11 from their 'natural' levels (lower solid curves) upwards towards their 'augmented' levels (upper dotted curves). That is, in the direction of greater skill levels and, as a consequence, improved performance. As the diagram shows, appropriate augmentation through

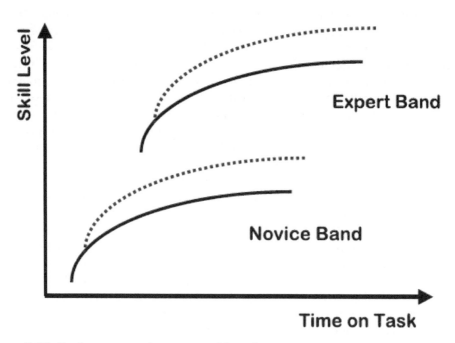

Figure 1.11 Performance plateaus and bands

performance support can be used to improve the quality of task execution for both novice and expert performers. This maxim also applies to people in general – and the problems they face. Obviously, the extent of the improvement that is made will depend critically upon the nature of the performance interventions that are introduced.

For various reasons, as people grow older, their skill levels can start to 'fall off'. For example, there comes a time when their vision, hearing and information-processing speed (amongst other things) start to deteriorate. For example, older people find it increasingly difficult to read the small print instructions on medicine bottles – or to determine the denomination of coins (other than by their physical size). Failing faculties can lead to a deterioration in the quality of an aging person's lifestyle. In order to combat this (in the context of sight and hearing), various visual and acoustic performance improvement interventions have been developed (such as spectacles, magnifying glasses and hearing aids) that enable failing faculties to be compensated for. These performance-improving aids can obviously help to restore an aging person's quality of life. Of course, even people with normal vision and hearing will often have to use special types of aid to improve their performance. For example, an astronomer may use an optical telescope (or a radio telescope) in order to get a better view of distant stars and planets. Similarly, a doctor is likely to use a stethoscope in order to listen to a patient's heartbeat.

Another extremely important reason for wanting to improve performance comes from a consideration of the many problems that are inherent in overcoming human disability. This area of study is not unrelated to the 'aging problem' that was described above. During their lifetimes people can become afflicted with a wide range of impairments, resulting in disability; unfortunately, some people are born with these. A considerable amount of research and development effort is put into creating performance aids that will help disabled people cope with the problems they have. A particularly interesting example of this is described in the following section; this involves combining computer and robotic technologies to create performance aids that will help stroke victims to regain the use of their limbs. Further examples of the use of EPSS in helping people overcome disabilities are discussed later in the book.

Of course, there are numerous other reasons why improving performance should be considered as imperative within many domains. Indeed, some increasingly pressing problems are to be found in the areas of *resource conservation* and *cost minimisation* – especially in the commercial and business sectors. When solving problems we always try to minimise the cost and time involved in realising a particular goal. Achieving this often depends upon minimising energy, effort and material utilisation. Invariably, improving the overall performance of a system can often lead to a reduction in its energy consumption or its material requirements – thereby leading to a subsequent reduction in the cost of running that system. A simple example can be used to illustrate this point.

Consider the amount of energy involved in heating a house; much of the heat that is 'injected' into a house often escapes through the walls, roof, windows and doors. By improving the thermal efficiency of the house (through the use of wall cavity insulation, loft insulation, double glazing and draft excluder) the heat loss can be substantially reduced. Less energy would therefore be needed to heat the house – thus leading to an overall reduction in energy costs.

There are, of course, many areas where a global improvement in performance is needed – for example, in reducing carbon emission in order to try to halt the process of global warming. There is a growing body of evidence to suggest that there is a relationship between the world's carbon dioxide production and the rapid changes that are taking place in the earth's form (melting polar ice caps and rising sea levels) and climate. There is therefore a tremendous performance support problem inherent in solving this problem – namely, finding mechanisms of energy production and use that are safe and do not generate carbon dioxide.

In this section we have tried to use appropriate examples and illustrations in order to explain some of the reasons why performance support and performance improvement are so important. The 'bottom-line' is, of course, that improvements in the performance of a system can lead to a reduction (either directly or indirectly) in the costs associated with that system.

The Role of Technology

In a modern, technology-driven society, much of what we do depends critically on the use of appropriate technology to support the tasks and activities that we have to undertake. For example, distant travel depends upon the use of a bicycle, motor-cycle, automobile, bus, train, ship or aeroplane. Similarly, effective communication depends upon the use of computer systems, radio, television and a telephone network. Maintaining our gardens is also very dependent upon the availability of appropriate tools and machines – such as a spade, a rake, a wheelbarrow and a motor-mower for cutting the grass. In his famous book, *The Age of Automation*, Sir Leon Bagrit (1965) advocated the thesis that all technology was essentially an extension of human faculties. This is a view to which we strongly subscribe.

Naturally, 'history moves on'! It is therefore important to remember that the ways in which we lived 100 years ago are not necessarily the same as how we live today. For example, we had no television, no motor-cars and certainly no computer systems. Bearing this in mind, it is highly unlikely that today's ways of living will be similar to those that will be experienced 100 years hence. Indeed, the kinds of problem we will face and the types of task that we will need to perform in the future will, in all probability, be very different from those which we undertake now. As an example, think of the ways in which the process of 'writing' has changed during the time human beings have existed – that is the transition from markings on sand or the walls of a cave to the use of electronic symbols within a computer. Bearing this in mind, it is important to realise that, as new types of problem-solving task emerge (due to the evolution of new industries and new directions of human development), so there will be an ongoing need for the development of new types of tool and machine to perform the tasks that human beings are unable to perform in an unaided way.

Within the area of performance support, technology (in the broadest sense) is extremely important because it provides the necessary resources from which many different types of internal (within the human body) and external performance aids can be constructed. From the particular perspective of this book, computers (and their related infrastructures) are undoubtedly the most important type of technology – but it is not the only technology that we need to consider. In order to produce the most effective solution to a performance support problem it will usually be necessary to seek a solution in which some form of computer technology is combined with other types of relevant technology. This is a topic which is further considered in Chapter 3.

USING COMPUTER TECHNOLOGY

The major thrust of this book deals with the use of computer technology for developing performance support systems. We therefore need to consider the basic nature of this technology. There are three major functions that a computer can perform: computation, data storage and communication. Computation uses the machine's ability to perform pre-programmed mathematical calculations at high speed; it also deals with the ability of a computer to 'take decisions' and therefore control other devices attached to it. Data storage refers to the ability of a computer to store large quantities of data, information and knowledge in electronic form – and make this available at any particular point of need, when required, to those who need it. Communication refers to the potential of a computer system to send messages to other computers and devices – thereby indirectly facilitating human communication.

Computer technology can manifest itself in a variety of forms. The most obvious of these is the explicit form; this category is represented by such artefacts as personal desktop computers (PCs), laptop systems and hand-held devices like a personal digital assistant (PDA). A typical example of this type of device is shown in the photograph in Figure 1.12.

In the illustration presented in Figure 1.12, the 'pencil-like' stylus device lying beneath the PDA is used to facilitate its user's interaction with it. This can be achieved in two basic ways: first, by means of pointing operations made on its screen; and second, using various forms of writing activity on the surface of the screen. Some PDAs are equipped with a miniature keyboard that enables its user to type in information – in much the same

Figure 1.12 Example of an explicit computer system – a PDA

way as a conventional PC or laptop computer is used.

The other major form of computer-based facility is that in which the actual computer is itself embedded within some other kind of technology. Examples of embedded applications include: washing machines, microwave cookers and mobile phones. An interesting medical application of embedded computer support (within robotic devices) has recently been described by Young (2007) in which this type of electronic performance support technology is helping stroke victims to recover from their debilitating conditions. As is the case in this example, the optimal solution to this performance support problem has been achieved by combining computer technology with other types of support technology – an important point that was made earlier in this section.

USING EXPLICIT COMPUTERS AS SUPPORT TOOLS

There are a number of ways in which explicit computer technology (both hardware and software) can improve human performance. The term 'information and communication technology' (ICT) is often used to describe different approaches to combining computer-related technology and communication technology in order to create different types of performance-enhancing environment. Typical examples of these include the Internet, the World Wide Web and integrated information processing packages such as *Microsoft Office* and its Open Source counterpart (*StarOffice*). Software products such as these are examples of sophisticated, integrated electronic performance systems, in that they provide collection of software tools – each having a similar end-user interface and the ability to communicate with each other. Together, these tools enable people to enhance their performance in areas such as writing (using the word-processing facility), doing mathematical calculations (using the spreadsheet package), performing data collection, storage and recall operations (by means of the database tool), and so on. Much of the ongoing study in the area of electronic performance support is concerned with the design, development and use of software packages to enable people to improve their skills and performance and overcome their limitations in particular areas – as has been discussed earlier in this chapter. These software packages can vary considerably in terms of their sophistication and the facilities they offer. The range of capability extends from simple 'typing tutors' through computer games to complex, powerful and spectacular immersive virtual reality systems.

THE IMPORTANCE OF UBIQUITOUS COMPUTING

Performance support problems arise at all sorts of times in numerous different places and in very diverse situations. Characteristics of this sort place severe demands on the electronic support technology that is needed – in terms of both its global and temporal availability and, of course, its reliability. The term 'ubiquitous computing' is often used to refer to situations in which computer support technology is made continuously available to its users in all possible locations at any time of the day or night – in the home, at work, in shops, under the sea, on trains and aeroplanes, and so on. There are three basic requirements that need to be fulfilled in order to achieve this goal. First, there needs to be sources of electrical energy available; second, there should be appropriate communication network coverage and connectivity; and third, relevant computing equipment needs to be available at any particular point of need.

In many ways, the third of the above requirements is probably the most crucial. This requirement can be achieved through the use of 'mobile' or portable computing technology (such as laptop computers, PDAs, mobile phones and portable storage devices) that people can carry with them where ever they go. Ideally, these types of computing technology would normally be augmented with appropriate ICT infrastructures and the provision of suitable energy sources.

In situations where there is no computer network availability (or connectivity), through the deployment of portable storage devices (similar to those shown in Figures 1.13 and 1.14) people can take their electronic data and information with them – wherever

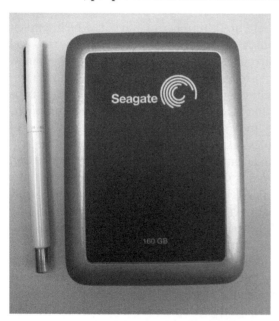

they have to go. These types of device are therefore having a substantial effect in terms of making collections of data and information available in a ubiquitous fashion.

Devices which have no moving parts (such as those shown in Figure 1.14) are particularly useful because of their high levels of reliability. However, their storage capacities (typically, 0.25 through 64 gigabytes) do not yet match the capacity of portable hard-disk drives such as that shown in Figure 1.13 – which has a capacity of 160 gigabytes.

Computer technology of the type described in this section is likely to show growing popularity in the development of future electronic performance support systems. PDAs, for example, are finding an increasing number of applications within both educational and commercial settings. The work described by Ketamo (2002; 2003) illustrates how PDA technology is being used within an educational context. This work demonstrates how adaptive software can be employed within a PDA in order to improve and enhance students' skills in the area of geometry study.

Figure 1.13   A typical portable hard-drive system

Figure 1.14 Examples of memory sticks

Conclusion

Human beings are each beset by the wide range of limitations that confronts them. These limitations can be of two basic types: they are either innate or acquired. Innate limitations arise from our natural shortcomings – for example, how quickly we can ambulate in an unaided fashion from one location to another, how much we can remember and how accurately we can perform mental calculations. Acquired limitations are those with which we are confronted as a result of the various goal-seeking and problem-solving activities in which we become involved. For example, suppose someone sets off to travel to a distant location using a motor-car and then, en-route, the vehicle breaks down. If the person involved in this scenario is not mechanically minded then it would not be possible for the journey to continue by motor-car since the person concerned would not know what is wrong with it and would probably not have the knowledge or skill needed to repair it. Fortunately, roadside services are often available in situations such as this – provided the person concerned has a mobile phone and knows the number to call.

During the history of the evolution of the human species, people have developed a wide range of tools and machines that can be used to enable them to overcome their difficulties and limitations. Many of these devices are also capable of providing us with opportunities for helping us to improve our performance in the tasks that we have to undertake. They can also extend the range of problems that we are able to solve. As has been stressed earlier in this chapter, the study of performance support is concerned with the design, development and use of performance aids that will enable us to improve what we do and how we do it. In many different ways, these performance aids are also likely to improve the quality of life for those involved in using them.

Because we live in a fast-changing, dynamic world, we will always be confronted with new situations and problems that we will have to solve. Of course, this will create a demand for new types of performance support intervention. Increasingly, computer-based systems are likely to figure prominently within the future systems that we build –

be these for use in the educational, medical, commercial or financial domains. Because of the future importance of 'Electronic Performance Support Systems', subsequent chapters of this book will deal with various aspects of the theory and practice of EPSS.

Acknowledgement

I am grateful to Paul van Schaik for his useful criticism and helpful suggestions for improving this chapter.

References

Ackerman, P.L. (2007). New Developments in Understanding Skilled Performance, *Current Directions in Psychological Science*, 16(5), 235–239.

Ackoff, R.L. (1972). Towards a System of Systems Concepts. In J. Beishon and G. Peters (eds), *Systems Behaviour* (pp. 83–90). London, UK: Harper and Row.

Bagrit, L. (1965). *The Age of Automation*, The BBC Reith Lectures 1964. London, UK: Weidenfeld and Nicholson.

Banerji, A.K. (1995). *Designing Electronic Performance Support Systems*, Ph.D thesis. Middlesbrough, UK: University of Teesside.

Barker, P.G. (1990). Designing Interactive Learning Systems, *Educational and Training Technology International*, 27(2), 125–145.

Barker, P.G. (1994). Designing Interactive Learning In T. de Jong and L. Sarti (eds), *Design and Production of Multimedia and Simulation-based Learning Material* (pp. 1–30). Dordrecht, The Netherlands: Kluwer Academic Publishers.

Barker, P.G. (1995). Electronic Performance Support Systems, Special edition of *Innovations in Education and Training International*, 32(1), 1–73.

Barker, P.G. (2006). Web Site Analysis – A Group Experiment in Data Quantification and Knowledge Engineering. In E. Pearson and P. Bohman, *Proceedings of the EDMEDIA 2006 World Conference on Multimedia, Hypermedia and Telecommunications* (pp. 2258–2263). Chesapeake, VA: Association for the Advancement of Computing in Education.

Barker, P.G., Schaik, P. van and Famakinwa, O. (2007). Building Electronic Performance Support Systems for First-Year Undergraduate Students, *Innovations in Education and Teaching International*, 44(3), 243–255.

Beacham, N. (1998). *Distributed Performance Support Systems*, Ph.D thesis. Middlesbrough, UK: University of Teesside.

Bezanson, W. (2002). *Performance Support Solutions – Achieving Business Goals Through Enabling User Performance*. Victoria, BC: Trafford Publishing.

Card, S.K., Moran, T.P. and Newell, A. (1983). *The Psychology of Human-Computer Interaction*. Hillsdale, NJ: Lawrence Erlbaum Associates.

Carroll, J.M. (1987). The Paradox of the Active User. In J.M. Carroll (ed.), *Interfacing Thought: Cognitive Aspects of Human-Computer Interaction* (pp. 80–111). Cambridge, MA: MIT Press.

Checkland, P.B. (1972). A Systems Map of the Universe. In J. Beishon and G. Peters (eds), *Systems Behaviour* (pp. 50–55). London, UK: Harper and Row.

Checkland, P.B. (2001). *Systems Thinking, Systems Practice*. Chichester, UK: John Wiley and Sons Ltd.

Checkland, P. and Poulter, J. (2006). *Learning for Action – A Short Definitive Account of Soft Systems Methodology and its Use for Practitioners, Teachers and Students*. Chichester, UK: John Wiley and Sons.

Famakinwa, O.J. (2004). *An Electronic Performance Support System for Library Systems*, MSc Thesis. Middlesbrough, UK: School of Computing, University of Teesside.

Flinders, S. (2000). *A Prototype Electronic Performance Support Facility to Support Web-based Information Retrieval*, M.Sc thesis. Middlesbrough, UK: School of Computing, University of Teesside.

Gery, G. (1991). *Electronic Performance Support Systems – How and Why to Remake the Workplace Through the Strategic Application of Technology*. Boston, MA: Weingarten Publications.

Jenkins, G.M. (1972). The Systems Approach. In J. Beishon and G. Peters (eds), *Systems Behaviour* (pp. 56–82). London, UK: Harper and Row.

Ketamo, H. (2002). Learning for Kindergarten's Mathematics Teaching. In *Proceedings of the IEEE International Workshop on Wireless and Mobile Technologies in Education (WMTE'02)* (pp. 167–168). Los Alamitos, CA: Institute of Electrical and Electronics Engineers Computer Society Digital Library.

Ketamo, H. (2003). An Adaptive Geometry Game for Hand-held Devices, *Educational Technology and Society Journal*, 6(1), 83–95.

Schaik, P. van, Barker, P.G. and Famakinwa, O. (2006). Potential Roles for Performance Support Tools Withn Library Systsems, *The Electronic Library*, 24(3), 347–365.

Schaik, P. van, Barker, P.G. and Famakinwa, O. (2007). Making a Case for Using Electronic Performance Support Systems in Academic Libraries, *Journal of Interactive Learning Research*, 18(3), 411–428.

Schaik, P. van, Pearson, R. and Barker, P.G. (2002). Designing Electronic Performance Support Systems to Support Learning, *Innovations in Education and Teaching International*, 39(4), 289–306.

Young, E. (2007). Tireless Reliable Physio-Robots Take on Stroke Paralysis, *New Scientist*, 193(2598), p. 3, 7th April.

Tabachnick, B.G. and Fidell, L.S. (2007). *Applying Multivariate Statistics* (5th Edn). Boston MA: Alyn and Bacon.

2 *Psychological Perspective*

PAUL VAN SCHAIK

This chapter aims to establish the psychological basis of electronic performance support and to present design guidance for incorporating this type of support in various application domains. After establishing the relationship between problem solving and electronic performance support, the main approach used by cognitive psychologists to study human problem solving is outlined. Psychologists' understanding of how problem solving can be improved as a result of learning – including how experts and novices differ in their performance – is then discussed. Based on the psychology of problem solving, guidelines for electronic performance support are proposed. Finally, conclusions regarding the psychological basis of electronic performance support are presented.

Introduction

This chapter is underpinned by the fundamental idea that all human task performance can be described by a range of levels commencing at novice problem solving to highly skilled expert performance. The goal of electronic performance support is to enhance task performance by changing the nature of performance from problem-solving-based to skill-based. There are two main approaches to achieve this goal. The first of these involves immediate support of task performance (for example, by providing the sequence of steps that make up a task procedure) without a course of instruction and, as a result, support for practising a correct or increasingly effective procedure for a task. The second depends upon providing instruction (or other learning activities) to enhance future task performance.

Information-processing Approach to Problem Solving

The dominant ('modal') approach to the study of human problem solving is the information-processing approach, originating from the Nobel Prize winner Herbert Simon and Alan Newell (Newell and Simon, 1972; see Mayer, 1992, Chapter 6, for a clear outline of this approach). In Newell and Simon's information-processing approach, two main types of thought process are involved in problem solving: (a) understanding, by building a problem space, and (b) finding a path ('searching') through the problem space, by using problem-solving techniques (see Figure 2.1).

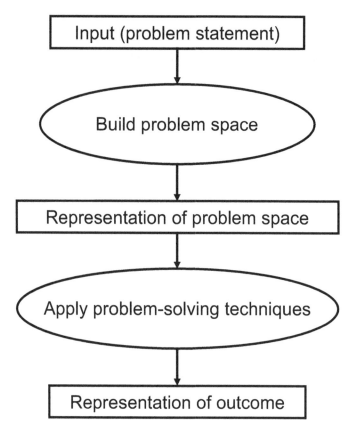

Figure 2.1   The problem-solving process

Source: Adapted from Mayer, 1992.

Various specific models of skilled performance in Human-Computer Interaction (HCI) have been postulated, for example, Goals, Operators, Methods and Selection rules (also known as GOMS, see Card, Moran and Newell, 1983 – discussed in Chapter 3), that are based on Newell and Simon's approach or share its goal-directed focus – for example, Norman's (1998) Model of Seven Stages of Action.

A *problem space* is a representation of the problem as the problem-solver understands it and this representation may not be (completely) accurate. The problem space consists of an initial state (the situation at the beginning of the problem-solving process), a goal state (the situation at the end of the process), a set of operators (actions that can be taken to solve the problem) and restrictions on the operators (stating when particular actions cannot be taken). Problems for which all elements of the problem space are available to the problem-solver are called *well-defined* problems; for example, a simple mathematical equation such as $7(x + 2) + x = 22$. Problems for which not all elements are available are called *ill-defined*, for instance, the problem: 'What policies should the government adopt to increase citizens' recycling of household waste?' Problems also differ in terms of the type of knowledge that is needed to solve them. Some problems, for instance, tic-tac-toe (noughts-and-crosses) can be solved using *generic* strategies that work across a variety of problems. Other problems, for example, solving a mathematical equation, require *domain-specific* strategies that work only for a particular type of problem. Problems also differ in the amount of knowledge possessed by the problem-solver. A problem is *semantically lean* when the problem-solver has very little knowledge or previous experience to solve the problem, for example, a person playing chess for the first time. On the other hand, a problem is *semantically rich* when the problem-solver has substantial knowledge to solve the problem, for instance, a chess master playing a game of chess – the master has substantial knowledge and experience regarding many aspects of the game, including opening, mid-play, end-play and strategy.

Generally, human problem-solvers use the following main sources of information to produce a problem representation (Robertson, 2001):

- the problem statement and its context;
- inferences about states, operators and restrictions not based on the problem statement;
- inferences based on the problem statement;
- previous experience in solving the problem;
- previous experience in solving similar problems;
- misconceptions about some aspects of the problem;
- more generally applicable procedures for dealing with aspects of the problem;
- external memory, that is, information in the environment – outside the problem-solver;
- instructions.

Several of these sources rely on a problem-solver's capabilities or experience, while others originate from outside and are external to the person. These external sources can form the basis for electronic performance support.

One of the best-known general *problem-solving techniques* is means-ends analysis. Employing this technique, a problem-solver attempts to reduce the difference between the current state in the problem space and the goal state. While doing this, the person breaks the problem down into sub-problems ('sub-goaling'). This is done by breaking a problem down into its structure of final goal and sub-goals. In means-ends analysis, there are three types of sub-goal: (a) to transform one state into another; (b) to reduce the difference between the current state and another state; and (c) to apply an operator. By applying a chain of subsequent operators, the problem-solver should eventually reach the goal state (that is a solution).

Different human-memory systems are involved in problem solving. They include *working memory*, which has a limited capacity,[1] and *long-term memory*, which has a vast capacity (see Figure 2.2). Slave systems of working memory hold the external description of the problem (in visual or auditory representation[2]). Long-term memory stores past experiences with problems, for example, facts, problem-solving techniques and related problems. In the central executive of working-memory, information from the slave systems and long-term memory interact and a path to a solution is usually generated and subsequently tested.

---

1   The size of the elements ('chunks') differs depending on a problem-solver's knowledge. Experts' chunks (for example, a configuration of pieces on a chess board) can be made up of various smaller elements (for example, the position of an individual piece). Novices' chunks can be smaller, composed of one smaller element (for example, the position of an individual piece) or a limited number of smaller elements.

2   There are two slave systems: the visuospatial sketchpad and the phonological loop. The first allows the rehearsal of visual information. The second allows the rehearsal of auditory information.

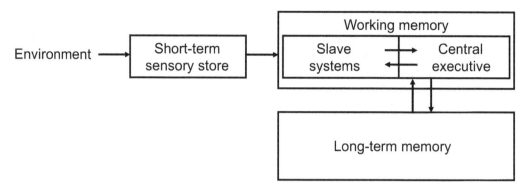

Figure 2.2   Components of memory

Source: Adapted from Mayer, 1992.

When applying a problem-solving technique – such as means-ends analysis – without external memory aids, a problem-solver holds the internal representation of the problem in working memory, including any sub-goals. Depending on the size of the problem representation and the number of sub-goals at any one time, the person's working memory may be overloaded and, as a consequence, problem-solving performance will be diminished. Indeed, task performance can be enhanced by providing the problem-solver with external memory aids as part of electronic performance support. Although most problem-solving research focuses on humans' (internal) memory ('knowledge in the head') rather than on external memory ('knowledge in the world'), use of the latter can enhance human task performance by reducing the problem of information overload (Norman, 1998). An outline of the tradeoffs between the two types of knowledge is presented in Table 2.1.

Improving Task Performance in the Information-processing Approach

Relevant to the study of electronic performance support is psychological research into the learning processes involved with problem solving and the study of differences in problem-solving performance between experts and novices. Both of these can be used as a vehicle for understanding how task performance can be improved.

LEARNING TO SOLVE PROBLEMS

According to research on problem solving, there are two main routes to acquiring expertise in problem solving: schema induction and the acquisition of cognitive skill.

In the context of problem solving, a schema is a knowledge structure consisting of elements of semantic knowledge (meanings of, for example, words or concepts) and the relationships among the different elements. According to Marshall (1995), the following four types of knowledge are represented in problem schemas:

1. Identification knowledge is declarative knowledge (of the type 'knowing what') and incorporates a configuration of various problem features and facilitates pattern recognition. Therefore, this type of knowledge helps problem-solvers perceive the

Table 2.1   Tradeoffs between knowledge in the head and knowledge in the world

Property	Knowledge in the world	Knowledge in the head
Retrievability	Retrievable whenever visible or audible.	Not readily retrievable. Requires memory search or reminding.
Learning	Learning not required. Interpretation substitutes for learning. How easy it is to interpret information in the world depends upon how well it exploits natural mappings and constraints.	Requires learning, which can be considerable. Learning is made easier if there is meaning of structure to the material (or if there is a good mental model).
Efficiency of use	Tends to be slowed up by the need to find and interpret the external information.	Can be very efficient.
Ease of use at first encounter	High.	Low.
Aesthetics	Can be unaesthetic and inelegant, especially if there is a need to maintain a lot of information. This can lead to clutter. In the end, aesthetic appeal depends upon the skill of the designer.	Nothing needs to be visible, which gives more freedom to the designer, which in turn can lead to better aesthetics.

Source: Norman, 1998.

most important part of a problem that needs to be addressed, and thereby limits the search for a solution to the most important parts of the problem space.

2. Elaboration knowledge is declarative knowledge of the main features of the problem. Knowledge elements include both specific instances and more general abstractions. Both types of element facilitate the creation of a mental model of the situation (a model 'in the head' of the problem to be solved), which, in turn, can help humans to access the knowledge required to identify a solution procedure.

3. Planning knowledge is a high-level form of declarative knowledge required to solve a problem and is used to create plans, goals and sub-goals. An example is knowledge about the 'precedence order' in which arithmetical operations should be applied (division, multiplication, addition, subtraction in this order), that is, when to apply an operation.

4. Execution knowledge is the procedural knowledge (of the type 'knowing how') of the process for solving a problem. It allows the problem-solver to carry out the steps derived through the application of planning knowledge. An example is knowledge about the manner in which to apply the operations (multiplication, division, addition, subtraction) used to solve a mathematical equation, that is, how to apply an operation.

There appears to be agreement on inclusion of the first three types of knowledge in problem schemas, but execution knowledge may be considered separate from a schema (Anderson, 1993). The reason for excluding execution knowledge is that the role of schemas is to identify the type of problem and specify, at a rather general level, how this type of problem is solved, but not how operators are applied. Therefore, the development of problem-solving expertise can be studied in terms of how people develop the high-level knowledge (schema induction) required to categorise and approach the solving of problems, as well as how people 'automate' (compile) problem-solving procedures (rule automation) as a result of acquiring cognitive skills. Schema induction and rule automation should be considered as complementary processes (van Merriënboer, 1997).

Schema induction

Schema induction is a form of learning where the solving of a new problem (this is called the target) is based on a previously solved similar problem (this is called the source or analogue). The idea is that, for the old problem, a problem-solver will have constructed an 'implicit' schema consisting of the problem statement (excluding the goal state), the solution procedure and the goal state. There are two routes along which the problem-solver can induce a schema for a new problem: principle cueing and example analogy (Robertson, 2001). Following the first route (principle cueing – see Figure 2.3), the person notices a strong similarity between the problem statement of the new problem and that of the old one. The schema of the old problem is then triggered and the solution procedure of the old problem is applied to the new problem. Following the second route (example analogy – see Figure 2.4), again the solver notices a strong similarity between the two problem statements; however, this time the solution procedure of the old problem, once triggered, cannot be used directly. Instead, the problem-solver adapts the procedure to the requirements of the new problem and then applies the adapted procedure to that problem. As a result of solving the new problem, the person adapts the schema so that it accommodates both problems. Consequently, having adapted a schema after solving several analogous problems, the problem-solver has created a schema that has increasingly become abstract and decontextualised (that is, depends less on the particular details of each problem).

The acquisition of cognitive skill

In order to understand the acquisition of cognitive skill, a basic understanding of the representation mechanism of procedural knowledge (which forms the basis of this type of skill) used in problem-solving research is important. In the information-processing approach to the study of problem solving, procedural knowledge for solving a particular problem is represented as a set of productions. A *production* (or production rule) is a condition-action pair of the general form IF conditions THEN action. The conditions (one or more) describe a situation and the action specifies what to do. A problem-solver checks if the conditions of a production match the content held in working memory. Only if the outcome is a match does the production apply and the problem-solver carries out the action. As a result, the problem representation is updated in working memory. This may involve the deletion of sub-goals or the creation of new sub-goals. A *production system* is then a set of productions that all are related to the same class of problem. Congruent with means-ends analysis, production systems set goals, recognise whether conditions have been met and carry out operations in order to solve a problem. However, cognitive skills are markedly more efficient than general problem-solving techniques such as means-ends analysis.

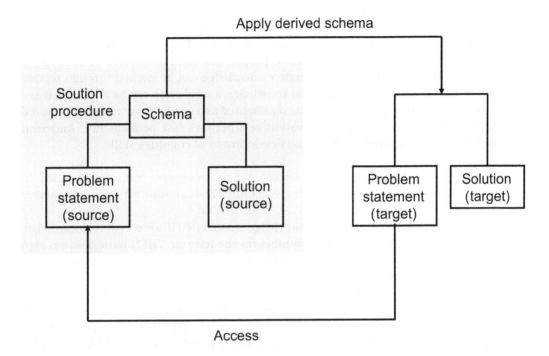

Figure 2.3 Schema induction – principle cueing

Source: Adapted from Robertson, 2001.

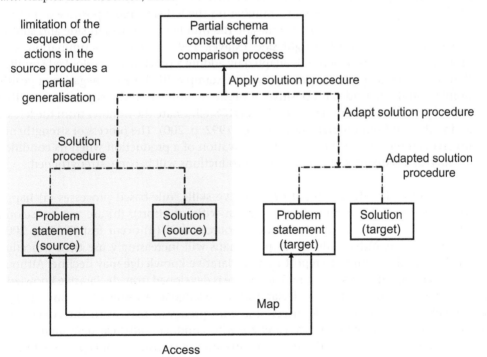

Figure 2.4 Schema induction – example analogy

Source: Adapted from Robertson, 2001.

According to Anderson (1983, 1990), when humans learn a cognitive skill, their declarative knowledge is converted into procedural knowledge. Individual elements of declarative knowledge can be represented as propositions and collections of this type of knowledge as networks. Humans' declarative knowledge can be elicited through reports in verbal or pictorial form. For procedural knowledge, a single step can be represented as a production and a whole procedure can be represented as a production system. Procedural knowledge can be assessed from observation of a person's task performance. Anderson proposes the following three stages in the development of cognitive skill:

1. *Declarative*. Task knowledge is still represented in declarative form, for instance, in the problem of solving a mathematical equation: 'You can subtract the same number from both sides of an equation' (Mayer, 1992: p. 200).
2. *Knowledge compilation*. Declarative knowledge is converted into procedural knowledge, for example, 'IF there is a positive number on the left side THEN write a minus sign followed by that number on both sides' (Mayer, 1992: p. 200). Proceduralisation is the process whereby productions are formed, based on declarative knowledge. Composition is the process in which several productions, that each separately have a different effect are combined into one, for instance, 'IF there is a positive number on the left side and a positive or negative number on the right side THEN eliminate the number from the left side and subtract it from the number on the right side' (Mayer, 1992: p. 200).
3. *Tuning*. Procedural knowledge is refined. Generalisation is the process whereby two or more similar specific procedures are combined into a more general one, for instance, 'IF there is a positive or a negative number on the left side and a positive or negative number on the right side THEN eliminate the number from the left side and subtract it from the number on the right side' (Mayer, 1992: p. 200). Discrimination is the process in which a production is adapted by adding a previously overlooked condition that is required to apply the production, for example, 'IF there is a negative or positive number on the left side and positive or negative number on the right side and [there are] no parentheses around the numbers THEN eliminate the number from the left side and subtract it from the right side' (Mayer, 1992: p. 200). The process of strengthening involves an increase in the amount of activation of a production when its conditions are met. Consequently, the most useful productions will become strengthened.

As a result of the development of cognitive skills, rule-based processes (a) happen without intention (or continue to completion without effort), (b) are not consciously monitored, (c) use few, if any attentional resources, and (d) occur fast (Feldon, 2007). Furthermore, as cognitive skills develop, humans will increasingly use their procedural knowledge and their ability to report their declarative knowledge may decline. Although Anderson has argued that procedural knowledge is developed from declarative knowledge, humans may develop some new declarative knowledge as a result of becoming expert at problem solving, for example, users of a word processor may learn the concept of a 'string' (Payne et al., 1990) and researchers who conduct statistical data analysis may elaborate their knowledge of the relationships among statistical concepts as a result of solving statistical problems.

The Power Law of Practice (Newell and Rosenbloom, 1981; also see Chapter 1) has been confirmed in many research studies as a way of expressing human task performance,

T (time taken to perform a task) as a function of practice P (time spent practising). The law describes the relationship as $T = cP^x$, with c a constant and x the slope of the line if T and P are presented using a logarithmic scale. Although the discovery of the power law predates Anderson's (1990) theory of Adaptive Control of Thought-Rational (ACT-R),[3] Anderson has used his theory to derive this law by applying the learning mechanisms of ACT-R to particular tasks, thereby providing a theoretical basis for the law.

DIFFERENCES IN PROBLEM-SOLVING PERFORMANCE

Expert versus novice problem-solvers

The following factors distinguish expert from novice problem-solvers.

Innate capacities and individual differences
Predispositions – such as intelligence, personality and motivation – and talent may account for differences in problem-solving performance, separate from the effect of knowledge that is specific to the problem that is being solved. However, there appears to be a lack of evidence that general intelligence is correlated with expertise at problem solving in specific domains and evidence for the transfer of skills developed in one domain to another is mixed (Robertson, 2001). Nevertheless, according to Gardner (1983), there are multiple types of intelligence underlying exceptional performance by humans in different domains. Exceptional performance in a particular domain becomes possible when a person's intelligence profile matches the demands of that domain. Furthermore, people differ in their ability to gain and exploit knowledge (Sternberg and Frensch, 1992). Some people are better at effectively organising the information they have encountered into their internal knowledge structures than others, even if they have spent the same amount of time practising. Although practice is essential, some learners are more talented than others and this allows them to achieve performance at a higher level and a faster rate (for example, Wynton Marsalis – see *http://en.wikipedia.org/wiki/Wynton_Marsalis*).

Level of skill development
The more problem-solvers use procedural knowledge (automatic procedures) as opposed to declarative knowledge, the more expert they will become. However, the development of problem-solving expertise may not be linear. This is demonstrated by the intermediate effect: a dip in performance may occur on particular tasks in specific domains, whereby novices outperform intermediates, although the latter have greater experience and, ostensibly, knowledge than the former. The likely cause for the effect is that intermediates have a greater knowledge, but this still lacks good organisation in memory (Patel and Groen, 1991).

Various 'staged' models of skill development have been proposed. Schumacher and Czerwinsky's (1992) (cited in Robertson, 2001) model focuses on the development of the human-memory representations of (external) systems and reflects the acquisition of problem-solving schemas discussed above. In the pre-theoretical stage, specific instances of problem features are retrieved from memory, based on superficial features of the current

---

3   The theory was developed to simulate and understand human cognition. Research using ACT-R focuses on understanding how people organise knowledge and produce intelligent behaviour.

situation and the instances stored in memory. This process is successful if the superficial features correspond with the underlying features of the system. In the experiential stage, learners start to develop an understanding of the causal relations within the system and begin to develop abstractions from their experience of solving problems in the domain. In the expert stage, learners can make abstractions across various system representations; therefore, their knowledge of the system is transferable. It may be possible to use experts' representations of systems (mental models) for teaching novices appropriate representations to understand complex systems in a particular domain. For this purpose, instructional materials can be developed from an expert's conceptual model. Hong and O'Neill (1992) demonstrated that this can be effective in the domain of statistics in terms of reducing learners' misconceptions.

Knowledge

The amount of knowledge and the elaboration of the specific knowledge structure increase with expertise in solving problems in a particular domain. Consistent with their expertise, in experts' long-term memory the elements are more interconnected than those in novices. For example, by combining several knowledge elements ('chunking' – for instance, the position of pieces on a chess board) experts develop a larger knowledge element ('chunk' – for instance, a configuration of chess pieces representing a particular stage in a game of chess) that they can employ as a single new unit in their problem solving.

As stated before, schemas can be useful because they store knowledge gained in a particular context in an abstract form so that it can be transferred to other contexts. However, because of the abstract nature of schemas they can result in rigid task performance by experts (Feltovich et al., 1997). Furthermore, experts may not be able to consciously access the elements of their knowledge that are compiled in schemas (Anderson, 1987). Therefore, experts may employ a certain regularly used procedure even though it is not always appropriate in a particular context.

Despite the possibility of rigid task performance, typically, an expert's performance is flexible. This apparent contradiction may be resolved by considering two different types of expertise. First, routine expertise is schema-based knowledge that experts use to solve standard problems efficiently, but – when applied inappropriately – can lead to rigidity. Second, adaptive expertise facilitates experts' flexible use of knowledge and allows them to find new solutions to non-standard problems. According to Feltovich et al. (1997), experts have many well-organised and highly differentiated schemas. Therefore, they are more likely to find apparent inconsistencies in the system state (for example, the anatomy of a patient) when solving a problem (for example, interpreting the result of a diagnostic test). As a result, they are more likely to make an extensive search of the problem space to resolve the inconsistencies and solve the problem, thereby demonstrating the flexibility of their performance.

Cognitive processes

Expert problem-solvers have developed problem-solving techniques that help them deal with difficult or new problems in their domain. Experts may represent a problem or plan their search through the problem space more effectively or more efficiently. Because of their superior experience and knowledge, experts may increase the information held in working memory (or, stated differently, reduce the load on working memory) by chunking and may perceive the problem state differently, which in turn can improve their performance when attempting to find a solution.

Experts have been found to be particularly efficient at perceiving and recognising patterns and categorising problems as a result of their expertise (Simon and Chase, 1973). However, the categories that experts use in making their judgements are based on goals and have been developed as a result of repeated use of these categories during many hours of previous problem solving. Therefore, when developing problem-solving expertise, problem-solvers change from using a classification based on surface features to one based on underlying features as a result of their search through the problem space from a multitude of previous problem-solving episodes.

Working-memory capacity was originally assumed to be around seven chunks (Chase and Simon, 1973). However, in order to account for results that are not consistent with this idea, more recent research has proposed a long-term working memory associated with skilled memory performance and expertise (Ericsson and Kintsch, 1995). In some circumstances, experts can store information in long-term memory rather than in working memory and, as a result, the amount of memory available to them for solving a problem increases, with subsequent greater efficiency or effectiveness.

Factors affecting the quality of non-experts' problem-solving performance

As stated previously, *working memory* is an important component of the human information-processing system involved with problem solving. In fact, it can be considered the 'bottle-neck' in problem solving. Therefore, by increasing *working-memory capacity*, human problem-solving performance should become more effective and efficient. Kyllonen and Christal (1990) demonstrated that working-memory capacity is highly correlated with reasoning ability. Their results are consistent with the idea that effective reasoning and problem solving depend on working-memory capacity. Unfortunately, although working-memory capacity – independent of a particular task domain – can be increased by training (Caretti et al., 2007), it is likely that continued training will be required to maintain an enhanced capacity (Willingham, 2004). Alternatively, it is possible to increase the amount of information held in working memory by chunking as a result of experience with solving multiple problems in a particular domain. However, this is the same as becoming an expert; therefore, it seems that there is no other means for non-experts to improve their working-memory capacity other than protracted experience and practising.

As stated previously, the *setting of sub-goals* is an important aspect of problem solving. Catrambone (1996) argued that problem-solving performance across problems in a particular domain would improve by teaching problem-solvers to set sub-goals. This teaching would be effective because problems within a domain typically share sub-goals even if the actions (steps) to achieve the sub-goals differ. Unfortunately, teaching people abstract procedures to find solutions to problems directly was reported to be ineffective (Reed and Bolstad, 1991). Nevertheless, Catrambone (1996) used a different method where groups of steps in sample problems were annotated with labels representing a sub-goal. The purpose of this method was that participants would combine these labelled grouped steps into a (higher-order) sub-goal (chunking), which Catrambone demonstrated to be successful. More generally, the teaching of strategic problem-solving procedures is the focus of instructional design-models for complex cognitive skills – see van Merriënboer

(1997) and van Merriënboer and Kirschner (2007) for a comprehensive, theory-based empirically validated model.

According to Gick and Holyoak (1983), transfer of learning to new problems occurs if a problem-solver possesses an abstract schema for a problem and its solution (the underlying structure of the problem). Therefore, problem-solvers should be encouraged to engage in schema induction by inviting them to compare problems that differ in surface structure, but share an underlying structure. However, Catrambone and Holyoak (1990) found that humans typically do not spontaneously apply previously learned problem solutions. Instead, it appears that humans rely on surface features of problems to draw analogies and appear to induce a schema only if explicitly directed. Nevertheless, research on the effectiveness of instructional-design models (van Merriënboer, 1997) demonstrates that this type of schema induction can be highly successful, but only if the instruction is based on an appropriate theory-based instructional design model.

In sum, non-experts' problem solving does not seem to improve, unless they invest the considerable effort required to become an expert by following a course of training involving protracted experience and practising. However, electronic performance support can provide a different and less cognitively demanding route to enhancing task performance.

The Application of Cognitive Psychology to Electronic Performance Support – How to Enhance Human Task Performance

Electronic performance support can be applied to many situations. The following four situations need to be distinguished regarding task performance before electronic performance support is introduced.

Situation 1. Unaided performance, in which no tools are used. This may be rare, but an example would be doing calculations 'in the head'. In Situation 1, electronic performance support can overcome or reduce the limitations of a human operator by providing declarative knowledge (of the type 'knowing what') or procedural knowledge (of the type 'knowing how').

Situation 2. Aided performance, in which the tools are not electronic. An example is doing calculations using a slide rule. In this situation, external electronic performance support (Gery, 1991) can be provided, where the original aid and the support system are two physically separated systems. This electronic support system can enable enhanced performance by providing more effective support, by either replacing or supplementing the existing tool(s). Although the significance of usability for successful task performance has been highlighted since the 1970s (Shneiderman, 1978), computer-based systems often still lack usability. An example is the use of non-standard language in menu options, such as those used in the statistical package SPSS (Field, 2009), that are unfamiliar to users. However, the less usable an artefact is, the more learning and (additional) performance support is required in Situation 2 or the following. The importance of usability applies more generally to computer-based systems, but also to electronic performance support in particular.

Situation 3. Aided performance, in which the tools are electronic, but they have not been explicitly designed with the goal of enhancing performance or are deemed to be insufficient for enhancing performance. (If the electronic tools had been designed to support task performance appropriately then no [new] electronic performance support would be necessary.) In Situation 3, intrinsic or extrinsic electronic performance support (Gery, 1991) can be provided, where the original aid and the support system are two physically integrated systems. An example of such an original aid is an electronic calculator. If the original tools and the Electronic Performance Support Systems (EPSS) are both running on the same machine (for example, a computer) then it is important to consider either (a) integrating the tools and the support system into one seamless system (intrinsic support) or (b) clearly presenting these as separate to the human operator and explaining how they are to be used together (extrinsic support).

Situation 4. Aided performance, in which the tools are specifically designed to enhance human task performance.

Generally, guidance for the design of electronic performance support would benefit a range of projects in different domains. This section presents design guidance, based on the analysis of human problem solving presented in this chapter.

As stated previously, there are two approaches to enhancing task performance. The first of these involves immediate support of task performance (for example, by providing the sequence of steps that make up a task procedure) without a course of instruction and, as a result, support for practising a correct or increasingly effective procedure for a task. The second depends upon providing instruction (or other learning activities) to enhance future task performance. The first approach is adopted by the field of HCI, whereas the second approach is adopted by the fields of Instructional Design (ID) and learning design (Barker, 2008). However, enhancement of task performance is typically not an explicit goal in HCI and ID. Electronic performance support uses these approaches in isolation or in combination, with the explicit aim of enhancing task performance. This chapter focuses on the first approach and for the second approach the reader is referred to several volumes on ID (for example, Reigeluth, 1983, 1987, 1999, 2008; van Merriënboer, 1997; van Merriënboer and Kirschner 2007).

Van Schaik, Barker and Famakinwa (2007) previously presented a set of design principles, but these were not based on an in-depth analysis of the psychological processes underlying electronic performance support. The generic principles stated by van Schaik et al. were: (a) enhancement of human task performance; (b) provision of data, information, knowledge and skills at a particular point of need; and (c) (optional) provision of a scaffolding function – see Cagiltay (2006) for example. The specific principles identified by van Schaik et al. were the following:

- explicit support for common tasks in the domain to be supported;
- presentation of step-by-step procedures;
- presentation of just-in-time information;
- integration of electronic performance support with the target application;
- simplicity and consistency of navigation and visual design.

Although the aforementioned principles remain useful, the application of the following guidance presented in this section is likely to be more applicable and useful for the detailed design of electronic performance support.

Many elements of instructional design models (in particular van Merriënboer's [1997; van Merriënboer and Kirschner, 2007] four-component ID model) can be applied to the design of immediate performance support without a course of instruction. An analysis of skills and knowledge is a prerequisite for any systematic attempt at supporting task performance.

ANALYSIS OF SKILLS AND KNOWLEDGE

In the first instance, when conducting an analysis, *principled skill decomposition* is required to identify, describe, classify and sequence the constituent skills of the task or task structure that is to be supported. Subsequently, several other types of analysis need to be conducted. First, *recurrent skills* need to be analysed. These are rule-based highly domain-specific, algorithmic procedures that guarantee that task goals will be reached. Recurrent skills are perfected by experts via automation (or compilation). Second, an analysis of *prerequisite knowledge for recurrent skills* is required. Prerequisite knowledge takes the form of facts, concepts, plans and causal principles. Third, *non-recurrent skills* need to be analysed. These consist of higher-level, strategic knowledge in the form of cognitive schemas used to solve unfamiliar aspects of problems; these schemas can be effective, but do not guarantee that task goals will be achieved. Non-recurrent skills are highly developed in experts through schema induction. Fourth, an analysis is necessary of *supporting knowledge for non-recurrent skills*. Supporting knowledge takes the form of conceptual models, procedural models, causal models and mental models[4] (van Merriënboer, 1997). The analysis of skills and knowledge that has been briefly discussed in this section is presented in greater depth in van Merriënboer (1997) and Clark et al. (2008).

SUPPORT FOR TASK PERFORMANCE

In terms of the effectiveness of support for task performance, a distinction needs to be made based on the type of skill that underlies task performance. In reality, many complex tasks include both recurrent and non-recurrent skills (van Merriënboer, 1997). If a comprehensive analysis of knowledge and skills has been conducted then it should be possible to support task performance (in an effective way) that is based on recurrent skills, as correct performance should guarantee that task goals are achieved. However, as stated previously, task performance that is based on non-recurrent skills can be effective, but success cannot be guaranteed.

Task performance can be enhanced by applying the following theoretical propositions. According to the *Component Fluency Hypothesis* (Carlson et al. 1990), the automaticity of recurrent skills greatly reduces cognitive load when humans are performing a complex cognitive skill. Because of the automaticity of recurrent skills, performance of a whole task that includes various recurrent and non-recurrent skills will be more fluid and less subject to errors caused by cognitive overload. Furthermore, given the automaticity of recurrent skills, cognitive resources are available for the performance of non-recurrent skills as well as the coordination and organisation of other skills that are part of the overall task. Electronic performance support that succeeds in making recurrent skills

---

4　Mental models are conceptualised as extremely complex schemas in which the nodes may be either facts, concepts, plans or causal principles linked by various types of relationship (van Merriënboer, 1997).

automatic is, as a result, likely to enhance task performance. This becomes more likely with repeated execution of the same task that includes the use of recurrent skills that are being supported. The *Understanding Hypothesis* (Ohlsson and Reese, 1991) holds that experts' understanding of content in a particular domain (for example, computer science) allows them to interpret a problem situation in general terms by using their relevant cognitive schemas. As a result, experts can monitor and reflect on their performance, and detect and correct their errors. Thus, experts can solve routine aspects of problems almost automatically. In addition, they can also evaluate the validity of the solutions they have produced and switch between problem approaches (from automatic task performance to performance based on strategic knowledge in the form of relevant systematic problem-solving approaches – that is prescriptive plans) when necessary. Therefore, electronic performance support that succeeds in developing relevant schemas in human operators is likely to enhance task performance. This becomes more likely when human operators perform a variety of tasks that require the use of the same underlying schemas (van Merriënboer, 1997). *Cognitive Load Theory* (Sweller, 1988; Leahy and Sweller, 2005; Kester et al., 2006; Feldon, 2007) suggests how cognitive load can be overcome by a systematic approach to the design of training, but this approach also applies in principle to other situations that involve the support of human task performance. Three techniques to control cognitive load are preventing cognitive load, redirecting attention and decreasing cognitive load. An electronic performance support system can apply the first technique (preventing cognitive load) by supporting tasks that are just beyond an operator's level of competence. The second technique (redirecting attention) can be applied by reducing cognitive load that is not associated with the task to be supported. Based on the 'Understanding Hypothesis', this can be achieved by providing information (including integrated information from difference sources) that is required for task performance and by presenting problem-solving procedures (systematic problem-solving procedures and heuristics rather than general procedures such as means-ends analysis) relevant to the task (van Merriënboer, 1997). Based on the *Component Fluency Hypothesis*, the third technique (decreasing cognitive load) can be applied by supporting full automation of recurrent skills. This can be achieved by extensive practice and the provision of prerequisite just-in-time information.

Support for recurrent skills

Frequently, the goal of electronic performance support is to achieve task performance in non-experts at a level that meets or surpasses that achieved by experts who do not use this support. The sequencing of tasks (or task steps) used by the support systems should then be the same as those used by the expert. If the use of the 'full' sequence is too complex for novices, then different techniques – such as segmentation, simplification and fractionation – can be used to work towards or approach experienced task performance (van Merriënboer, 1997).

For task performance that is based on recurrent skills, the required algorithmic procedures (with steps in sequence) or rules need to be presented (where possible in sequence). For instance, the steps of a procedure for formatting an electronic document would be presented in a given order. As another example, the rules used to solve simple arithmetic problems (previously presented to illustrate skill development in the section headed 'Learning to Solve Problems') would be presented without implying an order. This procedural information needs to be supplemented with prerequisite knowledge in the form of facts, concepts, plans or causal principles for carrying out each step or rule that has not been mastered by the target group. Examples are the concepts of 'paragraph' and 'document' as units that can be formatted using a word processor.

It is important to present feedback to promote learning (van Merriënboer, 1997) and motivation (Keller, 1983) wherever possible.[5] First, human operators should be informed regarding the accuracy or effectiveness of their task performance based on recurrent skills immediately after applying each step or rule. Feedback on errors should indicate why there was an error, so that it can be used as a basis for improving task performance. Second, motivational extrinsic feedback using verbal and non-verbal praise, encouragement and incentives should be given to enhance performance over time. Furthermore, operators should be informed that task performance based on recurrent skills guarantees that they will reach task goals, at least in principle.

Support for non-recurrent skills

If the use of the 'full' sequence of a complex task involving non-recurrent skills is too complex for novices then different scaffolding techniques – such as solving completion problems, which require the operator to complete a partially completed problem – can be used to work towards or approach experienced task performance (van Merriënboer, 1997).

For task performance based on non-recurrent skills, the required strategic knowledge in the form of systematic problem-solving approaches (prescriptive plans) and heuristics need to be presented. Systematic problem-solving approaches are general, but domain-specific procedures which, when applied, can result in effective task performance without guaranteeing success. An example is a plan for the playing phase of the card game of bridge.[6] Heuristics are principles that are applied within a systematic problem-solving approach, specifying how to achieve individual steps in such an approach, for instance, a rule for performing a two-way finesse in bridge. The presentation of strategic knowledge can be supplemented with supporting knowledge in the form of conceptual models, procedural models, causal models and mental models. For instance, in the field of experimental research design, researchers benefit from supportive knowledge in the form of a conceptual model of factors that affect the quality of research designs and a causal model of trade-offs between some of the factors (see Jennings, Kirkpatrick and Mohseni, Chapter 13 of this volume).

Again, it is important to present feedback to promote learning (van Merriënboer, 1997) and motivation (Keller, 1983) wherever possible. First, operators should be informed regarding the accuracy or effectiveness of their task performance based on non-recurrent skills when they have completed a whole task rather than after each individual step. The reason is that this type of task performance is effective (or less effective), as opposed to correct (or incorrect) and a judgement about effectiveness requires a whole task to be performed. Feedback on both the results (product) and the process of task performance are useful. Given that task performance based on non-recurrent skills is typically complex, 'complete' feedback may be precluded and feedback may be limited to most of the underlying non-

---

5   Feedback and motivational strategies can enhance self-regulation and self-efficacy, which in Social Cognitive Theory (Bandura, 1986) are two of the five uniquely human capabilities that provide people with the cognitive means to change their behaviour.

6   Readers not familiar with this card game can learn more at *http://www.pagat.com/boston/bridge.html*.

recurrent skills. Second, because task performance based on non-recurrent skills is typically naturally satisfying (intrinsically motivating) the need for extrinsic feedback should be reduced. However, other strategies from Keller's (1983, 1987) ARCS[7] model can be applied to increase motivation. These include attention (by capturing and sustaining interest of operators), relevance (by meeting the personal needs of operators) and confidence (self-efficacy – by assisting operators to believe that they will succeed). Furthermore, operators should be informed that task performance based on non-recurrent skills can be effective, but this does not guarantee that they will necessarily reach task goals.

DESIGN OF SUPPORT FOR USABILITY AND ACCEPTANCE

An analysis of skills and knowledge, and the design of task support are necessary conditions for successful task performance, but they are not sufficient. An electronic performance support system should also be designed for usability and acceptance. First, the electronic performance support system must be usable in terms of effectiveness and efficiency, which should be measured objectively and subjectively by assessing users' perceptions (Shackel and Richardson, 1991). Psychological principles, such as visibility, providing a conceptual model, good mappings and feedback (Norman, 1998) can be applied to promote usability. Second, usability is not sufficient and acceptance is also required, because the benefits of enhanced task performance will not be realised if a perfectly usable system is not accepted by its users. Major factors affecting potential users' decision to adopt a system include its perceived ease of use and perceived usefulness (Venkatesh et al., 2003). During the development process, users' acceptance should be monitored and their perceptions should inform the design in order to maximise acceptance.

Case Study

The theory presented in this chapter will now be illustrated by an example of electronic performance support for statistical data analysis, using two well-known websites: *Which Test?* (*http://www.whichtest.info/index.html*) and the *How To Guides* (*http://www.statsguides. bham.ac.uk/HTG/HTG_Home.htm*). For the purpose of this chapter, these sites illustrate the support of tasks based on recurrent skills (see the section entitled 'Support for Task Performance'). The electronic support systems for research design and analysis described by Jennings, Kirkpatrick and Mohseni (2009, Chapter 13 of this volume) illustrate the support of tasks based on non-recurrent skills (see 'Support for Task Performance').

Which Test? is an EPSS that supports the task of selecting statistical techniques for analysing quantitative data. The site presents a sequence of questions, each based on a rule used in the process of selecting the appropriate technique. The sequence is determined by the answers given to previous questions. The final result is the identification of the correct statistical analysis procedure, based on a particular research design and the type of data collected. Users can access prerequisite knowledge for most of the rules. For example, when identifying the level of measurement ('What sort of data have you?') users can request a description of each level (see Figure 2.5). Feedback on task performance is not

---

7   The components of ARCS are Attention, Relevance, Confidence and Satisfaction. The aim of the application of the model is to enhance learners' motivation to learn new skills and transfer the acquired skills to their work environment.

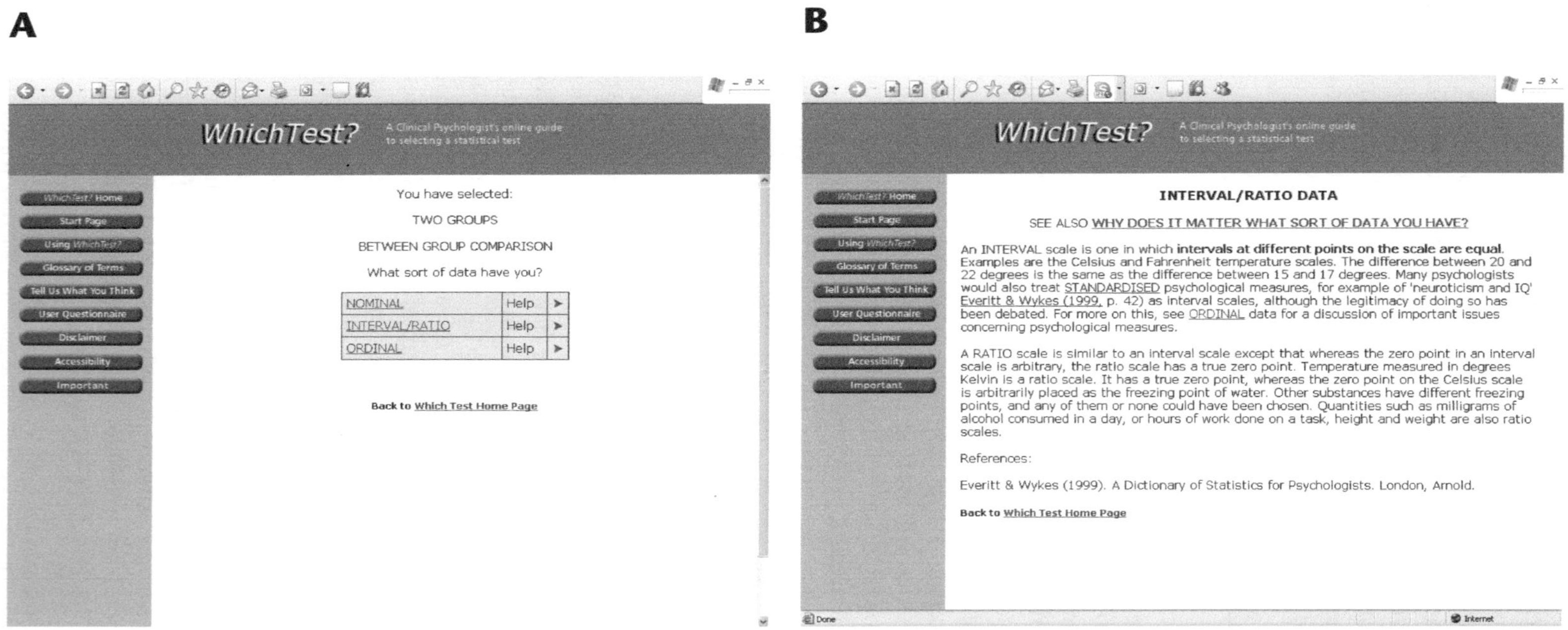

A

WhichTest? A Clinical Psychologist's online guide to selecting a statistical test

You have selected:

TWO GROUPS

BETWEEN GROUP COMPARISON

What sort of data have you?

NOMINAL	►	Help	►
INTERVAL/RATIO	►	Help	►
ORDINAL	►	Help	►

Back to Which Test Home Page

B

WhichTest? A Clinical Psychologist's online guide to selecting a statistical test

INTERVAL/RATIO DATA

SEE ALSO WHY DOES IT MATTER WHAT SORT OF DATA YOU HAVE?

An INTERVAL scale is one in which **intervals at different points on the scale are equal.** Examples are the Celsius and Fahrenheit temperature scales. The difference between 20 and 22 degrees is the same as the difference between 15 and 17 degrees. Many psychologists would also treat STANDARDISED psychological measures, for example of 'neuroticism and IQ' Everitt & Wykes (1999, p. 42) as interval scales, although the legitimacy of doing so has been debated. For more on this, see ORDINAL data for a discussion of important issues concerning psychological measures.

A RATIO scale is similar to an interval scale except that whereas the zero point in an interval scale is arbitrary, the ratio scale has a true zero point. Temperature measured in degrees Kelvin is a ratio scale. It has a true zero point, whereas the zero point on the Celsius scale is arbitrarily placed as the freezing point of water. Other substances have different freezing points, and any of them or none could have been chosen. Quantities such as milligrams of alcohol consumed in a day, or hours of work done on a task, height and weight are also ratio scales.

References:

Everitt & Wykes (1999). A Dictionary of Statistics for Psychologists. London, Arnold.

Back to Which Test Home Page

Figure 2.5 Identifying the level of measurement using *Which Test?*

A. Rule-based question; B. Prerequisite knowledge

provided. In sum, the supported complex skill of test selection consists of simpler steps (rules that can be seen as recurrent skills) that are presented in order. The supported prerequisite knowledge consists of concepts required in each of the steps.

The *How To Guides* is an EPSS that supports task performance in relation to various statistical procedures involved in using statistical packages – such as SPSS (Field, 2009). First, the site requires users to select a procedure by making two subsequent choices, where the second choice depends on the answer of the first choice – see, for example, Figure 2.6a. The choices broadly reflect, but do not literally present, the menu choices made in SPSS to access the particular statistical procedures. The choices are an improvement on the menu structure in SPSS because they better reflect the conceptual structure underlying statistical procedures. In sum, the supported complex skill of selecting statistical procedures that are conducted using SPSS consists of two steps which can be seen as recurrent skills.

After users have chosen a statistical procedure, the site presents the series of screens for that procedure in SPSS – see, for example, Figure 2.6b. Each screen is annotated with directions representing the steps involved with the statistical procedure to be carried out using SPSS. After the last step in the procedure has been completed, one or more screens (showing the output generated by the procedure in SPSS) are presented with annotations on how to interpret the results – see, for example, Figure 2.6c. The annotations identify particular elements in the results (such as descriptive statistics) or state a decision rule, for example, regarding the significance of a test result (for instance, a test of the equality of group variances). The *How To Guides* do not support prerequisite knowledge for task procedures or present feedback on task performance. However, the potential problem caused by this lack of availability would have been worse if some of the non-standard terminology employed by SPSS had been used. Instead, in the annotations the *How To Guides* use more common terminology used in statistical data analysis. In sum, the supported complex skill of conducting a test procedure using SPSS consists of simpler steps that can be seen as recurrent skills and that are presented in order. The supported prerequisite knowledge (in the annotations) consists mainly of facts required to interpret test results (identification of elements in the results).

Conclusions

This chapter has outlined the psychological basis of human task performance, based on the concept of problem solving and the development of expertise. Electronic performance support builds on and aims to enhance human cognitive structures (both declarative and procedural knowledge) and to reduce memory load. This is achieved by analysing skills and knowledge, and then presenting algorithmic procedures or rules for recurrent skills with prerequisite knowledge and feedback, and strategic knowledge for non-recurrent skills with supportive knowledge and feedback. As a result, human task performance, based on recurrent and non-recurrent skills, can be enhanced. This chapter has focused on the immediate support of task performance without a course of instruction, but this type of support can be complemented by instruction. Any electronic system to support performance should be designed with usability and acceptance in mind.

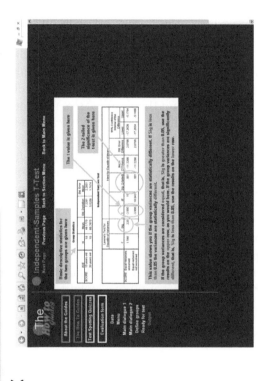

Figure 2.6   Conducting an unrelated t test in SPSS using the *How To Guides*

A. Selecting a statistical procedure; B. Conducting a statistical test; C. Interpreting test results

Acknowledgement

I am grateful to Darren Flynn and Philip Barker for their useful comments on previous drafts of this chapter.

References

Anderson, J. (1983). *The Architecture of Cognition*. Cambridge, MA: Harvard University Press.

Anderson, J. (1987). Skill acquisition: Compilation of weak method problem situations. *Psychological Review*, 94, 192–210.

Anderson, J. (1990). *The Adaptive Character of Thought*. Hillsdale, NJ: Erlbaum.

Anderson, J. (Ed.) (1993). *Rules of the Mind*. Hillsdale, NJ: Erlbaum.

Bandura, A. (1986). *Social Foundations of Thought and Action: A Social Cognitive Theory*. Englewood Cliffs, NJ: Prentice Hall.

Barker, P. (2008). Re-evaluating a model of learning design. *Innovations in Education and Teaching International*, 45, 127–141.

Cagiltay, K. (2006). Scaffolding strategies in electronic performance support systems: Types and challenges. *Innovations in Education and Teaching International*, 43, 93–103.

Card, S., Moran, T. and Newell, A. (1983). *The Psychology of Human-computer Interaction*. Hillsdale, NJ: Erlbaum.

Caretti, B., Borella, E. and De Beni, R. (2007). Does strategic memory training improve the working memory performance of younger and older adults? *Experimental Psychology*, 54, 311–320.

Carlson, R., Khoo, H. and Elliott, R. (1990). Component practice and exposure to a problem solving context. *Human Factors*, 32, 267–286.

Catrambone, R. (1996). Generalizing solution procedures learned from examples. *Journal of Experimental Psychology: Learning, Memory, and Cognition*, 22, 1020–1031.

Catrambone, R. and Holyoak, K. (1990). Learning subgoals and methods for solving probability problems. *Memory and Cognition*, 18, 593–603.

Chase, W. and Simon, H. (1973). Perception in chess. *Cognitive Psychology*, 4, 55–81.

Clark, R. E., Feldon, D., van Merriënboer, J. J. G., Yates, K. and Early, S. (2008). Cognitive task analysis. In J. M. Spector, M. D. Merrill, J. J. G. van Merriënboer and M. P. Driscoll (eds). *Handbook of Research on Educational Communications and Technology* (3rd edn) (pp. 577–593). New York: Routledge.

Ericsson, K. and Kintsch, W. (1995). Long-term working memory. *Psychological Review*, 102, 211–245.

Feldon, D. (2007). Cognitive load and classroom teaching: The double-edged sword of automaticity. *Educational Psychologist*, 42, 123–137.

Feltovich, P., Spiro, R. and Coulson, R. (1997). Issues in expert flexibility in contexts characterized by complexity and change. In P. Feltovich, K. Ford and R. Hoffman (eds). *Expertise in Context* (pp. 126–146). London: MIT Press.

Field, A. (2009). *Discovering Statistics Using SPSS for Windows* (3rd edn). London: Sage.

Gardner, H. (1983). *Frames of Mind: The Theory of Multiple Intelligences*. New York: Basic Books.

Gery, G. (1991). *Electronic Performance Support Systems – How and Why to Remake the Workplace through the Strategic Application of Technology*. Boston, MA: Weingarten Publications.

Gick, M. and Holyoak, K. (1983). Schema induction and analogical transfer. *Cognitive Psychology*, 12, 306–355.

Hong, E. and O'Neill, H. (1992). Instructional strategies to help learners build relevant models in inferential statistics. *Journal of Educational Psychology*, 84, 150–159.

Jennings, C., Kirkpatrick, A. and Mohseni P. (2009). Supporting expert work processes. In P. Barker and P. van Schaik (eds). *Electronic Performance Support: Using Technology to Enable Human Performance* (pp. 249–262). Aldershot: Gower.

Keller, J. (1983). Motivational design of instruction. In C. Reigeluth (ed.) (1983). *Instructional-design Theories and Models: An Overview of their Current Status* (pp. 386–434). Hillsdale, NJ: Erlbaum.

Keller, J. (1987). Strategies for stimulating the motivation to learn. *Performance and Instruction*, 26, 1–7.

Kester, L., Lehnen, C., van Gerven, P. and Kirschner, P. (2006). Just-in-time, schematic supportive information presentation during cognitive skill acquisition. *Computers in Human Behavior*, 22, 93–112.

Kyllonen, P. and Christal, R. (1990). Reasoning ability is (little more) than working-memory capacity? *Intelligence*, 14, 389–433

Leahy, W. and Sweller, J. (2005). Interactions among the imagination, expertise reversal, and element interactivity effects. *Journal of Experimental Psychology: Applied*, 11, 266–276.

Marshall, S.P. (1995). *Schemas in Problem Solving*. Cambridge: Cambridge University Press.

Mayer, R. (1992). *Thinking, Problem Solving, Cognition* (2nd edn). New York: Freeman.

van Merriënboer, J. (1997). *Training Complex Cognitive Skills: A Four-component Instructional Design Model for Technical Training*. Englewood Cliffs, NJ: Educational Technology Publications.

van Merriënboer, J. and Kirschner, P. (2007). *Ten Steps to Complex Learning: A Systematic Approach to Four-component Instructional Design*. Mahwah, NJ: Erlbaum.

Newell, A. and Rosenbloom, P.S. (1981). Mechanisms of skill acquisition and the power law of practice. In J.R. Anderson (ed.), *Cognitive Skills and their Acquisition*. Hillsdale, NJ: Erlbaum.

Newell, A. and Simon, H. (1972). *Human Problem Solving*. Englewood Cliffs, NJ: Prentice-Hall.

Norman, D. (1998). *The Design of Everyday Things*. Cambridge: Cambridge University Press.

Ohlsson, S. and Reese, E. (1991). The function of conceptual understanding in the learning of arithmetic procedures. *Cognition and Instruction*, 8, 103–179.

Patel, V. and Groen, G. (1991). The general and specific nature of medical expertise. In K. Ericsson and J. Smith (eds). *Towards a General Theory of Expertise* (pp. 93–125). Cambridge: Cambridge University Press.

Payne, S., Squibb, H. and Howes, A. (1990). The nature of device models: The yoked state space hypothesis and some experiments with text editors. *Human-Computer Interaction*, 5, 415–444.

Reed, S. and Bolstad, C. (1991). Use of example and procedures in problem solving. *Journal of Experimental Psychology: Learning, Memory, and Cognition*, 17, 753–766.

Reigeluth, C. (ed.) (1983). *Instructional-design Theories and Models: An Overview of their Current Status*. Hillsdale, NJ: Erlbaum.

Reigeluth, C. (ed.) (1987). *Instructional Theories in Action: Lessons Illustrating Selected Theories and Models*. Hillsdale, NJ: Erlbaum.

Reigeluth, C. (ed.) (1999). *Instructional-design Theories and Models (Vol. 2): A New Paradigm of Instructional Theory*. Mahwah, NJ: Erlbaum.

Reigeluth, C. (ed.) (2008). *Instructional-design Theories and Models (Vol. 3)*. Mahwah, NJ: Erlbaum.

Robertson, I. (2001). *Problem Solving*. Hove: Psychology Press.

Schaik, P. van, Barker, P. and Famakinwa, O. (2007). Making a case for using electronic performance support systems in academic libraries. *Journal of Interactive Learning Research*, 18, 411–428.

Schumacher, R.M. and Czerwinski, M.P. (1992). Mental models and the acquisition of expert knowledge. In R.R. Hoffman (ed.), *The Psychology of Expertise: Cognitive Research and Empirical AI*. New York: Springer.

Shackel, B. and Richardson, S. (1991). *Human Factors for Informatics Usability*. Cambridge: Cambridge University Press.

Shneiderman, B. (Ed.) (1978). *Databases: Improving Usability and Responsiveness*. New York: Academic Press.

Simon, H. and Chase, W. (1973). Skill in chess. *American Scientist*, 61, 394–403.

Sternberg, R. and Frensch, P. (1992). On being an expert: A cost-benefit analysis. In R. Hoffman (ed.). *The Psychology of Expertise: Cognitive Research and Empirical AI* (pp. 191–203). New York: Springer.

Sweller, J. (1988). Cognitive load during problem solving: Effects on learning. *Cognitive Science*, 12, 257–285.

Trask, R.L. (2002). *Mind the Gaffe: The Penguin Guide to Common Errors in English*. London: Penguin.

Venkatesh, V., Morris, M., Davis, G. and Davis, F. (2003). User acceptance of information technology: Toward a unified view. *MIS Quarterly*, 27, 425–478.

Willingham, D. (2004). *Cognition* (2nd edn). Upper Saddle River, NJ: Pearson Education.

3 *Technology Perspective*

PHILIP BARKER

This chapter provides a technological basis for the use and development of electronic performance support systems. It starts from a philosophical stance – by considering what may happen if people did not have any form of technology to sustain their lives and livelihoods. Having established the 'impossibility' of life without it, the chapter goes on to consider the basic nature of technology and the different forms that it can take. Particular emphasis is given to electronic technology in the guise of computers. Consideration is then given to the important topic of Human-Computer Interaction (HCI) as a means of providing a communication infrastructure for human use of computers (in general) and Electronic Performance Support Systems (EPSS) (in particular). Because communication and storage infrastructures are such an important aspect of modern life, society and the provision of performance support, special consideration is given to these topics. The final section of this chapter briefly describes and discusses some of the important models relating to the use of electronic performance support technology.

Introduction

While culture and religion provide a meaning for human life and for the creation of societies, it is technology that makes modern life possible. It also provides 'the fabric' from which human societies are built. Imagine a modern world in which there was no form of transport, no communication facilities, no buildings, no farm implements, no education, no medical systems, and so on. Existence would be a pretty difficult affair – if not an impossible one for most people. Technology is therefore an indispensable aid to modern living. However, having said this, it is important to remember that technology can also be used to destroy all that it has been used to create. An important corollary to this statement is the fact that electronic performance support can not only enhance people's ability to create various types of artefact, it can equally well promote their ability to destroy these assets. But, of course, these are relative things! For example, the destruction of a disease is a good thing even though the annihilation of a city would not necessarily be so.

Technology is everywhere about us and, in very many cases, within us and/or upon us. The evidence for this statement comes from the observation that most people wear some form of clothing or jewellery and very many people will probably have a dental filling or two! So, what exactly is this thing called *technology*? A typical dictionary definition of the term may read as follows: '*The application of scientific knowledge for practical purposes*'.

My dictionary also gives the following meaning: '*Machinery and equipment developed from scientific knowledge*'. Within the *Wikipedia* online encyclopaedia there is an extensive and illuminating discussion of this term (*http://en.wikipedia.org/wiki/Technology*). However, the reader is cautioned by the phrase: 'a strict definition is elusive'. Following on from this deliberation, one way in which to view technology is as a *process enabler*. That is, a mechanism that enables the realisation and/or the sustainment of various kinds of process – the types of process supported in any given context will define the particular field of technology involved (medical, educational, electrical, mechanical, bio-mechanical, and so on). It may be that the process(es) that a technology supports will result in the creation of a product of some sort – but this is not always a necessity.

Bearing in mind what has been said above, if an analysis is made of the important roles that technology can play in relation to human existence, it is possible to identify four major generic *strands of activity* to which the theory and practice of electronic performance support may be applied. These strands are depicted schematically in Figure 3.1 by arrows labelled A1 through A4.

Overall, this diagram is intended to portray the fact that ideas and methods for creating technologies originate from within the minds of people – that is, they are rooted within the 'people domain' that is located in the centre of the diagram. People therefore create technologies (such as those denoted by the labels T1 through T5 in the diagram) and then use these in various creative ways to fabricate many different sorts of *tool*, *society*, *product* and *service*.

From the perspective of performance support, the 'tool strand' (A1) in Figure 3.1 refers to a wide range of personal performance aids – such as mobile phones, digital cameras and PDAs. The importance of technology as an extension of human faculties (through

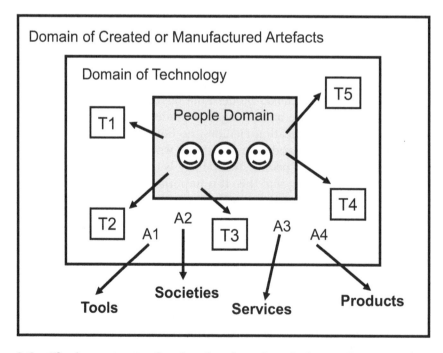

Figure 3.1   The important role of technology in relation to human existence

tool production and use) has been discussed earlier in this book (see Chapter 1). The second important application of technology shown in Figure 3.1 (labelled A2) is its use to produce artefacts to facilitate the creation, control and ongoing development of human societies – for example, the creation of houses, roads, hospitals, railway stations, airports, and so on. Various service industries (labelled A3) will then arise in order to support and maintain the embedded applications of the various technologies within any form of societal infrastructure. The other important outcome of technology application depicted in Figure 3.1 (labelled A4) is the creation of commodities (both products and services) that form the underlying basis for manufacturing and business organisations – such as banks, pharmaceutical companies, motor-car manufacturers and energy production companies – based on the use of wind, gas, electricity, nuclear power, and so on. Obviously, there is a tremendous range of opportunities in each of these activity strands (A1–A4) for the application of electronic performance support aids. Some of these are examined in the second part of this book.

Sometimes, many different technologies will need to be combined to create a desired artefact. A computer-based 'online community' (such as *MSN*), for example, needs to have *computer technology* and *communication technology* combined together in an appropriate way to create it. Of course, the computer technology will itself be dependent on two other important technologies – *hardware* (for example, the computer's screen and its keyboard) and *software* (such as its operating system and browser technologies).

The products that people create using technology do not always have to be 'touch and see' objects. They can be intellectual products or services – such as new ways of thinking about issues of importance, new theories and new knowledge and skills. These are often referred to as 'intellectual products'.

In general, any given type of technology will require the creation of a *technological framework* to support its application and utilisation. This framework will normally make available two essential commodities. First, it will provide a set of fundamental 'building blocks' (or components) that will enable the fabrication of larger, more functional, artefacts. Second, it will make available a set of 'tools' that will facilitate the application of the technology and the creation of these 'constructed' artefacts. The implementation and propagation of a technological framework will require an appropriate *knowledge base* and a supporting *skill base*. The first of these will embed relevant information and knowledge relating to the use of the underlying technology while the second will provide the means by which the technology is employed in effective and efficient ways during the process of artefact creation.

As a simple example of what has been said above, consider the process of painting a picture and the technological framework that is needed to support this activity. Essentially, two basic types of technology are needed to facilitate the creation of a painting: first, some form of *marking technology* (for example, a collection of paints or crayons) and second, an appropriate *recording technology* – a surface to which the paints/crayons can be applied – such as paper or canvas. When painting a picture, some tools will normally be required which will enable the paint to be applied to the surface. Most often, various types of brush are used – but there are many other possibilities (such as one's fingers and a spatula). Anyone can attempt to use these technologies to paint a picture. However, it is usually only an experienced artist who will have sufficient knowledge (about the techniques to be used) who will be able to create a worthwhile painting. And, of course, it is that person's skills with his/her brushes that will dictate how well the picture is actually rendered.

This book is primarily concerned with the use of electronic technologies for enabling and enhancing human performance. As is considered in the following sections, computers are the central technology for realising this objective. However, having said this, it is imperative that mechanisms and products are provided to facilitate human communication with these devices. This chapter therefore also considers the central issues involved in the study and use of HCI. In this context, special attention is given to human communication that is mediated by computer systems. Finally, to provide a basis for the second part of the book, some important models relating to the use of electronic performance support are presented.

Electronic Performance Support Technologies

Technology can take a wide range of different forms and there are many interesting dependencies between its various manifestations. For example, there is *building technology, transport technology, medical technology* and *educational technology*. Each form of technology has emerged for particular reasons and has a specific purpose. Educational Technology (ET), for instance, is concerned with the application of different types of tool and device for the support of teaching and learning processes. Naturally, computers figure prominently as an ET resource – as do marking technologies (chalk, pencils, pens, and so on) and recording technologies (such as paper, notebooks, blackboards, conventional whiteboards and interactive whiteboards). In distance learning situations, communication technologies (such as a postal service, computer networks, radio and TV broadcasting) are an important aspect of ET provision.

Because of the wide range of possibilities that exists for its use, computer technology can be thought of as a *universal performance support technology*. Indeed, it is our belief that there are very few forms of human endeavour which could not benefit from the application of computer-based performance support technology. Bearing in mind its tremendous impact and significance, the central role that computer technology can play in the area of performance support is depicted in a schematic way in the diagram presented in Figure 3.2.

As is shown in this diagram, computer systems of various forms are often the central core technology used for building electronic performance support tools and environments. Earlier in this book (see Chapter 1), mention was made of two different approaches for using computer technology within the context of performance support applications. One of these was as an explicit tool – as is illustrated by the *Information Processing* and *Office Management* tools listed in Figure 3.2. The other way of employing computer technology is as an embedded device that is 'hidden away' inside some other form of technology – for example, a digital camera, a mobile phone, an alarm clock or a washing machine. Bearing in mind these examples of the use of embedded computer technology, it is important to remember that in many situations, computer technology alone (as powerful as it is) will not always provide all that is needed to fulfil every performance enhancement need. Indeed, in many cases, one or more *adjunct technologies* (such as those listed in Figure 3.2) will be required to support and augment the facilities provided by the underlying computer technology.

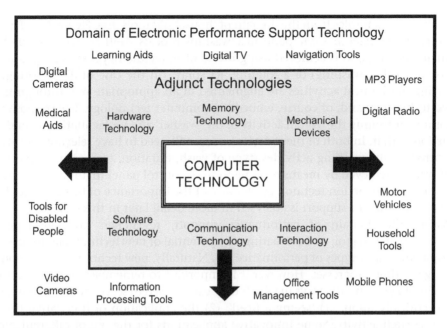

Figure 3.2   Examples of electronic performance support technologies

The way in which different technologies can be used to augment each other, to achieve a particular type of performance aid, can be illustrated by considering the way in which some of the component technologies shown in Figure 3.2 are integrated together within a mobile phone. Such a performance aid can be thought of as an example of a computer system that has been highly optimised for the purpose of facilitating communication between people who are remotely separated from each other. In order to function correctly, a mobile phone will require access to an appropriate telecommunications infrastructure – the *communication technology* shown in Figure 3.2. Indeed, in locations where a 'signal' is not available, the usefulness of this device will be reduced considerably. The utility and usability of a mobile phone will, to a great extent, be dependent on the quality and capability of its end-user interface (the *interaction technology* shown in Figure 3.2). Similarly, when a mobile phone is used for 'texting' purposes (using the SMS messaging facility), the success of this mode of operation will require an embedded text editing tool for the creation of messages – this reflects the importance of the *software technology* identified in the diagram. Many types of mobile phone are now able to take pictures; the amount of information (telephone numbers, addresses, photographs, and so on) that can be stored within a phone of this sort will obviously be a function of the *memory technology* that it employs. Finally, the 'look and feel' of a phone (and its robustness) will depend, to a large extent, upon the *hardware technology* that is used in its fabrication.

When two or more technologies are combined to produce an electronic performance aid, it is likely that one of the technologies will play a major role in the implementation of the underlying performance process while the other technologies will play a more subsidiary, but nevertheless necessary, role. For example, in office automation systems, explicit computer technology will provide the major performance enhancing function while other office technologies will play a more supportive role. As a further illustration of this principle, consider the underlying structure of a washing machine and electronic dishwasher – as examples from the domain of 'household tools' (see Figure 3.2). The main function of these machines is to perform a 'washing process' – either on clothes or dishes. Essentially, this process is achieved using mechanical technology – either 'agitation' (in the case of clothes washing) or a rotating 'jet spray' (in the case of dishwashing). The underlying mechanical activities are augmented in an appropriate way through the use of fluid technology and, of course, embedded computer technology. The purpose of the latter is for controlling the overall activity of the 'washer' and for facilitating an end-user's interaction with it. In both of these devices, users will need to have relevant mechanisms for controlling the washing activities (type of wash, duration, temperature, and so on). This is usually achieved by means of some form of control panel that is based on the use of appropriate interaction technology. Because of the importance of this latter topic, this aspect of performance support is analysed in more detail later in this chapter.

Within the domain of performance support, researchers and developers are continually searching for, and evaluating, the potential of new technologies for use in the development of new types of performance aid. Naturally, new technologies will continue to emerge as time progresses. However it is important to remember that the creation of new technologies (and the ways in which they can be used to solve problems) will usually depend critically upon: (1) 'seeing a need'; (2) the application of innovative thinking; and (3) research activity. Some innovative applications for the use of different types of technology for performance support purposes are discussed in the second part of this book.

The Importance of Computers

The underlying importance of computer technology in relation to its use within a performance support context has been established and briefly mentioned in an earlier section of this book (see 'The Role of Technology' in Chapter 1). In that section, it was emphasised that the utility of computers arose from their numerous 'attractive' capabilities in areas where 'native' human ability is often inadequate – such as performing numerical calculations (at speed and with accuracy), remembering and recalling things (when large numbers of items are involved) and decision making (in complex situations). Chapter 1 outlined the underlying rationale for using computers; this current section of the book now builds upon and expands the material that was previously presented.

There is a very wide range of computer technology available for use within the fabrication stages of a performance support project. Some of the possibilities that exist are illustrated in a diagrammatic way in Figure 3.3. As is illustrated in this diagram, it is customary to think of computer technology in terms of five basic dimensions. These are: *hardware* resources, *software* resources, *memory* resources, *interaction devices* and computer *infrastructures*. The diagram shows computer infrastructures at the top of the pentagonal structure to reflect (and emphasise) the point that this type of resource represents the various kinds of integrated system that can be generated by mixing together and consolidating the various component technologies signified by the other vertices of the pentagon.

Some examples of the different types of component that make up the five dimensions of computer technology listed above are presented in Table 3.1. It is important to emphasise that the various components listed in this table do not in any way represent a

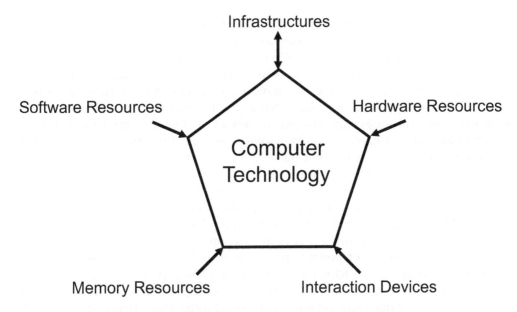

Figure 3.3   Five important dimensions of computer technology

Table 3.1   Examples of specific types of computer technology

Infrastructures	Hardware	Software	Interaction	Memory
Devices	Processors	Archiving	Acoustic	Embedded
- PDA	- single	Bespoke	- speech input	Removable
- Laptop	- multiple	Utilities	- speech output	Portable
- Desktop PC	Custom Boards	- Printing	- sound effects	Archival
Systems	- processor	- Editing	- music	Solid State
- bespoke	- memory	- Mapping	Tactile	Magnetic
- generic	Interfaces	Packages	- single touch	Optical
Networks	- internal	- Database	- multi-touch	- CD-ROM
- local	- external	- Email	Visual	- CD-R
- intranet	Communications	- Conferencing	- 2-D	- DVD
- global	- wire	- e-Commerce	- 3-D	
- private	- optical	- Financial	Gestural	
- public	- wireless	- Statistical	- hand	
	- satellite	- Graphics	- limbs	
	- broadcast	- VLE	- body	
	Servers	- LMS	Sensing	
	Modems	Web-based	- Motion	
	Storage	- Services	- Position	
	- online	- Social	- Location	
	- offline	- Webs	- Human body	
	- archival	- Weblogs	Scanning	
		- Wikis	- security	
		Intelligent	- identity	
		- tutoring	RFID tagging	
		- routing	- security	
			- identity	

fully comprehensive range of resources; the items presented are intended to be indicative (of the technology available) rather than definitive.

Essentially, the term 'infrastructure' is used to describe such artefacts as workstation clusters (as used, for example, in a bank, travel agent or design office), inhouse organisational networks (as may be employed in a hospital), distributed corporate networks and international networks (such as the Internet and the World Wide Web). Some examples of explicit computer systems (desktop PC, laptop computer and PDA) were briefly mentioned in Chapter 1 – as were some examples of the memory resources listed in Table 3.1. There are lots of other possibilities for using hardware technology – such as microprocessor chips (integrated circuits) and 'control boards' that can be embedded into consumer devices such as washing machines and mobile phones. The way in which the functionality of a device (such as a telephone) can be increased using this type of embedded technology (in conjunction with appropriate software) is considered in the short case study that is presented later in this section.

From the perspective of performance support, one particularly important area of software technology is that which deals with *application packages*. Essentially, these are software systems that have been developed for use in particular specialist areas. Most of these packages implement some form of *tool-set architecture*. That is, they provide a collection of tools, each one of which is intended to perform a particular function within its specialist domain. For example, in a graphics package – such as Adobe's *Photoshop* (Matthews et al., 2004) – there would probably be a 'rectangle' tool and an 'ellipse' tool which could be used to create instances of these objects on a computer's display screen. Similarly, in a statistical package such as *Statistical Package for the Social Sciences* (SPSS) there would be tools to facilitate a wide range of statistical procedures – such as correlation and regression analysis (Field, 2005). These two examples of software systems are illustrations of bespoke packages that have been designed for use in particular areas of human activity – graphical design and data analysis, respectively. In a similar way, packages like the *Virtual Learning Environment* (VLE) and the *Library Management System* (LMS) listed in Table 3.1 also provide infrastructures that embed tool-sets relevant to the processes of managing an organisation's learning resources and library-based materials, respectively. Generic software packages are also available (such as word-processing and spreadsheet systems) that have extremely wide utility since they can be used within many different domains of human activity.

Another very important type of resource depicted in Figure 3.3, and listed in Table 3.1, is that labelled 'Interaction Devices'. Resources in this category are needed for the facilitation of HCI – that is, people's use of computer systems of various sorts. Because of its importance within performance support systems, this topic is discussed in more detail later in this chapter.

Using Technology – An Illustrative Case Study

In order to illustrate how the resources listed in Table 3.1 can be used to create different sorts of electronic performance support environment, the remainder of this section is used to present a case study. It describes and discusses how an existing human-performance aid (a telephone) can be augmented with adjunct technology to extend its functionality.

This additional functionality would be able to improve human performance in relation to extending a person's ability to communicate a message successfully.

As a human-performance improvement tool, the conventional telephone was designed to enable people to project their voices (or other sounds) beyond their immediate locality. Its intent was therefore to enable people to send and receive spoken utterances – as can be seen in the upper part of Figure 3.4. However, there is a major problem with this 'simple' telephone tool. If one person makes a call to another, and the person being telephoned is not at his/her phone then the calling transaction cannot be successfully completed.

To overcome the above limitation, it is a relatively simple matter to augment the functionality of a conventional telephone by adding an 'answering' capability using some of the technological components listed in Table 3.1. Such a mechanism would enable a caller to leave a message for a recipient that cannot be directly contacted. A system diagram for a typical answering facility is presented in the lower part of Figure 3.4. The realisation of this performance improvement aid would involve the addition of (1) a microprocessor (for control purposes); (2) some memory (for storage of messages); (3) an end-user interface; and (4) appropriate software to control and coordinate the activity of the various components. After the system enhancement features have been added, the end-user interface to the augmented telephone would need to provide the following basic functions: (1) an audio message for the callers that would alert them to the availability of the messaging facility; (2) a simple visual and/or acoustic alerting facility for the owner of the phone – indicating the presence of new stored messages; and (3) a simple tactile

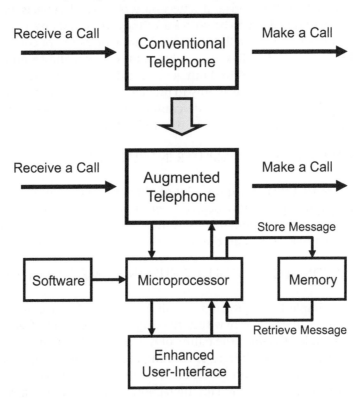

Figure 3.4   Augmenting a conventional telephone in order to improve its functionality

command facility that would enable the owner of the phone to retrieve and delete stored messages from the telephone's memory facility.

Of course, lots of extra facilities could be added to the augmented phone once the basic augmentation technology was in place. These could include such things as the storage of telephone numbers, call filtering and call re-routing. Appropriate extensions to the phone's end-user interface would be needed to accommodate these.

An alternative way of extending the functionality of a conventional telephone would be to provide these facilities through the medium of the telephone company that is responsible for supplying the phone service. In a similar way, large organisations may also offer their own inhouse message recording facilities – as a less expensive option than upgrading all their telephones. The way in which these support tools are provided would strongly influence the design of the end-user interface that provides access to them. The topic of human-computer interface design is outlined in the following section.

Human-Computer Interaction

HCI is a tremendously important aspect of electronic performance support environments. Its importance stems from the fact that the theory and practice of HCI can enable us to achieve two important goals. First, it provides us with a basis for designing effective and efficient mechanisms for facilitating people's use of electronic performance support tools. Second, it enables us to understand (and, if necessary, observe) the effects that performance support environments are likely to have on a user's cognitive and physical behaviour. The theory and practice of HCI are well documented in the literature of computing – see, for example, Smith-Atakan (2006), Dix et al. (1998) and Newman and Lamming (1995). The reader is referred to these sources for both general and in-depth treatments of this topic. The aim of this section of the book is only to provide an overview of the essential features of this discipline by introducing and describing some simple models and techniques – and the ways in which these are used in the study of HCI.

MODELS USED IN HUMAN-COMPUTER INTERACTION

Within the area of HCI there are quite a lot of different types of model. These are often used to describe and explain how people interact with computers and the effect that this interaction has upon them. In this section two basic models are described: the Information-Flow model (IFM) and the Human-Information Processor model (HIP).

THE INFORMATION-FLOW MODEL OF HUMAN-COMPUTER INTERACTION

This is one of the simplest, and probably, one of the most well-known models of HCI. The IFM is depicted in a schematic way within the diagram presented in Figure 3.5.

The IFM is intended to reflect the nature of the 'personal' (that is, an individual's) use of a computer facility for the purpose of realising the aided (see Chapter 1) execution of tasks in either of two broad contexts. These tasks may be: (1) internal to the computer and/or (2) external to it. An individual's interaction with a computer (as shown in Figure 3.5) will usually take place within the confines of some particular local environment – for example, a classroom, a home, a hospital, an airport or on a train. The model is

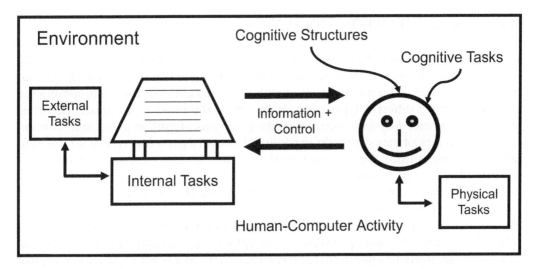

Figure 3.5   The information-flow model of human-computer interaction

referred to as an IFM because the basis of the human-computer activity taking place in the interaction depends upon the flow of information that takes place between the computer and its human user. This information could be of two basic types: that which is to be processed (as a result of task execution) and that which is needed for controlling the execution of tasks and other related activities.

There are four different types of task illustrated in Figure 3.5: first, the cognitive tasks taking place within the mind of the user (decision making, computation, recall of knowledge, and so on); second, the local physical tasks the user may have to perform (such as a mouse-move operation or a screen reading act); third, tasks that are internal to the computer system (for example, the creation of a text or graphics document); and fourth, tasks that are external to the local computer but which are mediated by it. These latter tasks may take place within the immediate environment of the computer (such as printing a document on a local printer) or they may be actioned in an entirely different 'remote' environment – for example, they could involve controlling the movement of a robotic device on the surface of a remote planet or deep beneath the sea.

When studying the model presented in Figure 3.5, one very important consideration that needs to be taken into account is the effect that the information flow (from computer to human) has on the *cognitive structures* and *cognitive activity* that is taking place within the mind of the computer's user. It is very likely that some of this information can be regarded as a source of experience and it could therefore be used to create, enhance and reinforce the user's *mental models* (see Chapters 2 and 4). However, there may be other situations in which the provision of too much external information could lead to the onset of *cognitive dilemma* (that is, not knowing the best course of action to take). This, in turn, could give rise to a reduction in human performance. This type of problem is a particularly important one in areas such as air-traffic control – see the work described by Waldron et al. (2007).

Later parts of this chapter will discuss how 'units' of the type shown in Figure 3.5 can be replicated and inter-connected (using a global communications network) to provide powerful environments for the support of Computer-Mediated Communication (CMC) and Computer-Supported Collaborative Working (CSCW) environments.

THE HUMAN INFORMATION PROCESSOR MODEL

The HIP model was introduced some decades ago by Card, Moran and Newell (1983). Essentially, this model was proposed as a mechanism for explaining human behaviour within the context of human interaction with computers. It does this by proposing the existence of three different types of memory within the mind of a human. The three memory types are: *long-term memory*; *working* (or short-term) *memory*; and *transient memory*. Each type of memory works in conjunction with a particular type of information processing mechanism: the *perceptual processor*, the *cognitive processor* and the *motor processor*. The way in which these memory and processing resources work together is described by a collection of ten Principles of Operation. One of these was referred to in Chapter 1: the Power Law of Practice.

The way in which the HIP model explains human information-processing behaviour is based on a three-step strategy involving perception, cognition and action. The human mind gains an awareness of internal and external events as a result of various perceptual processes; these are 'sensed' by the human body's sense organs (eyes, nose, ears, and so on). These 'leave' information in a set of transient information stores. The perceptual processor handles this material and extracts relevant and important items – leaving them in working memory. The cognitive processor analyses the material in short-term memory and decides what to do with it. This may involve either (1) coding it for storage in Long-Term Memory (LTM) for future use; (2) making immediate decisions; or (3) retrieving material from LTM that subsequently determines what actions need to be taken. If any physical action is needed, the motor processor is activated; this causes activation of the appropriate parts of the human body to implement the relevant activity.

The HIP model has been successfully used to explain quite a number of HCI activities – such as response times to a visual stimulus, reading rates and typing speeds. Within a number of areas, the model leads to quite good agreement between the theoretical predication and experimental observation of interaction parameters. Associated with the HIP model are a number of other important models such as the Goals, Operators, Methods, Selection (GOMS) rules and the Key-stroke Level (KLM) models. Again, each of these models can be used to predict and/or explain various aspects of HCI.

INTERFACE DESIGN

To facilitate the flow of information and control (I+C) between a computer system and its user(s), some form of *end-user interface* is needed. This requirement is illustrated in Figure 3.6. In this diagram, the target of the user's interaction is now depicted as a 'computer-based system' – since use of this term implies a broader range of target technology than is suggested by Figure 3.5. It could, of course, refer to both explicit computer systems and the use of systems and devices in which the computer technology is embedded within some other host technology.

The nature of the end-user interface to a computer-based system will depend to a large extent on three important factors: (1) the characteristics of the application domain involved; (2) the nature of the tasks that can be undertaken within that domain; and (3) the characteristics and intent of its users – that is, each individual's ability (or lack of) and what they want to achieve as a result of interaction activity. The ways in which interfaces are designed in order to achieve particular objectives, and the procedures involved, are

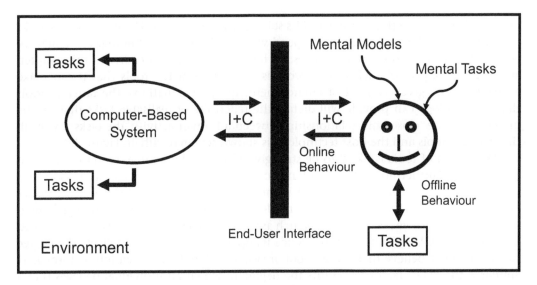

Figure 3.6   The function of an end-user interface

documented in the relevant literature of HCI – see, for example, Eberts (1994). One of the most important aspects of interface design is *task analysis* – which is discussed later in this section.

Once an interface has been designed, the 'interaction technology' described earlier in this chapter could be used to fabricate the various types of interface needed to facilitate interaction in any given context. The way in which these resources are assembled, the requirements they impose upon users and the functionality they provide access to will determine the *usability* and *utility* of the end-user interface that is created. Within explicit computer systems, the commonest types of interface hardware are keyboards/keypads, display screens and various types of mouse. In many systems that use this type of interface technology, much of the variability of the interface will be derived from the relevant use of embedded software technology in the form of general purpose or bespoke computer programs. Software programs can be employed in a variety of different ways to 'tailor' (or personalise) interfaces in order to meet the specific requirements of individual users or categories of user. This personalisation capability can be seen in devices such as digital cameras and DVD players intended for international markets – where its user is able to choose the language (say, English, French, German, and so on) that the end-user interface will use. Human disability is another very important area where both system and interface personalisation are important considerations. This topic is referred to in more detail in the second part of this book.

TASK ANALYSIS

Before an end-user interface for an application can be designed and fabricated, it will usually be necessary to identify and understand the nature of the underlying tasks that the user will be require to perform when using the interface. The process of identifying and describing the tasks involved in a particular human-computer activity is called 'task analysis' – the most popular approach being *hierarchical task analysis* (Diaper, 1989). Once a task analysis has been conducted, a *requirements specification* can be created. This will form the basis for interface design and its subsequent fabrication. The nature of the tasks that will need to be performed will depend very much on the technological framework within which their host activity resides. As has been mentioned earlier in this chapter, an important aspect of such a framework is the nature of the tools that it can make available in any given context or environment. In many situations, the range of tools that a technology can provide will dictate the repertoire of realisable tasks that can be undertaken. The 'close knit' relationship between a human activity, the tasks involved, the available tools and the host technology is shown schematically in Figure 3.7.

The design of tools is likely to be strongly influenced by a range of ergonomic and safety issues. Furthermore, the acceptance of these tools by an individual person or a workforce may need to be considered within the context of the *technology-acceptance model* described by Davies (1989). This model proposes that when users are confronted with a new technology, various factors such as its Perceived Usefulness (PU) and Perceived Ease-of-Use (PEOU) will strongly influence its uptake. The PU factor reflects the degree to which people believe that using a tool or system will enhance their job performance. Similarly, the PEOU factor represents the degree to which an individual believes that a particular tool or system would be free from substantial effort to use it.

To illustrate the important role that task analysis plays within the context of performance support (in general) and interface design (in particular), some consideration is now given to a simple 'copying problem'. This is depicted schematically in Figure 3.8. Solving the problem involves making one or more copies of the single page shown on the left-hand side of the diagram.

A range of technological possibilities exist for solving this problem. However, it is assumed that only six options are available. A copy of the document could be made:

[1]   manually using just a pencil (and paper);
[2]   manually using a ruler, compass and pencil;

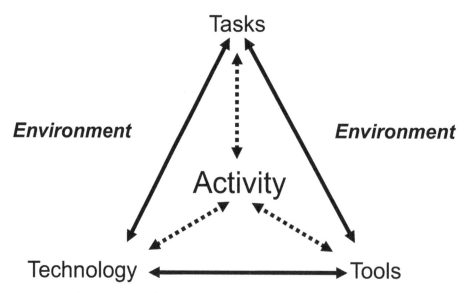

Figure 3.7   Tasks, tools and technology use within a domain of activity

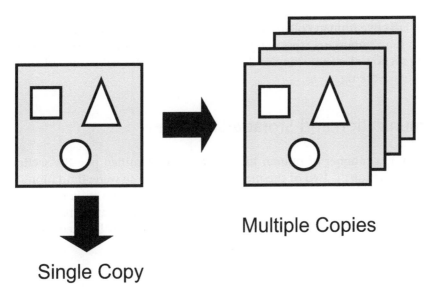

Multiple Copies

Single Copy

Figure 3.8   An example of task analysis

[3]   manually using tracing paper;
[4]   mechanically using a 'single-button' photocopier;
[5]   automatically using a 'multi-button photocopier with a display capability'; and
[6]   automatically using a personal computer fitted with a scanner and printer.

When contemplating the task analysis, it is necessary to think about the different copying technologies involved and the nature of the interfaces that would be required. It is also important to consider the nature of the knowledge and skills needed to use each of the copying technologies – and the quality of the results that would be obtained. The timescale involved may also be an important consideration. There are two broad options available: either using manual copying techniques or use some sort of copying machine. Of course, the nature of the interface required in a machine (options [4], [5] and [6]) would depend upon the functionality that it made available. A single-button photocopier (option [4]) may use a single depression of that button to produce a single copy of the document; producing 100 copies would therefore require a corresponding number of button presses. However, in option [5], an embedded microprocessor combined with a keypad interface and simple visual-display mechanism would enable the number of copies to be entered – the machine then being left to complete the photocopying task automatically. If extra functionality was needed (such as contrast settings, size reduction/ enlargement, collating, back-to-back copying, and so on) the nature of the end-user interface would need to be designed to accommodate this. Similarly, if it was required to do various sorts of image enhancement and manipulation then option [6] may be the best approach since different types of software tool could be made available within the computer to facilitate these requirements.

In the absence of options [4], [5] and [6], if it was required to produce a large number of copies using a manual approach (within a short timescale), then it may be necessary to 'employ' a group of suitably trained people to help perform the copying task. In a way, this would involve a group of people working in a collaborative way to solve the problem. Effective human collaboration within the context of problem solving and task execution is an important aspect of performance support. Because of its importance the following section discusses some of the issues involved in facilitating collaboration and collaborative working.

Communication and Storage Structures

In Chapter 1, a number of human limitations were identified (see the section entitled 'Human Limitiations'). Two of the most important of these were: limitations relating to the bounds of *human communication* ability; and shortcomings in *human memory* when remembering, recalling and sharing large volumes of data and information. This section briefly discusses some of the ways in which technology can be used to address these shortcomings.

IMPORTANT COMMUNICATION TECHNOLOGIES

The history of the development of human communication has evolved in four major phases. First, developing various forms of language and then learning how to speak, listen, read, write and use body language for the purposes of expressing ideas, emotions and the implementation of control activity. Second, creating and using 'mass communication' and broadcasting technologies – such as print, radio and TV. Third, developing and learning how to use personal communication technologies such as the telephone. Fourth, developing various kinds of computer and using these to achieve different forms of CMC.

Writing is an important human activity; originally, its power was to be found in its ability to overcome the transience of spoken forms of communication. Nowadays, this is less necessary – with the advent of powerful digital sound recording and editing technologies. As was described and discussed earlier in this chapter, conventional approaches to drawing (and writing) depend to a large extent on two basic technologies: a *marking technology* (such as a pen or pencil) and a *recording technology* (for example, paper). The advent of computer technology has changed the nature of many of the tasks involved in conventional approaches to writing – for example, the extensive use of a keyboard instead of a pencil. The use of a computer has also made available different forms of writing – for example, non-linear documents in addition to the conventional linear types (Barker, 1993). Computer systems are also changing the ways in which written documents are being delivered to their intended recipients.

Undoubtedly, one of the most important modern-day communication technologies is the *global communication network*, of which, the Internet is probably one of the most well-known examples (Hafner and Lyon, 1996; Naughton, 2000; Berners-Lee and Fischetti, 2000). Such networks provide us with a wide range of computer-based communication mechanisms that are broadly referred to as CMC. The principle underlying CMC is illustrated schematically in Figure 3.9. This shows how a basic personal-computer unit (shown previously in Figure 3.5) can be replicated and interconnected using a communication network in order to achieve local and/or global connectivity (and information sharing) – depending upon the type of communication network that is used.

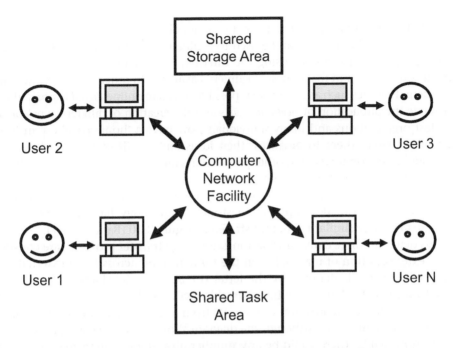

Figure 3.9   The basic principle of computer-mediated communication

One of the most popular and well-established approaches to CMC is probably electronic mail (email). This can be used to facilitate the exchange of a wide range of different types of message and electronic document. Digital networks also make it possible to implement various forms of real-time (synchronous) 'chatting' facilities (such as 'Internet Relay Chat' and Internet telephony – for example, using the VoIP approach). Systems of the type shown in Figure 3.9 are also important (from a performance support perspective) since they provide mechanisms for the support of CSCW – based on the availability of shared storage areas and shared workspaces (as discussed below).

Computer networks are also important from the perspective of implementing various approaches to e-commerce and e-business – and the resulting improvements in performance that can be achieved for consumers, manufacturers and suppliers. For example, use of the Internet can open up a far wider range of marketplaces (and hence, services and commodities) than may be available through conventional outlets (such as shops and stores) in any particular geographical area.

IMPORTANT STORAGE TECHNOLOGIES

As well as providing various mechanisms to facilitate human communication, another important facility that computer-based technology can provide is the ability to 'store' references to and representations of the various materials and artefacts that people create – thereby overcoming the shortcomings of their memory. Some of the important forms of personal electronic storage were introduced in Chapter 1 (see the section entitled 'The Role of Technology'). Bearing in mind that material, it is now necessary to discuss briefly the importance of computer networks (such as the Internet) as a medium for the storage (and publication) of digital resources (see Figure 3.9).

The ability of a communication network to provide electronic storage that can be accessed by any number of other people can be used to facilitate the creation of a 'personal' global publication facility. For example, using the Internet, an individual could store electronic documents on a *server* and make these documents available to others who are interested in reading them. Facilities such as this make it possible to create online *digital libraries*; they can also facilitate the publication of *electronic books* and the creation of different types of *virtual world*. Most organisations and many individuals now have a 'home page' on an Internet server which enables them to broadcast their ideas and details of their work and wares (either academic or commercial) to other people that could be based anywhere in the world – provided the locations at which they are based have suitable network connectivity. This represents a very powerful development in terms of human communication capability.

An equally powerful development in storage technology has been the advent of *shareable storage space* similar to that illustrated in Figure 3.10 (Barker, 2007).

In this diagram, three data/information/knowledge transfer processes are considered. First, the exteriorisation of material from the human mind across to an external private storage medium; this is denoted by the letter (E). Second, the sharing of some of this material by means of a dynamic public shareable medium; this process is labelled as (S) in the diagram. Third, the acquisition of material from a shareable medium; this is labelled as process (A) in Figure 3.10. Although the diagram shows only two users of the shareable medium, in principle, there could be any number. Examples of shareable media can be found in the many intranet systems, private networks and public networks (such as the Internet) that are now commonly available.

TECHNOLOGY TO SUPPORT COLLABORATION

The ability to use the Internet for storing, accessing and sharing information (see Figures 3.9 and 3.10) has made it possible to develop many different types of online collaborative

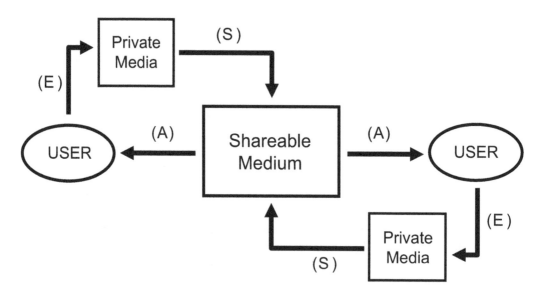

Figure 3.10 Using a computer network to store and share data and information

structure such as online conferencing, 'chat rooms', social websites, and so on. From a performance support perspective, two very useful online structures for the support of collaboration are *weblogs* (Doctorow et al., 2002; Clyde, 2004) and *wikis* (Klobas, 2006; Ebersbach, Glaser and Heigl, 2006).

A weblog (or 'blog') is essentially an online electronic journal (created by an author) that other people are allowed to access and to which they can add comments should they desire to do so. There are literally 'millions' of blogs on the Internet. A typical example of a community blogging facility within a particular region of the UK can be found at the following web address: *http://www.gazettelive.co.uk*. A specific example of a weblog from this online community (which is organised by postcode) can be found at the following address: *http://SRC-Weblog.blogspot.com*.

In many ways, a wiki is a more useful and a more powerful collaboration tool than a weblog. The most well-known example of a collaborative wiki is probably that known as *Wikipedia* – the online encyclopaedia. Indeed, at numerous places within this book, readers are referred to several references in this electronic sourcebook – see, for example, the 'Introduction' section of this chapter. Although wikis provide a useful framework for facilitating collaboration they can also be used in a variety of different ways for personal information management and electronic book publication (Barker, 2007).

Communication networks and shared resources of the types previously described in this section make it possible to implement many different types of CSCW environment in which the participants could be located at very different geographical locations. A typical CSCW environment is illustrated schematically in Figure 3.11.

This diagram shows how a set of shared resources can be used to facilitate and coordinate a team's efforts to solve a problem within a particular domain of activity. For example, the people involved could be using a shared electronic 'whiteboard' facility to create a concept map (see *Wikipedia*) to represent the important issues involved in the design of a new type of computer laser printer (see *Wikipedia*, again!). The tool-sets

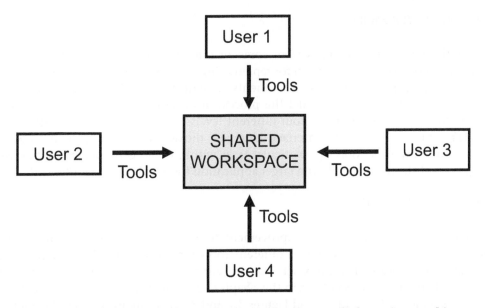

Figure 3.11 A typical shared-workspace approach to collaborative working

available to members of the problem-solving team may be different (depending upon each specific member's specialist skills) but they must all allow three basic functions: (1) communication between team members; (2) visualisation of the workspace objects; and (3) manipulation of these objects in various ways.

Models of Performance Support

This section introduces and briefly describes some of the underlying models often used when employing performance support technologies to improve the efficiency and effectiveness of both human and system performance.

THE INTENT-TECHNOLOGY-OUTCOME (ITO) MODEL

The 'Intent-Technology-Outcome' (ITO) model is a three-step representation of a technology-based approach to problem solving. It starts from identifying the *intent* of the performance project and then moves on to identifying appropriate combinations of *technology* that could be used for its realisation. These combinations are reviewed and assessed so that the likely *outcomes* from their use can be gauged. As an example, consider the problem of wanting to travel (the intent) from one location to another (the outcome). Some of the possibilities that exist (that is, the technologies) could be: walking, cycling, using a car, taking a train, using a bus, flying by aeroplane – or some appropriate and relevant combination of these. The ITO model is used to identify the most appropriate combination of resources that is needed to achieve the outcome – bearing in mind the availability and suitability of the resources and the time/cost frameworks involved in using them. The ITO model is often used in conjunction with, and as a precursor to, the use of the Performance Assessment model that is described later in this section.

THE FOUR-LAYER MODEL

One of the important outcomes from some of our early research into EPSS was the derivation of the 'Four-Layer' model for representing some of the different steps involved in developing support tools and environments (Banerji, 1995; Barker and Banerji, 1995). As its name suggests, in this model the process of developing a performance support environment involves the use of four different levels (or layers) of involvement. These are: (1) producing the end-user interface design; (2) the development of generic tools; (3) the creation of specific tools (for particular tasks within the target domain); and (4) the integration of the tool-sets into the target application for which they are intended.

THE TOOL-SET MODEL

The importance of performance improvement tools has been considered by Stevens and Stevens (1995). A collection of different tools for use in a particular application domain is often regarded as a tool-set. The concept of an 'application tool-set' has been mentioned on numerous occasions in this chapter – see, for example, the section entitled 'The Importance of Computers' and Figures 3.7 and 3.11. Normally, the results of a task analysis (as described in the section entitled 'Human-Computer Interaction') would be used to identify candidate tools for use within a given application domain; these tools would then be fabricated using an appropriate technological framework (see Figure 3.7). As was suggested above, individual tools and/or tool-sets can be either generic or specific. For example, in the context of software tools, a spreadsheet package is essentially a generic tool-set that can be used in any number of application domains that require numerical processing and data analysis. However, this generic software tool could be used to create specific support tools for use in particular areas of activity. A spreadsheet package could thus be used to create a specific tool-set for use in the areas of banking, accounting, and so on.

The rationale underlying the development and use of tool-sets is illustrated schematically in Figure 3.12.

This diagram shows how different technologies (either individually or in combination with each other) can be used to produce various types of performance improvement tool that collectively make up a tool-set. Essentially, within the above diagram, each realisable tool-set defines a domain of feasible tasks that it can be used to support. Of course, the effectiveness of any given tool-set will depend upon the various techniques that have been developed for using it to achieve particular outcomes. The effective use of these techniques will depend very much upon the skills and knowledge of the person (or team) involved in using the tools that make up a given tool-set.

THE TOOL-AUGMENTATION MODEL (TAM)

The Tool-Augmentation Model (TAM) was indirectly introduced earlier in this chapter when it was used as a basis for the 'telephone augmentation' case study that was presented in the section entitled 'The Importance of Computers'. Essentially, the TAM model is based on the principle of identifying shortcomings in existing performance tools and

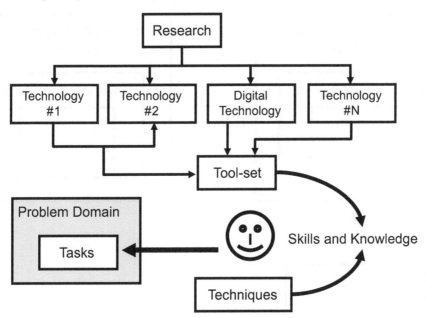

Figure 3.12 Rationale underlying the tool-set model

then designing appropriate augmentations (using suitable technologies) to overcome these. One of the most popular realisations of this model can be found in the provision of software packages for computers in order to meet particular needs that the available software does not fulfil. From a commercial perspective, the TAM also forms the basis for the many 'competitive' improvements that manufacturer's make to the consumer products they produce – such as motor-cars, digital cameras and mobile phones.

THE PERFORMANCE-ASSESSMENT MODEL (PAM)

In general, the theory and practice of performance support are concerned with improving human capability in particular areas of activity. As a corollary to this, performance support must also consider ways of improving the performance of the tools and systems that people employ. As was discussed in Chapter 1, in order to achieve this, the availability of various types of performance-assessment technique is an essential requirement. This need is summarised in the Performance-Assessment Model (PAM) which is illustrated schematically in Figure 3.13.

Essentially, the PAM provides us with a technique and strategy for deciding upon which performance interventions will be most suitable for improving the performance of a given human-activity system through the application of interventions such as new (or more effective) tools and/or environmental changes. It is important to regard performance assessment as an ongoing process of monitoring the performance of a given human activity (involving the use of a specific set of tools) within a particular environmental setting. In situations where it becomes necessary to improve system performance, it is necessary to design and introduce a performance-enhancing intervention. The ongoing performance-monitoring process shown in Figure 3.13 can then be used to justify the

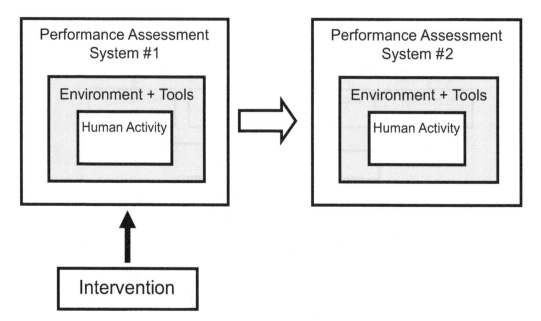

Figure 3.13 The principle underlying the performance assessment model

use of the intervention or, alternatively, indicate further weaknesses in the system where improvement is needed.

THE VIRTUALISATION MODEL

The principle of virtualisation involves identifying particular activities within a task environment (and interfaces to them) and 'shifting' the environment in which they are performed from one 'real' context to another 'simulated' one that is, for one reason or another, more advantageous in terms of performance improvement. For example, consider the physical activity of 'throwing' a switch from one position to another – in order, for example, to switch on a light. Because such a switch contains moving parts that 'rub' against each other, there is an intrinsic unreliability in such an object – due to wearing of the parts that contact with each other. The activity of throwing a switch could, in principle, be made more reliable (and its performance thereby improved) by removing any dependency on moving parts. This can be achieved by emulating the behaviour of a real switch by one that is simulated within a virtual (computer-based) environment.

COLLABORATIVE WORKING MODEL

There are very many situations in which problems require a team of people to be involved in problem-solving activity – as was depicted previously in Figure 3.11. Essentially, this diagram embodies the basic model underlying the concept of collaborative working. When applying this model to particular situations, it is necessary to give due consideration to the basic nature (and development) of both the specific and the generic tools that a team will need and the ways in which the various members of a problem-solving team may wish to communicate with each other. The types of tool-set and communication resources likely to be needed in any given situation will obviously depend upon the underlying nature and requirements of the problem-solving team. Generally, this can be of two broad types: (1) teams that meet in a face-to-face fashion and which are based in the same geographical locality; and (2) teams which are of a 'virtual' nature and which need to use the CSCW techniques described earlier in this section.

Conclusion

As was stated at the beginning of this chapter, technology is an indispensable component of modern living and of contemporary societies. It is therefore a necessary and fundamental 'building block' in the design and fabrication of electronic performance support tools and environments. Obviously, 'technology' covers a very broad range of possibilities. However, as its name implies, the effective deployment of *electronic performance support* will necessarily involve the use of some form of digital technology for its realisation. In many cases, the use of some form of computer technology will be central to the design and fabrication of a support environment. Having said this, it is also necessary to remember that a wide range of 'adjunct technologies' will be required to augment the underlying computer resources that are employed. Undoubtedly, in addition to the basic 'processing power' that computers provide, two other extremely important adjunct technologies are those that provide us with global communication capabilities and the ability to store substantially large volumes of digital data, information and knowledge. The effective use of the various support technologies described in this chapter depends critically upon the sound use of these resources according to established guidelines and 'good practice' – as are embodied in the established theory and practice of electronic performance support. Much of the experiential knowledge that has accrued in this area is embedded within the various models of technology utilisation that currently exist and which steer activity in this area. A number of the more important of these models have been briefly described in this chapter. Some of the ways in which these models are deployed in practical human-performance improvement situations will be described in the chapters that make up the second part of the book.

Acknowledgement

I am grateful to Paul van Schaik for his useful criticism and helpful suggestions for improving this chapter.

References

Banerji, A.K. (1995). *Designing Electronic Performance Support Systems*, Ph.D thesis. Middlesbrough, UK: University of Teesside.

Barker, P.G. (1993). *Exploring Hypermedia*. London, UK: Kogan Page.

Barker, P.G. (2007). Blended Learning the Wiki Way. In *Proceedings of the Second International Conference on Blended Learning – Supporting the Net Generation of Learner*, (pp. 60–71), 14th June 2007, The Fielder Centre. Hatfield, UK: University of Hertfordshire Press.

Barker, P.G. and Banerji, A. (1995). Designing Electronic Performance Support Systems, *Innovations in Education and Training International*, 32(1), 4–12.

Berners-Lee, T. and Fischetti, M. (2000). *Weaving the Web: The Original Design and Ultimate Destiny of the World Wide Web by its Inventor*. New York, NY: Harper-Collins Publishers Inc.

Card, S.K., Moran, T.P. and Newell, A. (1983). *The Psychology of Human-Computer Interaction*. Hillsdale, NJ: Lawrence Erlbaum Associates.

Clyde, L.A. (2004). *Weblogs and Libraries*. Oxford, UK: Chandos Publishing Ltd.

Davis, F.D. (1989). Perceived Usefulness, Perceived Ease-of-Use, and User Acceptance of Information Technology, *MIS Quarterly*, 13(3), 319–340.

Diaper, D. (1989). *Task Analysis for Human-Computer Interaction*. Chichester, UK: Ellis Horwood Ltd.

Dix, A., Finlay, J., Abowd, G. and Beale, R. (1998). *Human-Computer Interaction* (2nd Edn). Hemel Hempstead, UK: Prentice-Hall Europe.

Doctorow, C., Dornfest, R., Johnson, J.S., Powers, S., Trott, B. and Trott, M.G. (2002). *Essential Blogging*. Sebastopol, CA: O'Reilly and Associates.

Ebersbach, A., Glaser, M. and Heigl, R. (2006). *Wiki Web Collaboration*. Heidelberg, Germany: Springer.

Eberts, R.E. (1994). *User Interface Design*. Englewood Cliffs, NJ: Prentice-Hall.

Field, A. (2005). *Discovering Statistics with SPSS*. London, UK: Sage Publications.

Hafner, K. and Lyon, M. (1996). *Where Wizards Stay Up Late: The Origins of the Internet*. New York, NY: Touchstone.

Klobas, J. (2006). *Wikis: Tools for Information Work and Collaboration*. Oxford, UK: Chandos Publishing Ltd.

Matthews, C., Clarkson, M., Poulson, E. and Sahlin, D. (2004). *Photoshop CS Quicksteps*. New York, NY: Osborne/McGraw Hill.

Naughton, J. (2000). *A Brief History of the Future*. London, UK: Pheonix.

Newman, W.M. and Lamming, M.G. (1995). *Interactive System Design*. Wokingham, UK: Addison-Wesley.

Smith-Atakan, S. (2006). *Human-Computer Interaction*. London, UK: Thomson Learning in conjunction with Middlesex University Press.

Stevens, G.H and Stevens, E.F. (1995). *Designing Performance Support Tools – Improving Workplace Performance with Hypertext, Hypermedia and Multimedia*. Englewood Cliffs, NJ: Educational Technology Publications.

Waldron, S.M., Patrick, J., Morgan, P.L. and King, S. (2007). Influencing Cognitive Strategy by Manipulating Information Access, *The Computer Journal*, 50(6), 694–702.

4 *Learning, Instruction, Practice and Expert Behaviour*

PHILIP BARKER

Learning and instruction are important ways by which people acquire the skills and knowledge that they need in order to go about their daily activities. Of course, these resources are also critical assets from the perspective of problem solving, fulfilling ambitions and the realisation of the goals that individuals set for themselves. Bearing this in mind, this chapter explores the basic nature of learning and instruction from the perspective of providing background knowledge to support an understanding of expert behaviour and how this can be achieved through ongoing practice, problem-solving activity and the utilisation of electronic performance support technology. In this context, the MAPARI model of skill acquisition is considered and used to provide a basis for expert performance. A short case study is presented to illustrate how computer-based technology can be used to augment and promote expert performance in relation to a route planning and navigation scenario.

Introduction

As has been mentioned in some of the previous chapters, technology plays a fundamental and important role in the development of support aids for task performance in a wide variety of different contexts. Bearing this in mind, the concept map depicted in Figure 4.1 has been constructed to 'bring together' some of the material and ideas that have been presented in earlier chapters. This concept map also shows the relationship of some of the previously discussed material with the topics that are presented in this chapter.

Some of the earlier sections of this book have stressed the fact that computer technology provides the fundamental foundation upon which an Electronic Performance Support System (EPSS) is built. It is therefore important to explore the 'common ground' between computers and the people that use them. As has been said in the previous chapter, this common ground is often exploited through the study of Human-Computer Interaction (HCI). This topic is important because it enables people to study the effect that computer-based technology has on people and, of course, how people can use this technology (in

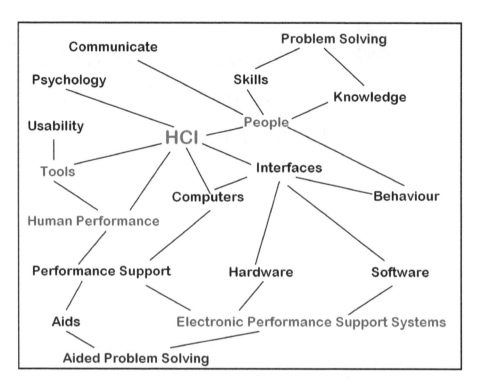

Figure 4.1   Concept map showing the relationship of human-computer interaction (HCI) to learning, problem solving and electronic performance support systems

either a native or embedded way – see Chapter 1) in order to solve problems and also to improve their knowledge and skill levels.

Problem solving is an important activity in which people participate either as individuals or in teams. This activity can take place in either of two ways – aided or unaided (depending upon whether or not any tools or problem solving aids are used). When tools or machines are used as support aids, it is necessary for us to consider the nature of the interfaces used to facilitate 'human-machine' interaction (generally) or HCI (in the case of computer systems). The usability and functionality of the tools are also important issues to consider. Naturally, if the tools needed to solve a problem are complex devices, then some form of learning (on the part of its users) may be necessary to gain an understanding of what the tools do and how to use them. It may also be necessary to provide some form of instruction, training and practice in order to achieve a required level of competent performance when using a particular kind of tool or machine. As an example of this type of situation, consider what is involved in learning to drive a motor-vehicle – as a machine for helping someone to move from one geographical location to another. In this example, a number of quite complex learning processes are involved – such as, understanding the motor-vehicle and how it works, learning the 'rules of the road' and knowing what to do in an emergency situation. The overall learning process usually involves three important procedures: first, receiving instruction from a (qualified) driving instructor; second, getting sufficient practice at actually driving the motor-vehicle; and third, learning about all the peripheral issues that need to be understood.

The learning processes involved will normally develop the competence and confidence needed to become a skilful driver.

Bearing in mind what has been said above, it is imperative that we understand the fundamental importance of skills and knowledge in relation to problem solving – and the roles that learning, instruction and practice play in developing expert behaviour and competent problem-solvers. The important relationships are illustrated schematically in Figure 4.2.

It is my conjecture that everything in a human's life is essentially a 'problem to solve'. Problems arise from goal-seeking activity, originating from a need to move from one state of existence to another. To achieve this transition, a problem-solver needs to gain the skills and knowledge required to create and execute an activity chain that leads him/her from one state of being towards the desired target state that is to be achieved – if, indeed, such an activity chain is possible. Later in this chapter we will see that the knowledge and skills a person has will depend critically on the experiences to which that person has been exposed. As a result of these experiences, a person will build (or extend) a set of mental models (see Chapter 3) and develop relevant skills appropriate to his/her area of study. Four very important skills that a problem-solver needs to have are: (a) the ability to be a creative thinker; (b) a critical and analytical approach to understanding situations, events and happenings; (c) the power to reflect on these issues; and (d) the ability to manage knowledge assets in appropriate ways.

This section has repeatedly emphasised the fact that three of the most important types of experience to which a person can be exposed are learning (either through a contrived learning event or a serendipitous one), instruction (from others – either in a direct or mediated way – or by self-instruction) and practice (again, either directly or through some form of artificially mediated technique, such as a simulator). There are many people who believe that every experience a person encounters is essentially a learning experience – a philosophy to which I subscribe. Indeed, every experience to which we are exposed

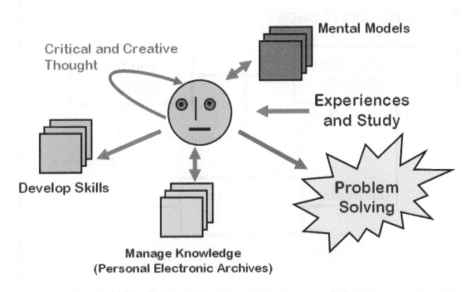

Figure 4.2   The importance of learning in relation to problem-solving activity

teaches us something; this could be something new that we did not know before or it could simply generate a deeper and more confident understanding of what we do and do not know. Because of their importance within the context of studying performance support and how it is used, these three types of educational experience (learning, instruction and practice) are examined in more detail in subsequent sections of this chapter.

What is Learning?

Learning is an intrinsic process that is a characteristic, to some extent or another, of all living species. Essentially, from a human perspective, learning is a set of processes which enable an individual or group of people to acquire the skills, knowledge, motivation, confidence and competence that is needed to perform one or more tasks in an effective and efficient way within some target application domain. As was mentioned above, the basic purpose of learning is therefore to acquire the skills and knowledge needed to solve a problem, realise a goal or fulfil an ambition.

In order to develop a generic approach to understanding the issues involved in a learning process, I consider, in the first instance, that any environment to which an individual (or group of people) is exposed will consist of a collection of three basic types of entity: objects, processes and relationships. Bearing this in mind, the first step in an individual's learning activity will involve the creation of an awareness (within that person's mind – as an observer) that an object/process/relationship actually exists within the given observation space of the individual (or group) concerned. This situation is depicted schematically in Figure 4.3

In this diagram I distinguish between three types of entity: *the observer* (as a learner) – who wants to learn about objects, processes and relationships within a given observation

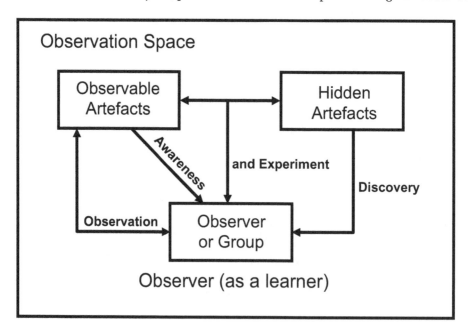

Figure 4.3   An observation space containing visible and hidden artefacts

space; artefacts which can be directly observed – the *observable entities*; and artefacts which, for some reason or another, cannot be directly observed – the *hidden entities*. Entities in this latter class may be either purposefully hidden for some reason, (as, for example, is the situation in a discovery game), or they may be hidden by natural phenomena (such as, their smallness or because they are embedded deep within some other system). Hidden objects will usually need to be 'discovered' by means of some form of discovery process (see below). It is important to remember that the process of observation described in Figure 4.3 will usually take place from within the context of a particular viewpoint or intellectual framework – such as that of a lay-person, a novice or an expert within the domain concerned.

The process of awareness generation (as shown in Figure 4.3) depends critically upon an individual's processes of perception. These are normally based upon our fundamental senses such as those of smell, vision, hearing and touch. Of course, following on from what was said in Chapter 1, there are a wide variety of tools and techniques available that enable these fundamental senses to be augmented in various ways so as to improve and extend their ability for observation and awareness generation in different contexts. For example, when the naked eye is unable to observe particular types of object, we may use a *telescope* (if the objects are distant from us) or a *microscope* (when they are extremely small). If the entities are invisible, some special sort of awareness generation equipment may be needed – for example, the use of x-ray and ultrasound technologies as are used in the field of medical science.

As can be seen in Figure 4.3, three important processes that need to be considered when discussing learning activity are *observation, exploration* and *discovery*. Although they are similar in intent, there are subtle differences between these three basic learning processes. Essentially, observation is a process of 'watching' a system (the observation space) – or an artefact within it –to develop an understanding of it or its behaviour. Exploration refers to the process of 'sifting through' the various artefacts contained in an observation space to find those that are of particular interest to us for the purpose of further study. Discovery refers to the mechanisms for finding some new object, process, property or relationship that we may previously have been unaware of. These activities are important because they can be used to help us extend the horizons of our knowledge.

Sometimes we can learn new things about a system that we are observing by means of various types of *experimentation* technique designed to augment the processes of observation, exploration and discovery described above. One way of doing this, for example, would be to apply different sorts of perturbation effect or stimuli to some of the objects in an observation space. This would enable us to see how those objects behave and react to any stimulus that has been applied. This approach therefore constitutes a particularly important aspect of both exploratory and discovery learning activities – and thus forms an important component of constructivist approaches to learning (Barker, 2004).

Having *identified* the important sets of entities within a given observation space, the next major task in a learning process will usually involve the application of different types of *analysis* and *classification* technique. The ways in which these are applied, and the basic nature of their underlying characteristics, will depend upon extant knowledge in the domain of interest and the learner's familiarity with and understanding of this. That is, the learner's intellectual framework. The processes of analysis and classification will enable us to *construct* appropriate *knowledge structures* that reflect the important properties and behaviour of the entities of interest and the relationships that exist between them. New *knowledge assets* can also be created by employing different types of knowledge construction techniques – such as inference and deduction. The main steps involved in this knowledge production activity and the relationships between them are illustrated schematically in Figure 4.4.

Once a collection of knowledge assets has been created (either in 'the head' or on various external media) it is important to apply appropriate (and ongoing) verification and validation procedures to ensure that they are correct, relevant, reliable and current. Naturally, because we live in a complex and changing world, it is imperative that we continually update the stock of knowledge that we have. The 'power' of knowledge lies within the spectrum of activities and applications that it can be used to support. It is therefore imperative that the knowledge assets that an individual (or a group of people) has created are deployed to solve problems and generate new knowledge artefacts of various types. This topic is discussed in the following sub-sections.

ACQUIRING, GENERATING AND MANAGING KNOWLEDGE

In principle, the learning processes that are inherent in Figures 4.3 and 4.4 will expand the levels of knowledge and expertise that a person has in the particular study domain in which the learning activity has been executed. It is important to remember learners in a particular area of study have to build a relationship with an existing corpus of knowledge and develop the necessary skills that are relevant to their domain of study. This situation is shown in a schematic way in Figure 4.5.

Undoubtedly, computer systems of various sorts are now becoming increasingly important for the storage of information and knowledge – and the creation of electronic

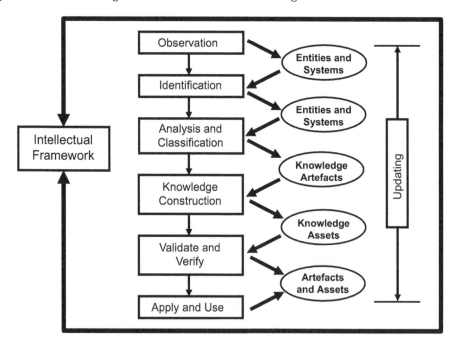

Figure 4.4   Basic steps involved in the creation of knowledge assets

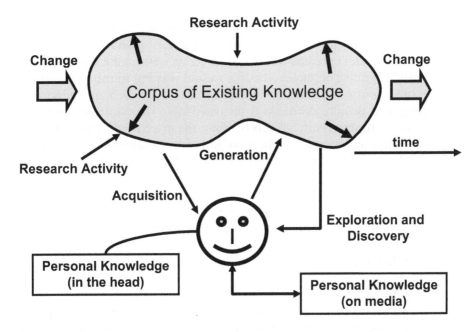

Figure 4.5   The acquisition, generation and management of knowledge

knowledge corpora. Computers are also now being used for providing access to a wide range of very powerful learning opportunities through the use of computational techniques to create simulations and provide access to various types of real-world and virtual experiences, such as collaborative social learning spaces. The use of computer systems in this way is often referred to as electronic learning or 'e-learning' (Holmes and Gardner, 2006).

The ways in which knowledge and information can be accessed from different sources, in both aided and unaided ways, is discussed in detail later in this book (see Chapter 6). The acquisition of knowledge (as shown in Figure 4.5) is believed to lead to the creation of a variety of different types of cognitive structure within the mind of the learner. As discussed in Chapter 2, some of the most important types of cognitive structure that we build in our heads are *mental models* of various sorts (Barker and van Schaik, 1999). However, because of the limitations of our memory, we often have to 'offload' some of our organic knowledge on to appropriately designed personal knowledge archives that reside on different types of media – for example, paper, magnetic, optical and electronic. This 'media dispersion' of our knowledge assets now raises the important issue of how they can be effectively and efficiently managed; this topic is considered in more detail elsewhere (Barker, 2008a; Al-Hawamdeh, 2003; Handzic and Zhou, 2005).

KNOWLEDGE STATES AND THE IMPORTANCE OF FEEDBACK

In an intellectual sense, a learning process will normally take a learner from a given state of knowledge (or capability) to another. In an ideal situation, the target skill/knowledge state that is achieved will correspond to that which is implied by the 'stated' objectives of the learning activity or the desired 'learning outcomes' of the learning process involved (for example, '*I want to learn to swim*', '*I want to understand computers*' or '*I want to be able to speak*

French fluently'). Unfortunately, the transition from a given skill/knowledge state to another (target) state is not usually a strictly 'linear' or direct process (Barker, 1994). The learning route towards a successful outcome will need to steer its way around all sorts of physical, motivational and cognitive obstacles. Also, for various reasons, learning processes can go wrong and result in outcomes which were not anticipated or which are undesirable (such as 'mal-learning' and demotivation). As is discussed later, the transition from novice to expert behaviour is thwarted with all sorts of *'distractive and corrective forces'* (Barker, 1994: p. 8). During a learning process it is therefore imperative that learners seek and receive appropriate *feedback* on their progress towards the realisation of a sought-after learning goal. This feedback should enable relevant decisions and (possibly corrective) actions to be taken in order to ensure that learning 'stays on track' and achieves the required outcomes. Essentially, feedback is usually generated as a result of comparing *where someone is* with *where they want to be* in terms of making a successful knowledge or skill transition.

POWER OF REFLECTION

Reflection refers to the ability of an individual (or group of people) to think about a given situation and what causal factors (or 'critical incidents') have led up to its emergence or appearance. The reflective process is also important when thinking about what actions need to be taken to change the status of the situation – if, indeed, the situation needs to be changed. Reflective thinking is a very important aspect of planning and the identification of activity chains that will lead to particular sorts of outcome. The importance of reflection in relation to learning is therefore of paramount importance and has been extensively researched and discussed in the literature of teaching and learning – see, for example, Schön (1983; 1987), Boud, Keogh and Walker (1985) and Lipman (1991). An extensive discussion of this topic and its importance can be found online: *http://www.infed.org/biblio/b-reflect.htm.*

ACQUIRING SKILLS

A skill is essentially a *dexterity* that a person (or a group of people) has when performing some particular task. Initially, skills are usually developed by 'mimicry'; that is, by trying to copy what someone else does or tells us to do – maybe a parent, a friend, a teacher, an instructor or an expert. This approach to skill acquisition is dealt with in more detail later in the chapter, where we will see that, as learners become more expert in a particular domain, so they are likely to generate new knowledge in that domain and contribute this to the dynamically changing corpus of existing knowledge (as depicted in Figure 4.5). Later in this chapter we will see that one of the essential components of skill development is the need, ability and opportunity to *practise* the skill and then apply it in different situations that reflect the level of expertise that has been acquired. Extensive and ongoing practise of a skill is essential to secure the transition from novice to expert performer – and subsequently maintain this latter level of performance.

LEARNING SPACES

As has been examined elsewhere (Barker, 1995, 2008b), there are basically two types of learning activity: planned (or contrived) and serendipitous. The latter type of learning activity is usually spontaneous and takes place as, when and where opportunities arise. However, a considerable amount of learning takes place in a pre-planned fashion and it usually occurs in an appropriately designed *learning space*. This may be in an actual physical classroom, in someone's home or a place of work; alternatively, the learning space may take the form of a computer program, a computer game, an online conference or a 'virtual learning environment' that only exists within a computer system (Secker, 2004; Catherall, 2005; Barker, 2007b). Indeed, many of the examples of learning spaces explored later in this book will take the form of 'virtual' spaces that are purposefully designed to generate learning and improve people's performance in cognitive and skill-based tasks.

Augmenting Learning with Instruction

In the previous section, a particular perspective on learning was presented in which the emphasis for skill and knowledge acquisition fell solely on the individual learner concerned. Of course, there are many situations in which a learning process may depend critically on an individual's ability to participate in various types of *instructional process* – including *self-instruction*. These processes may be very dependent on the availability of appropriate types of *instructional resource* – such as books, lectures, demonstrations and computer programs. Because instruction plays such an important role within an EPSS, this section of the chapter briefly explores what is meant by the above terms and how their associated products and processes can be used to augment learning activities (in general) and performance enhancement (in particular).

AN EXAMPLE – USING A MOBILE PHONE

Suppose I gave someone a fairly simple electronic device – such as a mobile phone. The person to whom it was given would usually be able to learn how to use it and would fairly quickly become a 'competent operative'. The processes involved in learning about the new phone would probably be based on two important factors: *intuition* and *prior experience*. However, suppose the mobile phone contained some new (and maybe complex) functionality that its user had never previously encountered. In this situation, some level of familiarity with the new functionality that is embedded in the phone would need to be acquired if its operator wanted to extend his/her level of skill – thereby making the phone a more useful device. Learning about the new functions of the phone may, in the first instance, be achieved through the processes of exploration and experimentation mentioned in the previous section. This approach could involve a considerable amount of *trial and error* – with the unavoidable costs of time (and expense) that may be involved. From a performance support perspective, this latter approach would not be regarded as a very efficient way of learning. In order to avoid the need to become excessively involved in trial and error learning, most mobile phones (and other more complex devices like digital cameras and computers) usually come supplied with a *manual*. The purpose of such a manual is two-fold: to *inform* and to *instruct*. It is used to inform its users about the basic characteristics of the mobile phone and the facilities that it offers. In addition, a manual would normally provide simple instructional details about how to use the facilities provided by the device in question. For example, if I wanted to learn how to use my phone's inbuilt text editor (to send a SMS text message), I may first attempt to do this using a trial and error approach. If, and when, I encountered any difficulties, I may then consult my manual and embark upon a process of self-instruction. These two learning approaches are illustrated schematically in diagrams (1) and (2) in Figure 4.6.

In general, a manual is essentially a learning resource that can be used to facilitate self-instruction on the functionality that a commodity (such as a mobile phone) provides. Of course, the level and quality of the instruction that is available within a manual will depend upon the way in which it is written and the *instructional strategies* embedded within it. Instruction manuals can be a very valuable resource once a learner moves beyond the simple and rudimentary functions that a commodity offers. However, in situations where a user lacks sufficient prior experience of a system, a manual can also be a useful way of reducing the trial and error involved in learning some of the simpler, more elementary functions. As the functionality of a device becomes wider and more complex, so the size of any associated instructional manual is likely to increase in a corresponding way. Because a mobile phone may have quite a substantial electronic memory, it may well be that some (if not all) of the paper-based manual will be replicated inside the mobile phone itself – in the form of an inbuilt 'help system' (see diagram (2) in Figure 4.6) which could be accessed by means of a particular, predefined combination of keystrokes.

Sometimes, other more sophisticated methods of instruction may also be needed for instructional purposes – such as the use of computer-based technology, access to an expert and discussion within a user-group forum and/or a social group (be this in an online or a face-to-face context). Sometimes, an appropriately designed instructional environment – for example, a classroom (real and/or virtual), a workplace and/or a laboratory may need to be employed. Diagram (3) in Figure 4.6 shows some of the additional instructional possibilities for learning about a mobile phone. The types of instructional resource

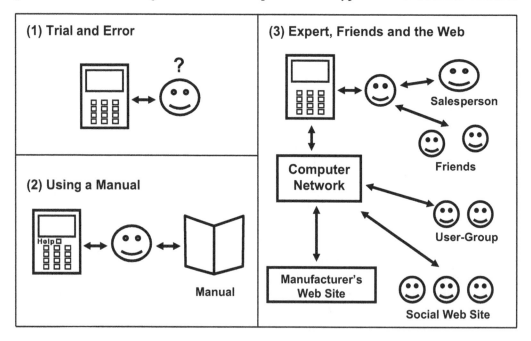

Figure 4.6   Learning to use a mobile phone – sources of instruction

shown in this diagram could, equally well, be used in any other kind of performance improvement situation.

THE RATIONALE FOR INSTRUCTION

The underlying rationale for wanting to design and implement opportunities for instructional activity arises from the potential effectiveness and efficiency that can be achieved when compared with the use of 'native' learning processes. This is especially so in 'mission critical' situations, where people have to acquire the knowledge and skills that they need in as short a timeframe as is possible. Using appropriate instructional methods is one way of achieving this.

Bearing in mind the importance of instruction within the context of creating an EPSS, I have summarised its pivotal role in skill and knowledge acquisition within the diagram presented in Figure 4.7 (Barker, 2007a).

Figure 4.7 shows how appropriately designed (or serendipitous) educational experiences may be used to stimulate and facilitate the development of skills and knowledge that is relevant to some particular target application domain (such as banking, medicine, computing, and so on). Notice how the central arrow in this diagram is labelled 'Ignore'. This situation is intended to illustrate what can happen if the educational experiences to which a learner is exposed are not designed correctly. This is likely to happen, for example, if they are not 'pitched' at the correct level – as would be the case if the cognitive complexity of the material is too high and requires a level of cognition that is beyond the intended recipients. Similarly, if users do not find the instructional resources stimulating and motivating, they may also be ignored in favour of some alternative mechanisms of skill and knowledge acquisition.

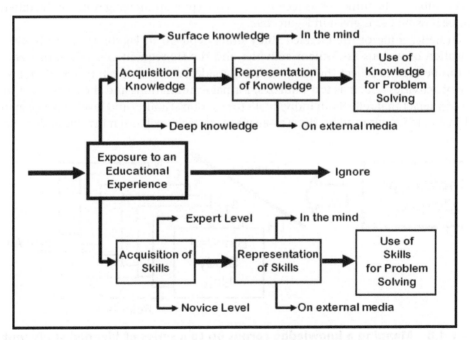

Figure 4.7   Basic rationale underlying the use of instructional scenarios

The 'educational experience' depicted in Figure 4.7 could refer to any number of different instructional possibilities – a single event or a composite, coordinated sequence of events involving a wide range of different resources. Typically, these educational events could include a series of lectures, workshops, seminars, guided reading, classroom or laboratory sessions, practical exercises and demonstrations, using a computer or a Virtual Learning Environment (VLE), and so on. In situations where a number of different types of instructional resource are used to achieve a particular educational objective, the resulting strategy is often called *blended instruction* (Barker, 2007a).

The 'conventional' way of providing instruction involves six basic steps: (a) identifying and specifying the context in which the instruction has to be given; (b) identifying the corpus of material that is to form the basis for instruction; (c) dividing this material up into a sequence of (blended) units; (d) presenting these units (to learners) in a logical sequence, within an appropriate timeframe, using a suitable learning space; (e) identifying appropriate assessment strategies that allow the impact of the instruction to be assessed; and (f) formulating various mechanisms for providing feedback to those who participate in the instructional processes. A simple model that can be used to depict the mapping of a knowledge corpus on to a sequence of blended study units is illustrated schematically in Figure 4.8.

The blended units involved in the kind of instructional strategy depicted in this diagram may be quite explicit (as in a series of lectures) or they may take on a more notional format (as in an educational computer game or an exploratory learning environment – where more complex issues may be hidden until the more rudimentary ones are mastered). Each of the blended study units shown in Figure 4.8 could consist of either a single type of resource or an appropriately selected mix of resources – depending upon the instructional objectives that are to be realised. In any given situation, it is imperative that an appropriate blend of resources is chosen – in a way that makes the instruction interesting, exciting, motivating and accessible to the minds of its recipients. A concept map showing some of the different resource possibilities is given in Figure 4.9.

Naturally, some of the blended study units depicted in Figure 4.8 will involve the application of various assessment activities and the subsequent generation of feedback that can be used to reflect the progress being made. Assessment can be based on a wide range of activities – such as tests, quizzes, formal examinations and the creation of some form of artefact that reflects an individual's (or a group's) ability and level of performance. Within an EPSS environment, these assessment strategies will often involve an individual

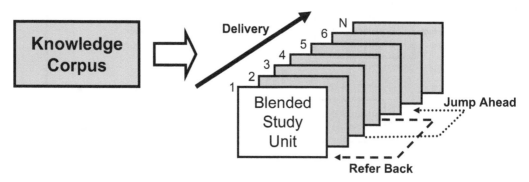

Figure 4.8   Mapping a knowledge corpus on to a series of blended study units

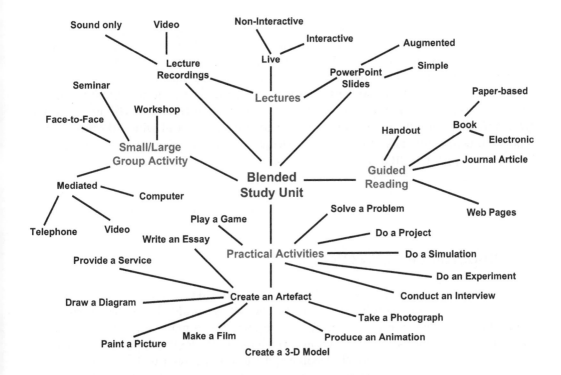

Figure 4.9   Candidate components for a blended study unit

or group actually performing 'on-the-job' tasks. These will sometimes involve assessing an operative's performance in a real operational environment (such as a manufacturing plant or a hospital). At other times, a simulated environment is used instead – especially in situations where the effects of an 'un-trapped' error made by an inexperienced operator could have detrimental or disastrous effects on a system or its level of performance.

APPROACHES TO PROVIDING INSTRUCTION

From the perspective of an EPSS environment, one of the most important ways of providing instruction is through the use of a computer system. There are two broad approaches: first, employing computer programs for the purpose of instruction; and second, using a computer to mediate between an instructor (or a group of instructors) and the people who are being instructed. Subsequent chapters of this book will consider and explore both of these approaches to providing instruction (in the form of EPSS) within various application domains.

In one of her early papers on EPSS, Gery (1995) describes three basic ways of providing instruction in relation to performance support: *intrinsic, extrinsic* and *external*. This taxonomy refers to the extent in which instructional materials are embedded within the tools and environment of the target application domain in which a given task is being executed.[1] Thus, in the mobile phone example, the manual shown in diagram (2) of

---

1   In her article, Gery (1995) describes intrinsic support as being support that is built into the system being used while extrinsic support is not embedded but can be accessed indirectly via the system being used. External support is not available either directly or indirectly via the system being used.

Figure 4.6 is an external instructional resource. Similarly, an inbuilt help facility (that is activated by a key-press combination) would be an example of an extrinsic instructional resource; however, an automated help system that was invoked when a user made an error would provide an example of an intrinsic instructional facility.

Two very important mechanisms for providing instruction within an EPSS environment are Just-in-Time (JIT) instruction and Just-in-Case (JIC) instruction.[2] The first of these (JIT) is used to provide a person/group with instruction as, and when, the need arises – but well before any lack of skills or knowledge would cause performance degradation. The second approach (JIC) is used in order to provide skill and knowledge development in case a particular eventually arises (such as a terrorist attack or a nuclear war). In this type of situation, it is necessary for an organisation to try to anticipate future events and situations and also identify the skill sets (and knowledge) needed to cope with them.

The Importance of Practice

During a learning process, it is essential to practise the skills that are being developed – be these physical or cognitive skills. Practice activities should also be accompanied by appropriate feedback and reflection on the progress being made towards reaching the desired level of performance. This section of the book illustrates the importance of practice activities within an overall model of skill acquisition that is referred to as the 'MAPARI'[3] model. A description is also given of an important technique (called 'scaffolding') that is often used to provide support for people during the early stages of skill development.

THE MAPARI MODEL

The MAPARI model is a generic conceptual tool that can be used to help explain the steps involved in skill acquisition (to a required level of performance) and the development of expert behaviour (if indeed, this can at all be achieved) in terms of six basic 'instructional' activities. It was originally introduced and used for explaining learning in an interactive learning environment (Barker, 1994). However, its remit is much broader than the particular context within which it was developed. The model is depicted schematically in Figure 4.10

As was stated earlier in this chapter, we believe that, initially, many skills are developed through a process of 'Mimicry'; that is, learners tend to 'copy' activities that an instructor (in the broadest sense of the word) demonstrates to them. Once some basic skills have been acquired, an individual's performance levels can usually be improved through a process of 'Apprenticeship' to an expert or master performer. Apprenticeship involves working with a domain expert to acquire the skills necessary to gain expert status and achieve an expert level of performance within a particular subject area. To realise this status it is necessary for an apprentice (a student or a trainee) to 'Practise' using his/her incipient skills for various purposes – such as problem solving. This facet of the route to

---

2   There is an extensive amount of literature available on these topics. Two useful sources of further information are: (a) the book by Marquardt and Kearsley (1999); and (b) the article by Harrison (2005). Details of these are given in the references section.

3   MAPARI is an acronym for Mimicry, Apprenticeship, Practice, Assessment, Refinement and Improvement.

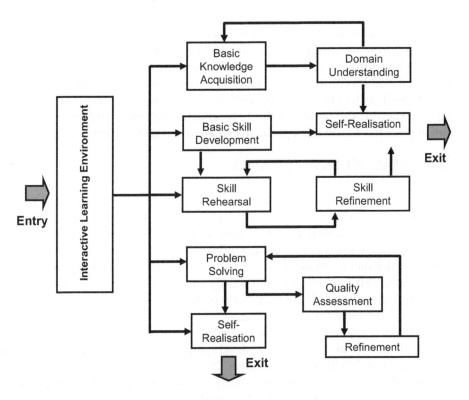

Figure 4.10 The MAPARI model of skill development

expert behaviour is probably the most important one from the perspective of this section of the book. To improve his/her performance, an individual has to practise, practise and practise! This practice is not only needed in order to achieve the limit of one's natural ability, it is also needed to maintain this level of ability. Skills that are not continually 'exercised' will start to decline in terms of the performance level that they can be used to achieve. The importance of practice has previously been discussed in the book within the context of the Power Law of Practice (Card, Moran and Newell, 1983); this law was used to explain how appropriately designed performance aids may be used to overcome an individual's natural, innate limitations.

The next important aspect of the MAPARI model is the process of 'Assessment'. This is used to gauge how closely the skills and knowledge that a person has acquired are approaching those that are characteristic of an expert in the domain of study. This aspect of the MAPARI approach can involve both self-assessment and peer-assessment processes.

Associated with assessment are the related processes of reflection – augmented in appropriate ways with the feedback that is derived from the skill assessment activities. Following each of the assessment stages, a process of skill and knowledge 'Refinement' takes place. This involves using the results of a particular assessment phase in order to refine skill development, that is, 'fine-tuning' the developing skills so that they fall into an appropriate 'region of acceptability' that would be deemed to be characteristic of expert behaviour – or some other required level of achievement. Of course, this may not always be possible to achieve without additional practice and application of the skills.

Indeed, in some cases it may be necessary to augment natural ability (or lack of this) with appropriate performance aids. Once a reasonable (or required) level of expertise has been achieved, graduates from the MAPARI model have to be encouraged to 'Improve' their knowledge and skill levels, in an ongoing way, in order to maintain them in an optimal condition. Indeed, as will be examined later in this chapter, an important characteristic of being 'an expert' is the need and ability to update one's skills and knowledge so that optimum approaches to solving a problem can be found and implemented.

PROVIDING PRACTICE ENVIRONMENTS

Within an electronic performance support system there will usually be a variety of different ways in which opportunities can be provided for practising skills. Two of these have already been mentioned earlier in this chapter within the context of assessing performance levels. These involved either using an operational, 'live' environment or by means of a simulated environment of some sort. Two extremely powerful ways of providing a simulated environment are: (a) by means of an educational/instructional computer-based game; and (b) through the provision of a virtual environment that closely simulates the behaviour of the real system for which training is being provided. These two approaches do not need to be mutually exclusive. The use of the game-playing approach is illustrated in our work on developing EPSS systems for use in academic libraries (Barker, van Schaik and Famakinwa, 2007). Within these systems, participants play educational games designed to develop the skills needed to perform the various tasks involved in using an academic library. The application of a virtual environment can be illustrated by reference to the *Second Life* Internet-based virtual world that is currently having a tremendous impact within a variety of different teaching, learning and training contexts – see, for example, *http://www.schome.ac.uk*.

SCAFFOLDING

The basic principle underlying the application of 'scaffolding' (as a support tool) arises from the advantages that can be accrued through the provision of a temporary 'assistive' environment that is able to offer (a learner) help and assistance during some period of learning or familiarisation activity. Within teaching and learning environments there is a variety of ways in which scaffolding can be achieved – depending upon the particular aims and objectives that its application are intended to fulfil. For example, SMS text messaging (based on mobile phone technology) is often used to scaffold new students who are making the transition from school to university life. This type of scaffolding is often called *global-generic* because the techniques can be employed over a large area of application within any subject domain. More specific scaffolding relating to a particular learning task or a particular course of instruction can also be provided. This is often referred to as *local-specific* scaffolding. Much of our work on EPSS deals with this latter type of mechanism of support provision.

As a pedagogic technique, scaffolding is a well-known method for providing various forms of support for learners while they are acquiring the skills and knowledge needed to become an expert performer in a given area of discourse. It is often used to provide help and rich feedback about problems that a learner may be experiencing. Cagiltay (2006), amongst others, has recently described how EPSS can be used effectively to provide scaffolding facilities within electronic learning environments. Our recent work in the area of pedagogic applications of electronic performance support has used this technique in a number of different areas. Some typical examples of the projects in which we have employed this technique include the design of support for electronic file transfer (Banerji, 1995), virtual study environments involving distributed performance support (Beacham, 1998), information retrieval using search engines (Flinders, 2000), quantitative research methods (Pearson, 2001; van Schaik, Pearson and Barker, 2002) and academic libraries (Famakinwa, 2004).

Within an EPSS environment, the underlying rationale for using a scaffolding facility is that it can be used to monitor a student's performance in a skill- or knowledge-based task. In situations where an underperformance is detected (and this is attributable to a lack of experience, knowledge or practice), a learning scaffold can be created which traps fundamental errors and mistakes (made by students) and then advises them on how to avoid or overcome these. In a similar way, underperformance as a result of a lack of relevant skill can also be used to initiate a scaffolding process. Normally, intervention by the scaffold is 'faded out' (that is, gradually decreased) as the student's performance approaches its 'plateau region' (see Figure 1.11, p. 22) for the task or skill that is involved – since further intervention would not achieve any significant increases in performance. However, if the EPSS detects any noticeable deterioration in on-task performance, it can reinstate the scaffold and use it in order to prevent further decline – again, fading it out when the user's performance becomes optimal.

We have incorporated the use of scaffolding techniques within our latest research into the use of EPSS in academic library systems. Our research in this area has been particularly directed (but not exclusively so) at undergraduate students. The system that we built is illustrated schematically in Figure 4.11 overleaf (Barker, van Schaik and Famakinwa, 2007). In this model, A, B and C represent the different channels of communication that the overall system interface needs to support. Channel A denotes a line of communication between the user and the EPSS through the system interface. Similarly, Channel B denotes communication between the user and library system (the target application) while C represents a dialogue between the system user and the scaffolding facilities provided by the EPSS.

The performance system shown in Figure 4.11, which is called *Epsilon*, will be described in more detail in Chapter 6 when the problems of accessing information within library systems (both conventional and electronic) will be analysed in more detail.

Expert Behaviour

An expert is usually regarded as a person who has developed highly specialised skills and knowledge relating to a particular subject area. Such a person would also be very adept at using these personal assets in order to solve problems in his/her area of specialism. Obviously, if the 'educational experiences' previously referred to in Figure 4.8 are to be designed in a way that will foster the development of experts in a given specialist field, then it becomes important for us to be able to characterise the essential hallmarks of 'expertise' and 'expert behaviour' within that domain of activity. Having identified these, we can then design the necessary instructional activities that will foster the development

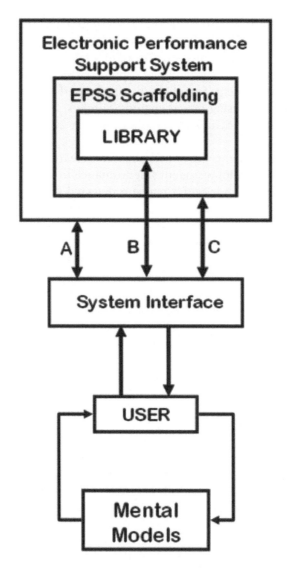

Figure 4.11 Use of scaffolding in an EPSS for academic libraries

of expert behaviour. Because of its generic nature, the MAPARI model could then be used to steer the application of the necessary instructional interventions that are needed. However, as Hoffman (1998) has indicated, strategies for helping to foster the development of experts are not without their complications.

The transition from being a novice (in a particular domain) to becoming an expert is ilustrated schematically in Figure 4.12.

Of course, the overall transition process shown in Figure 4.12 does not necessarily have to be a linear one; indeed, it can involve a range of non-linear activities (such as iteration, back-tracking and jump-ahead) in order to achieve particular learning or training outcomes. Naturally, in general, the desired learning outcome that we would wish to secure is a successful transition from 'novice' to 'expert' behaviour within a chosen skill domain. In Figure 4.12, this transition is depicted by multiple pathways

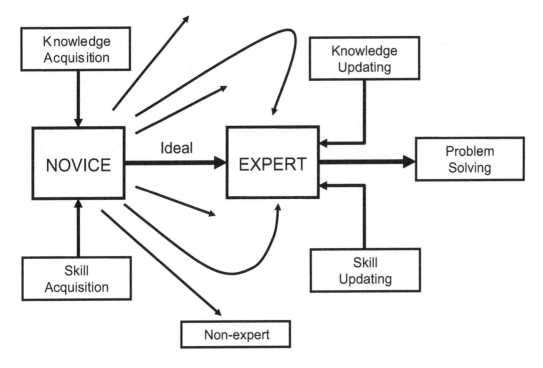

Figure 4.12 Learning transitions – from novice to expert

– each one of which denotes a different route to acquiring the expertise associated with being an expert. Different routes will usually require different times and different kinds (and amounts) of resource input.

Two important points emerge from Figure 4.12. First, not all the transitions that emanate from the novice state will automatically lead to the achievement of expert status within a particular domain; in some cases learning, training and instructional activity will fail – leading to the creation of a 'non-expert'. Second, the graph will exhibit a certain number of pathways of least resource requirements (one such traversal in Figure 4.12 has been labelled 'Ideal'). Obviously, the meaning of the term 'ideal' is likely to vary from one situation to another. For example, in some cases the ideal transition will be the path of minimum time; in other situations the ideal may be the path of minimum cost or the attainment of a particular pre-specified level of skill.

One of the important objectives of an EPSS is to embed expertise from different sources and pass this on to people who need to acquire it. Within many of the EPSS systems that we have produced, the MAPARI model has formed the basis for the development of high levels of expertise within the particular systems that have been built – thereby securing successful transitions between the two different levels of proficiency shown in Figure 4.12.

Experts will differ from novices in a number of important ways. For example, experts will usually have very rich mental models relating to the domain knowledge they have acquired. They will also usually have had a considerable amount of relevant experience and will have developed a set of skills that enable them to understand and solve problems within their specialist field. Experts will therefore be equipped with a 'tool-bag' of techniques that they can use for specialist problem solving. Futhermore, as is indicated in Figure 4.12, experts will also be aware of the continual need to update their knowledge and skills because otherwise, rapid 'progress' in virtually all areas of endeavour would soon render their skill sets and knowledge assets 'out of date'. This is especially true in most areas of science and technology.

An important aspect of being an expert in a particular domain is the ability to 'be creative' in terms of finding solutions to problems. This may involve 'borrowing' ideas from various other areas of activity in order to devise an appropriate solution pathway for a particular problem that has to be solved.

Another characteristic attribute of an expert is the ability 'to recover' (in a graceful and transparent way) from any awkward situations that may arise during problem-solving activity. Such situations may include, for example, unforeseen obstacles arising or any errors that are made. The implication of this is that the end result of an expert's action should not be significantly different in any way to that which would have been achieved if the error(s) or obstacles had not been encountered.

Experts are able to see the relevance and importance of various scientific and technical 'breakthroughs' in their areas of expertise and then apply these in order to improve the efficiency and effectiveness of what they do. This point is well-illustrated in the case study that is presented in the following section.

EPSS Case Study

This case study deals with the use of electronic performance support technology in order to solve some of the problems encountered by an outdoor leisure activities company. The business activity of the company involved organising various types of adventure holiday for its customers. For various reasons, the company wanted to introduce a more effective way of planning and executing some of the outdoor events that it had to organise for its client base. Some of the popular activities they wished to consider were: cycling trips, country walking events and mountain climbing. These activities are usually based in the UK but could involve travel to any country in which an appropriate holiday base was available. For each type of activity, the company employed appropriate 'experts' both to plan and conduct the events with various groups of clients. In this case study, just one particular type of activity (country walking) will be used to illustrate how the introduction of electronic performance support technology was employed to improve the efficiency and effectiveness of the company's overall organisational performance.

From the perspective of the leisure company, a walking event would involve a group of people setting off (with an expert leader) from one geographical location (the start) and subsequently arriving at another location (the finish) at some point later in the day. An important requirement of the company is that walking expeditions should make minimal use of roads and only employ terrain to which the general public has access rights. The length of any given walk and the magnitude of the vertical ascent that is involved would depend upon the nature of the client group for which the event is intended. Typically, the walks usually offered by the leisure company would fall into any one of three different categories (called X, Y and Z) – this was the terminology used in the catalogue that the company supplied to potential customers. The class into which a walk fell would depend upon the distance covered and the amount of climbing involved. The expert leaders of the walks were therefore responsible for planning the walking activities so that all events fell within the company's system for event classification. For the purpose of this case study, only walking events within the UK are considered.

Prior to the introduction of electronic performance support techniques, the walk leaders used conventional (paper-based) maps of various scales in order to plan their walks. Using various time-consuming measurement techniques, these maps were employed in order to make estimates of the distance and ascent involved in any given walking expedition. Subsequently, when any particular walking event was actually undertaken 'in the field', the walk leaders again used paper-based maps and a conventional magnetic compass in order to navigate their routes from start to finish. This approach to route planning and navigation is subject to a number of significant limitations. For example, as useful as it is, a conventional compass does not give any absolute indication of where a person happens to be. Similarly, a map and compass is only really useful in situations where a walk leader can actually see the surrounding terrain and any distinguishing features that can be recognised and then located on the relevant map. In the dark, or in mist, this approach to navigation is very difficult. It was difficulties such as these that prompted the leisure company to contemplate an alternative approach to what they were doing.

The electronic performance support system that was used to improve the company's overall performance was based on the use of two fairly recent developments in technology. The first of these was the widespread availability of the satellite-based Global Positioning System (GPS). The second was the availability of relatively low-cost digital maps, having different scales and wide coverage.

As a result of the changes introduced into the company by these developments, all leaders of walking activities were issued with personal satellite navigation ('sat-nav') systems similar to the one illustrated in Figure 4.13 (further details of these devices can be found at *http://www.garmin.com*). These hand-held navigation devices were used in conjunction with digital maps obtained via the Internet (or on CD-ROM) from a company called *Anquet Maps* (*http://www.anquet.co.uk*) who specialised in the creation of digital mapping systems.

One of the most attractive features of the type of navigator shown in Figure 4.13 is its ability to 'take in' a series of navigation points and then use these to direct its user from one point to another enabling navigation of a particular route. The navigation points can be entered into the device either manually (using the 'click-button' on its front surface)

Figure 4.13 Hand-held personal navigation system from Garmin

or automatically (by downloading them from a computer). A custom interface on the device and an associated cable is available to facilitate this connection. Another of the GPS navigator's attractive features is its ability to keep a fairly accurate 'tracklog' of where its user actually takes it. This facility is useful for keeping digital records of the walks that leaders undertake. The 'tracklogs' that are stored in the navigator's electronic memory can be uploaded to a personal computer and stored – both for the purpose of analysis and for future reference.

The way in which personal navigators of this type can be combined with a computer-based digital mapping system to create an electronic performance support environment for use by the leisure company is illustrated schematically in Figure 4.14. This diagram represents the activities involved in using the EPSS facility in terms of three major task execution areas. These are: (1) the route-planning phase; (2) the outdoor operational phase; and (3) the post-operational stage. Each of these aspects of the system is briefly outlined below.

The route-planning phase – diagram (1) in Figure 4.14 – is an interactive process in which a walk leader specifies a route that he/she will undertake at some future time. The computer-based mapping system allows a route to be defined as a series of mouse clicks on relevant screen-based digital maps. As this is being done, the route statistics (distance, ascent and an anticipated duration) are automatically calculated and displayed. A graphical height profile for the walk can also be obtained along with a 3-D visualisation of a 'walk through' of the route (if required). Once a leader is satisfied with the planning

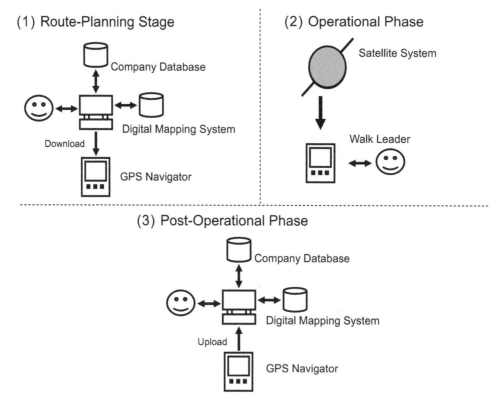

Figure 4.14 Rationale and logistics for electronic performance support system

of a particular walk, it can be downloaded to the GPS as a sequence of navigation points (previously defined in terms of mouse clicks). If it is required, and the particular GPS navigator (or GPS-enabled PDA) has the capability, relevant digital map sections can also be downloaded for use in the next stage.

The operational phase of the performance support process – see diagram (2) in Figure 4.14 – involves using the GPS device for navigation purposes on an actual walking event. During this phase the GPS tracking facility can be used to keep an accurate record of the walk. If a walk needs to be modified 'on the fly', new navigational data can be entered into the GPS and appropriate route amendments then made. The post-operational phase of the performance support activity – see diagram (3) in Figure 4.14 – involves connecting the GPS navigator to the computer-based mapping system so that the tracklog for the event (and other recorded data) can be uploaded to the computer. It can then be analysed and archived into the company's database for future use.

The new system that was introduced required the design and implementation of appropriate online instructional facilities so that company employees could learn how to use it – and acquire any necessary skills and knowledge they thought was appropriate. An important aspect of this EPSS was its use of simulation scenarios (using both 2-D and 3-D graphics) that involved both map reading and navigation exercises.

Conclusion

Learning is a fundamental process that takes place throughout an individual's lifetime. It may be executed in an explicit, conscious way (as in a lecture or a laboratory session in a college environment) or it may happen in a subconscious fashion – without a learner being explicitly aware that it is happening. It is through the process of learning that we acquire the knowledge and skills that we need to survive in our daily lives – both at work and during leisure. Of course, learning can be enhanced and it can be made more efficient and effective if it is augmented by appropriately designed instructional activities.

Skill and knowledge acquisition are an important aspect of becoming an expert in some particular area of endeavour. However, no matter what level and skill a person has, there will usually be natural, innate limitations that control what an individual is able to achieve. In many situations it is possible to overcome these limitations through the appropriate use of performance support aids – especially those that involve the use of electronic performance support techniques. The subsequent chapters of this book each illustrate how appropriately designed performance support environments can be used within particular specialist areas in order to improve and enhance human performance.

Acknowledgement

I am grateful to Paul van Schaik for his useful criticism and helpful suggestions for improving this chapter.

References

Al-Hawamdeh, S. (2003). *Knowledge Management – Cultivating Knowledge Professionals*. Oxford, UK: Chandos Publishing.

Banerji, A. (1995). *Designing Electronic Performance Support Systems*, Ph.D thesis. Middlesbrough, UK: University of Teesside.

Barker, P.G. (1994). Designing Interactive Learning. In T. de Jong and L. Sarti (eds), *Design and Production of Multimedia and Simulation-based Learning Material* (pp. 1–30). Dordrecht, The Netherlands: Kluwer Academic Publisher.

Barker, P.G. (1995). Evaluating a Model of Learning Design. In H. Maurer (ed.), *Proceedings of the EDMEDIA 95 World Conference on Educational Multimedia and Hypermedia*, (pp. 87–92), Graz, Austria, 17–21 June. Charlottesville, VA: Association for the Advancement of Computing in Education.

Barker, P.G. (2004). Implementing Constructivism using an e-Science Paradigm. In L. Cantoni and C. McLoughlin (eds), *Proceedings of the EDMEDIA 2004 World Conference on Educational Multimedia, Hypermedia and Telecommunications* (pp. 3803–3810), Lugano, Switzerland, 21–26 June. Norfolk, VA: Association for the Advancement of Computing in Education.

Barker, P.G. (2007a). Blended Learning the Wiki Way. In *Proceedings of the 2nd International Conference on Blended Learning – The Net Generation of Learner* (pp. 60–71), The Fielder Centre, University of Hertfordshire, 14 June. Hatfield, UK: University of Hertfordshire Press.

Barker, P.G. (2007b). Using Blackboard to Manage Students' Projects, In T. Bastiaens and S. Carliner (eds), *Proceedings of the E-LEARN 2007 World Conference on E-Learning in Corporate, Government, Healthcare and Higher Education* (pp. 621–629), Quebec City, Canada, 15–19 October. Chesapeake, VA: Association for the Advancement of Computing in Education.

Barker, P.G. (2008a). Using Wikis for Knowledge Management. In J. Luca and E. Weippl (eds), *Proceedings of the EDMEDIA 2008 World Conference on Educational Multimedia, Hypermedia and Telecommunications* (pp. 3604–3613), Vienna, Austria, 30 June – 4 July. Chesapeake, VA: Association for the Advancement of Computing in Education.

Barker, P.G. (2008b). Re-Evaluating a Model of Learning Design, *Innovations in Education and Teaching International*, 45(2), 127–141.

Barker, P.G. and Schaik, P. van (1999). Mental Models and their Implications for the Design of Computer-Based Learning Resources In G.M. Chapman (ed.), *Proceedings of the CBLIS 99 International Conference on Computer-Based Learning in Science* ([Paper A1), University of Twente, Enschede, The Netherlands, 2–6 July. Ostrava, Czech Republic: University of Ostrava Press.

Barker, P.G., Schaik, P. van and Famakinwa, O. (2007). Building Electronic Performance Support Systems for First-Year University Students, *Innovations in Education and Teaching International*, 44(3), 243–255.

Beacham, N. (1998). *Distributed Performance Support Systems*, Ph.D thesis. Middlesbrough, UK: University of Teesside.

Boud, D., Keogh, R. and Walker, D. (1985). *Reflection: Turning Experience into Learning*. London, UK: Kogan Page,

Cagiltay, K. (2006). Scaffolding Strategies in Electronic Performance Support Systems: Types and Challenges, *Innovations in Education and Teaching International*, 43(1), 93–103.

Card, S., Moran, T. and Newell, A. (1983). *The Psychology of Human-computer Interaction*. Hillsdale, NJ: Erlbaum.

Catherall, P. (2005). *Delivering E-Learning for Information Services in Higher Education*. Oxford, UK: Chandos Publishing Ltd.

Famakinwa, O.J. (2004). *An Electronic Performance Support System for Library Services*, M.Sc thesis. Middlesbrough, UK: University of Teesside.

Flinders, S. (2000). *A Prototype Electronic Performance Support System Facility to Support Web-based Information Retrieval*, MSc Thesis. Middlesbrough, UK: University of Teesside.

Gery, G. (1995). The Future of EPSS, *Innovations in Education and Training International*, 32(1), 70–73.

Handzic, M. and Zhou, A.Z. (2005). *Knowledge Management – An Integrative Approach*. Oxford, UK: Chandos Publishing Ltd.

Harrison, W. (2005). Do You Learn Just-in-time or Just-in-Case?, *IEEE Software*, 22(1), 5–7.

Hoffman, R.R. (1998). How Can Expertise be Defined? Implications of Research from Cognitive Psychology. In R. Williams, W. Faulkner and J. Fleck (eds), *Exploring Expertise: Issues and Perspectives* (pp. 81–100). Basingstoke, UK: Macmillan.

Holmes, B. and Gardner, J. (2006). *e-Learning: Concepts and Practice*. London, UK: Sage Publications.

Lipman, M. (1991). *Thinking in Education*. Cambridge, UK: Cambridge University Press.

Marquardt, M.J. and Kearsley, G. (1999). *Technology-based Learning – Maximising Human Performance and Corporate Success*. Boca Raton, FL: CRC Press.

Pearson, R. (2001). *An EPSS for Quantitative Research Methods and Statistics*, M.Sc thesis. Middlesbrough, UK: University of Teesside.

Schaik, P. van, Pearson, R. and Barker, P.G. (2002). Designing Electronic Performance Support Systems to Support Learning, *Innovations in Education and Teaching International*, 39(4), 289–306.

Schön, D. (1983). *The Reflective Practitioner: How Professionals Think in Action*. New York, NY: Basic Books Inc.

Schön, D. (1987). *Educating the Reflective Practitioner: Toward a New Design for Teaching and Learning in Professions*. San Francisco, CA: Jossey-Bass Inc.

Secker, J. (2004). *Electronic Resources in the Virtual Learning Environment – A Guide for Librarians*. Oxford, UK: Chandos Publishing Ltd.

PART II

Applications

5 Enhancing Educational Opportunities Using Electronic Performance Support Tools

PHILIP BARKER

Educational systems provide a vital resource that enables people to acquire the skills, knowledge and understanding they need in order to conduct their lives. Increasingly, computer-based performance support tools are being used in various ways in order to augment educational provision. This chapter discusses the basic nature of educational provision and describes some of the ways in which Electronic Performance Support Systems (EPSS) and/or tools can be used to enhance the educational opportunities that can be made available to their users.

Introduction

Education is something that everyone is likely to have experienced in one form or another. It may take the form of some explicit instructional activity, such as attending a lecture at a university, or it could be some less formal endeavour – for example, simply observing something and reflecting on the observations that have been made. Bearing in mind these two different types of scenario, it is easy to see that education can be both a *process* and a *system*. A university, its lecture courses and the students that attend them constitute an educational system (or part thereof). Observation and reflection are examples of educational processes – which people use in order to inform themselves, make judgements and, perhaps, change their views, values and attitudes. As a process, education can be thought of as a mechanism by which people gain an awareness of things and also develop their knowledge, understanding and skills. As a system, education can be thought of as an infrastructure that is used to provide an environment (and facilities) whereby the above commodities (skills, knowledge and understanding) can be acquired, applied and assessed.

The previous chapter considered a number of important processes upon which education and educational systems critically depend. These topics included learning and instruction – two fundamental and extremely important processes by which people acquire skills and knowledge. But, of course, education in the broadest sense of the word is much more than this; it is often considered to be a sort of 'umbrella' term that is used to group together a wide range of processes and systems – the ultimate aim of which is to achieve a facility for transferring skills, knowledge and culture from one generation to another. Equally important is the environment that education provides in order to create new knowledge through research, innovation and enterprise.

It is the responsibility of governments, societies and cultures to provide educational systems for the people they represent. In many societies, a multi-tier approach to educational provision is the norm. Such an approach is usually 'forced upon us' by the nature of people's developmental characteristics (Goswami, 2008). For example, a three-year-old child would not be sufficiently well-developed to understand the principles of calculus. Some ten to 15 years later, this situation is likely to have changed as a result of a prior 'build-up' of the necessary experience and background knowledge to make such a study meaningful. A typical multi-tier approach to educational provision is depicted schematically in Figure 5.1. This diagram has been derived by applying the 'life cycle model'[1] to the educational stages that people go through during their 'periods of existence'. In Figure 5.1, four basic tiers are depicted; however, in some systems a five-tier approach is employed – by including a pre-school level prior to the primary stage.

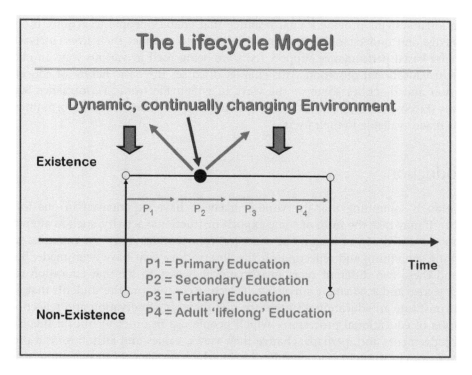

Figure 5.1   Applying the life cycle model to educational provision

---

1   In Figure 5.1, a particular point in the space of non-existence can represent either the conception of a new entity or the demise of an existing one. The vertical lines represent transitions from/to a state of non-existence to/from a state of existence. The verticality of the line and the escape velocity across the boundary (between existence and non-existence) can be correlated with various properties of the emergence and exiting processes. The horizontal line represents the traversal from 'birth' to 'death' and does not have to be a straight line; it can be any shape provided no point goes back beyond a previous one – as this would represent travel backwards in time.

In Figure 5.1, the large broad vertical arrows are intended to represent perturbations and forces acting on an individual (shown as a large solid circle) during his/her life-time. The thin arrows associated with this circle represent interactions between an individual and the environment(s) in which he/she exists. For each of the educational stages (P1 through P4) illustrated in Figure 5.1, a relevant curriculum is identified – containing both knowledge and skill requirements that are relevant to the developmental stage of the person involved. Naturally, in most cases, each phase builds upon the previous experiences that a person has been exposed to in the preceding stages. Each stage is usually accompanied by a series of assessment tasks. These are executed both within the educational stage itself and prior to leaving it – thereby ensuring that graduation on to the next stage of the educational process is soundly based (or otherwise!).

Within modern technology-driven societies, change takes place at a tremendous rate. As a natural consequence of this change, conventional formal education (as defined by Phases 1, 2 and 3 in Figure 5.1), will normally be unable to cope with the demands placed upon people in later life. There are two general ways in which this situation can be catered for: first, by instilling into students the basic principles of 'learning to learn' and encouraging them to apply these throughout their lifetime; second, by making available relevant 'adult courses' which enable people who have left formal education to 'come back' and learn more – as the demands placed upon them change. This latter approach is often called 'lifelong learning'.

It is our[2] contention that suitably designed EPSS and/or tools can help to improve educational opportunities in each of the life cycle phases (P1 through P4) shown in Figure 5.1. Of course, it is also very important to remember that as both a process and a system, education is itself a powerful performance enabler. In this chapter an attempt is made to show how electronic performance support technology (in its widest sense), when combined with appropriate educational paradigms, can be used to create very powerful skill and knowledge acquisition systems. At the same time, electronic performance support tools can be used to monitor learning processes, provide various types of assessment and offer appropriate performance-related feedback (advice and comments) to learners.

Taking into account the above scenario, the objective of this chapter is, therefore, to identify and briefly describe some of the ways in which electronic technology (in general) and electronic performance support (in particular) are influencing the nature and characteristics of current and emerging educational systems. Bearing this in mind, in the following section, an attempt is made to identify a theoretical basis for educational provision. Some principles, techniques and tools are then briefly described. Finally, a short sequence of vignettes is presented which demonstrate what can be achieved as a result of using EPSS and/or tools to realise particular educational objectives.

Rationale

As was suggested in the previous section, education is a complex process or system that people use in order to achieve an awareness of themselves and the environments in which they exist – both local and global; real and virtual. Education is thus a multi-dimensional phenomenon which allows people to acquire the skills, knowledge and

---

2   The word 'our', used in this context, refers to the editors of this book.

understanding they need in order to cope with the problems and issues of daily life – be these in a domestic, social or professional setting. The demands placed upon people (and what they need to know and do) will usually change over time – sometimes very quickly. An educational system may therefore have to respond dynamically and rapidly to changing requirements. The responsiveness of an educational system will often strongly influence the speed with which its target community can, for example, ward off some of the outcomes of an impending disaster (such as a hurricane, flood or outbreak of disease) or maintain its competitiveness within a given skill/knowledge marketplace. In situations such as this, it is imperative that appropriate (electronic) technology is embedded within the underlying systems so as to ensure that adequate levels of responsiveness can be achieved.

It is our contention that education itself is a valuable, generic and indispensible performance support tool. For example, when someone encounters a situation that requires skills and knowledge that he/she does not have, the obvious way forward is to acquire these resources. By doing this, if the situation arises again, it can be handled in an appropriate way – thereby achieving success rather than failure. In this way, education is the fundamental tool that enables performance improvement. The way in which an educational system achieves its objectives is through the deployment of appropriate 'educational experiences' – as was previously depicted in Figure 4.7.

Bearing in mind the rationale that is embedded in Figure 4.7 we suggest that 'an education' can be thought of as an appropriately designed sequence of educational experiences. This sequence will normally be designed in such a way that it will enable particular educational objectives to be achieved. These objectives will be identified and defined according to the educational phase (see Figure 5.1) to which they relate. In many ways, what constitutes an educational experience is 'open to debate'. For example, such an experience may involve attending a single lecture, a course of lectures or several courses of lectures – as in a university degree programme. It could involve going on a field trip, reading a book, playing a musical instrument or doing an experiment. If they are not ignored, at any given level of education, the educational experiences shown in Figure 4.7 will usually result in the development of some level of knowledge and skills for recipients. The levels of attainment likely to be achieved will depend critically on the nature, quantity and quality of the educational resources employed and the individual abilities of the cohort of learners that use them.

Within most educational environments it has become common practice to employ a 'blend' of different educational experiences in order to produce an optimal strategy for achieving particular educational objectives (Bielawski and Metcalf, 2005; Bonk and Graham, 2005). The underlying nature of this blending is depicted schematically in Figure 5.2. This shows how different types of educational resource can be combined in various ways to produce a blended approach to learning. This technique often requires the application of dynamic blending algorithms that can be used to tailor a resource blend both to the needs and the preferences of individual learners (Barker, 2006; Barker, van Schaik and Famakinwa, 2007).

Because of the underlying remit of this book, in Figure 5.2, particular emphasis has been given to the nature of educational experiences that are, in one way or another, based upon the use of some form of digital electronic technology. These are often referred to as *e-learning resources*.

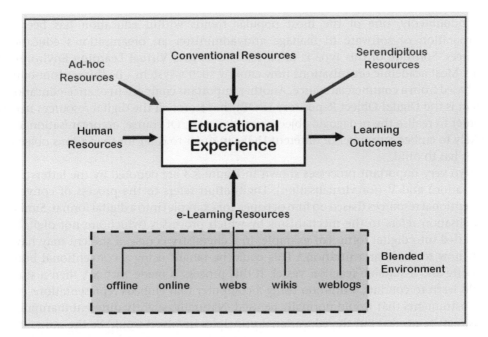

Figure 5.2 The role of blending in relation to designing educational experiences

Another fundamental concept that it is important to 'bring forward' from the first part of this book is the underlying importance of problem solving as a rationale for the provision of education. Problem solving was discussed extensively in Chapter 2 and its relationship to learning and instruction was described in Chapter 4. The significance of problem solving in relation to the four phases of education discussed in the previous section is illustrated graphically in Figure 4.2.

As has been suggested earlier, we strongly believe that achieving problem-solving efficacy (within individuals and/or groups) is one of the ultimate aims of an educational system. We also believe that electronic tools (in general) and EPSS (in particular) can help to produce educational environments within which this aim can be achieved. There is much evidence, both in the literature and elsewhere in this book, which supports this claim.

Bearing in mind the growing importance of electronic learning and the resources needed to support this technique, the following section discuses the ways in which these can be used and the impact they are having on the ongoing development of educational systems.

Principles, Techniques and Electronic Tools

Within all levels of education there have been substantial movements towards the introduction of electronic (digital) technology into educational systems. The ways in which this is being achieved is illustrated schematically in Figure 5.3[3] (Barker, 2009).

---

3   In this diagram (Figure 5.3), the un-arrowed lines represent structural relationships between the various components from which the system is comprised. Heavy arrowed lines represent either processes or instantiations of object classes or

Undoubtedly, one of the most popular trends within education has been the incorporation of software to manage and administer an organisation's educational resources. Software of this type is often referred to as a Virtual Learning Environment (VLE). Most academic organisations now employ such a system – be this custom-built or purchased from a commercial source. Another important component of an 'e-educational' system is the Digital Object Repository (DOR) that stores all the digital resources needed in order to realise the pedagogic objectives of its users. Of course, an organisational VLE is likely to embed a number of different DORs in order to cater for the various objectives that it has to fulfil.

Two very important processes shown in Figure 5.3 are denoted by the letters D (for digitisation) and V (for virtualisation). Digitisation refers to the process of converting conventional resources (based on film or paper, for example) into a digital format. Similarly, virtualisation refers to the mechanisms by which processes (which are not digital) are converted into digital form. For example, in a chemistry course, a student may have to learn how to perform a titration.[4] This could be taught using a conventional burette, a pipette and a suitable reaction vessel. If this process is made 'virtual', then a student would learn to conduct a titration using a computer that embeds representations of the real instruments that would normally be used. Naturally, slightly different manipulative skills may be needed but the educational principles involved would be the same. In the

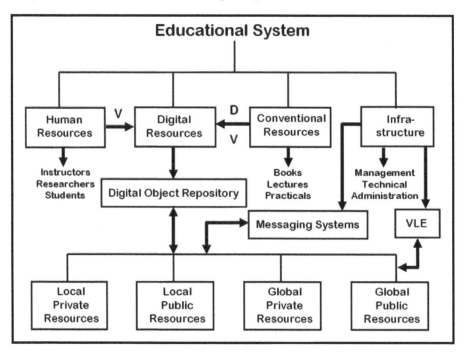

Figure 5.3   Introducing the 'e' word into education

dynamic interactions between system components. For a further discussion of this model, readers are referred to Barker (2008b, 2009).

4   Titration is a measurement technique that is used in analytical chemistry in order to estimate the amount of material that is contained in a solution. Further details on this technique can be found in the *Wikipedia* online encyclopaedia – see *http://en.wikipedia.org/wiki/Titrations* (accessed 3rd September, 2008).

following section we will see that the process of virtualisation often involves various types of simulation. The quality of the virtual experience that a person is exposed to will therefore depend, very much, upon the fidelity of the simulations that can be created.

An important aspect of the educational system depicted in Figure 5.3 is the various 'messaging facilities' that it embeds. These can be used to enable teachers and learners to communicate with each other for various purposes. Typical of the communication tools used are e-mail, real-time interactive chat and various forms of online conferencing. Facilities of this sort can provide mechanisms for debate, discussion and the exchange of messages and feedback. They can also be used to facilitate various forms of resource sharing.

An educational system, similar to that shown in Figure 5.3, is an example of a complex multi-component human-computer system. It is therefore imperative that the human-computer interfaces are designed in a user-centred fashion and show a high level of consistency, usability and reliability. Wherever possible, these interfaces should be intuitive and they should be supported by appropriate online 'help' facilities. These are important performance aids in relation to achieving smooth, efficient and effective end-user interaction with the system.

The natural extension of the processes embedded in Figure 5.3 is the creation of a Virtual Educational System (VES) that embeds within it all the tools and resources needed in order to execute and monitor educational processes of various sorts. The *VUSIL* (Virtual University Server in Lebanon) system that we built some years ago is an example of such a facility (Moukadem, Barker and van Schaik, 2003). Given that much of education is moving in the directions illustrated in Figure 5.3, it is important to consider the nature of the digital tools needed in order to support such a shift, and also, how the introduction of electronic performance support may be used to enhance the benefits that such a shift would bring.

Many educational paradigms, of necessity, have to be hosted by specific subject disciplines – and therefore require bespoke software for content delivery and, in some cases, specific digital tools. However, having said this, there is also a great deal within education that is of a highly generic nature – consider, for example, the widespread use of various forms of computer technology within virtually every subject domain. Everyone who has a computer has probably used a word-processing system, an e-mail package and a web browser (in order to access the Internet). Each of these items is an example of a performance support tool that can be used to enhance educational opportunities.

Like computer systems, many of the principles and techniques of performance support constitute a generic 'tool bag' that can be applied in a domain-independent way. Unfortunately, because of the space limitations imposed on this chapter, it is only possible to consider a small selection of the more general examples of performance tools and techniques. However, many of the subsequent chapters in this second part of the book will mention some of the more subject-specific issues and aspects of applying performance support techniques within particular domain contexts.

Some of the generic activities that need to be considered when applying electronic performance support technologies to educational processes are listed in Table 5.1.

In the following section, a set of vignettes is presented. These outline some of the ways in which electronic performance support techniques can be used within some of the contexts identified in Table 5.1. Many of these contexts are also addressed in subsequent chapters of this book – see, for example, Chapter 6 (information access), Chapter 10 (science and engineering) and Chapter 14 (observing and reporting).

Table 5.1   Generic educational activities

observing
reading
speaking
writing, drawing, presenting and publishing
calculating
simulating
gaming
measuring
constructing
accessing information and knowledge
managing collections of information and knowledge
interacting and collaborating with peers

Educational Vignettes

In this section, a series of short illustrations is used to demonstrate cases where performance support techniques and/or tools have been successfully used to augment educational processes.

VISUALISATION

Visualisation[5] is the collective name given to a particular type of data analysis and graphical display process that can be used in order to enable users to visualise (in a graphical way) the concepts embedded in a complex data collection. This data collection may be static or it may be time variant. Visualisation may involve the use of static images and/or dynamic images and animation. Similarly, 2-D, 3-D and 4-D techniques can also be applied. As is examined in the following vignette, visualisation is an important aspect of simulation.

Maps are an example of an important visualisation technique. A conventional map, for example, is a representation (in graphical form) of a section of the earth's surface. Various objects that exist at different locations are represented by different types of symbol. Colours are used to highlight different areas. The degree of detail that is shown on a map depends upon the scale that it is drawn at.

Electronic maps (see, for example, *Google Maps*[6]) provide a powerful performance tool in that they enable their users to visualise height profiles and the three-dimensional nature of the terrain they represent. When augmented with animation techniques, electronic maps can provide even more powerful performance tools by enabling users to perform a 3-D 'walk-through' of the terrain they wish to visualise.

---

5   There is an interesting entry on visualisation techniques and its various approaches in *Wikipedia*: see *http:// en.wikipedia.org/wiki/Visualisation* (accessed 3rd September, 2008).

6   *Google Maps* is just one example of an electronic mapping system. Further details can be found at *http://maps.google. com* (accessed 3rd September, 2008). Other examples of electronic mapping systems can be found at *http://www.anquet. co.uk* (accessed 3rd September, 2008) and *http://www.memory-map.co.uk* (accessed 3rd September, 2008).

SIMULATION AND VISUALISATION

Computer-based simulation techniques can be used in a variety of different ways to produce rich educational opportunities that may otherwise not be possible. As mentioned earlier in this chapter, when this technique is used, the quality of the learning experience that is achieved will depend critically on the fidelity level of the simulation. At the highest level a user should not be able to distinguish between a simulated environment and a real environment. However, this ideal is rarely, if ever, achieved in practice – nor is it necessary. Some well-known examples of the use of simulation include the use of a flight simulator (for training aircraft pilots) and an automobile simulator (used by driving instructors to train their clients). In our own university, radiography students who have to learn how to use complex X-ray machinery are first exposed to a simulated device (Cosson, 2007) which monitors what each student does and how his/her performance is changing with time. When a satisfactory level of performance is achieved they can progress on to using a real machine.

Simulation is closely related to the use of Virtual Reality[7] (VR). Within a VR system, users are allowed to interact with a real (via tele-presence) or computer-simulated environment. An interesting example of a simulated VR environment is that which is embedded within the *Second Life*[8] website. This is an Internet-based virtual world in which people represent themselves using electronic representations called avatars. A wide range of different educational facilities is available through this interactive virtual world.

GAME PLAYING

Within education, game playing is an important technique for knowledge creation and skill acquisition. By learning to play a game as skilful participants, people are able to acquire three important capabilities: first, they learn how to derive the rules that dictate how a particular gaming environment functions; second, they develop knowledge in the form of 'playing' strategies that are likely to lead to successful game outcomes; and third, they develop various manipulative and responsive skills that enable the rules and strategies to be put into practice.

Undoubtedly, over the last decade, computer games of various sorts have become tremendously popular. A wide range of gaming software is now available commercially – many of which have an educational orientation. Games can be single player or multi-player. Several multi-player games exist on the Internet.

There is also a good selection of hardware available for computer games[9] For many people (myself included), the popularity of computer gaming has been brought about by

---

7   Virtual reality has tremendous implications for education in terms of the development of electronic artefacts such as a virtual classroom, a virtual class, and so on. *Wikipedia* contains a useful description of virtual reality – see *http:// en.wikipedia.org/wiki/Virtual_reality* (accessed 3rd September, 2008).

8   *Second Life* is a very sophisticated example of a virtual world. Further details about this system can be found at *http://en.wikipedia.org/wiki/Second_Life* (accessed 3rd September, 2008).

9   Some examples of gaming hardware can be found in the following *Wikipedia* entries (accessed 3rd September, 2008): *http://en.wikipedia.org/wiki/Game_console* and *http://en.wikipedia.org/wiki/Handheld_game_console*.

the availability of (relatively) low-cost hand-held gaming devices such as the *Nintendo DS Lite*[10] – see the picture in Figure 5.4.

Systems such as as the *Nintendo DS Lite* have tremendous potential in relation to developing portable educational performance support systems based on the principles of gaming. Two examples of such packages that have been produced by Nintendo for the *DS Lite* are the *Brain Training* and *Sight Training* programs. Each of these contains exercises and activities intended to improve their users' performance in particular areas (mental skills and visual responsiveness, respectively).

As is discussed elsewhere (van Schaik, Barker and Famakinwa, 2006; van Schaik, Barker and Famakinwa, 2007), we have embedded various gaming elements within our *Epsilon* performance support system for use in academic libraries. This system is described in Chapter 6.

Figure 5.4   The Nintendo DS Lite hand-held gaming console

ACCESSING INFORMATION AND KNOWLEDGE

The widespread availability of the Internet in homes, workplaces and academic establishments has made access to stored information and knowledge much easier. Computer technology has therefore significantly improved people's ability to obtain the information and knowledge they need in order to solve problems (Barker, 2008a). By increasing the range and quality of the available information and knowledge, performance in problem solving can be improved both by reducing the time needed to solve a problem and by increasing the quality of the solution that can be achieved.

10   Details of the *Nintendo DS Lite* are given in the *Wikipedia* electronic encyclopaedia at *http://en:wikipedia.org/wiki/Nintendo_DS_Lite* (accessed 3rd September, 2008).

Two important aspects of information and knowledge access are the *search engines* and *databases* that are available. There are two broad approaches to the provision of databases: subject specific (such as *PsycINFO*[11] and *Chemical Abstracts*[12]) and general purpose archives. Ideally, all information that is published electronically would be indexed with relevant tags that would subsequently allow it to be retrieved by Internet search tools such as *Google*[13] and *Yahoo*.[14] Sometimes, information is 'brought together' and published in the form of electronic journals, electronic books and encyclopaedias that can be made available online (through the Internet, for example) or published on a medium such as CD-ROM or DVD. This chapter, for example, makes extensive use of the *Wikipedia* online encyclopaedia by giving readers access to information that it is not possible to include in the printed version of this book.

Further details on information access and a more in-depth discussion of the application of electronic performance support tools in this area is presented in Chapter 6 of this book.

MANAGING KNOWLEDGE

The previous vignette outlined how digital electronic technology makes it much easier for people to gain access to information and knowledge (in electronic form). Using this technology it becomes possible for people to build their own personal electronic digital archives containing material that is relevant to their own particular interests and needs. Reference has already been made to the concept of a Personal Electronic Archive (PEA) in Chapter 4 (see Figure 4.2). A PEA is defined as being a collection of digital information that has been collected by (and is accessible to) a particular individual. In a teaching and learning context, it is also possible for individuals to create a Personal Digital Archive for Learning – that is, a PeDAL (Barker, 2008b). PEAs and PeDALs are examples of performance support tools that can be used to support knowledge management.

The underlying building block for such performance support tools is a DOR – as described previously in this chapter (see Figure 5.3). However, a DOR only provides a basic storage and retrieval facility. In order to achieve more effective access and structuring of information and knowledge, it is necessary to superimpose some form of management structure on top of the DOR. This can be achieved in a variety of different ways using currently available content management systems or bespoke facilities (Barker, 2008a, 2008c).

---

11   *PsycINFO* is an important source of abstracts for psychological publications. Its database covers over 2,000 journals. The system is run by the *American Psychological Association* (APA). The homepage for *PsycINFO* is *http://www.apa.org/psycinfo/* (accessed 3rd September, 2008).

12   *Chemical Abstracts* is a database facility containing details of chemistry-related information. It is produced by the *Chemical Abstracts Service* (CAS) which is a division of the American Chemical Society. Further details on Chemical Abstracts can be found at *http://www.cas.org* (accessed 3rd September, 2008).

13   The *Google* search engine is probably one of the most popular of those currently available. Details of this performance support tool can be found on the *Wikipedia* site: *http://en.wikipedia.org/wiki/Google_search* (accessed 3rd September, 2008). There are country-specific versions of the search engine; one link into the system is *http://www.google.com* (accessed 3rd September, 2008).

14   A description of the *Yahoo* search engine can be found in *Wikipedia* at *http://en.wikipedia.org/wiki/Yahoo!_search* (accessed 3rd September, 2008). The search engine can be found at *http://search.yahoo.com* (accessed 3rd September, 2008).

DOING RESEARCH

People do research in order to collect data on a topic that is of interest to them. This data can be used in order to generate information, which, in turn, may lead to the creation of new knowledge or evidence that supports (or refutes) the validity of existing knowledge. Of course, research is an important part of problem solving and its application can lead to the development of new products of various sorts.

Research can be conducted in a variety of different ways – depending upon the results that are required, the outcomes to be achieved and the resources available. The 'classical' approach to research involves observing some process or artefact and collecting data about it and its behaviour. Sometimes, the research process requires an appropriate 'experimental design' to be conducted before the actual research is undertaken. After the observational phase of research has been completed, the data that has been accrued must be analysed for validity, correctness, consistency and reliability. Once the quality of the observational data has been established, it can be analysed in order to extract meaning from it. This can be done by using data mining techniques and/or statistical methods. An important outcome of these analytical processes is the creation of information that enables researchers to build models that reflect the meaning of the original data.

Because of the importance of research methods within undergraduate curricula in psychology, some time ago we built an electronic performance support system to augment the teaching of research methods (van Schaik, Pearson and Barker, 2002; Barker, van Schaik, and Pearson, 2005). The intent of the EPSS was to provide students with help in designing experiments and choosing appropriate statistical methods for analysing their data.

More in-depth treatments of the role of EPSS – as applied within a research context – are presented later in this second part of the book (Chapters 13 and 14).

PUBLISHING AND SHARING KNOWLEDGE

As was mentioned in the previous vignette, an important outcome of research activity is the observational data, information and knowledge produced. For a variety of reasons it is important that these resources are shared with those others who may be interested in them. This has usually been achieved by publishing the results of research in conventional paper-based books and journals. However, having said that, other publication media are also now being used to help in the dissemination process.

Because the publication cycle used in conventional paper-based publication involves a relatively slow process, electronic 'performance aids' based on computers and networks (such as the Internet) are now being used in order to 'speed up' the process of information dissemination. This has led to the creation of online databases (similar to those mentioned earlier in this section), electronic books (and related types of e-publication), conventional websites and a whole range of knowledge-sharing artefacts – such as weblogs and wikis (Barker, 2007a, 2007b; Bruns, 2008).

A weblog (or 'blog') is essentially a form of electronic diary/notepad that is published on the Internet. The entries that its owner makes can be read and commented on by those other people who are granted access to it. Weblogs are normally created and managed using an online publishing package such as *Moveable Type*.[15]

Wikis are a more powerful performance tool than weblogs. They provide an online web-based publishing environment in which information and knowledge can be created and shared across a community of authors and readers. The *Wikipedia* system (which has been extensively referred to in the footnotes accompanying this chapter) is a sophisticated example of a wiki. Performance tools (such as *MediaWiki*[16]) are usually used to provide the type of environment and infrastructure that is needed to create and publish wikis.

COLLABORATION

There are two broad ways in which people learn: first, as individuals; and second; as members of groups or teams. Group learning usually involves people working together in (a collaborative way) on the various activities that are needed to solve a problem or achieve an educational goal. Communication with peers is an important aspect of group problem solving – as is 'presence' within the shared space that the group uses to support its learning activities. In situations where group members cannot work together in a face-to-face fashion within the same physical (geographical) space, appropriate support tools are needed to facilitate these requirements. Within the context of educational tasks, there are many tools available to support the process of collaboration and collaborative learning. For example, the 'messaging' facilities depicted in Figure 5.3 can be used in various ways to provide a communication infrastructure to support collaboration.

E-mail is probably one of the simplest tools for the communication aspect of collaborative learning. Online conferencing systems (such as *FirstClass*,[17] for example) also provide a useful vehicle for the support of collaboration. Such environments usually provide a conventional e-mail facility and interactive chat tools, as well as support for synchronous and asynchronous conferencing.

The wiki and weblog performance support tools described in the previous vignette also provide powerful facilities for the support of collaboration. The way in which a wiki structure can be used to support collaboration is illustrated in Figure 5.5. In this diagram, the abbreviations WP and WW stand for 'wiki page' and 'wiki web', respectively.

The wiki structure shown in Figure 5.5 allows authors to add and edit the content contained within it. As an illustration of the power of this form of collaboration, the *Wikipedia* system is a very impressive example of a knowledge source that has been produced as a result of the involvement of over 75,000 people – most of whom have never met in a face-to-face context.

---

15   The *Moveable Type* system is one of many examples of commercially available weblog authoring systems. Further details on this system can be found both at the company's website *http://moveabletype.org* (accessed 3rd September, 2008) and in *Wikipedia* at *http://en.wikipedia.org/wiki/Moveable_Type* (accessed 3rd September, 2008).

16   The *MediaWiki* performance support tool is a popular wiki authoring and publishing system. It has been used, for example, to build the *Wikipedia* system. Further details are available at *http://en.wikipedia.org/wiki/MediaWiki* and *http://www.mediawiki.org* (both accessed 3rd September, 2008).

17   *FirstClass* is defined in *Wikipedia* as 'a client-server groupware, email, online conferencing ... system' (see *http://en.wikipedia.org/wiki/FirstClass* – accessed on 12th February, 2009). Further details of this system can be found at *http://www.firstclass.com* (accessed 12th February, 2009).

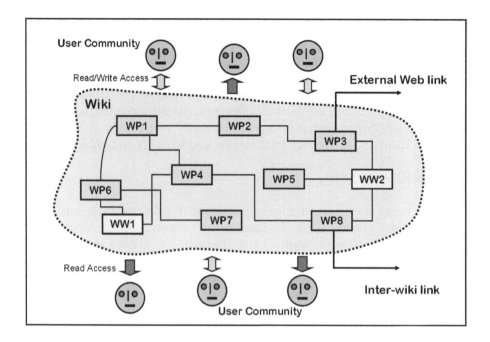

Figure 5.5   Using wikis to create and share knowledge

SOCIAL NETWORKING

Social networking is the term that is commonly used to describe the use of suitable computer-based tools (such as *MySpace, FaceBook, LinkedIn* and *Bebo*)[18] that enable individuals to project their presence into an online community. This can be achieved in a variety of different ways depending upon the type and level of interaction required. An online community usually forms because of its members' common interests. Professional people, for example, may belong to a Community of Practice (CoP). The objectives of such a CoP are to share experience and discuss particular topics of interest related to a specific area of discourse – such as medicine, physics, literature, languages, education, and so on.

Within many online communities, individual members each have a *profile*. This profile is likely to contain personal details (such as gender, age and contact details) and a record of the individual's qualifications, experience, special interests, and so on. In some communities, individuals may prefer to hide their real identity by using some form of pseudonym – such as *Charlie36* or *LilyAsh*; they can usually also choose which information about them is revealed to the group. Members' profiles can be used in various ways to enable the formation of sub-groups of people whose profiles match each other with respect to one or more attribute values. In some situations, membership of an online social networking group may depend upon applicants having a profile that is acceptable to the group's norms.

---

18   Social networking is discussed in considerable depth in *Wikipedia* at *http://en.wikipedia.org/wiki/Social_networking* (accessed on 12th February, 2009).

Within an educational setting, it is possible to use a wide range of criteria to create social groupings which support study groups for both teaching and learning. For example, 'records of achievement' could be used as part of a learner's profile. It is therefore feasible to set up social networking groups for members having a particular interest and/or ability level in a particular subject area.

ASSESSING ABILITY

Assessing the knowledge and skills that people have is usually thwarted with difficulties. In Chapter 1 we discussed 'performance' (see the sections entitled 'What is Performance?' and 'Why Improve Performance?') and its importance. There are four performance-related parameters that are often used to assess an individual's ability in relation to task performance: (1) the time taken to perform the task in question; (2) the number of errors made during task execution; (3) the quality of the results produced; and (4) the cost associated with producing a given outcome. Most people will be familiar with the limitations of tests and examinations – particularly the complex nature of the many factors that can influence the outcomes of these activities. It is also important to remember that the mechanisms used for assessment can themselves influence an individual's performance by perturbing the skills and knowledge that are being appraised.

In order to illustrate the unreliable nature of 'one-off' assessment, Figure 5.6 shows the results of a daily performance testing of ability for a person in relation to three dimensions of computational performance (A, B and C) over a period of time[19]. As can be seen from this diagram, the performance levels oscillate, sometimes quite widely from one level to another. As was mentioned above, these performance oscillations can be caused by a variety of factors – some internal (for example, emotional state and motivational state), some external (such as distractions and ambient conditions) and some historical factors (related to prior experience). Obviously, any single measurement is highly unlikely to represent the true performance of the person in the particular dimension concerned.

Assessing task performance is very important in applying EPSS techniques since, if it is not possible to do this, then it becomes almost impossible to measure the quantitative gains associated with the particular performance interventions introduced. Naturally, performance assessment in an educational context is an area where considerably more research needs to be undertaken.

One of the important roles of an EPSS in the domain of skill and knowledge assessment is to produce various types of tool for the accurate and reliable measurement of performance. Such tools may (1) facilitate self-monitoring of ability (and the provision of appropriate feedback to their users); (2) enable peer monitoring in various contexts (along with the provision of guidelines for improvement); and (3) enable their users to document and maintain records of achievement in relation to skill and knowledge acquisition and their application to problem solving (for example, the creation of personal websites, weblogs, wikis and e-portfolios).

---

19   The results shown in this diagram are based on unpublished research data obtained in an experiment conducted by the author in August–September, 2008. In the experiment the subject was working in the plateau region of the upper curve shown in Figure 1.11 and was therefore considered to be an expert performer. Observations were made over a period of 29 consecutive days.

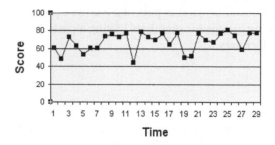

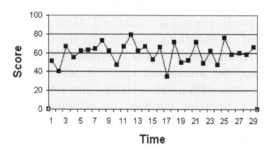

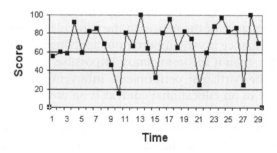

Figure 5.6 Results of daily arithmetic testing

Conclusions

This chapter has tried to identify some of the more important concepts and trends involved in the application of electronic performance support tools within the context of educational settings. It is our belief that performance support tools can be used at all levels of the 'lifelong' educational curriculum that was identified in Figure 5.1. Furthermore, our thesis is that these performance tools can be deployed both by teachers and by students within virtually any subject area.

The important underlying strategy that should be adopted when using this approach is: first, to identify an educational need (arising from either an individual or a group of students/teachers); and second, to design and build an appropriate performance aid that will enable the identified shortcomings to be overcome. In this way, the use of EPSS tools can be used to enhance the educational opportunities that are made available to all those who wish to benefit from using them.

The impact of technology (in general) and of EPSS tools (in particular) has far-reaching ramifications for the future of education. Indeed, Bruns (2008: pp. 341–343) calls for a radical change in educational philosophy from the conventional 'production-based' models to one which involves the '5Cs' – thereby, producing students who are able to be *creative*, who can be *collaborative, critical, combinatory* and *communicative*. Increasingly, bearing this in mind, we see the future of educational performance support as being one of providing tools and infrastructures to facilitate the development (and enhancement) of these capabilities.

Acknowledgement

I am grateful to Paul van Schaik for his useful and supportive comments on previous drafts of this chapter.

References

Barker, P.G. (2006). Motivation, Learning Spirals and Blended Learning. *Proceedings of the 1st International Conference on Blended Learning – Promoting Dialogue in Innovation and Practice* (pp. 91–97). Hatfield, UK: University of Hertfordshire.

Barker, P.G. (2007a). Using Wikis as a Teaching and Learning Resource. In C.P. Constantinou, Z.C. Zacharia and M. Papaevripidou (eds), *Proceedings of the CBLIS 2007 International Conference on Computer-Based Learning in Science – Contemporary Perspectives in New Technologies in Science and Education* (pp. 12–23). Nicosia, Cyprus: Learning in Science Group, University of Cyprus.

Barker, P.G. (2007b). Blended Learning the Wiki Way. *Proceedings of the 2nd International Conference on Blended Learning – Supporting the Net Generation Learner* (pp. 60–71). Hatfield, UK: University of Hertfordshire.

Barker, P.G. (2008a). Using Wikis for Knowledge Management. In Luca, J. and Weippl, E.R. (eds), *Proceedings of the ED-MEDIA 2008 World Conference on Educational Multimedia, Hypermedia and Telecommunications* (pp. 3604–3613). Vienna, Austria. Chesapeake, VA: Association for the Advancement of Computing in Education.

Barker, P.G. (2008b). Blended Electronic Learning – Managing the Blend. *Proceedings of the 3rd International Conference on Blended Learning – Enhancing the Student Experience* (pp. 45–53). Hatfield, UK: University of Hertfordshire.

Barker, P.G. (2008c). Using Weblogs and Wikis to Enhance Human Performance. In Bonk, C.J., Lee, M.M. and Reynolds, T. (eds), *Proceedings of the E-Learn 2008 World Conference on Electronic Learning in Corporate, Government, Healthcare and Higher Education* (pp. 581–588). Las Vegas, NV. Chesapeake, VA: Association for the Advancement of Computing in Education.

Barker, P.G. (2009). Using Metanotation as a Tool for Describing Learning Systems. In Fu Lee Wang, Joseph Fong and Reggie C. Kwan (eds), *Handbook of Research on Hybrid Learning Models: Advanced Tools, Technologies, and Application*. Hershey, PA: Information Science Reference, IGI Publishing.

Barker, P., Schaik, P. van and Famakinwa, O. (2007). Building Electronic Performance Support Systems for First-Year University Students. *Innovations in Education and Teaching International*, 44(3), 243–255.

Barker, P., Schaik, P. van and Pearson, R. (2005). An EPSS for Learning Psychological Research Methods. *International Journal of Continuing Engineering Education and Lifelong Learning*, 15(1/2), 19–29.

Bielawski, L. and Metcalf, D. (2005). *Blended e-Learning – Integrating Knowledge, Performance Support and Online Learning*. Amherst, MA: HRD Press Inc.

Bonk, C.J. and Graham, C.R. (2005). *The Handbook of Blended Learning: Global Perspectives, Local Designs*. San Francisco, CA: Pfeiffer.

Bruns, A. (2008). *Blogs, Wikipedia, Second Life and Beyond, From Production to Produsage*. New York, NY: Philip Lang Publishing.

Cosson, P. (2007). Virtual Education: A Reality or Radiography?, *Synergy News*, 20–21, August 2007. Available online at: *http://www.shaderware.com/live/graphics/p20-21_SynNews_Aug07.pdf*. [Accessed on 11th February, 2009].

Goswami, U. (2008). *Cognitive Development – The Learning Brain*. Hove, UK: Psychology Press, Taylor and Francis Group.

Moukadem, I., Barker, P. and Schaik, P. van (2003). Evaluation of the VUSIL Virtual Learning Environment. In D. Lassner and C. McNaught (eds), *Proceedings of World Conference on Educational Multimedia, Hypermedia and Telecommunications 2003* (pp. 1340–1343). Chesapeake, VA: AACE.

Schaik, P. van, Barker, P. and Famakinwa, O. (2006). Potential Roles for Performance Support Tools Within Library Systems. *The Electronic Library*, 24(3), 347–365.

Schaik, P. van, Barker, P. and Famakinwa, O. (2007). Making a Case for Using Electronic Performance Support Systems in Academic Libraries. *Journal of Interactive Learning Research*, 18(3), 411–428.

Schaik, P. van, Pearson, R. and Barker, P. (2002). Designing Electronic Performance Support Systems to Support Learning. *Innovations in Education and Teaching International*, 39(4), 289–306.

6 *Information Access*

OLADEJI FAMAKINWA AND PHILIP BARKER

Information and knowledge are fundamental resources that provide the underlying basis for all human activity. Because of their intrinsic value in relation to problem solving, these commodities often have to be stored for future use. Subsequently, when they are needed, appropriate retrieval mechanisms must be used in order to extract relevant items from within the archives in which they are stored. This chapter discusses some of the problems associated with information access and retrieval within the context of library systems. The role of performance support tools within libraries is briefly discussed and a case study is presented which illustrates how an electronic performance support system can be used to help people locate information that is of interest to them.

Introduction

As is discussed in Chapter 7, communication is a fundamental human activity. It can take place in a variety of different ways and in a range of contexts. Essentially, communication involves the transfer of *signals* (and/or messages) between a sender and one or more recipients. Signals and messages can exist in various forms; they are usually embedded within an appropriate medium or *communication channel*. According to the early work undertaken by Shannon (1948), the way in which a communication process takes place can be represented using a model similar to that depicted in Figure 6.1.

A signal is usually defined in terms of the changes in state that can take place within a given communication channel. From a scientific perspective, signals arise from the various types of observation that are made on the entities, processes and events that people choose to study. Because of the inherently transient nature of signals, they often have to be stored for future use. The act of storing signals on a storage medium produces *data*. This data has no intrinsic meaning. When meaning is added to data, it is converted into a semantically richer resource called *information*. This latter resource is important because it facilitates decision-making processes. That is, it enables people to make decisions about what they have to do in relation to the different types of situation that arise as they navigate through the various problem spaces encountered during their problem-solving activities (Barker, 2008a). The nature of problem solving has been discussed in some detail in Chapter 2.

As is indicated in Figure 6.1, signals, data and information can also be generated by the human mind. In this situation, these resources are derived from the *knowledge* that people have accumulated as a result of the experiences to which they have been exposed during their lifetime. As has been discussed in earlier chapters of this book, knowledge

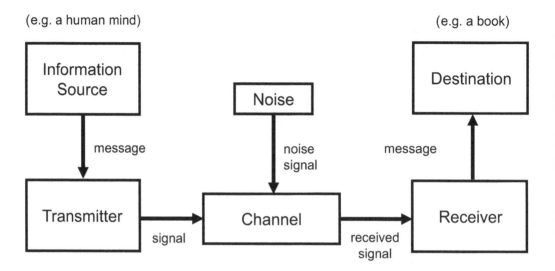

Figure 6.1   Shannon's basic model of communication

is acquired through various types of learning process. The relationship between data, information, knowledge (and wisdom[1]) is often expressed in terms of the *DIKW hierarchy* diagram that is shown in Figure 6.2 (Ackoff, 1989; Zeleny, 2005). DIKW is an acronym for Data, Information, Knowledge and Wisdom.

Within Figure 6.2, a 'pyramidal' structure is used to reflect the fact that more of the lower-level elements in the pyramid are required to synthesise the higher-level components. Also, as has been mentioned previously, elements near the base of the pyramid are less semantically rich than those near its apex.

Despite the tremendous creative power of the human mind, it does have a number of shortcomings. These include: (1) its limitations in relation to computational capability and (2) its restricted ability to remember substantial volumes of detailed material. This latter limitation is imposed on people due to the human brain's storage capacity and – most important – its retention and recall characteristics. Naturally, various types of performance support tool can be used to compensate for many of these shortcomings – thereby enhancing people's individual performance in these areas. Due to these natural 'memory limitations', the human brain often has to 'off-load' (or exteriorise) some of the material that it contains. This exteriorisation is necessary to prevent material from getting lost as a result of becoming forgotten (Barker, 2008a). Various types of ancillary storage medium can be used to support exteriorisation processes – for example, notebooks, sketchpads, film, computers, audio recorders and, of course, books. Books are important because they have always been a well-established mechanism by which data, information and knowledge have been stored for posterity. Increasingly, however, 'electronic books' are beginning to play an important role in relation to knowledge and information storage (Barker, 1997).

The growth in the number of books available for public consumption has led to the formation of various types of private and public *library*. Public library systems are important

---

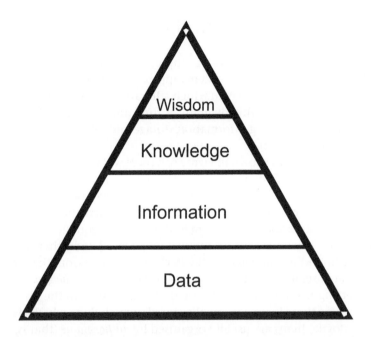

Figure 6.2   The Data, Information, Knowledge and Wisdom hierarchy

because they provide mechanisms for sharing data, information and knowledge within those societies that support them. Private libraries are usually used to support closed groups of people and/or individuals. During the course of their studies, most scholars will build their own *personal* library systems containing books (and other artefacts) related to the particular domains that they study.

As has been mentioned earlier, once material has been stored in an appropriate archive (such as a library), appropriate retrieval mechanisms need to be put into place so that particular items of interest can be retrieved – as and when they are needed. The nature of the retrieval processes employed will depend upon how the material in an archive is structured and organised. The structuring of recorded knowledge is usually achieved by means of a suitable *taxonomy* or *classification* system. This enables items having similar characteristics to cluster together within a common category. Particular items of knowledge will usually be identified by way of a *naming convention* – that is, the names that people assign to them. When used in conjunction with a naming convention, taxonomies can be used to provide a method by which particular items of information or knowledge can be retrieved from within the host archive that houses them.

From what has been said above, it is easy to see that libraries, in themselves, are powerful performance aids for enhancing people's ability to store and access knowledge and information. However, because libraries can be quite complex, both in relation to their organisation and their structure, various sorts of performance support tool are often needed in order to make it easier for people to access the stored materials that they contain. Bearing this in mind, this chapter discusses some of the roles that an Electronic Performance Support Systems (EPSS) may play within a library system and then goes on to describe and discuss the development and use of a prototype performance support tool (called *Epsilon*) for use within academic libraries.

Libraries as Enablers of Information Access

A library is essentially a repository for storing collections of recorded information and knowledge (Barker, 1997). Using the 'systems approach' that was advocated in Chapter 1, a simple model that illustrates the way in which a library operates is depicted schematically in Figure 6.3. As is shown in this diagram, a fundamental and inherent aspect of all library systems is the underlying information storage and retrieval processes they employ as part of their basic operation.

Within the library system shown in Figure 6.3, there will usually be a collection of *library staff* responsible for its overall management and operation. The library's staff will also control the input and output of its resources. In an 'ideal' system, each user would specify the nature of the items that they wish to retrieve. The system would then automatically retrieve these items from within its store and deliver them to the user that requested them. Unfortunately, most libraries do not have this level of 'automation'; instead, users themselves have to play a significant role in finding and fetching the items they require from the information store. These processes are usually facilitated by means of the library's *catalogue*.

A library catalogue is essentially a list of all the items held in the library along with a description of where these items are actually stored – which floor, which aisle, which shelf. Within the catalogue, items are usually organised by *author-name* (that is, the identity of the person[s] that created it) and also by *title* (in other words, what a particular item is 'called'). Therefore, if a user knows the name of the author who created a particular sought-after item, the library's catalogue can facilitate a search by author-name. Similarly, if a user knows the title of the required item then the material could also be located by means of this information. Also, a sub-set of the *keywords* embedded in an item's title may also be used for retrieval purposes. Once a library user knows the '*shelf-location*' of a required item, the retrieval process now simply involves going to the relevant area (within the library system) where the item is located and 'pulling' it off the shelf upon which it is stored. Obviously, the discussion presented here is only relevant to a conventional library system; digital libraries would not require users to 'fetch' material from shelves. However,

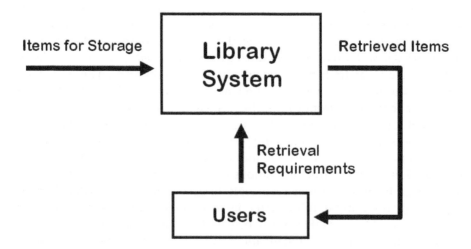

Figure 6.3   Schematic representation of a library system

having said this, in a virtual library, users may undertake a simulated 'walk through' of the library involved (Barker, 1997).

Naturally, within the scenario described above, there are numerous ways in which performance support tools could help users to overcome any difficulties they may encounter – be these associated with the 'usability' of a library system or as a result of a user's limitations in possessing the relevant skills and knowledge to use that library. The types of problem that library-users are likely to face are discussed in the following section while the application of performance support systems for overcoming some of these problems is discussed in more detail later in the chapter – and will be illustrated by means of a case study. However, before pursuing these issues, it is necessary to say a little more about how classification systems are currently used within conventional libraries. This background is needed since it forms the basis for the case study that is to be presented.

As has been mentioned earlier in this chapter, knowledge classification is usually an integral aspect of any stored archive. Classification is an important mechanism that facilitates the rapid retrieval of material as and when it is required.

Many classification systems involve some form of *hierarchical arrangement* of the items they describe. As an example of this, consider the way in which this book is organised: it is sub-divided into a number of *parts*. Within each part the material is organised into *chapters* – each one of which deals with a particular topic area. Each chapter is then divided into a series of *sections* that cover particular aspects of the chapter's topic area. Sections are then divided into *sub-sections* – and so on. Another important component of a book is its *index*; this serves to enable its users to locate the pages upon which particular topics are discussed. In many ways, the pages of a book are analogous to the shelves of a library – in that they store the items of knowledge that the author has committed to them.

In a similar way, within a library system, the overall knowledge that it contains can be sub-divided into subject areas; these can then be sub-divided into different topic, sub-topics, and so on. Material that is related to a particular subject area could now be located within a specific section of the library. A library's catalogue is analogous to the index of a book – it enables library-users to locate where particular items reside within the storage hierarchy (building, floor, section, aisle and shelf).

Most of the established institutional libraries use either a nationally or an internationally recognised classification system. Two examples of such systems are the *Dewey Decimal Classification* (DDC) (Satija, 2007) and the *Library of Congress Classification* (LCC) (Chan, 1999). The LCC system divides knowledge into broad groupings corresponding to social sciences, humanities, and the natural and physical sciences. These areas of knowledge are distributed over 20 large classes – with an additional category for general works. Each of the classes is assigned a letter of the English alphabet to denote it. Within these classes, there are further sub-divisions which allow for more specific groups. In a similar way, the DDC system uses the decimal number system for its groupings. The DDC system divides human knowledge into ten main sub-divisions – each one of which is assigned 100 numbers. These main classes are then sub-divided in order to accommodate more specific groups. Table 6.1 shows some examples taken from the DDC and LCC schemes.

An attractive consequence of the classification system used in a library is the fact that it helps people to *browse* through related items of knowledge – since all the items related to a particular topic will usually be located in the same shelving area. In addition, libraries also provide an index or a catalogue of all the items available within its stock. As has already been discussed, a library's catalogue will normally contain two main components: an

Table 6.1   Examples of classification systems commonly used in libraries

Dewey Decimal Classification		Library of Congress Classification	
400	Languages	P	Language and Literature
410	Linguistics	P101-410	Linguistics
411	Writing systems	P327-327.5	Writing systems
500	Science and Mathematics	Q	Science
510	Mathematics	QA	Mathematics
512	Algebra	QA150-272	Algebra

alphabetical list (by *title*) of all the items held in the library and an alphabetically organised list of all the authors who have produced these items. These lists function as performance aids in that they enable the library stock to be searched quickly by its users – either manually or electronically. If a library catalogue exists in electronic form (and an appropriate access system is available), then it would be possible to use additional search parameters – such as the year of publication of an item and/or its subject-domain keywords.

Another important feature of modern, academic library systems is the *online databases* they provide access to – such as, *MEDLINE, PsycINFO, Chemical Abstracts*, and so on. These can be used to access particular research items held within bibliographic retrieval systems. These online databases thus provide another dimension to the information access possibilities that exist within a library system. The case study that is presented later will also discuss this aspect of information access.

Earlier in this section, mention was made of the various types of problem that may arise when people use libraries for accessing information. It was suggested that these could be attributed to two broad sources: the usability of the library system itself and/or a lack of skills and knowledge on the part of library users. The following section briefly discusses some of the problems that commonly cause performance-related problems in the context of library usage. The ways in which some of these problems can be overcome are then considered in the case study.

Problems Related to Information Access in Libraries

Most modern academic libraries provide access to a vast collection of different types of media object. These include books and journals, audio and video tapes, compact discs (CDs) and digital video discs (DVDs), microfilms and microfiches, and various online resources such as databases and electronic journals. Usually, these libraries also make available a wide range of services and facilities for storing and retrieving information. Unfortunately, many library-users often find the plethora of resources rather daunting (van Schaik et al., 2007; Famakinwa, 2004; Hull, 2000). To combat this problem, many libraries have strived to improve the ease-of-use of their services by making skilled library-staff available to train users and provide appropriate user-support where required. In order to avail themselves of this type of support, library-users usually have to be physically present. For a variety of reasons, this may not always be possible. In addition, with the advent of computer networks, many users now want to have online access to their library's resources; this situation often adds to the problems of providing adequate training and user-support. To cater for the needs of these 'online users', many libraries have produced electronic training materials in the form of *e-manuals* and digital video presentations (Library and Information Services, 2008). Despite all these very laudable efforts, many novice library-users still experience significant problems when trying to use library facilities (Carlson, 2003; Hull, 2000).

The types of problem that novice library-users usually experience include: (1) a lack of awareness of the services and facilities available to them and (2) their inability to locate the information resources they require – typically, books that reside on the library's shelves and journal articles held in databases and electronic journals (van Schaik et al., 2007). Many novice library-users also have difficulty using the classification systems used by libraries – particularly those based on the decimal numbering system used by the DDC scheme (van Schaik et al., 2006; Hull, 2005). In addition, novice users also seem to experience problems in formulating keywords when conducting online searches; this invariably leads to either too few or too many results being retrieved.

Library-users who are actually working within the confines of their local library can seek help from the librarians who are available to assist them. However, many users often rely on other alternative 'coping' strategies – such as purchasing the book they require from a local bookstore or by using an Internet search engine (such as *Google*). Of course, one of the problems of using an Internet search engine is the lack of control that exists over the 'quality' of the information retrieved from the multitude of websites that now exist. Very often, many of the items obtained will be of a much lower quality and standard compared to those held in peer-reviewed electronic journals and online databases.

The use of *online services* (such as the electronic journals and online databases mentioned above) introduces yet another problem with respect to information access. This arises from the lack of standardisation that exists in the nature and functionality of the end-user interfaces these search engines employ. Furthermore, these interfaces tend to change quite frequently as new developments take place.[2] While experienced library-users often find the flexibility offered by these interfaces very powerful, novice users usually encounter difficulties because they provide too many confusing options. Many of these are (in most cases) not required for the more rudimentary types of search that novice library-users want to conduct. These users are therefore more inclined to use the 'easier to use' Internet search engines – often being unaware of the reduced quality of the results they are likely to get. It is therefore imperative that users should be made aware of this so they can assess the value of their findings very carefully. Another problem here is the volume of search results that most Internet searches produce. When this is substantially large, it is necessary for users to understand how they can 'fine-tune' their searches to produce more manageable results.

It must be emphasised that, from the perspective of information retrieval, Internet search engines are not 'all bad'! On the contrary, they can be a very powerful tool when used by experts and experienced users who understand their limitations and how to 'tweak' them. Indeed, expert users often take advantage of Internet search engines to find specific journal articles which they cannot otherwise locate via online databases.

---

2   During a period of less than a year while the author of this chapter was researching the problems of information access, the *CINAHL* database's interface changed twice. This is a significant contrast to the very popular *Google* Internet search engine – which has used the same interface since its inception in 1998. The acronym *CINAHL* stands for *Cumulative Index to Nursing and Allied Health Literature*; further details are available online at the following Web address: *http://www. ebscohost.com/cinahl/* (accessed 23 October, 2008).

Like a web browser, an Internet search engine is an example of a performance support tool in that each of these resources can be used to enhance people's ability to access information. However, like all tools, if they are not used correctly, they can produce more problems than they solve. Of course, there is no reason why browsers and search engines themselves could not be augmented with appropriate performance enhancing features so that the effects of these problems could be minimised.

In order to resolve some of the difficulties that library-users encounter when accessing information, appropriate electronic performance support interventions can be introduced into a library system. The following section uses a case-study approach to illustrate how this can be achieved and the kinds of results that can be produced.

Performance Support in Libraries – A Case Study

Within the schematic library system depicted in Figure 6.3, there are two broad areas where performance support tools could be utilised. First, embedded within the library system itself: Gery (1995) refers to these as being either *intrinsic* or *extrinsic* support tools – depending upon their level of binding to the host application. Second, the tools may exist in an environment that is external to the library system; that is, (in Gery's parlance) they are *external* support tools that form part of the local environment in which the user of the library system happens to be. A built-in 'help' system that is embedded within an online electronic application that runs within a library system is an example of an intrinsic tool. In contrast, a separate online help manual that is available to a user of the application provides an example of an extrinsic support aid. However, a conventional paper-based manual that is located on a near-by library shelf would constitute an external support aid for the application. Similarly, a tool that is embedded in a remote library-user's personal computer (or in a portable computing device such as a mobile phone) could also be thought of as an example of an external support aid. For example, a software package (running on a Personal Digital Assistant or PDA) that directs its users towards the resources available in a particular library would be an instance of an external tool. Some tools are referred to as being *quasi-intrinsic*. Thus, a tool that exists in a portable device (such as a mobile phone or PDA), that guides a library-user to the particular shelf where an item is stored, would be an example of a quasi-intrinsic support aid. The distinction between intrinsic, extrinsic and external performance support aids is further discussed in Chapter 12.

Bearing in mind the problems relating to information access described in the previous section, the remainder of this chapter discusses some of the ways in which intrinsic and extrinsic electronic performance support tools can be developed for use in library systems.

THE EPSILON PROJECT

Our EPSS in libraries project (called *Epsilon*) began in 2004.[3] Its intent was to explore potential uses of performance support interventions as a means of helping novice library-

3   The *Epsilon* Project is a collaborative venture between the School of Computing and the School of Social Sciences and Law at the University of Teesside in the UK. It started as a Masters project and was subsequently funded by grants from the University of Teesside and the UK's Higher Education Academy. The latter grant was awarded to Professor Philip Barker in 2005 as part of a National Teaching Fellowship award.

users access and retrieve information within the setting of an academic library. The project commenced with a detailed exploratory investigation of the performance problems faced by students when using an academic library. The findings enabled a prototype EPSS to be built; this was called *Epsilon 1*. The system provided access to a range of electronic tools that were designed to offer help and assistance with the various types of library-task that users wanted to perform. It was a web-based system that was able to integrate with the library's pre-existing services – such as the online catalogue. Some screen shots from the *Epsilon 1* system are presented in Figures 6.4 and 6.5.

As shown in Figure 6.4 overleaf, the help facility is contained in the screen-panel shown on the right-hand side of the diagram. When in use, it is continually updated to provide relevant tips and advice – depending on the nature of the task that its user is performing.

Figure 6.5 illustrates how the *Epsilon 1* system integrates with other library services – in this case the library's online catalogue.

The *Epsilon 1* system was tested and evaluated to assess its impact, utility and effectiveness. The results showed that students' task performance improved with the use of the *Epsilon 1* tool. The evaluation group also reported that they found the *Epsilon* tool helpful and would use it if it was made available as a fully supported operational system.

During the research that was undertaken with the *Epsilon 1* tool, it was found that library-users often had difficulties locating books on the library-shelves – as many of them were confused by the decimal number system that was used to identify a book's shelf location (Famakinwa et al., 2007a; van Schaik et al., 2006). Bearing this in mind, a new version of the system was produced – this was called *Epsilon 2*. The intent of this revised version of the EPSS facility was to provide library-users with a sound understanding of the DDC system – as used in the academic library where the research was undertaken. This objective was achieved through the use of interactive, online instructional materials that embedded both a didactic strategy (presented by means of an online tutorial) and a gaming element that provided a competitive practice environment wherein students could self-assess their skills and the progress they were making. The competitive element within the games was reflected in the time measures for sorting books into order and the time taken to find a book within a simulated library.

The interactive online tutorial was based on the use of text, graphics and animation. Its content was designed to inform users about the rationale underlying the DDC system. They were also given exercises to perform in order to assist their understanding of the system and improve their confidence in applying what they had learnt within an actual library. Subsequent developments of the *Epsilon 2* system incorporated audio (see Figure 6.6) and a video presentation (see Figure 6.7) to expand students' learning options.

The gaming module that was provided with the *Epsilon 2* system was designed to give students practice at using the DDC system by requiring them (1) to sort 'books' into shelf-order (as depicted schematically in Figure 6.8) and (2) find the locations where particular books would be located on the shelves of the library (see Figure 6.9).

As was the case with the previous prototype system, it was necessary to conduct an intensive evaluation of the *Epsilon 2* system. This evaluation involved both psychology students and staff from the Teesside University. The members of staff thought the system was interesting and, in principle, potentially useful for their students. However, they did suggest that it would be better if the tool could be adapted to meet the needs of specific subject areas. The results from the evaluation by first-year students indicated that they found the EPSS 'exciting and easy to use', and believed it helped them to improve

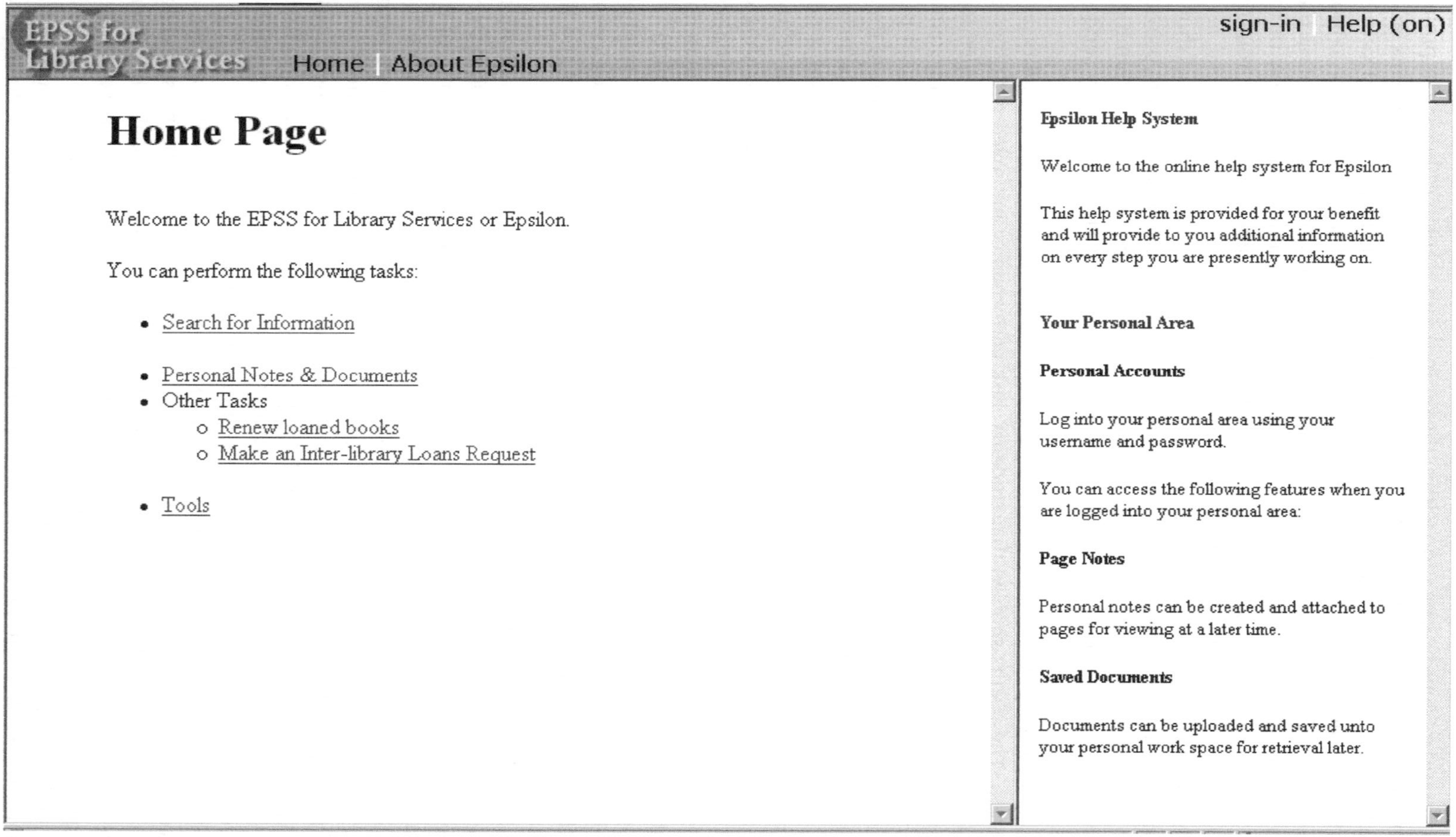

EPSS for
Library Services   Home | About Epsilon

Home Page

Welcome to the EPSS for Library Services or Epsilon.

You can perform the following tasks:

- Search for Information

- Personal Notes & Documents
- Other Tasks
  - o Renew loaned books
  - o Make an Inter-library Loans Request

- Tools

Epsilon Help System

Welcome to the online help system for Epsilon

This help system is provided for your benefit
and will provide to you additional information
on every step you are presently working on.

Your Personal Area

Personal Accounts

Log into your personal area using your
username and password.

You can access the following features when you
are logged into your personal area:

Page Notes

Personal notes can be created and attached to
pages for viewing at a later time.

Saved Documents

Documents can be uploaded and saved unto
your personal work space for retrieval later.

Figure 6.4   The help facility provided by the *Epsilon 1* system

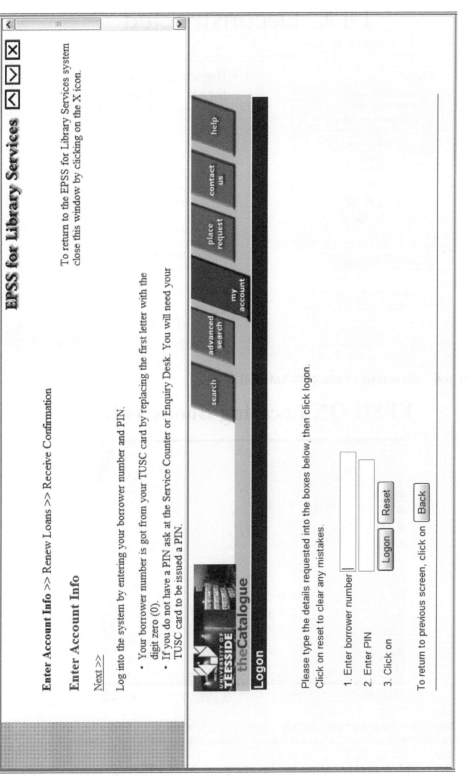

Figure 6.5 Integrating *Epsilon 1* within the library system

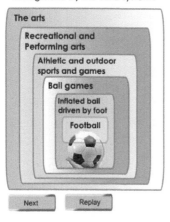

DDC Deconstructed

How is the game of football
categorised by the DDC system?

The arts

Recreational and
Performing arts

Athletic and outdoor
sports and games

Ball games

Inflated ball
driven by foot

Football

Next   Replay

Click on the *Replay* button to
watch the animation

Slide 11 of 15

- The idea behind the DDC is
  that it classifies things first
  very broadly and then
  more specifically
- These classifications are
  then assigned numbers
  - The topmost categories have
    numbers 000, 100, 200, 300, etc
  - The next categories beneath
    these have numbers 10, 20, 30, 40,
    etc
  - Categories beneath these
    continue with 1, 2, 3, 4, etc

Figure 6.6   A section of the DDC tutorial

EPSILON Locating Books Video

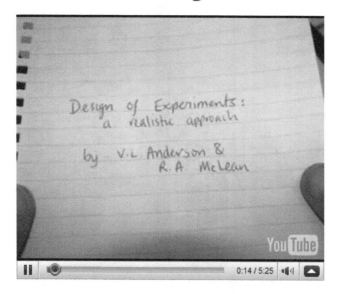

When you have finished watching the video, return to the presentation by clicking on this hyperlink,
then select Open on the dialog box that appears. Continue with the next slide of the presentation.

Figure 6.7   Video presentation for locating books in a library

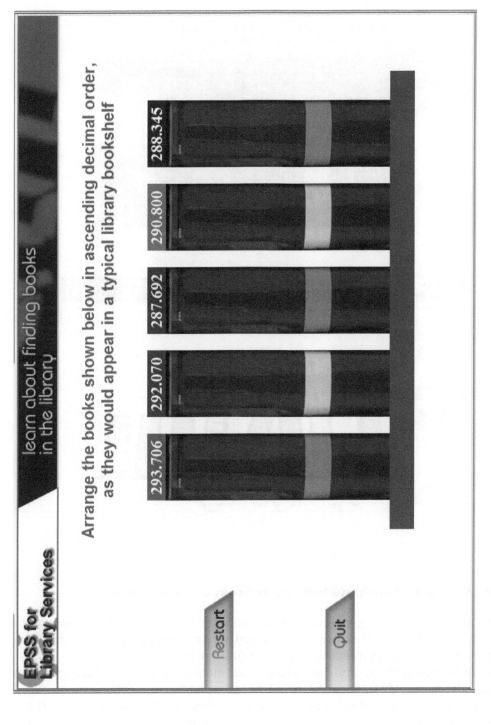

Figure 6.8   Game to help students understand decimal numbers

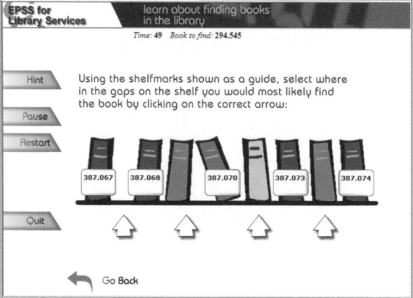

Figure 6.9   Game to help students locate books on library shelves

their confidence in locating books within the academic library. Detailed accounts of the research, development and evaluation conducted in relation to the *Epsilon 2* system have been presented elsewhere (Famakinwa et al., 2007a; van Schaik et al., 2006).

Within virtually all aspects of modern-day life, mobile computing technology is now playing an increasingly important role in its use for performance enhancement. This is especially so in its application for the support of teaching and learning activities. This is manifest in the increasing level of interest that is now being shown (both by students and staff) in the use of various types of pervasive portable device – such as mobile phones,

PDAs, portable audio devices and video players (Barker, 2008b). Bearing in mind these developments, it was important to consider how they could be utilised within the *Epsilon* project. The decision to explore the use of mobile technology therefore triggered the design and development of a new version of the *Epsilon* system for use on mobile phone technology; this 'mobile' version of the system was called *Epsilon 3* (Famakinwa et al., 2007b; Onibokun, 2006).

When designing the *Epsilon 3* system, it was necessary to take into account many of the challenges of mobile-device platforms. Some of these challenges included small display-screen sizes, restricted input options, limited storage space, intermittent reliability of wireless communication networks and the lack of standard micro-browsers and application development tools. As a result of these limitations, the content had to be adapted for use on mobile devices. The changes made included (1) optimising the content for users who would most likely have limited time to read the information and (2) displaying the information in a manner that would ensure consistent presentation across different types of mobile device. Other modifications included redesigning many of the graphics elements so they could be viewed on the small display screens of mobile devices. The reduced storage requirements of the modified graphics and sound elements then allowed them to be stored easily on the mobile device. The navigation system and presentation of each page were redesigned to ensure that users always knew 'where they were' in the system. Figure 6.10 shows an example of a screen shot of the *Epsilon 3* system running on the *Openwave*[4] mobile-phone simulator.

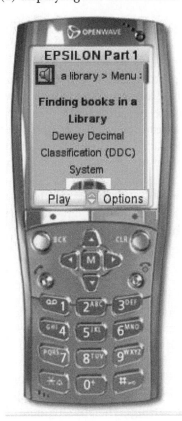

Figure 6.10 Accessing the DDC tutorial on a mobile phone

The mobile *Epsilon* tool was evaluated with a cohort of students using the simulator shown in Figure 6.10. A pre-test and post-test evaluation design was used. The results obtained from the evaluation indicated that the confidence of the users was higher as a result of the use of the mobile *Epsilon* tool. In addition, users also stated that they found the system helpful and they would make use of an operational version of the system if it was made available to them. During the evaluation, most of the problems encountered by the evaluation group arose from the desktop simulator rather than from the application tool itself. Further, more detailed descriptions of the design and development processes – and the evaluation results – relating to the *Epsilon 3* performance enhancement tool are presented elsewhere (Famakinwa et al., 2007b; Onibokun, 2006).

---

4   The *Openwave* phone simulator is a set of development tools that is used for building, debugging and testing mobile applications on a personal computer system. Further details on this software can be found online at the following Web address: *http://developer.openwave.com/dvl/tools_and_sdk/phone_simulator/*.

FUTURE WORK

As has been described earlier in this chapter, development of the *Epsilon* system has been ongoing since 2004. Each new release of the system has incorporated various enhancements based on the findings of the evaluative studies that have been undertaken. The current version of the system (*Epsilon 4*) extends the facilities offered by previous releases by addressing the information access problems associated with online information retrieval from electronic journals and online databases. Some of the important issues addressed by *Epsilon 4* include:

- combined searches across multiple online databases;
- tutorials and help on the correct search criteria to apply when using an online database or search engine;
- advice and assistance with database selection;
- tutorials and help with subject-specific searching; and
- tutorials about (and help relating to) how to locate a journal article from a reference to it.

Figure 6.11 shows an illustrative screen shot from the prototype version of the *Epsilon 4* facility that has been developed. The 'application' window (shown on the left-hand side) is used to display the online database being used (and its related interactive dialogue), while the help window (shown on the right-hand side of the screen display) provides appropriate procedural support for the user. The buttons located in the toolbar (that runs along the top of the screen) can be used to activate the other functions provided by the tool – such as the tutorial and help facilities.

Further details of this work and suggestions for how the underlying research can be extended to apply to new developments in library systems (such as digital libraries, networked libraries, and so on) are presented elsewhere (Famakinwa, 2010).

Conclusion

Libraries provide a powerful and well-established mechanism for the storage of knowledge artefacts such as books, journals and other media objects of various sorts. However, despite their utility and usefulness, they are often difficult systems to use. This chapter has identified the important roles that electronic performance support tools can play in overcoming some of the problems that people encounter when using a conventional library system. A case-study approach has been used to show how an EPSS can be integrated into an operational library system (within an academic setting), thereby augmenting and enhancing the facilities available to library-users. The interventions introduced have served to achieve two major benefits. First, improving the overall usability of the library system; and second, providing bespoke electronic tools that could be used to enable library-users to overcome any shortfall in knowledge and skills they may have when accessing the various types of information that is held within the library. The work that has been described in this chapter has depended critically on appropriate evaluative studies; these have steered the direction of development of the EPSS tools and ensured that they meet the needs of their users within the context of information access.

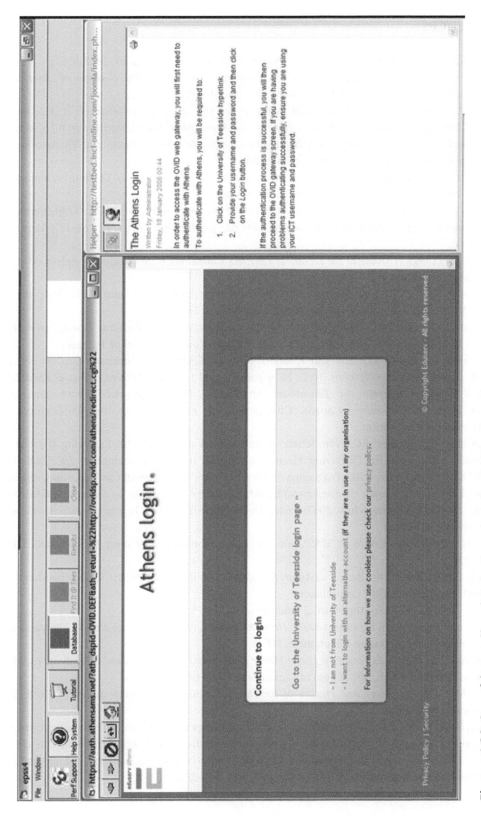

Figure 6.11 Searching online databases using the *Epsilon 4* system

References

Ackoff, R.L. (1989). From Data to Wisdom, *Journal of Applied Systems Analysis*, 16, 3–9.

Barker, P.G. (1997). Electronic Libraries of the Future. In A. Kent (ed.), *Encyclopaedia of Library and Information Science*, 59(S59), 119–152. New York, NY: Marcel Dekker.

Barker, P.G. (2008a). Using Weblogs and Wikis to Enhance Human Performance. In C.J. Bonk, M.M. Lee and T. Reynolds (eds), *Proceedings of the E-Learn 2008 World Conference on E-Learning in Corporate, Government, Healthcare and Higher Education* (pp. 581–588). Chesapeake, VA: Association for the Advancement of Computing in Education.

Barker, P.G. (2008b). Mobile Computing – Critical Factors Influencing Success. Keynote Presentation. *ICTE 2008 Conference*, September 2008, Sardinia, Italy.

Carlson, C. N. (2003). Information Overload, Retrieval Strategies and Internet User Empowerment. In Haddon, L. (Ed.), *Proceedings of 'The Good, the Bad and the Irrelevant'*, 1(1), 169–173. Helsinki, Finland.

Chan, L.M. (1999). *A Guide to the Library of Congress Classification* (5th Edition). Englewood, CO: Libraries Unlimited.

Famakinwa, O.J. (2004). *An Electronic Performance Support System for Library Users*, M.Sc thesis. Middlesbrough, UK: School of Computing, University of Teesside.

Famakinwa, O.J. (2010). *Using Electronic Performance Support Systems to Facilitate Information Access*, draft Ph.D thesis. Middlesbrough, UK: School of Computing, University of Teesside.

Famakinwa, O., Barker, P.G. and van Schaik, P. (2007a). Electronic Performance Support and Its Role in Future Library Systems. In C. Montgomerie and J. Seale (eds), *Proceedings of EDMEDIA 2007 World Conference on Educational Multimedia, Hypermedia and Telecommunications* (pp. 216–223). Vancouver, Canada. Chesapeake, VA: Association for the Advancement of Computing in Education.

Famakinwa, O.J., Barker, P.G., van Schaik, P. and Onibokun, J., (2007b). Exploring the Use of Mobile Technology for Delivering Electronic Support. In C.P. Constantinou, Z.C. Zacharias and M. Papaevripidou (eds), *Proceedings of the 'CBLIS 2007 International Conference on Computer-Based Learning in Science: Contemporary Perspectives on New Technologies in Science and Education'* (pp. 256–264), 30 June–6 July, 2007, Crete, Greece. Nicosia, Cyprus: Learning in Science Group, University of Cyprus.

Gery, G. (1995). The Future of EPSS, *Innovations in Education and Training International*, 32(1), 70–73.

Hull, B. (2000). *Barriers to Libraries as Agents for Lifelong Learning*. Final Project Report. London, UK: Library and Information Commission.

Hull, B. (2005). I Don't See the Point..., *Adults Learning*, 16(7), 29–30.

Library and Information Services. (2008). *Help and Support*. Available online at: *http://lis.tees.ac.uk/help/default.cfm*. (Accessed: 7 September, 2008)

Onibokun, J.A. (2006). *Exploring the Use of Mobile Devices for Delivering E-learning Applications*, M.Sc thesis. Middlesbrough, UK: School of Computing, University of Teesside.

Satija, M.P. (2007). *Theory and Practice of the Dewey Decimal Classification System*. Oxford, UK: Chandos Publishing.

Schaik, P. van, Barker, P.G. and Famakinwa, O. (2007). Making a Case for Using Electronic Performance Support Systems in Academic Libraries, *Journal of Interactive Learning Research*, 18(3), 411–428.

Schaik, P. van, Barker, P.G. and Famakinwa, O. (2006). Potential Roles for Performance Support Tools within Library Systems, *The Electronic Library*, 24(3), 347–365.

Shannon, C.E. (1948). A Mathematical Theory of Communication, *Bell System Technical Journal*, 27, 379–423, 623–656.

Zeleny, M. (2005). *Human Systems Management: Integrating Knowledge, Management and Systems.* Singapore: World Scientific.

7 *Human Communication*

NIGEL BEACHAM

Human communication is a fundamental activity that facilitates the exchange of signals, information and knowledge between groups of people. The effectiveness of communication can be influenced by a variety of different factors related to the nature of the people involved and the types of mechanism used for its facilitation. This chapter discusses the nature of human communication and the ways in which electronic performance support tools can be used to influence its effectiveness in terms of Communication Competence (CC). A case study is presented which describes how an Electronic Performance Support System (EPSS) environment can be used to provide support for people who are involved in providing an awareness and understanding of dyslexia and the effects that it can have on communication competencies.

Introduction

As was described in Chapter 1, human-activity systems form the underlying basis for all human endeavours. Naturally, within such systems, human communication plays a major role. Because of its importance in relation to human existence, this chapter discusses the nature of human communication, some of its strengths and weaknesses and the underlying roles that electronic performance support tools (e-tools) may play in its achievement.

Human communication is based upon the sending and receiving of messages. This can involve a single individual or a group of people. Adler and Rodman (1994: p. 18) illustrate the types of activity associated with communication in the form of a *transactional model*. Figure 7.1 builds on this model and demonstrates the types of communication aid and tool which can be used to facilitate such activities – and the ways in which these interventions can be used to support communication processes.

Figure 7.1 depicts the sending and receiving of messages (by a Sender) to themselves (Sender), to another individual (Receiver A), to a group of individuals (Receivers A and B) and to the public (Receiver C). In the case where the sender and receiver are the same person, this is referred to as *intrapersonal* communication. Alternatively, in a situation where the recipient is one or more other people (that is, Sender sending messages to Receivers A–C), the communication is said to be *interpersonal*. A wide range of technologies and support tools are available to facilitate each of these types of communication.

As is discussed in the following section, within a human communication system there can be various 'deficiencies' associated with the sender of a message, its recipient and the

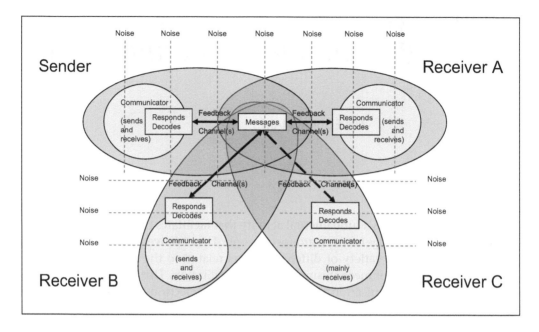

Figure 7.1   Communication aspects

Source: Adapted from Adler and Rodman, 1994.

mechanism by which that message is transported between them (see, for example, the 'noise' in Figure 7.1). Naturally, any of the shortcomings identified can, in principle, be overcome by an appropriately designed performance support aid. The rationale underlying this and the ways in which this can be done are discussed later in the chapter.

When sending signals or messages, it is possible to use either a single communication channel or multiple channels. Examples of the use of more than one channel include (1) the simultaneous use of speech and gestures and (2) an automated slide projection system that is accompanied by a pre-recorded audio narrative. Each channel that is used within a communication event will have both advantages and disadvantages. Important factors that need to be considered include: cost, range, reliability, security, privacy, representational capability, ease of use, and so on. Bearing this in mind, it is often necessary to consider very carefully the combination of channels that is most appropriate for any given situation. The complexity of the issues involved provides a good case for the provision of advisory tools that can be used to assist people in selecting the most appropriate 'media' combinations and the best channels to use for the transmission of any particular type of message. This is particularly important in the case of educational messages embedded in books, lectures or e-learning resources – especially in situations where 'disabled' students are involved. In situations of this sort it is imperative that the expressiveness of different media is considered along with the cognitive load placed on individuals when sending and receiving messages in this category (Beacham and Szumko, 2003; Beacham and Alty, 2004, 2006; Alty et al., 2006; Perkin et al., 2007).

When considering interpersonal communication, three important aspects that need to be examined are (1) the size of the group involved; (2) the location of its members; and (3) the level and type of information exchange that can be employed (for example, one-way, two-way, and so on). These factors will strongly influence the nature and types of tool that will be needed to facilitate the exchange of messages and also enhance the efficiency and effectiveness with which this can be achieved.

In terms of supporting two-person (that is, dyadic) exchanges and group communication, e-tools that facilitate the sending, receiving and conveying of messages are often referred to as *Computer-Mediated Communication* (CMC) tools. The two main modes of messaging associated with CMC are called *synchronous* and *asynchronous* communication (Sharp et al., 2007). Synchronous communication relates to interactions between two or more people in real time – for example, video conferencing and real-time chat. Asynchronous communication relates to interactions (between two or more people) in which there is a time delay between messages – for example, texting (using a mobile phone), electronic mail, wikis, weblogs and asynchronous conferencing. Collis and Verwijs (1995) have discussed some of the important e-tools for supporting group communication activities – such as email, video conferencing, bulletin boards, discussion boards, shared knowledge bases and document sharing tools.

Because of its intrinsic importance, the subsequent sections of this chapter discuss human communication in terms of the concept of *communication competencies* and how e-tools may be used to improve an individual's performance when composing and sending messages and, of course, when receiving and understanding them. A case study is then presented which describes a visual EPSS facility (called *DyslexSim*) which illustrates the application of the performance-orientated approach in assisting people who are involved in creating an awareness and understanding of dyslexia and the effects that this can have on an individual's ability to communicate with others.

Communication Competencies

This section discusses the concept of communication competency and how this can be influenced both by disability (on the part of the people involved) and by the availability of e-tools that can compensate for the shortcomings imposed by some form of communication disability. A broader discussion of disability and its impact on people's ability to communicate is presented in Chapter 8.

CC refers to an individual's ability to communicate with other people in an effective and efficient way. Naturally, people show considerable variation in terms of their competency with regard to their ability to create, process and understand messages. Obviously, in situations where a deficiency in one or other of these tasks can be identified, e-tools and EPSS can, in principle, be designed to overcome them.

In the CC model, messaging partners will have two levels of competence. First, the ability to create an effective message based upon the communication resources available (*message coding*) and second, the ability to derive the correct meaning from an incoming message (*decoding*). Performance in these areas may be affected by a number of disabling conditions – such as a limited vocabulary range, low reading ability and any physical and mental disabilities that people may suffer from. Examples of such disabilities include visual impairment, speech impairment, restricted movement or mobility and perceptual/cognitive impairments. As has been stated earlier, shortcomings in either of these areas (message coding and decoding) can be overcome through the application of an appropriate supportive intervention – such as an augmented e-tool or a fully-fledged EPSS. Some of the ways in which an EPSS can be used to support and/or augment human communication within the contexts previously discussed in this chapter are depicted schematically in Figure 7.2.

An important disabling condition that can significantly influence a person's communication competencies is dyslexia. According to the British Dyslexia Association (BDA) (2008):

> *Dyslexia is a specific learning difficulty which mainly affects the development of literacy and language related skills. It is likely to be present at birth and to be lifelong in its effects. It is characterised by difficulties with phonological processing, rapid naming, working memory, processing speed, and the automatic development of skills that may not match up to an individual's other cognitive abilities. It tends to be resistant to conventional teaching methods, but its effects can be mitigated by appropriately specific intervention, including the application of information technology and supportive counselling.*

Consequently, the BDA claim that individuals with dyslexia may have underlying difficulties that affect their communication competencies. These difficulties include reading hesitantly, misreading (thereby making understanding difficult), problems with sequences (for example, getting dates in order), poor organisation and time management, difficulty organising thoughts clearly and erratic spelling. Fortunately, many individuals with dyslexia are extremely adept at developing coping strategies and using additional support aids and e-tools to overcome their communication difficulties – thereby improving their communication performance. The aids and tools that are currently being deployed are usually based on the EPSS strategies illustrated in Figure 7.2.

Unfortunately, within the UK there is not a widespread understanding of dyslexia. Such an understanding is of paramount importance when teaching and learning activities

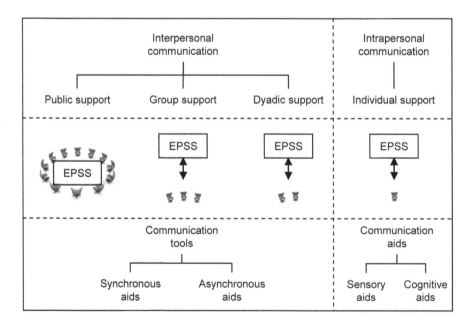

Figure 7.2   Configurations of EPSS for human communication

(that, essentially, involve the transference of educational messages) and the design of resources for use by dyslexic students. To help improve the level of awareness of dyslexia within the UK and Europe, the author of this chapter has been involved in the design and creation of a performance support tool called *DyslexSim*. The development and use of this system is described in the following section.

DyslexSim – a Visual Performance Support Aid

Improving communication in terms of raising awareness and understanding of dyslexia issues has become an important issue in recent years. This importance has been heightened by the publication of the Singleton Report (1999) and the introduction of the *Special Educational Needs and Disability Act* (SENDA, 2002). These events have together resulted in a requirement to deliver effective education and training within academic and industrial organisations – in order to ensure they do not fall foul of the law. Staff development workshops have been one way in which Higher Education Institutions in the UK have addressed this issue. However, it can be very difficult to communicate even a small part of the experience of dyslexia to people who have little or no understanding of it.

One solution to this problem has been to develop a computer-based performance support tool called *DyslexSim* for use in workshops and public lectures (Beacham and Szumko, 2003). The EPSS that was produced embedded various animations and simulations designed to illustrate the various kinds of effect experienced by some of those who suffer from dyslexia. Underlying the *DyslexSim* system is a 'visual and perceptual problems simulation' (VAPPS) package – see *http://www.brainhe.com/resources/beacham2003.html*. A screenshot of the start-up pages of the *DyslexSim* system is shown in Figure 7.3 (a and b). The intention behind the development of this tool was to improve the way in which communication about dyslexia could be achieved through the use of visualisation. This involved moving away from the presentation of abstract ideas in favour of concrete learning, based on the use of images and experiential exercises (Boyle, 1997). Focusing on the visual and perceptual problems which dyslexic individuals can experience seemed an obvious and practical way to begin (West, 1997).

The remainder of this section outlines the development and use of the *DyslexSim* system as an example of an interpersonal group communication tool (see Figure 7.2) that can be used to help raise awareness of the visual and perceptual problems (and other difficulties) usually experienced by people who are dyslexic.

SYSTEM DESIGN AND DEVELOPMENT[1]

As well as some of the standard sources of material on dyslexia (Ott, 1997; Proustie, 2000; Reid, 1998), much of the underlying knowledge that is embedded within the *DyslexSim* system was derived from work undertaken by researchers such as Evans (2001), Irlen, (1991), Jordan (2002), Snowling (2000), Stein et al. (2000) and Witton et al. (1998). These

---

1   *DyslexSim* is distributed on CD-ROM along with an extensive pack of supporting information and materials. The *DyslexSim* pack is available either through Loughborough University or iANSYST Ltd. To order *DyslexSim* or to obtain further information, either contact: (1) Loughborough University Enterprises Limited, Loughborough University, Ashby Road, Loughborough, Leicestershire, LE11 3TU, Tel: +44 (0) 1509 222 452, Web: *http://dyslexsim.lboro.ac.uk/* or (2) iANSYST Ltd. Fen House, Fen Road, Cambridge, CB4 1UN, Tel: +44 (0) 1223 420 101, Web: *http://www.iansyst.co.uk/*.

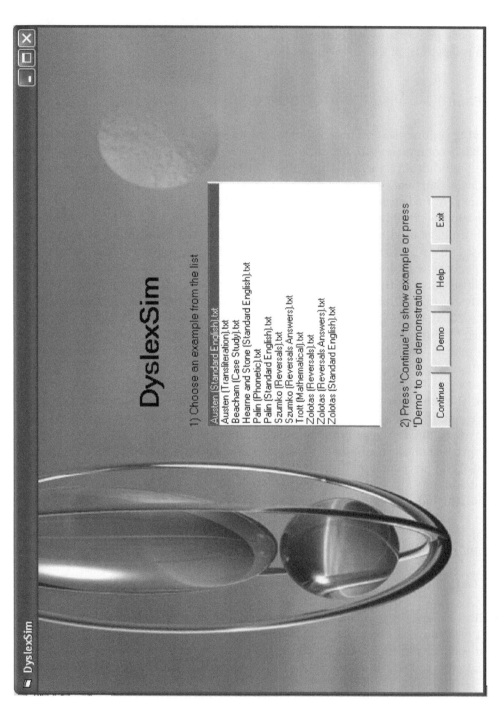

Figure 7.3a Screenshot of *DyslexSim*

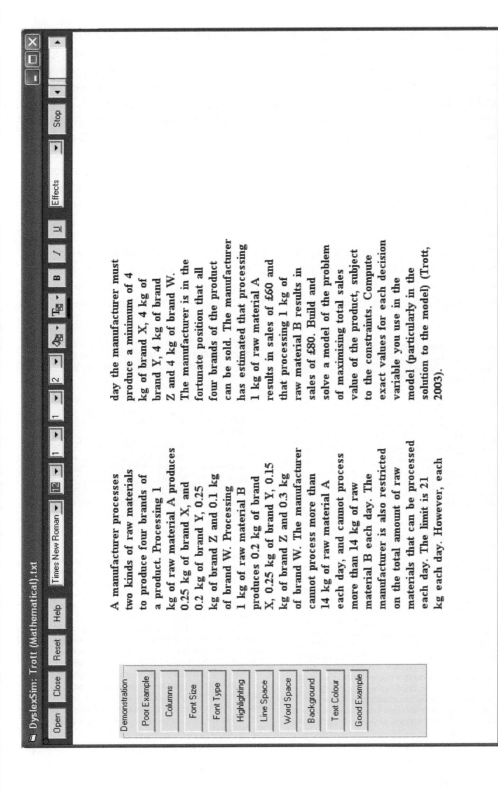

Figure 7.3b Screenshot of DyslexSim

researchers have written extensively about the problems associated with dyslexia. Some of the perceived symptoms of dyslexia have been illustrated by Proustie (2000), Ryden (1992) and Morgan and Klein (2000). Their illustrations were used as a basis for the animations that were produced for use with the *DyslexSim* system. Examples of some of the distortion effects that a dyslexic person can experience are shown in Figure 7.4.

Simulation tools can be particularly effective at conveying information that is otherwise difficult to communicate or demonstrate (Barker, 1989; Collins et al., 1997; Mayer and Gallini, 1990; Preece, 1994). Simulation tools are also another important type of generic tool found in EPSS facilities (Banerji, 1995: p. 27). The *DyslexSim* system was therefore developed using various types of simulation to reflect some of the visual and perceptual distortion effects dyslexic individuals experience. Besides containing simulations of the effects illustrated in Figure 7.4, simulations were also provided to demonstrate other conditions such as the overlap effect, the disappearing effect and the floating line effect (Evans, 2001; Irlen, 1991; Proustie, 2000).

The simulations provided by *DyslexSim* represent difficulties individuals with dyslexia experience when reading printed text. Such difficulties are experienced not only when text is presented on paper, but also on screen devices (such as desktop, laptop and palmtop computers), signpostings, cloth and other forms of fabric and materials. It is

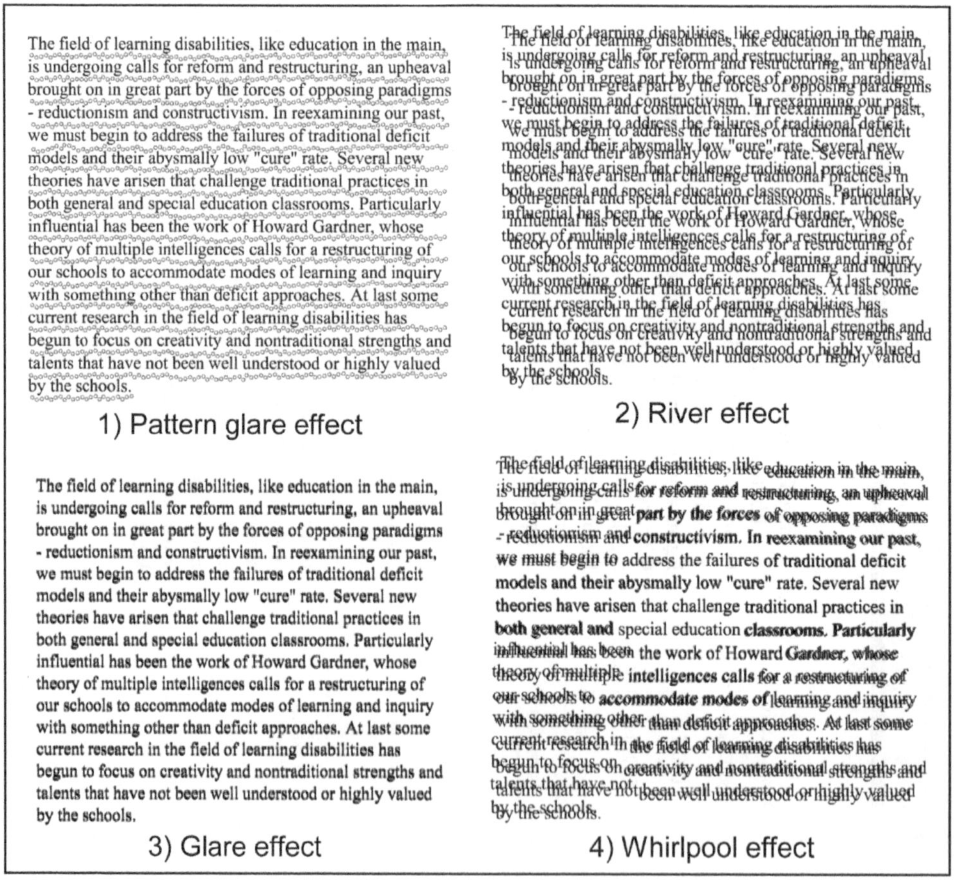

Figure 7.4   Visual and perceptual distortion effects

therefore important that such difficulties be considered whenever and wherever text is used – particularly when used to represent information for teaching and learning.

The simulations described above were intended to illustrate what many dyslexic individuals actually perceive. Unlike long-established examples illustrating these effects as static images, *DyslexSim* provides a dynamic representation of each effect (Tyre, 1998). The benefit of this is that it shows people how difficult text is to read and understand and how this inhibits both the communication competencies of sufferers and, of course, the learning processes in which they partake. Using simulations of this sort helps to make the experience more realistic and therefore more engaging and memorable for those who use them. The simulations also provide a basis upon which to explain how and why particular modifications to learning materials and methods can improve the learning performance of dyslexic students.

Although simulations form the main component of the *DyslexSim* system, additional integrated components can be added to meet the requirements laid down by potential end-users. Additional components that have been added include a text-reversal component, a text-flow component and a font-comparison component. A more detailed account of *DyslexSim* (its development and use) has been reported by Beacham and Szumko (2003).

EVALUATING THE DYSLEXSIM SYSTEM

Various studies have been conducted in order to assess what potential end-users of *DyslexSim* thought about it – whether they liked it, found it helpful and could see a real need for the tool. The results obtained from these studies have provided a growing stock of evidence in support of the tool's effectiveness to facilitate communication (about dyslexia) from the perspective of staff development workshops. The information that has been gathered has also helped to further improve and develop the tool itself. To illustrate the way in which *DyslexSim* has been evaluated, the remainder of this section presents a summary of the findings obtained from a typical evaluation study[2] in which the tool was used as a group communication aid (see Figure 7.2).

The study involved two workshops, each of which involved a small number of teams – as shown in Figure 7.5. Both workshops covered issues related to improving participants' knowledge and understanding of dyslexia – and the tools available to achieve this. During each workshop, *DyslexSim* was used to demonstrate the types of visual and perceptual problem that dyslexic learners encounter. At the end of the workshops, each of the participants was asked to complete a *DyslexSim* evaluation questionnaire; accounts of the perceived effectiveness of the tool were also provided by the two tutors[3] who presented the workshops.

Of the 29 participants who took part in the study, the majority (52 per cent) performed a dyslexia support role. Within the remainder, 34 per cent were lecturers,

---

2   The study referred to here involved two workshops on dyslexia run within two UK universities. The first workshop was held at De Montfort University (DMU) and the second at the University of Hull. Twenty-nine participants took part in the workshops. Of these, 17 attended the workshop at DMU and 12 attended the workshop at the University of Hull. Participants had similar backgrounds in relation to their job context and background knowledge relating to dyslexia. For this reason, the results from the two workshops were aggregated and are discussed as a whole. Two participants in the DMU workshop were dyslexic.

3   The two tutors who presented the workshops were both from the English Language Study Unit at Loughborough University. They had co-taught together for many years and used *DyslexSim* on a regular basis as part of staff development workshops and contributions to continuous professional development activities.

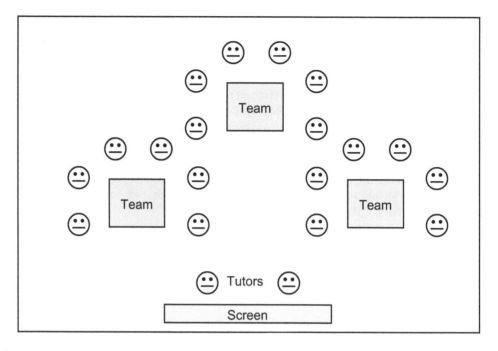

Figure 7.5   Workshop arrangement

21 per cent played a disability advisory function and 24 per cent stated that they undertook some other role – such as a special-needs assessor or an examination assistant. There was a broad variation in knowledge of dyslexia among the participants; however, the majority had a good understanding of it (and also worked in this field). Although a few participants possessed some knowledge, hardly any of them felt that they were experts in this area. Most participants (69 per cent) felt that they had some knowledge of visual and perceptual problems – within this group, 17 per cent said they knew a great deal and 14 per cent said they knew a little; none of the participants felt they knew nothing about these problems.

Even though the majority of participants reported that they possessed some knowledge of visual and perceptual problems, all respondents confirmed that *DyslexSim* considerably improved their understanding. Many of the participants felt taken aback by the extent to which such visual effects could influence learners with dyslexia. When asked if they were aware of, had seen or used any other support tools that could show these types of visual and perceptual problem, the majority of participants (69 per cent) reported that they did not know of any available tools and 31 per cent were aware of just a few examples. However, within this latter group, all respondents felt that *DyslexSim* communicated the issues better than any of the other tools they had previously encountered. All of the participants liked *DyslexSim* – with 83 per cent liking it a great deal. The same view was reflected in the results relating to the helpfulness and practicality aspects of *DyslexSim*. All participants felt that the tool increased their communication competency as it motivated them (1) to ask questions; (2) to formulate 'what-if' scenarios (based upon their prior knowledge and past situations); (3) to discuss their feelings (both before and after experiencing *DyslexSim*); and (4) to discuss changes that they would make based upon what they had learnt. None of the participants felt that *DyslexSim* was in any way unhelpful or impractical. When asked whether they would use the system, 93 per cent of the participants reported that they would. Of these, the majority (55 per cent) felt they would use it often. Even the small minority who said that they would not use it explained that this was due to the type of work roles they performed – they would, however, recommend the tool to their colleagues.

Each of the tutors involved in the *DyslexSim* evaluative study felt that the tool could be used as an effective mechanism to facilitate group communication about dyslexia. In the following section, some of the reflections made by one of the tutors are summarised and discussed.

Reflections

DyslexSim is a computer-based performance support aid that is accessible at any time, in any place and at any point of need throughout any organisation that uses it. The system provides fast access to visual simulations for staff-development purposes relating to dyslexia. It has been used predominantly by university tutors in an 'on-the-job' context to help them to communicate to other people[4] the types of communication difficulties that dyslexia can cause. Although it is most often used in a group tutorial mode, there is no reason why the system could not be used in a one-to-one situation or in a 'self-study' mode of operation.

Because of the nature of the material that it embeds, the *DyslexSim* EPSS can be used to substantially reduce the amount of time it can take for a tutor to explain the difficulties experienced by individuals with dyslexia. It also reduces the complexity and difficulties associated with performing similar tasks manually or by using conventional presentation mechanisms – such as the use of overhead transparencies.[5]

Flexibility and adaptability are two of the other attractive features of *DyslexSim*. All of the examples (of the different dyslexic effects) that are embedded within the system can easily be changed and adapted to suit the needs of any particular type of audience – and the roles that its members carry out. For instance, if the participants in a workshop consisted of mathematics lecturers, examples using mathematical materials could be used. Alternatively, if a workshop involved administrative staff, examples relating to student services could be presented. In situations where workshops consist of people from different backgrounds, it is possible to use the same simulation with different discipline-specific examples. In extremely rare cases (where relevant examples are not available within the system) it is possible for end-users to augment *DyslexSim*'s facilities by adding their own materials. When using different types of simulation material, audience participants would not need to learn (and would not be distracted by) irrelevant information or jargon. The system tailors the text it uses to the prior knowledge and level of understanding of its

---

4   In this context, the people involved would normally be staff within an academic organisation whose role involves creating and disseminating information.

5   In the past, tutors would try to describe (in words) what it was like for a person with dyslexia. They later used overhead transparencies to help them – for example, two overhead transparencies (overlaid on top of each other) were often used to try to simulate the difficulties people with dyslexia experience. Much of the time the experience was frustrating both for the tutor and for the workshop participants. Often the participants remained unclear about what it is like to be dyslexic, why they needed to make adjustments, and how to go about implementing the changes. When *DyslexSim* became available, it changed the entire communication experience that took place in workshops.

audience – thereby placing participants in a better position to discuss with each other the implications of what they have experienced.

The adaptability of the system is also reflected in its ability to accommodate different learning styles. For instance, it can help individuals who have a visual learning style by actually illustrating what a tutor has said. Similarly, for individuals with a verbal learning style, *DyslexSim* can help them to realise that people often see text in a different way to them. The system can also show how important it is to supplement textual information with visual representations – particularly in a learning context. In cases where an individual's learning needs are not adequately catered for, *DyslexSim* could be used to address the situation. For example, if a person was only partially sighted, it would be possible to customise the text size in the material to suit that individual's particular requirement.

As was mentioned earlier, simulations are one of the most important aspects of *DyslexSim*. Because they are so powerful, they not only depict what it is like to suffer from dyslexia (and what it is), but can also be used to justify (within a teaching context) why it is important for lecturers to make adjustments to their learning materials (and for support staff to make appropriate modifications to administrative materials). *DyslexSim* has also helped to dispel the often-misunderstood claim that people with dyslexia are not as intelligent as non-sufferers. It has also helped to show participants how to adjust their learning and teaching materials through the use of an integrated demonstration component.

DyslexSim helps generate ideas for modification of learning materials by teachers and others by simulating the reading difficulties individuals with dyslexia experience when changing the nature of the text. This includes comparing the difference between text that is arranged in single or multiple columns, comparing different font types, sizes and colours, comparing different background colours and shades, comparing different formats such as paragraphs, bullet points, and comparing text which is underlined, bold and/or italic. *DyslexSim* also helps to generate ideas for modifications of learning materials for different subjects. For example, mathematical texts often contain many abbreviations and units presented after numbers and words. *DyslexSim* helps teachers and others modify learning materials by simulating the reading difficulties individuals with dyslexia experience when changing the spacing between words, numbers and units, and between lines of text. As a result, what makes this tool particularly useful is its ability to represent any combination of text arrangement and format in order to explore the most appropriate representation of text for a particular context.

Another useful feature of the *DyslexSim* tool is the manner in which it provides different ways for accessing its embedded information. Users can access this according to: subject, content, type of demonstration, visual stress effect, reading difficulty and various kinds of user-specific selection criteria. This is very useful when a presenter has to respond to an impromptu question using a demonstration (or other resource) that is embedded within the system – for example, '*How does someone with dyslexia see underlined text?*'

In many ways, *DyslexSim* resembles a decision support system that helps participants in a workshop to communicate and decide upon the most appropriate formatting actions for a particular set of conditions. This is particularly useful for encouraging participants to reflect on the decisions they make about their current practice and to highlight the fact that there may not always be a solution for all situations.

From a financial perspective, *DyslexSim* can be used to reduce the cost of training by decreasing both the time it takes to explain things and the number of times information needs to be repeated to participants. Furthermore, participants are more likely to remember and recall the key points because of the visual style used in presenting the information. As a result, the production of course materials is more likely to be in accordance with the needs of learners with dyslexia. This in turn improves the communication competency and learning performance of the students with which the participants interact. Because the examples presented by *DyslexSim* are so vivid, when new lecturers have to develop their own course materials, they are likely to require a minimum amount of external intervention or training. This can therefore lead to a reduction in the time that experienced lecturers need to spend helping their less-skilled colleagues.

Undoubtedly, exposure to the *DyslexSim* system enables participants (especially new lecturers) to design their materials more quickly and more accurately than they could without it. It also helps them to learn more about the people that they are teaching. Subsequently, armed with awareness and insight, it is hoped that participants' beliefs and behaviours towards individuals with dyslexia will change for the better.

Although the *DyslexSim* system had been specifically designed and developed to help tutors communicate very complex and important (dyslexia-related) information to new employees in a university setting, there is no reason why it could not be used in other professional fields. For example, it could be a useful asset for helping human-computer interface designers to understand the difficulties that dyslexic individuals can have when using particular computer systems. It is therefore a good example of a performance support aid that facilitates human communication.

One important implication arising from this work (for dyslexic learners) is likely to be an improvement in the quality of the learning materials that they are given – arising as a result of a reduction in the visual and perceptual difficulties normally experienced by dyslexic learners. Another implication for dyslexic learners is that as academic staff become more aware of dyslexia and its consequences, so dyslexic learners are more likely to be identified and subsequently supported during their time at school and university – and beyond.

Although *DyslexSim* provides numerous benefits, it also possesses a number of limitations. This includes not addressing/presenting all reading problems experienced by dyslexics – such as mathematical formulae, tables and graphs. Also, the tool currently only addresses difficulties associated with reading visual-verbal information in the form of text, and does not display difficulties related to reading graphical textual information such as banners and signs. Finally, the tool is developed specifically for tutors whose role involves informing individuals about dyslexia and visual stress. It is only meant to be used by qualified support teachers and practitioners.

Conclusions

The rationale underlying the development of the *DyslexSim* tool was not to provide an exact representation of every aspect of visual perceptual difficulties – which is a major research undertaking in itself – but to provide a useful and practical communication tool for staff-development workgroups within a university setting. Bearing this in mind, dyslexia support tutors who have used the *DyslexSim* tool have reported that they have found it useful in helping them to communicate about important aspects of dyslexia. Most of the people who have attended staff development sessions also found the tool useful for helping them to visualise and understand some of the problems that dyslexic learners experience.

Based upon the positive support that has been given to the *DyslexSim* system, quite a number of educational organisations within the UK are now using it to facilitate communication in their workplaces. It has also been used to demonstrate the needs of end-users in other areas where visual and perceptual problems and dyslexia awareness is required – such as end-user interface design and inclusive education.

Like many aspects of the modern world, education is changing extremely rapidly. A shift is now taking place from a *what you know* paradigm to a *how you know what you know* situation that is based on information accessing strategies (see Chapter 6) and critical thinking skills. Consequently, some people have suggested that the traditional ways of teaching and learning can no longer adequately cater for the future needs of society. If this is indeed the case, then new ways of providing educational support for people will need to be developed. In the future, it is likely that personal EPSS facilities will need to provide individuals and groups of individuals with all the necessary support and tools that they need – as and when required at any point of need.

The introduction of the SENDA initiative is just one example of the changes that are taking place and which are having an impact on the way in which technology is designed and used. Research studies such as those carried out by Banerji (1995) and Beacham (1998) into the use of EPSS in education have shown that significant benefits can be gained in relation to both staff- and student-performance. The *OASIS*[6] system (Barker et al., 1995, 1997), the *Epsilon* system (see Chapter 6) and the support aids for using communication tools (Banerji, 1995) illustrate the type of developments that have been taking place. However, with the recent introduction of new legislation such performance support systems and tools are subject to the same requirements. Performance support systems that facilitate human communication must not only be accessible to users as and when required, they must also take into consideration each user's individual accessibility difficulties and needs. This issue is further discussed in Chapter 8.

Inclusive practices that build on the changes introduced by SENDA have the potential to impact further on the design and use of performance support systems. Inclusive educational practice relates to the access, collaboration, and tolerance and diversity of individual learners within an organisation. In an educational context, it is no longer acceptable that performance support systems (and their associated support aids) are just accessible. Any support aid (such as the communication tools described earlier in this chapter) should facilitate collaboration, tolerance and diversity. Undoubtedly, there is a need for further research into ways to accommodate these additional aspects into performance support systems in order to facilitate trust and co-agency for everyone involved in an organisation.

Finally, the underlying philosophy of electronic performance support is to bridge the performance gap between novice users and expert users – to provide the necessary support and scaffolding to enable a novice user to become a skilled performer at a suitable level. One aspect of this is to reduce the need for novice users to take up the valuable time and effort of expert users from their primary roles. Consequently, at one level, an electronic

---

6   OASIS is an acronym for Open Access Student Information System.

performance support approach could be perceived as being contradictory to the activity of human communication by limiting interaction between people who, for example, work closely together. That said, there is a balance to be made between the performance of an individual and the performance of a group – particularly where an individual's performance may be poor for an activity carried out alone, but excellent in terms of group activities. This is because we have shown in this chapter that at another level, to limit the level and amount of interaction is not the intention of such systems, but to improve all aspects of user-performance at individual, group and organisational level.

Acknowledgements

I am grateful to Kenneth McIntosh for his valuable comments and support during the writing of the chapter. I am also indebted to Philip Barker – whose editorial skills reduced the size of the manuscript to one half of its original value and Paul van Schaik for his editorial comments.

References

Adler, R.B. and Rodman, G. (1994). *Understanding Human Communication* (5th Edition). London, UK: Harcourt Brace College Publishers.

Alty, J. Al-Sharrah, A. and Beacham, N. (2006). When Humans Form Media and Media Form Humans: An Experimental Study Examining the Effects of Different Digital Media Have on the Learning Outcomes of Students who have Different Learning Styles, *Journal of Interacting with Computers*, 18(5), 891–909

Banerji, A. (1995). *Electronic Performance Support Systems*, Ph.D thesis. Middlesbrough, UK: School of Computing, University of Teesside.

Barker, P.G. (1989). *Multi-media Computer-assisted Learning*. London, UK: Kogan Page.

Barker, P.G., Beacham, N.A., Hudson, S. and Tan, C. (1995). Document Handling in an Electronic OASIS, *The New Review of Document and Text Management*, 1(1),1–18.

Barker, P.G., Richards, S., Beacham, N.A., Tan, C.M. and Hudson, S. (1997). Knowledge Sharing through Electronic Course Delivery, *Innovations in Education and Training International*, 34(1), 3–10.

BDA (2008). *What is Dyslexia?* British Dyslexia Association. Available online at: *http://www.bdadyslexia.org.uk/whatisdyslexia.html*. [Accessed on 5 February, 2009].

Beacham, N. (1998). *Distributed Performance Support Systems*, Ph.D thesis. Middlesbrough, UK: School of Computing, University of Teesside.

Beacham, N. and Alty, J. (2004). Media Efficiency During Learning Using DAB Radio: An Initial Educational Study, *Interactive Multimedia Electronic Journal of Computer Enhanced Learning*, AACE, 6(2), December 2004. Available online at: *http://imej.wfu.edu/articles/2004/2/02/index.asp*. [Accessed on 5th February, 2009].

Beacham, N. and Alty, J. (2006). An Investigation into the Effects that Digital Media can have on the Learning Outcomes of Individuals who have Dyslexia, *Computers and Education*, 47(1), 74–93.

Beacham, N.A. and Szumko, J.M. (2003). The VAPPS Prototype: A Computer-based Staff Development Tool for Dyslexia. In D. Pollak (ed.) *Proceedings of a Joint Conference: Supporting the Dyslexic Student in HE and FE: Strategies for Success*, 12 June 2003 (at De Montfort University) and 19 June 2003 (at the University of Hull).

Boyle, T. (1997). *Design for Multimedia Learning*. London, UK: Prentice Hall.

Collins, J., Hammond, M. and Wellington, J.J. (1997). *Teaching and Learning with Multimedia*. London, UK: Routledge.

Collis, B.A. and Verwijs, C. (1995). A Human Approach to Electronic Performance and Learning Support Systems: Hybrid EPSSs, *Educational Technology*, Jan–Feb, 5–21.

Evans, B.J.W. (2001). *Dyslexia and Vision*. London, UK: Whurr Publishers.

Irlen, H. (1991). *Reading by the Colour*. New York, NY: Avery Publishing Group Inc.

Jordan, I. (2002). *Visual Dyslexia Signs, Symptoms and Assessment*. Barnetby-le-Wold, UK: Desktop Publications.

Mayer, R.E. and Gallini, J.K. (1990). When is an Illustration Worth Ten Thousand Words?, *Journal of Educational Psychology*, 82(4), 715–726.

Morgan, E. and Klein, C. (2000). *The Dyslexic Adult in a Non-Dyslexic World*. London, UK: Whurr Publishers.

Ott, P. (1997). *How to Detect and Manage Dyslexia*. Oxford, UK: Heinemann Educational Publishers.

Peoples, D.A. (1992). *Presentations Plus* (2nd Edition). Chichester, UK: John Wiley and Sons.

Perkin, G., Beacham, N. and Croft, A.C. (2007). Computer-assisted Assessment of Mathematics for Undergraduates with Specific Learning Difficulties – Issues of Inclusion in Policy and Practice, *International Journal for Technology in Mathematics Education*, 14(1), 3–13.

Preece, J. (1994). *Human-Computer Interaction*. Harlow, UK: Addison-Wesley.

Proustie, J. (2000). *Literacy Solutions: A Practical Guide to Effective Strategies and Resources*. Taunton, UK: Next Generation.

Reid, G. (1998). *Dyslexia, A Practitioner's Handbook*. Chichester, UK: John Wiley and Sons.

Ryden, M. (1992). *Dyslexia, How Would I Cope?* London, UK: Jessica.

SENDA. (2002). *Special Educational Needs and Disability Act*, Available online at: *http://www.opsi.gov.uk/acts/acts2001/ukpga_20010010_en_1*. [Accessed on 5 February, 2008.]

Sharp, H., Rogers, Y. and Preece, J. (2007). *Interaction Design: Beyond Human-Computer Interaction* (2nd Edition). Chichester, UK: John Wiley and Sons Ltd.

Singleton, C.H. (1999). *Dyslexia in Higher Education: Policy, Provision and Practice*, Report of the National Working Party on Dyslexia in Higher Education, Published by University of Hull on behalf of the Higher Education Funding Councils of England and Scotland, UK.

Snowling, M.J. (2000). *Dyslexia* (2nd Edition). Oxford, UK: Blackwell Publishers.

Stein, J., Talcott, J., and Walsh, V. (2000). Controversy about the Visual Magnocellular Deficit in Developmental Dyslexics, *Trends in Cognitive Sciences*, 4(6), 209–211.

Tyre, C. (1998). *Dyslexia, A Staff Development Handbook*. Lichfield, UK: QEd.

West, T.G. (1997). *In the Mind's Eye: Visual Thinkers, Gifted People with Dyslexia and Other Learning Difficulties*. New York: Prometheous Books.

Witton, C., Talcott, J.B., Hansen, P.C., Richardson, A.J., Griffiths, T.D., Rees, A., Stein, J.F. and Green, G.G.R. (1998). Sensitivity to Dynamic Auditory and Visual Stimuli Predicts Nonword Reading Ability in Both Dyslexic and Normal Readers, *Current Biology*, 8(14), 791–797.

8 *Disability*

STEVE GREEN AND ELAINE PEARSON

This chapter considers the concept of disability in the context of electronic performance support. Terms such as *disability, accessibility, exclusion, inclusion* and *community* are explored together with ideas such as *adaptability, personalisation* and *universal design*. We describe some of the existing categories of device that are often used as *assistive technologies* and also consider novel uses of standard computer and mobile technologies (as performance support aids) in the context of disability and accessibility. These are particularly important in relation to developing *personal* and *adaptive learning environments* for people with special needs – thereby providing 'access for all' through the use of appropriately designed performance aids.

Introduction

In Chapter 1 mention was made of some of the innate limitations that people are born with or which they succumb to in later life. At birth people have the capacity to acquire a number of remarkable abilities which they then further develop as they grow older. Typically, they learn new skills such as how to walk, how to talk, how to recognise and name different objects and how to interact with their environment and each other. Invariably, people's skills and abilities should improve over time, but then, as they grow older some of their abilities peak and begin to decline.[1] In some situations, experience and/or a suitable support aid can often be used to counteract declining ability – thereby maintaining a satisfactory performance. For example, as people grow older their vision deteriorates; this deterioration can usually be compensated for by wearing spectacles – or by using a magnifying glass. Similarly, the experience accrued by older automobile-drivers can often make them safer on the roads than younger, less experienced ones. However, if a person has an innate or acquired disability then they may never be able to acquire the necessary experience and skills. Thus, a person with poor eyesight, limited mobility and unusually slow reactions may be considered to be unsafe and may never be allowed to drive a motor-car. Such an individual is therefore *excluded* from the community of motor drivers – as would a blind person.

---

1   In Figure 1.11 (p. 22) performance plateaus are shown. However, if performers do not maintain their levels of skill, their performance is likely to decline; this can certainly happen in relation to visual and many physical skills as a person ages.

Inherent in the concept of *disability* is the notion of *exclusion*. Of course, everyone will be *excluded* from some communities – simply because of their inability to perform certain actions; these may include not being able to run a mile in under four minutes, being unable to play a piano to a reasonable level of skill or their total lack of ability to speak French or to read Chinese. Most people probably do not consider themselves to be excluded from society in general. However, the likelihood is that most people will acquire some level of disability sooner or later in their lives. Everybody is ultimately categorised by their abilities, their disabilities and by the communities which accept them as members.

Bearing in mind what has been said above, it would seem more reasonable that people with a level of disability should be categorised by what they can achieve, rather than what they cannot do. For example, someone with a hearing impairment may be able to communicate using British Sign Language (BSL) at a rate that most hearing-able people could never follow. Similarly, a person using specialist screen-reader software may be able to listen to its audio narrative at an extremely fast rate. Of course, because of most people's lack of fluency in BSL, or limited experience with a screen reader, they would probably be excluded from deaf or blind communities (see Figure 8.1). *Disability* can therefore be considered as the mismatch between the abilities of individuals within a context – or more accurately the expectations of specific communities which lead to accidental or deliberate exclusion. It is this mismatch which results in *exclusion,* and hence, the concept of disability.

The view outlined here is compatible with current thinking and leading research in the area of disability, in which function is most important (Martin, 2006). This position is reflected in the *International Classification of Function, Disability and Handicap* (ICF) (World Health Organisation, 2001). In this context, functioning is positive health and dysfunction or disability is negative health. The ICF discusses disability at three levels. First, *impairments* are problems with body structures and body functions. Second, *activity limitations* are problems with capacity. Third, problems with performance are *participation restrictions*. As a consequence of this view of disability and the ICF, a number of different approaches have been tried which help people to understand the nature of disability and also to help them to design for accessibility, inclusion, personalisation and enhanced performance in order to alleviate or overcome participation restrictions. The ability to understand the capacities of

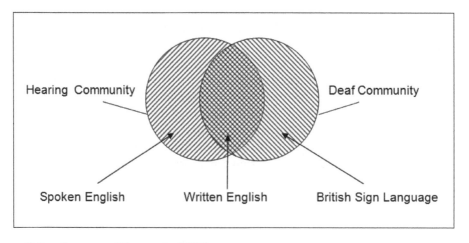

Figure 8.1   Communities and abilities

others and the likelihood of exclusion is an important issue in designing for inclusion and for developing performance support aids. Sometimes *disability simulations* are used to help raise awareness amongst communities such as teachers or designers. The best simulations do not try to give their users an experience of a disability, but instead, they illustrate the likely effects that a bad design or a poor support aid may have on its users (Colella, 2000; Pearson and Koppi, 2006a). Some examples of this approach can be found in the *DyslexSim* system described in Chapter 7. Consequently, designers, programmers, computer scientists, teachers, learners, users or any *community of practice* are better able to support themselves – to express design concerns or to optimise their environment for better use of electronic performance support tools. The involvement of users in design decisions is a basic principle of *user-centred design*.[2] Naturally, if users are drawn from the widest possible circles then it could be claimed that the principles of *inclusive practice* or even *universal design* are being upheld. Many believe that truly universal design is impossible, given the mismatch in abilities between diverse communities. Nevertheless, designers should always try to be aware of who they may be including and excluding as a consequence of their actions – and take measures to minimise arbitrary exclusion.

Assistive Technologies

Assistive technologies are often defined as being 'any technology which can be used to help someone with an innate (or acquired) disability to overcome the limitations typically associated with that disability'. Two common examples are: spectacles for the large number of people who are short- or long-sighted and hearing aids for those who suffer from hearing loss. However, for many people that have severe disabilities, their ability to move, speak, communicate or interact with their environment may depend on a range of assistive technologies. These could include mobility devices (such as electric wheelchairs, scooters or adapted cars), interface devices (for example, adapted keyboards, joysticks and switches), communication technologies (such as speech tablets and screen readers) and mobile devices (mobile phones, *iPods*, PDAs, laptops, and so on). The latter type of device can be used 'as is' or adapted in various ways. Assistive technologies, such as those depicted in Figure 8.2, can therefore be considered as Electronic Performance Support Systems (EPSS) specifically designed for people with a recognised disability. These are generally hardware devices and software systems designed or employed to help an individual to perform ordinary actions or to help in that individual's rehabilitation.

In many instances, the assistive technology that is employed may not be specifically designed for use with disabled people in mind. For example, a computer programmer who has dexterity problems may be quite happy to use a standard keyboard and mouse to carry out the tasks involved in their profession or to write e-mails and printed notes, whereas that same person may have great difficulty when signing a form or handwriting a letter. Similarly, a researcher with dyslexia (see Chapter 7) may happily prepare reports with the help of a tablet computer, word-processor and spellchecker; however, the font choice and paper colour may be configured to suit their special needs. As another example,

---

2   An introduction to user-centred design can be found in the *Wikipedia* online encyclopaedia (accessed 3rd October, 2008) at the following Web address: *http://en.wikipedia.org/wiki/User-centered_design*. Details on this approach to design can also be found at *http://www.usabilityprofessionals.org* (accessed 3rd October, 2008).

Figure 8.2   Examples of devices used as assistive technologies

a young person who has to use a wheelchair may find it easy to go 'virtual bowling' with friends (when using a *Nintendo Wii*), but would find great difficulty when using the ramp used to deliver the balls in a real bowling alley. Disabled people, teachers, helpers and support agencies are always looking for ways in which emerging technologies similar to those illustrated in Figure 8.3 can be utilised in innovative ways.

Given the wider definition of assistive technologies (as discussed above), almost all technology can be considered assistive under the right conditions. Taking the more conventional definition, assistive technologies may be viewed as performance support systems designed specifically with disability and access in mind. Devices of this type are often classified under a number of headings – as shown in Table 8.1.

In the sense that assistive technologies are designed to allow individuals to overcome limitations or improve access, they can obviously be considered to be specialist forms of electronic performance support tool. They can also be seen as being an agent of fairness and equity – which is important from the perspective of employment. It is a principle of anti-discrimination law both in the UK (the DDA – *Disability Discrimination Act*) and in the USA (the ADA – *Americans with Disabilities Act*) that employers are normally expected to make reasonable adjustments to workplace equipment to accommodate for disability. As a matter of principle, within most societies, it is both an ethical and a moral requirement that exclusion should be avoided wherever and whenever this is at all possible. Undoubtedly, assistive technologies and EPSS can help people take their rightful place within a community.

It is an irony of the modern world of changing technologies that while some people's quality of life can be improved enormously by these advances, others are left bemused by the shifting world around them. For example, an elderly man (living in the UK) who

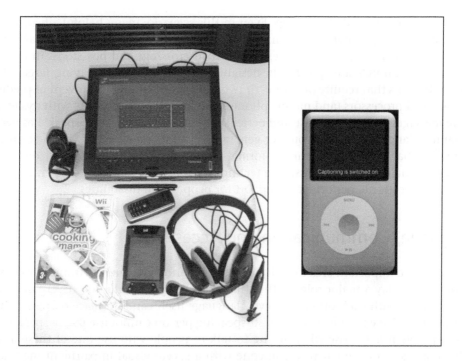

Figure 8.3   Alternative assistive technologies

Table 8.1   Device categories for assistive technologies

Device Category	Purpose	Examples
Mobility	To aid in physical movement and independent living	Electric wheelchair, mobility scooter, adapted car, robot arm, crutch, walking stick, prosthesis
Input/Output and Control	To allow connections with computers and other intelligent or control devices	Adapted keyboards, button switches, suck-blow switch, head switch, tracker-ball, adapted mouse, eye-tracker, touch-screen, concept keyboard
Display and Sensory	To display, read or show results. To provide augmented or alternative sensory experiences	Large screen displays, screen magnifiers, screen readers, Braille output, GPS position reader, echo-location, eye-glasses, hearing aid
Communications	To allow individuals to communicate via language and speech	Adapted speech boards, e-mail, SMS, mobile phones, symbol-systems, alternative or augmentative communication devices

suffers from dementia may not be able to find a telephone box on the street to call his daughter – possibly because they are no longer the red colour[3] he was familiar with as a child. Maybe his daughter gave him a mobile phone – but he may not be able to see the numbers or remember where he put it. Furthermore, he may not remember to carry it or

---

3   Until recently, most telephone boxes within the UK were painted a distinctive red colour – as were the posting boxes used by the UK's postal service. At the time of writing (October, 2008), the latter are still this colour.

keep it switched on and charged up. Even in this scenario, many helpful advances have been made: town planners are beginning to look at the effects of using familiar markers to indicate items such as telephones, curbs, road crossings and bus stops. In addition, some mobile phones are specifically designed for older adults – having large, clearly labelled buttons that require only one- or two-button operation. The advent of predictive text on word-processors (and mobile phones) can help people (possibly with dyslexia) to create messages with greater ease and better spelling. In contrast, 'text-speak' has become a common language among younger generations, some members of which seem to be unable to change register for more formal communication. Nevertheless, despite the various anomalies that arise, assistive technology can be considered to be an important element of electronic performance support for people with disabilities.

Language, Communication and Accessibility

Language is an important area in which assistive technologies and electronic performance support tools play a major role. Without language people would find it very difficult to communicate with each other. However, language itself can also place barriers between communities. For example, if an English-speaking person cannot use BSL or speak French then a problem may arise when trying to talk to people who use one of these as their only language. In a similar way, someone with a severe visual impairment may not be able to read a passage of English even if they understand the language. The individual may not have a problem seeing the text but may have an innate learning disability which means that their reading abilities are poorly developed. The medium used, the language employed, its level of complexity and the context in which it is used are all important factors in relation to establishing effective communication. Assistive technologies and performance support tools can be used to support people's language underperformance by providing assistance within each of the problem areas listed above.

When considering the *communication medium*, for example, it is often possible to change the basic nature of the communication channel that is used. Thus, written text (from a computer screen) can be automatically converted into spoken form using a screen reader such as *JAWS*[4] or it may be converted into embossed Braille dots. Similarly, spoken text may be converted into a text transcription using either automatic speech recognition or human speech recognition (Papadopoulos and Pearson, 2007; Wald, 2004; Wald and Bain, 2008). A transcript or set of captions may be provided, possibly in the same or an alternative language.

When considering the language and *level* associated with a communication process, it is important to remember that translations between languages are nowadays quite common and may be performed automatically or by an experienced translator working from text or spoken sources. Automatic text translation can be an invaluable performance aid for most people – whether disabled or not. The use of *signing* services such as BSL or American Sign Language (ASL) can be a tremendously important tool for deaf communities – these transform spoken utterances into gestural movements of the hands, head, face and arms.

---

4   *JAWS* is an acronym for *Job Access with Speech*. A useful summary of the history, background and uses of JAWS can be found in the *Wikipedia* online encyclopaedia at the following Web address: *http://en.wikipedia.org/wiki/JAWS_(screen_reader)*.

Various types of handheld mobile device are now used to provide dictionaries for those who need to translate words or signs into another language or for those whose level of language is relatively low. Additionally, some signing systems can be used to help people understand English or another native language by providing further pictorial reinforcement of nouns, verbs or whole sentences – as is depicted in Figure 8.4. Both the *Widgit* Picture Communication Symbols (PCS) and the *Rebus* symbol sets are used in this way – as well as being a language in their own right (Stephen and Linfoot, 1996; Widgit, 2000). Iconic English (as depicted in Figure 8.4) can also be used in this way as a sort of intermediate language.

An important recent development that is likely to have significant ramifications for the use of language within the context of disability is the concept of 'blended communication'. Using multiple communication modalities or 'blended strategies' (Barker, 2006), it is possible to create mechanisms by which shortcomings in one modality can be compensated for by a richness in others. Similarly, where disabilities are concerned, it may often be possible to achieve a communication blend that can enable each different disability to be overcome by changing the nature and composition of the blend that is used. The way in which this blended approach can be used is discussed later in the chapter.

The communication techniques described above have been used extensively to facilitate the development of personalised communication tools (for disabled people) that can interface with other types of electronic environment – such as the World Wide Web. As a learning environment, the Web has become an extremely useful resource. However, accessing many web sites (and the various materials embedded within them) can be an extremely difficult task for people who have a communication disability – blind users are a case in point. Consequently, appropriate guidelines – such as those listed in

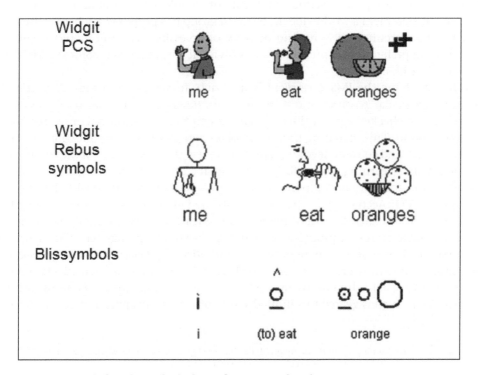

Figure 8.4 Example of symbols-based communication

Table 8.2   Accessibility guidelines

- Provide appropriate alternative text to non-text content in web pages
- Provide headings for data tables
- Ensure users can complete and submit all forms
- Ensure links make sense out of context
- Provide captions and a transcript for videos and live audio
- Ensure accessibility of non-HTML content, including PDF files, *Microsoft Word* documents, *PowerPoint* presentations and *Adobe Flash* content
- Allow users to skip repetitive elements on the page using a 'Skip to Content' or 'Skip Navigation' option at the top of the page
- Do not rely on colour alone to convey meaning
- Make sure content is clearly written and easy to read
- Make JavaScript accessible
- Design to standards and check your work

Source: WebAim, 2008.

Table 8.2 (WebAim, 2008) or guidelines developed for use by specific groups (Pearson and Koppi, 2001) – need to be applied to improve the accessibility of these resources by users who have a shortcoming in their communication ability.

Even if designers follow these guidelines, and even after a professional accessibility audit of a web site, there may still be inherent problems with the content as it is offered. Obviously, this can pose a serious problem for people with disabilities. In order to overcome this problem a worldwide *AccessForAll* group has proposed a scheme which will allow for the searching, locating and delivery of accessible learning material based on the needs and preferences expressed by an individual within a given context (IMS, 2004; Nevile et al., 2005).

When applying the IMS *AccessForAll*[5] approach, to achieve an *accessible relationship* between a particular resource and a specific user, descriptions of that user's needs and preferences are checked against the metadata descriptions of resource components until a match is found. This matching process involves comparing the specification of a user's control, display and content needs (and preferences) with a description of the components of a sought-after Learning Object (LO) (Nevile et al., 2005). When a match is found, the delivery of the appropriate component will form an accessible relationship between the user and the LO. According to the *AccessForAll* metadata overview, accessible systems should be able to adjust the user-interface to the learning environment, locate needed resources and alter resource properties to match the needs and preferences of the particular user involved. This process may require the *substitution*, *augmentation* or *transformation* of the components within a resource – such as changes in its format or the media that it uses. Within our own establishment[6] we use a Transformation, Augmentation and Substitution Service (TASS) which is geared to a limited subset of e-learning applications and contexts.

---

5   IMS is a global learning consortium involved in the development of international standards for learning technologies. Originally, 'IMS' stood for 'Instructional Management Systems'.

6   We refer here to our (that is, the authors') work at the Accessibility Research Centre at Teesside, Middlesbrough, UK.

This approach can thus be thought of as a special instance of an *AccessForAll* service (Green et al., 2006a, 2006b; Gkatzidou et al., 2006).

Our work to date has focused on applying the TASS to LOs. To make rich online content match individual needs and preferences, this approach requires a basic resource to be created from existing or newly authored components; the appropriate adaptations (transformations, augmentations and substitutions) then need to be identified and applied. Examples of these adaptations are given below.

A *transformation* may occur when text is rendered visually (as characters or in a sign language) or aurally (perhaps by a screen reader). It can also be transformed into a tactile form (such as Braille) or simply changed with respect to its colour, size and other display features. Sometimes the end result of a transformation and a substitution (see below) may be very similar. However, the processes by which the results are achieved will be different.

An *augmentation* involves the optional addition of a feature to a primary resource, for instance, a textual caption could be added to a video when required by a user with a hearing impairment or when having to contend with a noisy environment.

A *substitution* usually involves a replacement of one component by another equivalent component. For example, this may occur when a user requires non-visual access to a resource – as may be the case with a blind person or in an 'eyes-busy' situation. Similarly, an interactive exercise requiring a mouse for operation could be substituted by an exercise that could (instead) be controlled using a keyboard or a keyboard emulator. In the case of visual substitution it would be necessary to replace the visual element of a LO with components that match the user's preferences for non-visual access.

Using this idea of a TASS, it is possible to build an EPSS that incorporates the elements of personalisation in relation to the specific needs or preferences of individuals in a given context. Although the primary focus of our work is on supporting people with disabilities, everyone has preferences and/or changing needs, so these adaptable systems could ultimately benefit everyone.

Accessible and Personal Learning Environments

In many ways, accessibility relates to the capability of a learning environment to adjust to the needs of its users. This characteristic is determined by the flexibility of the environment (with respect to presentation, control and access methods) and the availability of adequate *alternative-but-equivalent* content (Heath et al., 2005). The individual needs and preferences of a user may arise from (1) the context in which that user happens to be; (2) the tools available (such as assistive technologies, mobile devices, electronic performance support); (3) the nature of the environment that is involved; and (4) any relevant disability from which the user suffers. The *AccessForAll* movement separates descriptions of needs and preferences into *display*, *control* and *content* characteristics. Of course, an individual's declared needs and preferences may change according to context (Nevile, 2005; Pearson and Koppi, 2006b); they should also be *anonymous* in that there is no requirement for the system to know why any particular individual (in a specific context) has those needs or even who the individual is. For a variety of legal and ethical reasons, environments should therefore only maintain the limited information needed for users to be able to express their needs and preferences.

Interestingly, many of the requirements which have been listed above have been embedded within the *Bodington*[7] Virtual Learning Environment (VLE). This provides a number of *skins* that are capable of transforming the system's end-user interface in various ways to meet the different interaction preferences of its users. For example, a skin may be designed to allow a person with a visual impairment to read text using a very large font size; another skin may be designed for people with dyslexia. In addition, in situations where none of the available skins are appropriate to a particular user, the option exists for that user to suggest alternatives. Any new skins that are developed can then be offered to all subsequent users to choose from if they so wish. It is important to note that *Bodington* does not require its users to declare why they have chosen any particular skin.

The principle of involving users in the design of a system (particularly its end-user interfaces) is a very important one. Sometimes systems need to be designed specifically to cater for a particular need while at other times they can be adapted in appropriate ways to meet this need. It is often the case that it is not just the interface, as described above, but the entire environment which needs to be designed with a particular group of people in mind – an example of this approach is described below.

Recently, our research group[8] was asked to design a VLE for a special needs college in the UK – known as Portland College. Our user-centred design took a very specific and pragmatic approach to the development of an adaptable environment (Harrison et al., 2008). The resulting VLE that was developed (see Figure 8.5) is an example of a Personalised VLE. Each student has an individual learner-profile that tailors his/her personal learning environment to meet the particular learning needs that the student has.

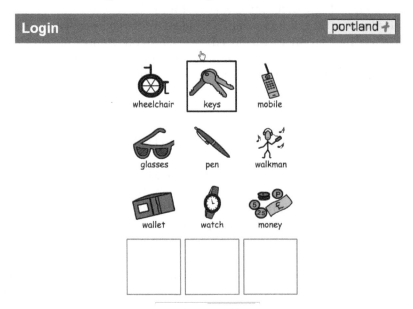

Figure 8.5   The Portland VLE symbolised log-in screen

---

7   *Bodington* is a free open source VLE developed at Leeds University and known as *Bodington Common* (*http://www.bodington.org/index.php*). It allows its users to choose an appropriate 'skin' for their personal use. A number of skins are provided using the HTML facilities of the web site. These allow different fonts, text size, colours and layout to be defined by using Cascading Style-Sheets (CSS).

8   We refer here to our (that is, the authors') work at the Accessibility Research Centre at Teesside University, Middlesbrough, UK.

The unique features of the Portland VLE have resulted in an accessible and adaptable personal learning environment that meets the needs of learners with severe learning difficulties and/or physical disabilities. The system encourages a greater level of independence for learners by ensuring that the VLE and its embedded LOs are accessible – with the appropriate input device, language tools and layout required by each individual user.

Within the UK, the Joint Information Systems Council (JISC) has suggested the concept of a Personal Learning Environment (PLE) (JISC, 2005). This proposal goes one step further than an adaptable VLE because most aspects of such an environment (including functions such as e-mail, discussion boards, diary and calendar) could be actively modified by its individual users. A PLE can be developed from an adaptable VLE (like the Portland VLE described above) if a common set of standards can be identified for component interoperability and each individual is allowed to build their personal set of functions from the available components (Green et al., 2006ab; Pearson et al., 2008).

The bespoke system that we developed for Portland College has demonstrated that a VLE can be created that is adaptable to the needs of a particular group of learners having complex physical and/or cognitive disabilities. If we converted our VLE to an Open Source facility, and adopted the JISC concept of a PLE, the result would be the creation of an Adaptable Personal Learning Environment (APLE) that could be used by many other groups of learners having particular needs and preferences. This issue is further discussed in the following section.

Adaptable Personal Learning Environments

One way of achieving an APLE is to extend the concept of a TASS to deal with both the features of a learning environment as well as its content – and then to embed the TASS into a PLE (Green et al., 2008; Pearson et al., 2008). Such an arrangement is illustrated schematically in Figure 8.6.

The suggestion outlined above is based on the principle that learning content can be generated from adaptable LOs. Any such LO can be thought of as an aggregation of media components based on a proven learning pattern (Jones, 2004; Green et al., 2006a).

In turn, a learning pattern can be considered to be a template into which the learning activities and materials can be slotted. For example, a learning pattern may start with a *brief introduction*, a *description of the concept*, an *illustration*, a *practical exercise* and a *self-test*. This pattern could now be applied to a variety of subjects or topics and could meet the teaching style of many teachers, and possibly, the learning style of many students too. Using a variant of the IMS *AccessForAll* concept (as mentioned previously), the TASS would work on available descriptions of LOs (in the form of metadata) and user-profiles (anonymous profiles of users' needs and preferences) to generate alternative, equivalent learning experiences relating to a user's declared needs, preferences and learning styles (Jones and Pearson, 2006). Because adaptable LOs are based around patterns, it is possible to replace or augment material or content (which may be seen primarily as meeting accessibility requirements) and, in addition, use an alternative learning pattern corresponding to a particular student's learning style.

The proposal outlined above may provide a more pragmatic, adaptable and accessible learning environment than could be achieved by using the current PLE concept alone.

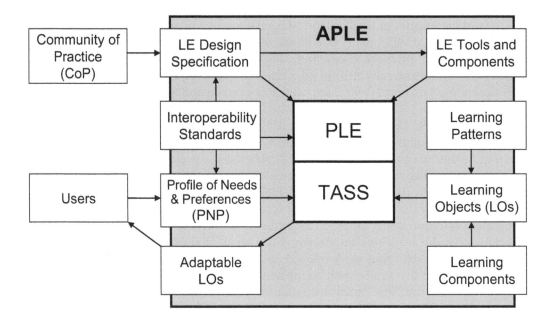

Figure 8.6 An Adaptive Personal Learning Environment (APLE)

Although the JISC PLE proposals consider the concepts of personal choice, no specific account has been taken of the work on adaptability that has been undertaken by the IMS *AccessForAll* group. The PLE proposals are based on a well-recognised (and understood) need to make learning environments more usable for individuals – or better suited to their learning and research needs. A logical next step is to make this more accessible by adapting both content and functions to the needs and preferences of users.

With the concept of adaption in mind, we believe that the APLE concept can be applied in a wider sense as an accessible personal electronic performance support tool for use in a variety of contexts. This would make it an Accessible Personal Environment (APE) that is not specially geared to learning. The user-profiles, the components and the design realisation would depend upon the specific community of practice, but the principles would remain the same – specifically those of matching delivered content and tools to meet the needs and preferences of its users. However, at the moment, because many PLEs, APLEs and APEs are largely conceptual, additional work is needed to make them a practical reality and it is important that this is undertaken by communities involving developers, tutors, designers, practitioners, students and disabled groups.

Similar approaches have also been tried in adaptive e-assessment in education – where users have a degree of control over the level and complexity of the problems and questions that they tackle. In such an environment, some individuals may feel that they do not need revision or testing on the easy questions or that they are not yet ready to tackle the more advanced areas. This form of assessment is often said to be *formative* in that it helps individuals to understand their current level of attainment so that they can take the opportunity to focus on aspects that need more work. As has been suggested in Chapter 5, formative e-assessment is very much an aspect of electronic performance support in that its very purpose is to improve future understanding and task performance.

Using a profile-driven technique, every learner could define a profile that is based on their current educational experience, knowledge and preferences. An assessment method, which adopts standards such as IMS QTI (Question and Test Interoperability), can then take account of this information in order to present a personalised assessment (Lazarinis et al., 2009). Combining the prior experience of students with their performance on a test would then produce an accurate picture of each student's current understanding and areas for further work. This can be particularly effective where the assessments are built up into a full educational history or an e-portfolio of educational achievements – as has been discussed in Chapter 5. These are areas of ongoing research which are expected to make a significant contribution to the APLE model that is depicted in Figure 8.6.

Conclusion

In the first chapter of this book, it was suggested that EPSS facilities are essentially technologies which, as their name implies, support or improve human task performance. Electronic performance support tools fall within the ever growing category of *aiding environments* which are designed to help people overcome inherent or acquired limitations. For people with a disability, such support systems have a special importance because of the increased likelihood of experiencing difficulties with unaided activities: consequently, performance support is crucial and levels of performance improvement are likely to be quite significant. Disability encompasses a wider range of people than may be initially anticipated. Even though total blindness, profound hearing loss, extreme physical incapacity or severe learning difficulties are (thankfully) rare, the likelihood of some level of disability is high and increases with age. Most people will experience physical, visual, auditory and cognitive impairments as they age. It may therefore be better for people to classify themselves as either *partially-abled* or *not-yet-disabled*.

Given the wide spectrum of ability that can exist within any given human society, it becomes very apparent that the accepted 'standards of performance' are relatively arbitrary and personal. What may constitute a bad performance for one person could be acceptable or good for another. For example, if a disabled person takes 30 minutes to write an e-mail message (using a head-mounted switch) this may constitute good performance – whereas for an able individual using a standard keyboard, such a time would be barely satisfactory. Similarly, on one occasion we[9] watched a young man (with a severe motor disability) type a sentence on a laptop computer by painstakingly 'hitting' a key, waiting for the letter to register and repeat a variable number of times (while the key was held down); he then had to press and hold down the 'delete' key long enough to (hopefully) end up with just one instance of the required letter on the screen. This was an extremely frustrating process but it was a strategy that worked for him. However, by simply turning off the keyboard's auto-repeat function his performance was improved and his level of frustration reduced. A simple change in his support system thus improved his performance enormously.

Computers, computer technologies, embedded and ubiquitous systems all have a significant role to play as electronic performance support facilities for people with disabilities. These resources may be employed as originally anticipated or adapted in

---

9   We refer here to our (that is, the authors') work at the Accessibility Research Centre at the University of Teesside, Middlesbrough, UK.

some way to make them more usable by a disabled person. In addition to these 'standard' technologies, a very wide range of assistive technologies is also available. These can be used to support performance and act as an enabler that makes access possible and easier. They can also be used both for rehabilitation and for supporting subsequent improvement in performance. With the necessary, newly acquired skills, tools like screen readers, eye-tracking devices and head-mounted switches can enable users to reach or even exceed normal performance levels in certain situations. For example, people who use a screen reader to listen to text (read from a screen at 200–300 hundred words per minute) can often perform faster than a sighted person can read. Similarly, communicating with sign language in a noisy environment can often be much more effective than speaking or shouting. Deaf people are now able to use video technology for remote communication by posting sign language videos to online websites such as *YouTube* (see *http://www.youtube.com*) and by using video phones (Deaf News Network, 2007). This, of course, means that deaf people can now converse in real time without having to be present in the same room. Furthermore, web-enabled mobile phones are now being adopted by deaf people to support e-mail conversations and instant messaging.

Combined with EPSS, assistive technologies have much to offer people with disabilities. Undoubtedly, in the future, the advent of truly adaptive electronic environments and personalised technologies is likely to produce significant benefits both for able and disabled people. If concepts such as disability, exclusion and limitations are discarded and replaced with terms like accessibility, inclusion and capability it would open up a tremendous opportunity for removing artificial barriers between communities and achieving real breakthroughs in adaptive, accessible EPSS.

Acknowledgements

The authors are grateful to Philip Barker and Paul van Schaik for their useful comments and editorial contributions to the previous drafts of this chapter.

References

Barker, P.G. (2006). Motivation, learning spirals and blended learning, 91–97 in *Blended Learning – Promoting Dialogue in Innovation and Practice, Proceedings of the First Annual Conference on Blended Learning*. 15th June, 2008, The Fielder Centre, University of Hertfordshire, Hatfield, UK.

Colella, V. (2000). Participatory simulations: building collaborative understanding through immersive dynamic modeling. *The Journal of the Learning Sciences,* 9(4), 471–500.

Deaf News Network (2007). *Sign of the times: Video, email are boons to the deaf.* Available online at: http://deafnn.wordpress.com/2007/06/09/sign-of-the-times-video-email-are-boons-to-the-deaf/. *[Accessed on: 5th February, 2009].*

Gkatzidou, S., Pearson, E. and Green, S. (2006). The use of learning object patterns and metadata vocabularies to design reusable and adaptable learning resources in *ED-MEDIA, Proceedings of World Conference on Educational Multimedia, Hypermedia and Telecommunications, 2006* (1), 2928–2933. Orlando, FL.

Green, S., Jones, R, Pearson, E. and Gkatzidou, S. (2006a). Accessibility and adaptability of learning objects: responding to metadata, learning patterns and profiles of needs and preferences. *ALT-J, Research in Learning Technology*, 14(1), 117–129.

Green, S., Jones, R., Pearson, E. and Gkatzidou, S. (2006b). Learning patterns and learner profiles in learning object design. *ALT-J, Research in Learning Technology*, 14(2), 217–221.

Green, S., Nacheva-Skopalik, L. and Pearson, E. (2008). An adaptable personal learning environment for e-learning and e-assessment in *Proceedings of ACM (Bulgaria) CompSysTech'08*. June 2008, International Conference on Computer Systems and Technologies, Gabrovo, Bulgaria.

Harrison, M., Stockton, C. and Pearson, E. (2008). Inclusive, adaptive design for students with severe learning disabilities in *Proceedings of ICALT, 2008*, 1023–1027. 8th IEEE International Conference on Advanced Learning Technologies (ICALT), Santander, Cantabria, Spain.

Heath, A., Treviranus, J. and Nevile, L. (2005). *Individualised adaptability and accessibility in e-learning, education and training, part 1: framework*. Available online at: *http://web.archive.org/web/20070808071714/old.jtc1sc36.org/doc/36N1024.pdf* [Accessed on: 10th February, 2009].

IMS (2004). *IMS AccessForAll metadata specification. IMS Global Consortium*. Available online at: *http://www.imsglobal.org/accessibility/* [Accessed on: 5th February, 2009].

JISC (2005). *Personal learning environments. Joint Information Systems Committee*. Available online at: *http://www.jisc.ac.uk/index.cfm?name=cetis_ple* [Accessed on: 5th February, 2009].

Jones, R. (2004). Designing adaptable learning resources with learning object patterns. *Journal of Digital Information*, 6(1). Available online at: *http://jodi.tamu.edu/Articles/v06/i01/Jones/.* [Accessed on: 5th February, 2009.]

Jones, R., and Pearson, E. (2006). *Designing Adaptable Learning Resources*. World Conference on Educational Multimedia, Hypermedia and Telecommunications (EDMEDIA). Orlando, Florida.

Lazarinis, F., Green, S. and Pearson, E. (2009). Measuring the performance of hypermedia assessment tools to QTI.[10] *International Journal of Innovation and Learning*, 6(2).

Martin, D. (2006). Physical therapy and pain management with the elderly. In G. McCleane and H. Smith (eds), *Clinical Management of the Elderly Patient in Pain* (pp. 207–218). New York, NY: Haworth Press.

Nevile, L. (2005). Anonymous Dublin core profiles for accessible user relationships with resources and services. Paper presented at the *International Conference on Dublin Core and Metadata Applications*, Madrid, Spain.

Nevile, L., Cooper, M., Heath, A., Rotherberg, M. and Teviranus, J. (2005). Learner-centred accessibility for interoperable web-based educational systems. Paper presented at the *1st International Workshop on Interoperability of Web-based Education Systems, 14th International World Wide Web Conference*, Chiba, Japan. Available online at: *http://l3s.de/~olmedilla/events/interopPapers/paper08.pdf*. [Accessed on: 5th February, 2009].

Papadopoulos, M. and Pearson, E. (2007). *Innovative Practice in Education: Exploring the pPotential of Human and Automatic Speech Recognition in the University Classroom*. Association for Learning Technology ALT-C, Nottingham, England.

Pearson, E. and Koppi, T. (2001). Developing inclusive practices: Evaluation of a staff development course in accessibility. *Australian Journal of Educational Technology*, 19(3), 275–292

Pearson, E. and Koppi, T. (2006a). A pragmatic and strategic approach to supporting staff in inclusive practices for online learning, *Australasian Society for Computers in Learning in Tertiary Education (ASCILITE)*, Sydney, Australia.

---

10   QTI refers to IMS Global Learning Consortium Question and Test Interoperability Specification, which is a data model for the representation of test and assessment information.

Pearson, E. and Koppi, T. (2006b). Supporting staff in developing inclusive online learning, In M. Adams and S. Brown (eds), *Towards Inclusive Learning in Higher Education*. London, UK: Routledge Press.

Pearson, E., Green, S. and Gkatzidou, S. (2008). Widening participation through adaptable personal learning environments, accepted by the *HEA ICS Conference*, August 2008, 2(4), 244–255.

Wald, M. (2004). Using automatic speech recognition to enhance education for all students: Turning a vision into reality. 34th ASEE/IEEE Frontiers in Education Conference, Savannah, GA.

Wald, M. and Bain, K. (2008). Universal access to communication and learning: The role of automatic speech recognition. *International Journal Universal Access in the Information Society*, 6(4), 435–447.

WebAim (2008). *Introduction to web accessibility*, WebAIM – Web Accessibility in Mind. Available online at: *http://www.webaim.org/intro/#principles*. [Accessed on: 5th February 2009].

Widgit Software (2000). *Choosing the right symbol software*. Available online at: *http://www.widgit. com/products/choosing-software.htm*. [Accessed on: 5th February 2009].

World Health Organisation (2001). *International Classification of Functioning, Disability and Health: ICF*. Geneva: World Health Organisation.

9 Medical Applications

JEAN ROBERTS

This chapter examines various aspects of performance enhancement in the domain of health care. It uses case studies from the UK – but many are replicated in international locations. In many ways, most activity in the clinical domain relates to the application of clinical expertise and technologies to realise effective, efficient and efficacious health care. These activities may relate to the prevention of illness, interventions to 'treat' an ailment and bring about recovery from it and to facilitate coping strategies – if the clinical condition is chronic or enduring. The use of computing technologies, tools and solutions has become an important intervention within a wide range of medical, clinical and care contexts. This chapter examines the effectiveness and efficiency of clinical activities (from a patient's perspective) and also explores the management of health processes to support clinical practice.

Introduction

The approach used in this chapter not only examines medical aspects of performance enhancement but also covers the full spectrum of clinical activities – including situations where the work of nurses, paramedical professionals, laboratory staff, doctors and other care professionals can be enhanced by the use of appropriate technologies. It covers the full range of health care – including primary care (available to the public without a professional referral) and secondary care (where one clinical professional may introduce a patient to an expert in a particular area for a specialist consultation). For a chronology of IT-related developments in the health domain in the UK, the recent *British Computer Society Health Informatics Forum*[1] book is a recommended source (Hayes and Barnett, 2008).

The material presented in this chapter is divided into three parts; they overlap to some extent because every clinician is also a member of the public and access to virtually all the information sources is open and transparent. The three parts cover: enhanced support for clinical professionals; performance-enhancing informatics for domain management; and clinical information to support patients and effective contributions from individuals to the maintenance of their own health status.

---

1   The British Computer Society (*http://www.bcs.org.uk*) is a professional organisation for people who work with and apply computer systems and information technology within various application areas. There are numerous 'specialist groups' – such as the Health Informatics (Nursing) Group that exists within the BCS Health Informatics Forum (see *http://www.bcshif.org*). These groups provide a focus for people with common interests in a particular area of computing.

Enhanced Support for Clinical Professionals

Clinical decision making is based on both specific patient-information (a clinical history and a description of their current condition) and an underlying evidence base that has many facets. In addition, clinical decisions will usually be framed by the health technologies available in any particular environment, the management policies involved and the availability of human resources. Each of these will influence the decisions that are made for a given patient. Decisions about actual care and treatment are thus based on many factors including the types of equipment the health facility has in operation, the drugs in the pharmacy stock, the types of clinical intervention available and the types of operation that the staff of the organisation have the competency and the licence to perform. Public perceptions of 'good' health care are increasingly based on information that patients have acquired from Internet sites. These may refer to activities in facilities of different types, staff with other skills and interventions that are not carried out locally at all. General practitioners (family physicians) are frequently berated for not 'prescribing the innovative new drug' about which patients have found articles via an Internet search engine, and which may not (yet) be proven or acceptable in the patients' own country or practicable in local circumstances. Health care professionals are thus challenged to defend their actions, explaining in lay language why something that may, superficially, seem to be the 'magic bullet' is not appropriate in specific cases.

ELECTRONIC PATIENT-RECORDS – ESSENTIAL FOR EFFECTIVE CLINICAL PERFORMANCE

Over a lifetime, an individual may receive care interventions and treatment from many clinical practitioners, be prescribed innumerable pills and potions, and have differing outcomes as a result of interaction with health care facilities. Any of these entities may have an impact on the efficacy of a subsequent decision to treat. It is therefore necessary to bring all these elements together into a record of the clinical history of that patient. Up until relatively recently, unconnected IT systems in health care across the world were, at best, focused on collecting data (reported symptoms, vital signs, test results, operating theatre interventions, clinical assessments, locations of interventions, medical consultations and nursing orders) individually. They may have shared or mirrored demographics to identify uniquely the patient to whom the data referred. We are now striving for full 'womb to tomb' lifelong clinical histories being readily available to all authorised and technologically authenticated professionals with a need to know about a particular person during a specific episode of care. This cannot be achieved without major investments in technologies, the development of 'fit for purpose' informatics solutions and trained practitioners who have appropriate competencies to design, deliver, operate and use those solutions to support effective care of patients. Typically necessary solutions have been developed over time. One such incremental development – that of the NHS in England – the National Programme for IT (NPfIT) – is charted in Brennan's book (Brennan, 2005). The goals of NPfIT are laudable and in essence are very similar to those of the different parts of the UK[2] – although the strategic model chosen for development varies. The goals include:

- supporting the delivery of care and services around each patient's choice, 24/7, 'just-in-time', conveniently and seamlessly regardless of sectoral boundaries;
- supporting professional staff through electronic communications, better knowledge management, faster access to essential information (notes, test results in appropriate presentational formats), routine access to specialised expertise, evidence and guidance; and
- improving the management of services by providing good-quality data to support National Service Frameworks (national standards and targets for individual clinical conditions), clinical audit, good governance and effective management information.

The above goals will have a significant impact on the effectiveness, efficiency and efficacy of health care. However, the challenges involved in moving towards their achievement are pervasive.

EVIDENCE-BASED OPERATIONAL CLINICAL GUIDANCE

Clinical protocols that can be used like telesales scripts in professional hands are based on good practice sanctioned by experts and grounded in an analysis of what actually works effectively in real care situations. Clinical guidelines are developed in the UK under the aegis of the National Institute for Health and Clinical Excellence (NICE, *http://www.nice.nhs.uk*), presented worldwide in systematic reviews by The Cochrane Collaboration (*http://www./cochrane.co.uk/en/collaboration.html*) and are based on evidence, research and expert opinions. Having such guidance available facilitates the setting of national standards and, within those, targets for local achievement. NHS organisations then use audits and business intelligence functions to determine how changes that they make move them towards their target over time.

Technology can present selected scientific facts culled from many sources and many countries. Complex search strategies using Internet sites can be employed to identify more publications than could ever be read and assimilated by a clinician – even if they did not have a day job to do. Anecdotally, it is said that if a GP (general practitioner or family physician) was to read everything printed about their specialism then they would be 'a month behind in a week'. It is therefore imperative that relevant technologies are used to draw important pertinent material directly to the professional's attention. There are risks, for both professionals and lay people, from interpretation and assessment of the value of material on clinical topics that is available on Internet sites. As is the case when evaluating other subjects, typical concern surrounds biased or unbalanced material, material without expert provenance or material that is perhaps not the most up-to-date (Roberts and Copeland, 2001). There are additional issues for clinical searches including alternate Greek and Latin stemmed terms *nephro* (Greek) and *renal* (Latin) – both referring to the kidneys; and spelling differences – demonstrated by *fetal* (US) and *foetal* (UK) and

---

2   In the UK, There are four health areas – one for each of the member countries, namely England, Wales Scotland and Northern Ireland. Details of the national health programmes in these areas can be found at the following Web addresses (accessed on 13th August, 2008): *http://www.connectingforhealth.nhs.uk; http://www.hscni.net; http://www.show.scot.nhs.uk* and *http://www.ihc.wales.nhs.uk.*

anemia (US) and *anaemia* (UK) – which could artificially limit the results of searches. Most peer-reviewed scientific articles are classified using *Medical Subject Headings* (MeSH), an extensive controlled vocabulary/metadata system. It was created and is updated by the National Library of Medicine in the USA and is used by the *Medical Analysis and Retrieval System* (*MEDLINE*) article database (for which *PubMed* is the public 'face').

Scientific papers can now be accessed online in abstract or full form. This is useful for collating material on a given topic – thereby enabling rapid increases in knowledge by practitioners. It is also important that research and operational findings are added to the knowledge base in an appropriate form and on a regular basis. Whilst other countries have a tradition of presentation, publication of and citation in sources like *MEDLINE* (*http://www.ncbi.nlm.nih.gov*) and *BioMed Central* (*http://www.biomedcentral.com*), there appears to be less encouragement to disseminate findings in the UK relating to health topics by those operationally active in (direct support of) care areas.

Papers can be either invited for conferences or conferences can seek material via a call for papers. If scientific papers are accepted by conferences then they become part of the proceedings which can be made available on CD-ROM or in hard copy, contemporaneously or after a certain period for free access over the Web. Searching such a plethora of sources can be risky and time-consuming, so clinicians must take care in selecting keywords to search (and find) and, as authors, in giving their contribution an explicit title which describes clearly the main themes of their paper. Effective searching and access to a wide range of full papers, not just short abstracts, are usually facilitated by various access management systems such as *ATHENS* (*Athens Access Management System* – see *http://www. athensams.net*) for publishers' bodies of work.

Performance Enhancing Informatics for Domain Management

It must not be forgotten that health care is a business. For example, the position of the NHS as an employer is variously claimed (apocryphally) to be 'second only to the Indian Railway or the Red Army'. Even the NHS 'free at the point of delivery' must be properly managed, and demonstrate corporate probity and good governance. Like any corporate entity, the NHS needs technologies to support its business functions in an efficient way. These include:

- activity management, audit and monitoring;
- data sharing between departments (about staff, resource use and patient-related issues);
- 'just-in-time' ordering of supplies (for example, drugs, food and consumables);
- fee-setting, bidding for commissioned business and the management of payment claims;
- commissioning services (covering pricing, charging, contract negotiation and ongoing monitoring);
- tactical operational support for managing facilities and strategic planning of new developments (based on the population demands and needs within a 'political' context);
- complex programme and project management (from 'design and build' of hospitals to implementation of computing, health technologies and medical devices); and

- research into best practice (which may use, for example, queuing theory, geographic information systems, population analysis and concepts such as capability maturity modelling).

The health care delivery organisations (both public and private) need market intelligence to project demands and estimate needs (based on epidemiology) and monitor actual operational performance (both commissioning and purchasing services).

HEALTH VARIANTS OF BUSINESS FUNCTIONS

Variants of many business functions that require high performance (similar to those used in other businesses) may have to occur differently in the health domain. For example, the additional pressures placed on performance monitoring functions (similar to those used in other industries) make them the subject of very close scrutiny within the context of health care. The additional pressures that are placed on health monitoring processes can be illustrated by the statement *'people will die if health organisations get their information handling wrong'* in the health domain. Some of the important performance monitoring issues in relation to health care are described and discussed below.

National targets are set for the maximum amount of time that patients will have to wait for treatment once they have been diagnosed with specific clinical conditions. NHS organisations are recompensed by virtue of a financial process that includes recognition of their performance against targets that are set differently for primary and secondary care. The complex rule base for the funding process is annually reviewed and will not be described here[3] but examples of outline performance targets are considered. For instance (as of early 2008), patients in emergency (trauma) departments must be seen within four hours and performance against this target is rigorously monitored. Planning documents[4] for the NHS in England state that:

> *In the early 1990s waits of more than six months for your first outpatient appointment were not uncommon, and tens of thousands of you waited more than two years for their operation. By December 2008, the longest you will wait after being referred by your GP until you start your treatment will be 18 weeks – that is, unless it is clinically appropriate to wait longer, or you choose to delay treatment. Wherever possible you will wait less than this. Any hospital appointments, tests, scans or other procedures that you may need before being treated will all happen within this maximum time limit.*

Gathering all the information needed to monitor waiting times requires data from many sources, benchmarking of indicators on a regular basis and early alerts if any of these are likely to breach targets – so that remedial avoiding action can be taken. Similarly, the NHS Cancer Plan sets out the long-term goal that, *'no patient should wait longer than one month from an urgent referral by their GP with a suspected cancer diagnosis, to the start of*

---

3   Further details on the rule-base underlying the funding process can be found at the following website (accessed on 13th August, 2008): *http://www.dh.gov.uk/en/Managingyourorganisation/Financeandplanning/NHScostingmanual/DH_4065475.*

4   The NHS planning documents referred to here were published on the Internet at the following Web address (accessed on 13th August, 2008): *http://www.18weeks.nhs.uk/Content.aspx?path=/What-is-18-weeks/patient/.*

treatment, except for a good clinical reason, or through their personal choice' (Department of Health, 2000: p. 11, 2008) – and this too needs close management.

Other aspects of strategic health management capitalise on technologies over the longer term, for example, bringing data together across national boundaries in order to maximise the response to international disasters necessitates message-passing between disparate system architectures. This might involve having to coordinate resources, track progress of the incidents (natural or societal) and identify the populations affected by critical occurrences – which may frequently be in inaccessible areas. Satellite technology and telehealth processes for 'on-the-spot' assessment are crucial, as are virtual-reality scenarios for the preparation of disaster plans and training to deploy these in situations that may occur infrequently – such as war zones and disaster areas. Similar processes can be brought to bear in disease-tracking across continents (such as HIV/AIDS) and in managing outbreaks of (possibly) life-threatening conditions in an enclosed area (such as the Ebola hemorraghic fever virus or winter influenza).

Telehealth includes an element of 'remoteness' linked to accessibility. This could involve anything from vast geographic distances, the risk status of a patient's location (such as in a war zone) or logistics due to traffic gridlock in a holiday period – all of which make it difficult for a clinical specialist and a patient to be in the same place at the same time. Limited financial and business evaluation has formally been carried out, but there is strong evidence of a performance impact on service provision as well as the quality of eventual outcomes from enabling telehealth activities (Cornford and Klecun-Dabrowska, 2001). There are benefits to immediate clinical assessment carried out through webcams operated by paramedics at an accident scene. In this way experts can apply their clinical expertise from their office – rather than having to waste valuable time in travelling to the scene of an incident.

Strategic national databanks such as *UK-Biobank* (see *http://www.ukbiobank.ac.uk*) and the *Icelandic DeCODE* (see *http://www.decodegenetics.com*) also need effective technologies to manage their extensive subject databases and, under ethical research consent, correlate their data with other sources such as the national censuses and demographic market profiles.

ENHANCING SUPPORT FOR THE MANAGERS OF CLINICAL AREAS

Decisions always need to be informed by evidence, whether direct patient-care decisions made by clinicians regarding the most appropriate interventions for individuals, management decisions that affect the facilities and resources deployed overall, or the populations that potentially make demands on care delivery. According to Bernard Crump, the Chief Executive of the NHS Institute for Innovation and Improvement, *'We need our teams and organisations to be able to capture, interpret and communicate the essence of any situation in order to make the right decisions at the right time.'* (Pencheon, 2008: p. 2)

General principles of data guidance were established in the 1980s by the late Dame Edith Korner (Mason and Bishop, 1983) stating that health care deliverers should be collecting, *'the minimum amount of information without which it is not deemed possible to manage effectively'*. In effect this should have removed (and in practice did greatly reduce) any need for ad hoc investigations of health data for one purpose, such as a Parliamentary Question, after which such data was never used again. The plethora of statistical returns on performance issues that are necessary today could not be delivered without modern informatics systems.

The NHS is awash with (ever-changing) indicators and targets. Information systems must be able to capture, collate, analyse and present information in the most effective manner across all sectors of care – and be able to correlate this information with that held by local authority services and social care agencies. The basic questions asked of management information systems in the health domain that need to be answered are three-fold:

- What services are health organisations providing and what outcomes arise from them for defined populations?
- Can it be proven that organisations are actually doing what they say they are doing and doing it effectively?
- Are they using appropriate resources and methods to gain 'gold-standard outcomes' (as defined by national service frameworks)?

Indicators are frequently used to highlight where a situation is in 'a warning mode' (and requires investigation) rather than in 'a mandatory stop mode' (which indicates an immediate cessation of process is necessary). I well remember my own hospital being taken to task when it was thought that we were not efficient – we were (allegedly) taking three times as long to handle a third of the patients as a neighbouring organisation. Further reasoned investigation showed that we were carrying out the particular process of clinical stabilisation by 'suspending inpatients', whilst in fact they went home for short periods of time to see if they could cope with their medications before returning to hospital, whereas the other location formally discharged and readmitted the same types of patient in the same circumstances!

An example of another challenge to health information systems relates to the very large hospitals that have international renown in certain clinical procedures. In many cases they also support the local population within their catchment area with less complex or critical procedures – routine maternity services, general medical outpatient clinics, and accident-and-emergency services. Asking such hospitals to *prove* that they provide effective services to their own local communities requires the informatics system to be able to segment information that describes the performance for each population. This system must also show how hospitals are performing for routine services on a regular basis – looking at turnover, length of stay, health resource (usage) grouping by clinical diagnosis and other factors.

The examples presented in Figure 9.1 show that interpretation of figures *in context* is crucial to good decision making. Deming (1993) rightly said, '*Ultimately, the ability to lead depends on one's ability to understand variation.*' The context of interpreting performance data in the health domain will include social factors, familial factors right through to statistical differences from an expected norm of 'outliers' (occurrences of clinical cases that were unpredicted). If we are to calculate evidence-based targets we must use understanding of the context of past activity and projected profiles to generate information with integrity. Such evaluations and calculations are beyond the scope of this chapter and cannot be done informally 'on the back of an envelope' but require sophisticated informatics systems and competent information and business analysts to do the work.

Patients originate from both the local community and as a result of specialist external referrals

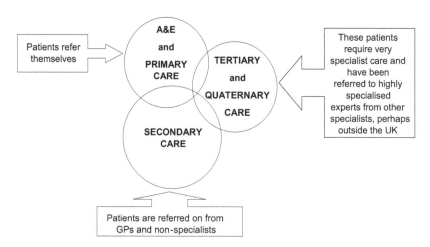

Figure 9.1   Performance analysis of a complex range of types of patient

The NHS is, some would say, beset with targets and indicators of effective service provision. The levels aspired to may be local measures of performance which, in major clinical areas, are informed by past performance and set in the context of national prescribed standards of good practice or required performance. 'Progress towards national targets' is only one performance indicator. Others include 'rate of readmittance' – which may reflect too much haste to discharge patients from a hospital episode.

Monitoring can also cover, for example, waits for certain types of patient in an accident-and-emergency department being under four hours from arrival to admission/discharge or transfer to another facility, or the monitoring of ambulance responses within 14 minutes to emergency calls. Indicators need to be monitored frequently and those giving potential cause for concern (flagged as amber) and those that have breached targets (flagged as red) brought to the attention of the senior officers in the organisation, so that action can be taken. Areas performing within limits would be flagged as green and therefore would not be highlighted. These alerts are referred to operationally as either 'traffic lights' or 'RAG' reports (for obvious reasons).

Clinical Information to Support Patients and Patients' Effective Contribution to their Care

Patients are both subjects of health care interventions and can be involved in that care and the understanding of their clinical conditions. There are innovative technological developments that improve the effectiveness and efficiency of clinical processes, ensure decisions are well-grounded in evidence, and demonstrate new tools and techniques at the leading edge of research. These are described in outline in this section. More detail can be found in the referenced sources and by using an Internet search engine to find other occurrences of similar work. Performance enhancement for health services includes both the 'corporate' efficiency considered in the preceding section (entitled 'Enhancing support for the managers of clinical areas') and – in a patient-related context – 'efficacy' with regard to outcomes for patients/clients.

TECHNOLOGIES FOR PATIENTS

Technologies that enhance the quality of life for those with clinical conditions are becoming prevalent but not yet ubiquitous (Roberts, 2006). This section explores situations in which appropriate technologies can be used to extend the opportunities for patients and their carers to be involved in care interventions and in performance-enhancing lifestyle maintenance.

Sources of information that enable the public to be involved in, rather than just the object of, more effective health care are increasing. They range from the wide-ranging triage (first line assessment) service 'NHS Direct' (now merged with 'NHS Choices') to single-issue Internet sites for specific clinical conditions – such as the Diabetes UK site (*http://www.diabetes.org.uk*). Guidance that is publicly available includes Internet sites from various sources both within and outside of the NHS. Technologies and informatics applications, in addition to empowering clinicians to provide interventions that bring about satisfactory outcomes for patients, increasingly support patients in bringing about positive outcomes for themselves by their actions (alone or in conjunction with their clinicians). Effective self-management and involvement by patients can have a contributory, but not necessarily positive, effect on the performance of health services overall. This section covers some of the areas where such benefits can be identified.

Evidence-based clinical guidance for patients

Clinical protocols developed by experts can be used to create interactive tools (based on hierarchical branching through a preset script – depending on answers given to sequential questions) for patients/clients, resulting in recommendations for the next steps in diagnosis or treatment. For example, multimedia NHS Direct (UK telephone number: 0845-4647; Web address: *http://www.nhsdirect.nhs.uk*) provides a telephone advice line, Internet site and phone triage service for 'common clinical conditions', a web-based protocol-driven general information site and NHS Direct Interactive on digital TV. The service also extends to dental advice, an appointment-and-advice line (non-clinical) linked to the NPfIT Choose and Book national electronic booking service, phone support for patients with long-term conditions, assessment of patients over the telephone to prepare them for operations and give aftercare and support, and specific 24-hour helplines giving coordinated advice and information around local and national health scares (for example, swine flu, meningitis in children or MRSA). In order to reduce the number of times patients have to travel for check-ups to specialist clinics, NHS Direct also carries out hearing tests over the telephone so that NHS clinics can check that patients' hearing aids are properly fitted and comfortable.

Under NPfIT, a project called *HealthSpace* is piloting patients' 'view only' access to their own summary care records – functionality that was first introduced operationally in the GP system operated by Dr Hannan (*http://www.tamesideandglossop.nhs.uk*) in 2006. Commercial suppliers have also launched personal-health-record initiatives, using secure Internet sites (or in some, as yet non-validated, ways involving patient-held smart cards) that allow users to store and share their health records using a free online service.

End users (patients themselves) can capture monitoring data on, for example, glucose and cholesterol levels or download clinical information, such as laboratory results or x-rays, from the websites of their health care provider – which ultimately patients themselves will be able to selectively share (or not) with their doctor, family member or carer. This development offers a huge step forward in relation to people's involvement in health, ownership of personal data, self-management and compliance with (agreed) care programmes. If informal care (by patients, friends and family) happens safely and effectively, the time released from NHS and other health delivery agencies can be targeted in other ways, thereby increasing their performance and coverage and improving efficacy of available services. It must be recognised that such shared services must be monitored for safety and responsibility for decision making. Moreover, the technology that is used must capture *all* interventions, results and outcomes if a comprehensive patient-record is to be maintained.

Single-issue Internet sites – information for expert patients

There are many motives for making health topics widely available on Internet sites or via the World Wide Web – including service support, transparency of corporate or NHS comparative performance profiles, commercial promotion of, for example, drug products and medical devices, and for sharing experiences with fellow sufferers from particular conditions or diseases. Sites can become specialist repositories of information relating to a single theme and are informative to both specialist professionals and so-called 'expert patients' and their family. However, it is important to be aware of the limitations of sources such as personal co-morbidities or complex confounding factors which may make some suggested interventions less than efficacious or inappropriate – regardless of claims that are periodically seen in the media. Indeed, media claims can sometimes be 'selective with the truth'. An interesting example of this situation arose in a national newspaper article[5] – the title of which read '*Beefed up Broccoli to Fight Cancer*'.

Although there is some truth in the body of the article concerned, the evidence underpinning the claim (that the suggested actions will only be effective in some circumstances, with certain cancers at particular stages and in limited situations) needs to be considered very carefully. To counter situations such as this, the Internet site *http:// www.healthdirect.co.uk/index.html* contains useful evidential commentary (collated by an academic source on behalf of the UK's Department of Health) that sets into context any claim relating to 'hot' clinical topics currently in the eyes of the media.

Self-monitoring by patients

Patients with long-term chronic conditions such as diabetes or asthma often use facilities to monitor their own conditions on a day-to-day basis. These 'expert' patients can take steps to intervene personally if their clinical condition escalates and gives cause for concern. This can result in a reduction in the number of visits that need to be made to health care practitioners for routine confirmation of their clinical state. Interactions

---

5   The headline referred to here appeared in an edition of the *Daily Mail* newspaper that was published in the UK during 2005. Further details of the 'broccoli' issue can be found at the following websites (accessed on 13th August, 2008): *http://news.bbc.co.uk/1/hi/health/4688854.stm* and *http://news.bbc.co.uk/1/hi/health/4502404.stm*.

with clinical professionals will still be required if a patient's clinical state becomes more critical or intense. Visits to a clinic therefore become more effective and productive – as the *'come back and see me in six months'* advice can be extended or reserved for *'if you feel your condition has changed significantly'*. Redistribution of the deployment of scarce expert resources can thus improve the quality of care and the support for other people who may be at risk

Previously, it was a patient's own responsibility to monitor their status between appointments at a clinic. Technology has made it possible for test results to be input to patient records via phone links, the Internet or even satellite connections. This means that without leaving their clinical base, specialists can still monitor progress and, if necessary, call a patient in on an ad hoc basis or send a text reminder or email to stress the need to comply (*'have you taken your medication today?'*). This represents the best use of limited clinical expertise and is less invasive to patients, whilst still clinically acceptable practice. Similar technologies can be used to manage stress and anxieties in pregnancy – reassurance can be given to patients by remote analysis of foetal vital signs expressed as signal traces transmitted via computer networks. Where a family has a child in hospital and home commitments to other family members, the Internet and webcams can be used for regular updates and comfort, for example 'the virtual goodnight kiss' (Gray et al., 2000) which has been proven to reduce lengths of stay in hospital and improve the quality of a patient's hospital experience.

For those focused on health maintenance, technologies can also assist – for example, the elite athlete whose vital signs (blood pressure, heart rate) can be monitored in training to indicate risk or performance enhancement. This technology can increasingly be purchased over a shop-counter by those who may have underlying conditions and engage in lone pursuits such as walking in less-populated countryside areas. Any change in clinical status from a personal norm can be used to activate an 'emergency' procedure and, in an extreme case, can trigger a medical evacuation or recovery.

REMOTE AND EXTERNAL SUPPORT FOR IMPROVING QUALITY OF LIFE

Those who live independently may have clinical conditions that normally are manageable but could give rise to concern. In these cases 'smart home' technologies that can monitor and manage room temperature, switch on the oven or open the garage door remotely are already being deployed. Research, such as that at the University of Ulster (Augusto et al., 2005), is deploying communication technologies, sensor technologies and intelligent user-interfaces (rather than pure software solutions) in order to emphasise the intelligent aspects of a smart home. The researchers recognise that *'translating information into accurate diagnosis when using non-invasive technology is full of challenges'* (p. 164) and claim justifiably that *'smart home technology offers a viable solution to the increasing needs of the elderly, special needs and home based-health care populations'* (p. 164). Use of such technologies may decrease reliance on NHS (and other) services, in addition to increasing opportunities to maintain independent living.

Those patients with post-operative problems or needing rehabilitation after a trauma (Murray et al., 2006), muscle problems during pregnancy, back problems or just wishing to perfect their golf swing can increasingly call on relevant technological support to help them overcome their difficulties. Such technological aids can, over time, plot movement visually and analyse gait, stance, muscle development/degradation or areas where clinical problems can be addressed by exercise, rehabilitation or alterations to ways of, for example, moving or sitting. Technologies can scan the body and produce virtual-reality three-dimensional images that graphically show body changes (*http://www.wwl. co.uk/3dbodyscanner.htm*) in a similar way to the models of geographical topography that are used in news bulletins. The progress of muscle distortion to cope with the weight of a developing foetus can be similarly visually monitored, and actions that potentially ease discomfort can be taken. The precision of the images is such that slight changes (immeasurable by the naked eye) can be identified through digital analysis. This type of investigation can be either preventative (thereby reducing the impact on the NHS's performance and, in addition, improving a patient's quality of life) or rehabilitative (especially in cases where a patient's demotivation could lengthen recovery time due to lack of perceived improvements – for example, in cases of remobilisation after amputations).

Virtual Reality (VR) can help Parkinson's disease sufferers to improve their mobility and ability to enter ordinary life situations which would otherwise cause them difficulties. Because of perceptual difficulties, someone with Parkinson's disease can have a tendency to 'freeze' unexpectedly or to adopt a shuffling gait. Building on a Fifth Framework European Union project called PARREHA,[6] a prototype set of glasses was developed to support the use of VR (see *http://www.parkaid.net*). These have been used to provide visual cues to trigger a response and encourage better walking patterns in people with the disease. The Institute of Neurology at University College London is involved in evaluating this technique, which is claimed will help one in 20 Parkinson's sufferers to lead a more normal life. The deliverables from these projects, like many others carrying out homecare research,[7] are likely to have quite an impact on health services as social, clinical and other support provision will be reduced – improving situations for patients and their informal carers and reducing costs of service providers.

Conclusion

However a definition of performance enhancement is crafted, there are significant benefits from applying technologies in health care. These are observable in real-life situations around the world as well as within leading-edge research projects. Value may come from cost reduction, resource release where alternative deployment may realise additional benefits, and/or from quality improvements that result in positive changes in patients' behaviour or effectiveness of clinical practice.

Deployment of technologies in health care is as volatile and fast-moving as it is wide in scope. This chapter has only highlighted a limited number of aspects of application which can be (and are being) replicated in other clinical areas, both currently and in the future. The caveat, to the positives described, is that technologies alone cannot solve the performance challenges faced in the domain of health care. Rigorous evaluation of emerging technologies, safety, robustness criteria and attention to patients' sensitivities

---

6   Further details of the PARREHA project can be found at the following Web address (accessed on 13th August, 2008): *http://www.fastuk.org/research/projview.php?id=676.*

7   See, for example, the health applications described at the following website (accessed on 13th August, 2008): *http://cordis.europa.eu/ist/ka1/health/projectbooklet/patients.htm.*

and clinical attitudes will all need to be deployed in order to maximise opportunities for performance enhancement.

Acknowledgements

I am grateful to colleagues in the British Computer Society Health Informatics Forum and colleagues both in the NHS and elsewhere (in the UK and abroad) for sharing their health informatics experiences with me over the years.

References

Augusto, J.C., Nugent, C., Martin, S. and Olphert, C. (2005). Software and Knowledge Engineering Aspects of Smart Homes Applied to Health. *Studies in Health Technology and Informatics,* 117, 164–171.

Brennan, S. (2005). *The NHS IT Project: The Biggest Computer Programme in the World ... Ever!* Oxford, UK: Radcliffe Publishing.

Cornford, T. and Klecun-Dabrowska, E. (2001). Ethical Perspectives in Evaluation of Telehealth, *Cambridge Quarterly of Health Care Ethics,* 10(2), 161–169.

Deming, W.E. (1993). *The New Economics for Industry, Government, Education.* Cambridge, MA: MIT Press.

Department of Health (2000). *NHS Cancer Plan: A Plan for Investment, A Plan for Reform.* Available online (and as a PDF download) at: *http://www.dh.gov.uk/en/Publicationsandstatistics/Publications/PublicationsPolicyAndGuidance/DH_4009609* (accessed 14th August 2008).

Department of Health (2008). *Cancer Wait Times.* Available online at: *http://www.performance.doh.gov.uk/cancerwaits/index.htm* (accessed 14th August 2008).

Gray, J.E., Safran, C., Davis, R.B., Pompilio-Weitzner, G., Stewart, J., Zaccagnini L. and Pursley, D.W. (2000). Baby CareLink: Using the Internet and Telemedicine to Improve Care for High-risk Infants. *Pediatrics,* 106(6), 1318–1324.

Hayes, G. and Barnett, D. (eds) (2008). *UK Health Computing: Recollections and Reflections.* Swindon, UK: BCS Books.

Mason, A. and Bishop, P. (1983). *Developing a District IT Policy* (pamphlet). London, UK: Kings Fund.

Murray, C.D., Patchick, E., Pettifer, S., Caillette, F. and Howard, T. (2006). Immersive Virtual Reality as a Rehabilitative Technology for Phantom Limb Experience: A Protocol. *CyberPsychology and Behavior,* 9(2), 167–170.

Pencheon, D. (2008). *The Good Indicators Guide,* NHS Institute for Innovation and Improvement. Available online at: *http://www.institute.nhs.uk/* (accessed on 14th August 2008).

Roberts, J. (2006). Pervasive Health Management and Health Management Utilizing Pervasive Technologies: Synergy and Issues. *Journal of Universal Computer Science,* 12(1), 6–14.

Roberts, J.M. and Copeland, K.L. (2001). Clinical Websites are Currently Dangerous to Health. *International Journal of Medical Informatics,* 62(2–3), 181–187.

10 *Science and Engineering*

ASHOK BANERJI

This chapter examines various aspects of performance support within the domain of science and engineering. The important characteristics of performance-enhancing task-execution environments are reviewed and a unified support model is presented in order to describe them. Activities in science and engineering involve different degrees of information processing. Information and knowledge support are therefore a crucial aspect of the work undertaken by modern science and engineering professionals. The engineering domain is further complicated by the need to provide performance support facilities that meet the requirements of a wide spectrum of skills and expertise on the part of their users. For this purpose a broad range of support tools and technologies are available to facilitate effective and efficient performance. Various examples of performance enhancement are described and a short case study is presented.

Introduction

In recent years, computers and communication technologies have been increasingly used to facilitate and automate many common tasks that people perform. In fact, nowadays, technology has become almost ubiquitous and people are often unaware of its underlying utility. Consider, for example, the everyday task of withdrawing cash from a bank. Instead of going into a particular branch of the bank and embarking on a face-to-face transaction with a bank clerk, many people now use an ATM – that is, an 'automated teller machine'. This involves inserting an appropriate personal identity card into the machine, using a keypad to enter the access code for the account to be debited and then specifying the amount of cash required. Provided that the access code the customer enters is correct and sufficient funds are available in the customer's account (and in the ATM), the required amount of cash is dispensed almost immediately. In this example, many of the tasks that were previously performed manually by a clerk in the bank have now been replaced by equivalent tasks involving the use of ATM technology. Originally, these tasks involved: using a customer's signature (for identity and account verification), checking and updating the balance in the customer's account and the manual 'handover' of cash to the customer. Nowadays, these operations are all performed automatically using computer and communication technologies. The ATM-based transaction system has removed the need for any face-to-face human interaction (between the bank clerk and the customer) by making the cash withdrawal process an automated self-service activity. One of the advantages of the ATM automation process is the reduction in errors that can arise as a result of shortcomings in unaided human performance (in terms of the mistakes that might be made by the bank clerk). Furthermore, the automated system has enhanced the level of convenience for its customers as a result of increased accessibility – by enabling them to withdraw cash at any time of day and at a wider range of service locations.

The ATM example described above illustrates how the deployment of computer and communication technologies can be used to enhance the performance of both a banking organisation and its customers. This is an important type of application in business and commerce; further examples of applications in these areas are discussed in Chapters 11 and 12. In contrast, this chapter deals with performance support applications in science and engineering. Applications in these areas are becoming more involved and demanding. This has therefore had a significant impact on the performance of the researchers and engineers involved in these areas. Bearing this in mind, the underlying goals of this chapter are: (1) to explore the processes involved in the application of science and then identify possible computer-supported activities where performance support techniques may be applied, and (2) to discuss computer support in engineering processes – particularly those used in industrial contexts. Because of their importance, this chapter describes examples of performance support within each of the above types of application area. It also describes their advantages and offers suggestions for developing appropriate technology-based support facilities within science and engineering settings.

The Unified Model of Performance Support

Originally, the concept of *performance support* was introduced to address problems associated with: improving the ease-of-use of technology-based systems, providing support for task performance and helping to facilitate learning processes. Keeping these requirements in mind, it is widely agreed that performance support systems should have three primary characteristics (Barker and Banerji, 1995):

- they should enable people to perform tasks quickly (because performance-enhancing tools should be able to provide integrated task structuring, data, knowledge and tools at the time of need);
- they should not tax the performer's memory, nor should they require performers to manipulate too many variables; and
- they should enable task completion with learning as a secondary consequence.

Based on the notion of a human-activity system (as described in Chapter 1 of this book), a *unified model of performance support* has been proposed (Banerji, 1999). A fundamental assumption that is inherent in this model is that the tasks to which it refers are all computer mediated. That is, the human activities involved are all 'routed' through appropriate computer and communication facilities. Bearing this in mind, it is important to realise that successful task completion depends on the permeability of the barriers that exist between the person involved in executing a task and the actual task that is being executed (see Figure 10.1).

To improve the permeability to the barriers depicted in this figure, effective performance support will invariably employ a broad range of processes, technologies and methods to support its users. Undoubtedly, the most effective performance support systems will be

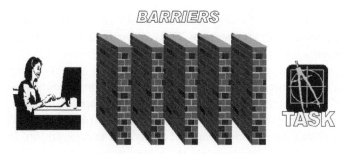

Figure 10.1 Barriers to performance

those that are designed around their users' needs and will thus involve user-centred design principles. Furthermore, such systems will embed processes of incremental improvement which enable continuous ongoing refinement – as a result of feedback relating to the target system's performance.

In a performance support system, many of the constraints imposed by the performance barriers described above can be reduced (if not entirely removed) by 'scaffolding' – that is, the provision of appropriate support infrastructures. Examples of these can be found in use in many diverse disciplines. Typical examples include business systems development, data modelling and processing, management information system design, executive information system design, decision support, expert systems, artificial intelligence, computer-based learning systems, multimedia systems, process modelling/re-engineering, and virtual representation – to name just a few. Generic support tools typically generated by these disciplines include the examples listed in Table 10.1. Within this table each column (A through F) represents a particular generic approach to providing a performance support solution. These six categories do, in fact, represent the complete performance support spectrum – from training to task-automation tools.

Table 10.1   The spectrum of performance support possibilities

A	B	C	D	E	F
Training, e-learning and just-in-time learning facilities	Infobases/ Reference/ Hypertext	Knowledge Management Systems	Workflow Management/ Process Support Tools	Decision Support Tools/Expert Systems	Process automation tools/ Job aids/ Wizards

Within the unified model, the concept of 'performance deficiency' is introduced. This is defined, for any given task-execution process, as the difference between the *ideal state* (excellent task completion) and the *actual state* (which a performer happens to be in during task execution):

$$performance\ deficiency = \{ideal\ state - actual\ state\}$$

Measuring the quantity (*ideal state – actual state*) is central to performance-problem analysis and identifying performance gaps. This requires monitoring the performance of those who solve problems and, where applicable, measuring the effect that their solutions have on overall organisational performance. In this context, the gap (and therefore performance deficiency) can be measured both in quantitative terms (*time, quality, error count, accident or failure rates* and *cost*) and in qualitative terms (*convenience* and *satisfaction level*) – both from the perspective of an employee/problem-solver and an employer/client. Of course, it is also important to consider the *resultant state* that arises after task execution. If, for some reason, it is not possible to achieve the *ideal state*, then the difference between the *resultant* and *ideal* states will reflect a shortfall in performance that may show up as a reduction in quality of the final outcome of task performance. For example, a swimmer who is not able to achieve a previously attained 'personal best' represents a shortfall in performance.

The barriers to performance depicted in Figure 10.1 can arise from a number of sources, for example:

- the gaps that exist in a person's knowledge of the work/problem space;
- a lack of access to relevant information and data;
- an inability to make accurate/correct decisions;
- a lack of understanding of workplace processes;
- an inability to establish personal/organisational goals; and
- an inability to solve problems within the work domain.

Within the context of a human-activity system, performance support can be thought of as a set of processes that are designed to improve the permeability of the performance barriers (see Figure 10.1) which a person encounters as they attempt to accomplish a problem-solving task. In most situations, effective performance support will depend critically upon a designer's ability to: (1) model the task in question; (2) build a profile of the person involved in performing the task; and (3) identify an appropriate performance-improvement intervention. It also involves measuring key performance indicators and using the results of these observations to provide continuously applied corrective actions that support the overall performance of the person who is executing the task. Naturally, improving the permeability of the performance barriers involves continuously measuring a problem-solver's state with respect to their position within the relevant task space. This may require, for example, measuring the time it takes for the person involved to discover a solution (to the problem in hand) plus the time it takes in order for that person to execute the actual solution that has been selected. During the task execution process, the support system must continually compare the actual current system state (at any particular time) with the ideal (target or sought-after) state – and then respond in an appropriate way by providing the information that is needed for emerging states of the system to map on to the ideal state – if indeed, this is feasible.

In many performance improvement situations, corrective action has to be applied in order to realise an improvement in behaviour – this is essentially a 'control situation' from the perspective of using an Electronic Performance Support System (EPSS). In most control situations, positive feedback is used to reinforce the direction of progress to which it refers. Similarly, negative feedback is used to inhibit progress in an incorrect direction. As depicted in Figure 10.2, negative feedback is used to prevent the onset of undesirable states. In this situation, negative feedback leads to corrective action.

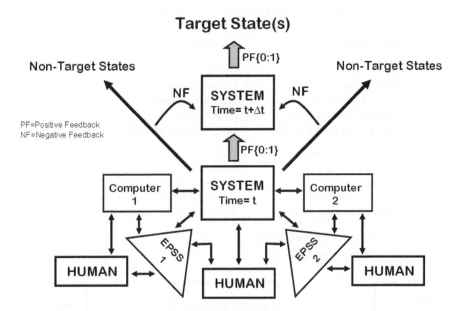

Figure 10.2 Human activity and the unified model of EPSS

Within any human-activity system to which performance support is being applied, it is important to consider the roles played by both the human and the computer components in relation to the realisation of the overall system goals. Thus, in a performance support situation, the human and computer components each represent resources that are available to augment the underlying host system. The ability of the augmented 'system' to complete tasks more accurately and efficiently depends on monitoring, feedback and the application of appropriately designed interventions. Therefore, performance support can be viewed as having been enacted by the unification of human and computer components. Of course, it is assumed that the human component is not fully competent in completing the task in an unaided way. The feedback loop helps to increase competence continuously. The *total* system performance therefore improves continuously – which means that the system's performance improves continuously. In this sense, the Unified Model is an adaptive model, with the human being a variable component. The human-computer collaboration inherent in Figure 10.2 (sometimes this is referred to as human-computer symbiosis) combines the strengths of both human and computer components (as listed in Table 10.2) to optimal advantage.

The forgoing discussion of the unified model of performance support is particularly relevant for the domain of science and engineering. In the following sections of this chapter, the underlying processes involved in science and engineering activities will be examined – with a view to discussing how these can be supported within the unified framework presented earlier in this section. The focus in these sections will therefore be to explore the aspects of performance problems relevant to science and engineering activities. Broadly, the performance problems for each of these domains are more or less similar – as shown in Figure 10.3. This diagram will be the starting point to investigate and reveal the aspects of support required for scientific activities.

Table 10.2   The properties of the primitive components of an EPSS system

	Strengths	Weaknesses
Humans	Pattern recognition Selective attention Capacity to learn Infinite LTM[b] capacity Multiple type data in LTM	Low STM[a] capacity Decaying memory Slow processing Error prone Unreliable access to LTM
Computers	High-capacity memory Permanent memory Fast processing Error-free processing Reliable memory access	Weak even in simple template matching Limited learning capacity Limited capacity LTM Limited data integration in decision making Inefficient pattern recognition

Source: Adapted from Banerji and Ghosh, 2010.

[a] Short-Term Memory; [b] Long-Term Memory.

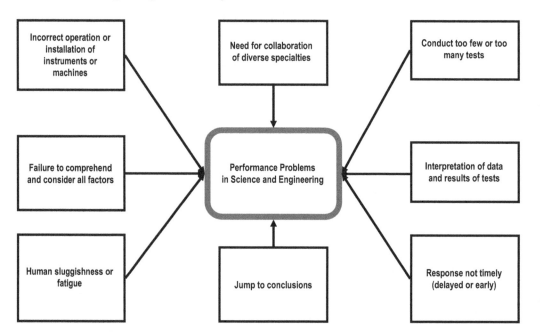

Figure 10.3 Performance problems in science and engineering practices

Performance Support in the Science Domain

Science is a branch of knowledge or study dealing with a body of facts or truths systematically arranged and showing the operation of general laws. It is systematic knowledge of the physical or material world gained through observation and experimentation.[1] Scientists create knowledge. They study the world and seek to understand and explain natural

---

1   Useful definitions of the terms 'science' and 'scientific method' can be found in online resources such as *http://dictionary.com* and *http://www.reference.com*.

phenomena. Thus scientists are trained in scientific methods which involve the design of experiments to test theories. This is a complex process because it does not always follow any fixed path. There are many possible strategies in any scientific investigation. However, it is evident that scientists build on previous work and current knowledge. For this reason, open communication among scientists is very important. In fact, three of the remarkable approaches and technologies developed in the last century were basically targeted at meeting this need. These involved: first, the concept of hypertext – proposed by Vannevar Bush (1945) – which evolved out of the need to promote information access between scientists engaged in nuclear research in the USA during the Second World War; second, the development of the Internet (Internet Society, 2007); and third; the subsequent creation of the World Wide Web. These latter two developments[2] also evolved out of the need to support collaborative communication between researchers and scientists (Berners-Lee, 1989).

Scientific activity usually involves searching for a cause for a given effect or phenomenon. The key steps involved in the process of science are: (a) making observations; (b) asking questions; (c) forming hypotheses; (d) making predictions; and (e) conducting tests or experiments. Often the first step in the scientific process is an observation of some phenomenon. The observation process then leads to a question such as 'Why did it do that?' or, 'What made that happen?' These questions might suggest an answer or an explanation. Any possible explanation is called a hypothesis. This process is often called inductive reasoning. Quite often a number of specific observations may lead to the formulation of a general hypothesis. If the hypothesis is sound, it should allow 'predictions' to be made. Thereafter, tests and/or experiments are performed to confirm the hypothesis or refine it further – based on the generalised results of the tests that are made. Finally, theories or laws can be formulated. The method of scientific investigation described above involves the application of five basic categories of scientific skill. These are listed in Table 10.3. The skills (and tasks) listed in this table form the foundation of problem solving in science and the underlying scientific methods that are employed.

Table 10.3   Categories of scientific skill and their associated tasks

Acquisitive	Organisational	Creative	Manipulative	Communicative
Listening	Recording	Planning ahead	Using instruments	Questioning
Observing	Comparing	Designing	Demonstrating	Discussing
Searching	Contrasting	Inventing	Experimenting	Explaining
Inquiring	Classifying	Synthesising	Constructing	Reporting
Investigating	Organising	Inferring	Calibrating	Writing
Gathering data	Outlining	Predicting	Measuring	Criticising
Researching	Reviewing	Hypothesising	Interpreting	Graphing
	Evaluating			Teaching
	Analysing			

Source: Adapted from Trowbridge et al., 2000; Bobrowsky, 2007.

---

2   The Internet is the name given to an international network of computer systems. Running on top of this underlying hardware/software configuration is a whole range of applications – one of which is the World Wide Web.

Communication among scientific communities is an essential part of the inquiry process. The values of independent thinking and reporting the results of observations and measurements are essential in this regard. Mental models of the thinking processes are an integral aspect of scientific inquiry. These processes include inductive reasoning, formulating hypotheses and theories, deductive reasoning – as well as the use of analogy, extrapolation, synthesis and evaluation. The choice of experiments (or models for exploration) and subsequent data collection, ordering, structuring and analysis of data are just some of the essential processes that can be facilitated through the appropriate use of the performance support techniques described in this chapter and elsewhere in this book. Indeed, computer-based support has become necessary for most of the tasks presented in Table 10.3 due to the increasing complexity of the science domain. Figure 10.4 illustrates some of the typical classes of performance problem that scientists often face. It also shows some of the possible causes of these problems and the types of support needed for solving performance problems in this area.

Information access, support for collaboration, decision support and experimental support for testing and calculation are the main areas of science where computers can be used to aid and facilitate the scientific skills and tasks shown in Table 10.3. The way in which scientific inference and decision making can be supported is illustrated by websites such as 'Which Test?' (*http://www.whichtest.info/index.html*) and 'The How To Guides' (*http://www.statsguides.bham.ac.uk/HTG/HTG_Home.htm*). These examples of performance support for statistical data analysis have been described earlier in Chapter 2 of this book.

Another example of how computers have become an essential tool in scientific exploration is the Human Genome Project (Braun et al., 2003). The objective of this project was to determine the complete nucleotide sequence of the human genome. This process involved approximately three billion nucleotides of the human genome. Addressing these challenges required the use of high-performance computing techniques (Braun et al., 2003). As a result of widespread international cooperation and advances in the field of genomics (especially in sequence analysis), as well as major advances in computing technology, a 'rough draft' of the genome was finished in the year 2000. There are currently hundreds of databases containing biological information that may contain data relevant to the identification of disease-causing genes. Interested readers will find detailed discussion of the computational process in the paper by Swidan et al. (2006). The genetic sequence of human DNA is now stored in databases that are available to anyone who has Internet access (see, for example, *http://www.ncbi.nlm.nih.gov*). These have been used in developing useful performance-enhancing tools that are now within easy reach of researchers in this area. An example of such a tool is the electronic Polymerase Chain Reaction (e-PCR). This PCR technique is now an absolutely routine component of practically every molecular-biology laboratory. e-PCR empowers scientists by providing them with a flexible alternative for the conventional method. It is a computational procedure that is used to identify Sequence-Tagged Sites (STSs) within DNA sequences (*http://www.ncbi.nlm.nih.gov/sutils/e-pcr/*). The *NCBI GenBank* is an excellent example of computer support for biologists and genetic scientists. Naturally, knowledge discovery using these databases holds enormous potential.

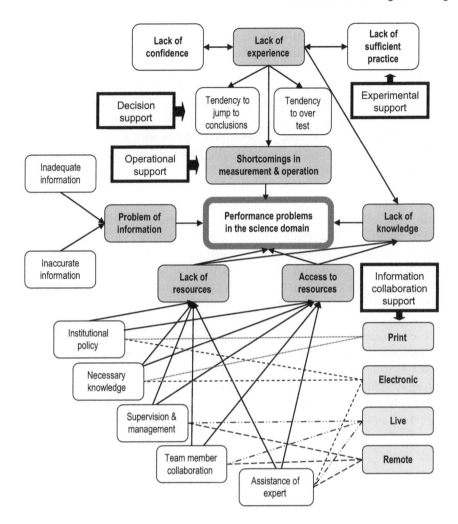

Figure 10.4 Typical performance problems arising in the science domain

Performance Support in the Engineering Domain

Originally, engineering meant the art of managing engines. In its modern and extended sense, engineering is the art and science by which the mechanical properties of matter are made useful to humans in structures and machines.[3] Indeed, according to Barker,[4] '*In its very broadest sense, the discipline of engineering is concerned with that body of knowledge (both theory and practice) that is relevant to the design and fabrication of real-world artefacts arising from human endeavour.*'

Engineering is a problem-driven discipline. Engineers apply the knowledge created by scientists and create engineering knowledge. They design and build devices or machines

---

3   A useful definition of the term 'engineering' and a description of the methods it employs can be found in online resources such as *http://dictionary.com* and *http://www.reference.com*.

4   This definition is based on a personal communication entitled 'On the Nature of Engineering' that was sent to Bani Battacharya and which was reproduced in a paper that was published in 2008 in the journal *Innovations in Education and Teaching International*, 45(2), p. 93.

and operate these for improving the quality of human life in general. With the development of human knowledge-engineering, engineering processes are also getting complex. In many situations, this has necessitated the use of human-computer symbiosis as well as computer-based process automation. In fact, the early references to performance support systems were concerned with supporting engineering processes such as: the Integrated Circuit (IC) chip manufacturing processes in Intel (Gery, 1991), the Service Diagnostic System in the Ford Motor Company (Bielawski and Lewand, 1991), just-in-time help in Renault (Pring, 1992) and the creation of simulation-based performance support tools for the marine industry (Banerji and Bhandari, 1997).

Broadly, engineering processes that often require support include activities such as design, development, operation, testing, fault diagnosis, repair and maintenance. In all these areas the chief concern is usually reducing the probabilities of error. Within many systems, errors can arise as a result of the inherent weaknesses of the human components of the system, for example, a lack of responsiveness ('sluggishness'), forgetfulness, inability to comprehend, and many others (such as those listed in Table 10.2). In particular, limitations in a human's ability to perceive, attend to, remember, process and act on information are all potential sources of error within systems in which there is a human element. Stranks (2006) outlines a number of factors which can contribute to human error. These include: *inadequate information, lack of understanding, inadequate design, lapses of attention, mistaken actions, misperceptions, mistaken priorities* and *wilfulness*. A diagram that illustrates some of the different types of performance problems that can arise within engineering systems is presented in Figure 10.5.

An appreciation of the causes of error is important because they are significant sources of performance problems, performance shortcomings and accidents in the workplace. It

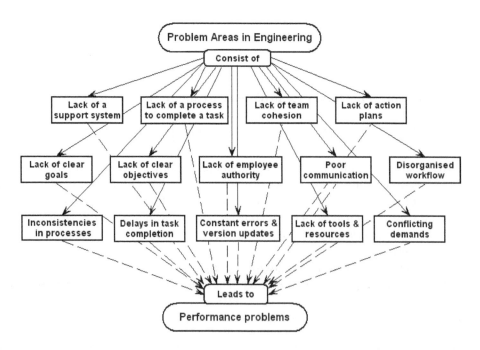

Figure 10.5 Potential application areas for performance support in engineering

has been estimated that up to 90 per cent of all workplace accidents arise as a result of human error (Feyer and Williamson, 1998). Bearing this in mind, performance support interventions for engineering processes will usually include strategies for reducing errors that arise from the following six sources: (1) learning-gap; (2) memory-gap; (3) inconsistency; (4) application; (5) decision making; and (6) omission. Performance support interventions for use in an engineering context could include appropriate combinations of the generic types of tool that were previously listed in Table 10.1.

Various computer-based performance-enhancing support systems for engineering applications are available from a number of different sources. For example, simulation tools like *MATLAB*[5] *(http://www.mathworks.com/)* and *LabVIEW (http://www.ni.com/labview)* and design tools such as *AutoCAD (http://www.autodesk.com)*, and many others, now greatly simplify the *design* process within engineering projects. In addition, many of these tools allow engineers to visualise new products and test their performance before actually building them. Another example, the *Supervisory Control And Data Acquisition* (SCADA) system greatly simplifies engineering-plant *operation*. Such systems collect data from various sensors at a factory, plant or other remote location and then send this data to a central computer which then manages and controls the plant while displaying data at a supervisory control desk. Engineering *maintenance* tasks are aided by *monitoring* the state of the equipment. For example, computer-based vibration analysis of rotating equipment alerts the operator about the possible need for preventive maintenance when the vibration goes beyond a set limit.

Fault diagnosis and repair is another class of problem that often challenges engineers. A typical fault diagnosis process is presented schematically in the diagram shown in Figure 10.6.

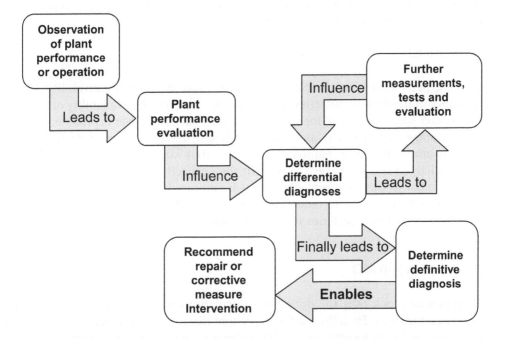

Figure 10.6 Flow diagram to facilitate problem diagnosis in a process plant

5   Please see also Chapter 13 in this volume for further details about applying performance support techniques when using MATLAB.

Depending upon the level of sophistication of the equipment involved, the diagnostic processes that need to be applied can become quite complex. In order to combat this complexity, most of the functions depicted in Figure 10.6 would be augmented through the use of appropriate performance support tools. As a way of facilitating this, a considerable amount of effort has been devoted to developing computer-based maintenance systems. One example of such a system is the *Advanced Integrated Maintenance Support System* (AIMSS) from Raytheon (*http://www.raytheon.com/capabilities/products/aimss/index.html*). AMISS is an Interactive Electronic Technical Manual (IETM) authoring tool set. It uses an object-oriented database that can store, retrieve and display information, data and documentation relating to the particular engineering systems for which it is being used. Diagnostic information that is needed by an engineer can be displayed on a workstation or on an engineer's personal computer. Systems of this sort can also be augmented by the use of an expert system, a decision support system, knowledge management tools and case-based reasoning techniques to create an integrated fault diagnosis system. Such a system could be based on the use of the unified performance support model that was described earlier in this chapter. The case study described in the next section will elaborate on this.

Case Study – Battery Maintenance

This case study illustrates how the ideas discussed in the previous parts of this chapter can be brought together to create an operational performance support system. The case study is based on the work of Gerald Damschen (2008) as related to the author of this chapter, while Damschen was a student at Jones International University.[6]

BACKGROUND

As a young petty officer in the Navy, Damschen was assigned responsibility for the maintenance of the back-up batteries on a nuclear submarine. The availability of a reliable back-up power source is critical for ships of this sort. Back-up power is provided by large powerful storage batteries that are carried on-board the ship. These batteries require continuous monitoring and maintenance so that they stay at peak capacity. They are frequently charged and discharged to prevent their capacity loss. The underlying reason for this is similar to the 'memory' effect (that is commonly seen in rechargeable laptop batteries) which causes severe reduction in their capacity. Each charge and discharge cycle of the submarine's batteries requires numerous calculations to characterise their condition.

DEVELOPING A JOB AID

When Damschen took over the duties, the calculations were performed manually and recorded in a log book. He followed the procedure like many of the petty officers before him but soon he began looking for an alternative way to perform the tedious calculation

---

6   Further details about the history and current role of Jones International University are given in the *Wikipedia* online encyclopaedia at: *http://en.wikipedia.org/wiki/Jones_International_University*. [Accessed: 29th January, 2009].

tasks that sometimes had to be carried out multiple times a day. As a solution he wrote a simple computer program to do the calculations on a personal computer. This allowed him to enter all of the measurements that had been taken; it would then display them on the computer's screen so that he could verify their correctness. Thereafter, the computer program performed various calculations which were previously done manually. Thus he off-loaded the calculation tasks to the computer. This decreased the possibility of calculation errors, freed him of the time that was earlier required for calculations and made him more efficient since the task could be completed more quickly. Thus, in its first incarnation, Damschen's battery calculation program was a simple procedural *job aid* serving as a performance support tool.

AN INFORMATION MANAGEMENT TOOL

As the ship's batteries were nearing the end of their normal life, he had to monitor them more closely. Often he had to respond to the Captain's critical questions and submit details of the batteries' conditions and their performance trends. Answering these questions required going through historical data, searching through the battery log and performing additional calculations. To simplify these tasks he wrote another computer program to store the results of the calculations to a disk and display the data as graphs for easy visualisation of the trends. This allowed him to retrieve data as needed for whatever period, present these in the required format and observe the trend. Thus, in its second incarnation the battery calculation *job aid* became a simple *information management system* that stored information about the ship's batteries and helped in task performance.

A KNOWLEDGE MANAGEMENT SYSTEM

Satisfied with the results of the battery monitoring program and its ability to easily identify trends, Damschen began to look for reasons for the trends. At one point he found that part of the battery was not performing as well as the rest. While looking for the reason he could not make sense of the readings. Finally, he realised that the information about the different battery blocks as recorded and displayed on the screen of his computer was actually different from the way the batteries were physically installed. The discrepancy looked somewhat similar to the location arrangement shown in Figure 10.7 (a) and (b).

Thus, correspondence of the physical location of the batteries with those used for analysis caused confusion. To solve this problem, Damschen added another component to his program; this created three-dimensional graphs of the parameters ordered in the way the battery parts were physically installed in the ship (Figure 10.7b). With this revision, the location and cause of reduced capacity became visually clear – there was a problem with the part of the system that kept the battery acid mixed. The graph showed the exact location of the problem and indicated which one needed to be fixed. In addition to the revised display, he added another component to the program for storing notes, observations and experiences. So, in the third incarnation, the *information management system* evolved into a *knowledge management system* supporting the battery maintenance and monitoring task.

1	2	3	4	5
6	7	8	9	10

(a)

1	2	8	7	5
10	9	3	4	6

(b)

Figure 10.7 (a) Location arrangement of batteries as recorded and displayed on the computer screen and (b) the actual physical location arrangement of the batteries

THE FINAL ELECTRONIC PERFORMANCE SUPPORT SYSTEM

Eventually, when it was time for Damschen to leave the ship he gave the final touch to the system by adding additional components to the program. He knew that his replacement would not have much time to learn about the battery system before taking over the duties so he made a digital battery manual which could be easily searched and referred to; it could also provide a quick 'newcomer' orientation. Damschen also converted the troubleshooting section of the manual into electronic form and linked it to the calculation program. He created triggers in the program to alert its user to any out-of-specification readings discovered during the calculations. The software could then 'step' the user through the appropriate troubleshooting process to correct the problem. So finally, the knowledge management and performance support system became a full-featured *EPSS* that incorporated information support, procedural support and support for decision making, coaching, learning and job aids.

The benefit of the program was acknowledged by the ship's Captain who remarked that the battery maintenance system had added several months to the life of the ship's batteries and allowed the submarine to meet additional commitments that would not have been possible otherwise. The improved performance saved the Navy several million dollars by not having to take the vessel out of service prematurely in order to replace its batteries.

EPILOGUE

The system worked very well for Damschen because it was designed to perform tasks he needed to do – in the way that he preferred to do them. He visited the ship a little over a year after his transfer. He enquired how his successor was using the battery maintenance system – a system that he developed so elaborately. To his surprise the reply was that his replacement had not used it because he was not comfortable with computers. Moreover, he did not have time to learn how to use it, and he did not really see much use for it anyway. Thus, a very well-developed performance support system was left unused!

The EPSS was designed by the user around his work process but it was not made a part of the work-process policy. The subsequent user did not have any input into the design of the software, therefore, he did not understand how it could help him. Also, he was not motivated to work differently, unlike his predecessor. The software was not designed around its user, and in the absence of management policy, it went unused and was discarded. By not involving all the possible users, the design was not user-centered.

Thus a successful system had fallen victim to the common problem of EPSS design and implementation.

THE MORAL OF THE STORY

When planning for the integration of an EPSS into the daily life of workers, it is crucial to begin with a user-centred approach and involve users early and often in the process of designing the EPSS. Adopting such an approach is likely to minimise misconceptions about the intended uses and roles of the EPSS.

Conclusion

Great breakthroughs in science are made through systems of scientific enquiry. These have led to new ways of thinking about and understanding both the natural and artificial systems that make up the Universe. Undoubtedly, advances in science have helped to address many of the problems encountered in (and have contributed to) the development of engineering and technological practices. As the complexities of both science and engineering processes have increased, the need for computer support – both as a means of understanding them and of controlling them – has become very evident. Indeed, without the synergy that exists between computers and human minds, many of the scientific and engineering feats that have been achieved in the modern world would not have been accomplished. However, most of these developments have evolved as a consequence of attempting to use available technology in an ad-hoc way to meet performance needs. These developments have lacked a coherent and integrated design framework – similar to that which is embedded in the unified model of performance support that has been outlined in this chapter.

Because of the potential that it has as a basis for designing EPSS, this chapter has reviewed the unified model of the performance support concept and has illustrated areas in which the model may be used. In order to do this, the characteristic processes involved in scientific investigations have been identified and examples have been given of how computer-based performance support tools may contribute to the different activities involved in this domain. A similar approach was then adopted for the characteristic activities involved in the engineering domain. Finally, a simple case study was then presented to illustrate the way in which an EPSS can evolve in an incremental fashion using a step-by-step engineering approach.

Of course, it is important to realise that the type of performance support that is used in the science domain is fundamentally different from that required in engineering. This is due to the nature of the activities involved and the people who participate in them. Scientific activities mainly require knowledge and information support. However, the activities involved in engineering often require a wider range of support functions – because the target users range from 'white collar' to 'blue collar' – each varying in knowledge and skill levels. Naturally, in situations of this sort, appropriate performance support design would benefit from the application of the unified support model together with a judicious mix of the toolsets listed in Table 10.1 (p. 195). To facilitate this objective, the set of ten EPSS design principles identified by Barker and Banerji (1995) and Banerji and Scales (2005) may prove useful. Eventually, this may lead to the vision of HAL (Clarke,

1968) as a ubiquitous performance support environment, reducing, if not eliminating, every possible performance gap within a given target system.

Acknowledgements

The author is indebted to Philip Barker and Paul van Schaik for their help in relation to writing and completing the manuscript upon which this chapter is based.

References

Banerji, A. (1999). Performance Support in Perspective. *Performance Improvement Quarterly*, 38(7), 6–9. Available online at: *http://www.pcd-innovations.com/piaug99/PSinPerspective.pdf*. [Accessed on: 27th January, 2009].

Banerji, A. and Bhandari, R. (1997). Designing EPSS for the Marine Industry. *International Conference on Computers in Education*, December 2–6, 1997, Kuching, Sarawak, Malaysia. Available online at: *http://www.sp.edu.sg/resources/images/schools/sma/papers/epss.pdf* [Accessed on: 29th January, 2009].

Banerji, A. and Ghosh, A.M. (2010). *Multimedia Technologies* (Chapter 13). New Delhi, India: Tata McGraw Hill.

Banerji, A. and Scales, G.R. (2005). Interactive Multimedia for Learning and Performance. In S. Mishra and R.C. Sharma (eds), *Interactive Multimedia in Education and Training* (pp 47–59). Hershey, PA: IGI Publishing.

Barker, P. and Banerji, A. (1995). Designing Electronic Performance Support Systems. *Innovations in Training Technology International*, 32(1), 4–12.

Berners-Lee, T. (1990). Information Management: A Proposal. CERN March 1989, May 1990, W3 Archive. Available online at: *http://www.nic.funet.fi/index/FUNET/history/internet/w3c/proposal.html*. [Accessed on: 29th January, 2009].

Bielawski, L. and Lewand, R. (1991). *Intelligent Systems Design – Integrating Expert Systems, Hypermedia, and Database Technologies*. New York, NY: John Wiley and Sons.

Bobrowsky, M. (2007). *The Process of Science and its Interaction with Non-Scientific Ideas*. Washington DC: The American Astronomical Society. Available online at: *http://aas.org/files/The_Process_of_Science.pdf*. [Accessed on: 29th January, 2009].

Braun, T.A., Scheetz, T.E., Webster, G., Clark, A., Stone, E.M., Sheffield, V.C. and Casavant, T.L. (2003). Identifying Candidate Disease Genes with High-Performance Computing. *The Journal of Supercomputing*, 26(1), 7–24.

Bush, V. (1945). As We May Think. *Atlantic Monthly*, July issue. Available online at: *http://www.theatlantic.com/doc/194507/bush* [Accessed on: 29th January, 2009].

Clarke, A.C. (1968). *2001: A Space Odyssey*. New York, NY: The New American Library.

Damschen, G.A. (2008). *Designing Information and Performance Support Systems*. EDU652 Course project for the M.Ed programme. Centennial, CO: Jones International University.

Feyer, A.M. and Williamson, A.M. (1998). Human Factors in Accident Modelling. In Stellman, J.M. (ed.), *Encyclopaedia of Occupational Health and Safety, Fourth Edition*. Geneva: International Labour Organisation.

Gery, G.J. (1991). *Electronic Performance Support Systems – How and Why to Remake the Workplace Through Strategic Application of Technology*. Boston, MA: Weingarten Publications.

Internet Society (2007). Histories of the Internet. Available online at: *http://www.isoc.org/internet/history/* [Accessed on: 30th January, 2009].

National Center for Biotechnology Information (NCBI) Details available online at: *http://www.ncbi.nlm.nih.gov/*. [Accessed on: 30th January, 2009].

Pring, I. (1992). *Digital Vision DVI Project Directory*. London, UK: Digital Vision International.

Stranks, J. (2006). *Health and Safety Handbook: A Practical Guide to Health and Safety Law, Management Policies and Procedures*. London: Kogan Page.

Swidan, F., Rocha, E., Shmoish, M. and Pinter, R. (2006). An Integrative Method for Accurate Comparative Genome Mapping. *PLoS Computational Biology*, 2(8): e75. Available online at: *http://www.ploscompbiol.org/article/info%3Adoi%2F10.1371%2Fjournal.pcbi.0020075*. [Accessed on: 26th September, 2009].

Trowbridge, L., Bybee, R. and Powell, J. (2000). *Teaching Secondary School Science: Strategies for Developing Scientific Literacy*. UpperSaddle River, NJ: Prentice-Hall. [Cited in *Building Science Process Skills* by A.V. DeFina, The Science Teacher, January 2006, 36–41.]

11 *Business and Commerce*

BARRY IP

The aim of this chapter is to examine the increasing permeance of Electronic Performance Support Systems (EPSS) from previously standalone entities into new and exciting applications in the world of business and commerce. The first section provides a brief overview of EPSS and related tools, including, where available, specific examples within business and commerce. This is followed by a discussion of the impact of EPSS systems on those who employ their use in terms of planning, management and evaluation. The last section explores emerging avenues of development, with particular emphasis on the growth of new technology and ubiquitous computing, and their contribution towards expanding the provision of computer-based systems for performance improvement.

Overview of Electronic Performance Support Systems in Business and Commerce

As mentioned in Chapter 1 (p. 23), EPSS is underpinned by the fundamental aim of performance improvement, of which there are three basic measures: quantity of output, financial income and customer-satisfaction. For businesses, these parameters may be extended to include other relevant aspects such as the quality of service and/or products, operational efficiency, customer retention and market share, all of which provide a strong motivation for the development of increasingly sophisticated EPSS and EPSS-related tools. Performance support has been defined as: 'A helper in life and work, performance support is a repository for information, processes and perspectives that inform and guide planning and action' (Rossett and Schafer, 2007: p. 2), but, more specifically in this book as '[...] computer-based systems that are intended to improve the performance of human beings within some particular task domain' (Barker, Chapter 1: p. 27).

In the context of computer-based performance support, numerous advances have taken place to facilitate heightened performance. In commerce, the use of Business Information Systems (BIS) is, of course, well documented. The general spectrum of BIS incorporates the principal areas of transaction processing, management information, decision support, executive information, end-user information and special-purpose applications (such as virtual reality, artificial intelligence and expert systems) (Bocij et al., 1999: pp. 31–4; Regan and O'Connor, 2002: p. 12; Stair and Reynolds, 2001: pp. 20–6, 29–30). However, the purpose of BIS is not necessarily that of performance enhancement, but rather to offer a set of interrelated components to support the collection, manipulation and dissemination of data (Bocij et al., 1999: p. 27; Stair and Reynolds, 2001: p. 4). Hence, while BIS facilitate across numerous business processes, EPSS is distinguished on the basis that it offers a richer integration of information, tools and methodology in a specific domain (Gery, 1991: p. 34; Regan and O'Connor, 2002: p. 181; Rossett and Schafer, 2007: p. 17). One major advantage of EPSS is considered to be its ability to deliver dynamic, context-specific training, especially for complex jobs requiring high levels of expertise (see Karat, 1997; Regan and O'Connor, 2002: p. 181, pp. 242–4). Similarly, Regan and O'Connor (2002: pp. 242–4) situate EPSS as one of two methods (the other being that of 'live', help-desk systems) which offer a just-in-time, context-sensitive mode of learning. These viewpoints are reinforced by the application of EPSS in specific learning environments, as documented in the seminal work of Gery (1991: pp. 53–178), where numerous case studies highlight the use of EPSS to deliver performance improvements for a range of companies. Further in-depth studies have since been conducted to demonstrate the use of EPSS to help improve work performance in factories (Ockerman et al., 1999), aircraft management (Winslow and Caldwell, 1992), coastguard leadership (Rossett and Schafer, 2007: pp. 11–3) and general on-the-job training (Ryan, 1995; Rossett and Schafer, 2007: pp. 9–11), thus underlining the flexibility of EPSS to be adapted for a variety of complex situations.

Beyond training applications, EPSS has been used to aid creativity and decision making. Brusilovsky and Cooper (2002) describe the use of an 'intelligent' EPSS which combines online information with problem-solving features. The system, named *ADAPTS* (Adaptive Diagnostics and Personalised Technical Support), enables maintenance technicians to troubleshoot and determine informed actions for complex machinery. Similarly, Francisco-Revilla and Shipman (2000) outline an adaptive medical EPSS to help users with varying ability to gain knowledge about medical procedures and aid in their diagnosis of illnesses (a more extensive overview of medical applications of EPSS can be found in Chapter 9). As for creative applications of EPSS, these have been evidenced in New Product Development (NPD) (Massey et al., 2002) and in the assistance of technicians during computer-aided design (Rossett and Schafer, 2007: pp. 194–5). In particular, Massey et al. (2002) demonstrated how EPSS could be used to systematically integrate and structure knowledge-intensive, ill-structured processes (here, in the context of NPD, which requires the use of information and knowledge in creative ways) to enhance all aspects of business performance.

The unique feature amongst these examples is the extent to which EPSS utilises, typically, cutting-edge computer and multimedia technology to enhance users' performance. This intricate link between technology and delivery of performance benefits thus requires users and usability issues to be taken firmly into account (see Chapters 1 and 2), a point which has been acknowledged by numerous researchers in the field. Both Gery (1997) and Karat (1997) describe numerous commonalities between EPSS and user-centred design, but the need to incorporate context- and task-relevant systems which, in turn, offer tools and present information in such a way to enhance performance, makes EPSS, at the very least, a more complex design proposition. Such is the significance of end-users and usability, that Regan and O'Connor (2002: pp. 10–11) consider performance support tools to be a subset of End-User Information Systems (EUIS). EUIS encompass text and data handling software, multimedia/graphic design, communication tools, collaborative systems, time and knowledge management systems, and, of course, dedicated performance support systems, all of which are aimed at enhancing various aspects of workers' performance, and require careful planning and design.

Planning, Management and Evaluation of Electronic Performance Support Systems iIn Business and Commerce

The above examples draw attention to the complexities involved in the design, development and implementation of EPSS, the challenges of which place a considerable impact on decision makers and potential users, as the failure of an EPSS project will not only culminate in a failure to enhance performance, but is likely to incur valuable time and resources. Consequently, it may not come as a great surprise that there are often reports of uncertainty over proposals to embark on new EPSS projects. The research of Bastiaens (1999) and Bastiaens et al. (1995) highlights numerous problems encountered during the application of EPSS. Although this research was based on relatively small studies and some marked benefits of EPSS were observed, the findings warn against expectations that EPSS will necessarily lead to positive results. Some of the key concerns reported include the system's potential lack of a clear focus, a relatively limited use of in-built help features, the feeling from users that EPSS should only assist in performance enhancement and that the system should not replace any provisions for human support or intervention (Bastiaens, 1999; Bastiaens et al., 1995). However, the broader issue highlighted by Bastiaens (1999) and Desmarais et al. (1997) is that more research and evidence is needed to validate the true effectiveness of EPSS.

In response to these reservations, others have pointed towards a more thorough planning procedure and the need for EPSS to be linked directly to a company's change-management philosophy. Gery (1991: pp. 195–204, 214–30), Benko and Webster (1997) and Bezanson (2002: pp. 32–5, 113–20) chart, in detail, the various stages and key roles for the planning and implementation of EPSS, including the need for the involvement of instructional designers, technical analysts, online developers, programmers, graphic artists, quality assurance specialists and subject experts. An extensive methodology is also proposed by Goodman (1998), developed at SmithKline Beecham, which stresses the need for performance support measures (in general) to be integrated with change management, particularly with the view to encourage the adoption of new technologies in the case of EPSS. A similar approach is fervently promoted by Rossett and Schafer (2007: pp. 178–82), which suggests that the strategies of change management for performance support should include the following:

1. State the advantages – including a justification for the new system, how it will make a difference to the company and workers, organisational fit (does the system serve a clear purpose?) and a demonstration of successful applications in similar contexts.
2. Establish compatibility of the proposed system with company strategy and workers' requirements, and the degree of integration with existing company systems, procedures and working practices.
3. Simplify the system – any proposed performance support system (especially electronic systems) must be easy to use, contain easy-to-understand language and terminology, and offer appropriate guidance to users and monitoring of progress.
4. Test the system – this should be carried out regularly and by the target users to highlight areas for improvement.
5. Communicate the impact of the system to the company. This is to ensure that everyone in the company is aware of the benefits of the new system and to encourage feedback for further improvements.

Concomitantly, Wisener (2002) reiterates many of the above points specifically in the context of EPSS. Wisener provides a broad summary of the common barriers against the adoption of EPSS, and claims that organisations are often resistant to change because key decision makers are not always fully aware of the benefits of performance support systems. Amongst the proposals to help overcome the barriers to EPSS, Wisener (2002) and Massey et al. (2002) urge businesses with the view of using EPSS to make a clear financial and strategic case with which to present to decision makers. By emphasising the positive links between human performance and business output, especially via the use of accounting and performance measures for intangible assets such as return on investment, cost-benefit analysis and an assessment of a firm's human-resource competencies (see Beatty et al., 2003; Bezanson, 2002: pp. 58–60; Desmarais et al., 1997; Driscoll and Hynes, 2002; Wisener, 2002) planners will be able to demonstrate the inherent value of EPSS to senior management, and to therefore spark the process of change.

Beyond financial and strategic evaluations, other methods have been offered to provide a more contextual analysis of EPSS. Gery (2002) recommends that Performance-Centred Systems (PCS) (in general) or EPSS should be evaluated in the context and situations in which they are used. Here, four dimensions of evaluation are of significance: performance support tools offered by the system, reference material provided by the system, the provision of instructional courses to promote learning and the system's ability to encourage users to collaborate with others to gain information, solve problems and create new challenges. So, in addition to financial and performance measures, a well-supported case for the introduction of EPSS is likely to include extensive insight into the specific design of the system, and, where possible, a demonstration of how the benefits will be delivered in practice.

A broader reflection of the potential impact of EPSS may also be derived from the work of Mudambi et al. (1997). As mentioned earlier in this chapter, three of the basic measures of performance are defined as quantity of output, financial income and customer-satisfaction. Up to this point, the evaluative approaches considered relate predominantly to the assessment of output and/or income. In contrast, the element of customer-satisfaction is critical for not only helping companies maintain their customer-base, but also to enhance value in the eyes of consumers, especially in homogeneous markets where products and/or services may be difficult to differentiate between competitors. Yet somewhat conspicuously, customer-satisfaction has received comparatively little research with respect to EPSS. Nevertheless, Mudambi et al. (1997) propose that a company's performance comprises of four parts (company-performance, product-performance, distribution-performance and support-services-performance), which together contribute towards customers' perception of the company or brand. For each part, a further distinction is made between tangible and intangible attributes which a firm may directly influence to enhance brand value. Rossett and Schafer (2007: pp. 133–4) also highlight how specific customers may be targeted using performance support systems, such as the recording of customers' preferences to enable companies to produce personalised recommendations to inform customers about new product lines (an issue which will be explored further in the next section).

In summary, EPSS or PCS (in general) requires a myriad of factors to be considered, from planning to evaluation, design to formulating new strategy, such that the chosen performance measure (output, income, customer-satisfaction, quality of product and/or service, customer retention and so on) may be suitably enhanced. The following section examines some emerging developments in EPSS and how they contribute towards the added provision of performance support for the benefit of businesses and, in particular, general consumers.

Emerging Developments in Electronic Performance Support Systems for Business and Commerce

So far, the examples presented in this chapter have outlined applications of EPSS and general PCS in largely traditional and established business contexts. However, recent technological advances (especially those fuelled by the phenomenon of ubiquitous computing, as described in Chapter 1) will enable EPSS to expand beyond conventional boundaries. The widespread adoption of portable devices such as laptop computers, personal digital assistants (PDAs), mobile phones, *iPods*, MP3 players and games consoles, combined with the increasing availability and convenience of Internet access opens up a wealth of possibilities for businesses and the wider public. In addition to affording users with greater flexibility and access to online resources, new technologies have the potential to allow more enjoyable user-experiences to be created, particularly in terms of the ability for consumers to gather and use information on demand, facilitating interaction between users across social networks and the customisation of these technologies according to the specific requirements of users. Consequently, the increasing possibilities offered by a range of existing and emerging technologies are likely to lead to significant improvements in the use of EPSS for the enhancement of customer-satisfaction.

Two recent examples where ubiquitous technology (also referred to as pervasive and persistent computing) has been adapted to offer clear and direct performance benefits include Radio-Frequency Identification (RFID) and Global Positioning Systems (GPS). Their application in business contexts has been described as belonging to a broader concept known as ubiquitous commerce (u-commerce) (Lee et al., 2007; Watson et al., 2002), defined as: 'The use of ubiquitous networks to support personalised and uninterrupted communications and transactions between an organisation and its various stakeholders to provide a level of value over, above and beyond traditional commerce' (Watson et al., 2002: p. 332).

RFID entails minute memory chips embedded into physical objects to enable data contained in them to be captured by a reading device. The introduction of RFID in a commercial context has largely been met with enthusiasm, a point illustrated by its adoption across a broad range of areas including tourism (Hsi and Fait, 2005), education (Yoder, 2006), healthcare (Miller et al., 2006; Wu et al., 2005) and, of course, business (see, for example, Jurishica and Schwieters, 2004; Niederman et al., 2007; Ruta et al., 2007). Among the benefits, RFID's most significant contribution to date appears to be that of enhancing supply-chain performance in terms of providing a more dynamic method of stock control, efficient use of warehouse/storage space, and reducing time and labour requirements (see Bendavid et al., 2006; Lee et al., 2004; Niederman et al., 2007; Simchi-Levi et al., 2004: pp. 256–7).

Similar levels of dramatic growth have also been observed in the use of GPS technology, especially in the field of consumer transport and transport management (Rocha et al., 2007; Stopher et al., 2007; Taylor et al., 2000). The performance benefits of GPS are illustrated in no better way than through its importance in a military context, from where the technology originates, to enable various forms of military equipment (such as land vehicles, ships, aircrafts and missiles) to be tracked and located with great precision – for a history of GPS, see Pace (1996), Shaw (2004) and Theiss et al. (2005). Outside military uses, GPS expanded into commercial applications in the early 1990s from where it began to transform into an accessible, everyday tool as evidenced by its application in industries including logistics (for stacking problems in warehouses and deployment of public transport), security (for tracking of sensitive or potentially dangerous material), marketing (for time and consumer-sensitive advertising) and banking (for the synchronisation of transactions across multiple branches) (Theiss et al., 2005). However, primarily in the form of satellite navigation systems (as described in Chapter 4), the technology is becoming a highly desirable and affordable feature in modern cars due to the clear performance benefits afforded to general consumers, which range from relatively simple route finding to the avoidance of congestion hot spots. With the expected rise in its adoption, numerous initiatives have been proposed and implemented by governments to use GPS for traffic control and to help alleviate congestion problems (BBC, 2007; Rincon, 2005).

But despite the marked benefits of these new technologies, the ubiquitous nature of RFID and GPS (specifically) and u-commerce (in general) have raised concerns in relation to consumers' privacy and the potential abuse of personal data gathered using pervasive technology (Eckfeldt, 2005; Günther and Spiekermann, 2005; Lee et al., 2007; Ohkubo et al., 2005). According to Roussos and Moussouri (2004), consumers' concerns can reside in any of three areas: continuous and unwarranted monitoring of consumption patterns, direct marketing (such as targeted junk mail, unwanted advertising and other invasions of privacy) and the use of data for personalisation (that is, information about a person's private life may be captured without their knowledge or consent). Hence, despite the clear benefits to companies which employ the use of u-commerce applications and related technologies, businesses must develop careful approaches for implementation, and ensure consumers are made aware of the use of any ubiquitous technology and be offered the choice to deny participation (see Greenfield, 2006: pp. 246–7). Unlike traditional performance support systems which may be chiefly focused on enhancing business performance, the wider implications of the expansion of technology into the everyday lives of consumers (as in the case of u-commerce) necessitates a delicate balance between corporate and financial benefits on the one hand, and personal privacy and consumers' acceptance on the other.

U-commerce aside, other notable developments have taken place for the enhancement of customer-services and for the creation of richer interactive experiences for consumers. Information kiosks are an example of where multimedia technology has been employed in a range of scenarios to supplement numerous business services. Borchers et al. (1995) offer a useful categorisation of kiosks according to their primary function, which may be providing information or a service, delivering advertising or offering entertainment. A further taxonomy is also offered by Rowley and Slack (2007), which examines the design and use of kiosks according to their location, the type of user they hope to attract, key tasks and the technology used. In business, the vast majority of multimedia-based kiosks are used to provide information to customers, which firmly situates their use within the context of performance support. The most common applications of information kiosks include trade exhibitions to provide details about product-lines (Guinn and Hubal, 2004), and airports and cities to provide public transport and tourist information (see Johnston and Bangalore, 2004; Slack and Rowley, 2002) but these have been further extended to health centres and hospitals to provide information and advice on medical issues (Nicholas et al., 2002, 2004), as well to the wider community (such as employment, shopping and community centres) to enhance social inclusion and the public's access to information (Boudioni, 2003). Being aimed at a wide range of users, and particularly the general public (some of whom may have little or no IT knowledge), multimedia kiosks represent a highly demanding challenge for businesses which employ them, as they must be designed to be user-friendly and intuitive whilst also providing key information about products or services.

Another effective approach for the enhancement of user-experiences is the use of web-based chat applications for live customer-service. Here, established tools such as *MSN Messenger*, *ICQ* and *Skype* are used by companies to provide consumers with speedy and direct access to help services (Saha et al., 2003; Stockburger and Fernandez, 2002; Totty, 2004). Instant chat facilities can also make the general process of customer-service appear more seamless and user-friendly to consumers (Qiu and Benbasat, 2005; Stockburger and Fernandez, 2002; Van Slyke et al., 2004). The recent emergence of Web 2.0 is also significant, as it incorporates a multitude of dynamic, user-centred applications such as social networking (for example, *Facebook*, *MySpace*, *Bebo*), personal blogs, user-generated content and file sharing (O'Reilly, 2005). These, coupled with the delivery of content via digital, online distribution for products previously sold only through tangible formats such as music, film and games, have contributed towards richer interactive experiences for consumers. In terms of performance improvement, these applications (information kiosks, live chat, Web 2.0 and so on) offer users, at the very least, complete flexibility to access relevant, domain-specific (and typically, free) information which, in turn, can contribute towards enhancing memory, knowledge and motivational shortcomings (see Chapter 1). And while these tools do not necessarily teach users any new skills (in contrast to some of the examples given in the section entitled 'Overview of electronic performance support systems in business and commerce'), they each demonstrate certain characteristics which define performance support systems, outlined by Bezanson (2002, p. 15, pp. 104-8) and Gery (1995), which include intuitive design, the ability to obtain immediate performance benefits, and/or features that enable task automation and system customisation.

From a commercial standpoint, there is great potential for these new technologies to become even more integrated into business practices. Instances where this is becoming a reality can be found in the development of virtual worlds, usually in the form of three-dimensional, interactive environments. The emergence of 'serious games' – that is, games designed strictly for training and simulation purposes, not entertainment (Narayanasamy et al., 2006; Raybourn, 2007; *www.seriousgames.org*) – is a prime example of highly realistic, game-like software which resides at the cutting-edge of EPSS technology. While the use of serious games is, at present, largely confined to educational, military and health applications, the technology on which these games are produced is commercially available to general users in the form of PCs and games consoles. Via these platforms, commercial developments such as Nintendo's motion sensing interface on the *Wii*, Sony's recently released *Home* on the *PlayStation 3* and Microsoft's *Xbox LIVE Marketplace* open up a breadth of new features for consumers. These range from games such as *Trauma Center*, based on performing surgical procedures, and *Fit*, which promotes general health and fitness (both on *Wii*) to general-purpose features for social interaction, entertainment and shopping (*Home*, *LIVE Marketplace* and *Wii Channel*). Developments such as these firmly illustrate the rapid growth of mass-market, interactive applications for a range of performance-related benefits, but perhaps more importantly, begin to establish stronger and clearer links between business- and customer-focused applications of EPSS.

Figure 11.1 provides an overall reflection on the main issues explored in this chapter, encompassing design, evaluative and planning procedures in relation to the goal of performance improvement.

Conclusion

This chapter has presented a broad overview of EPSS in business and commerce. One of the most telling observations is the apparent polarisation of EPSS between business- and customer-focused applications. It appears that the majority of EPSS or PCS can be

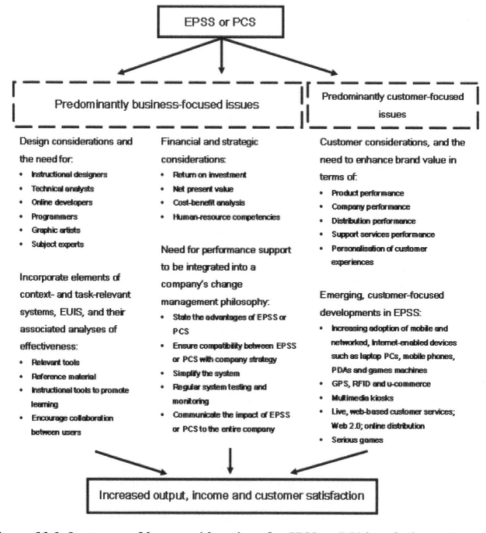

Figure 11.1 Summary of key considerations for EPSS or PCS in relation to performance improvement

placed neatly into two main categories: those which contribute towards increased output and/or income, and those for the enhancement of customers' satisfaction. However, the emergence of new technologies and innovative applications are allowing the principal components of performance improvement to become more integrated, such that a broader range of benefits may be delivered to both businesses and general consumers. The increasing development and uptake of interactive applications which encourage the production and sharing of creative content by users (such as social networking and content-sharing websites, and interactive games) stimulates alternative and exciting ways for businesses to communicate to their customers, as well as greater freedom in terms of how products and services can be marketed to target audiences.

However, new possibilities will also bring about fresh challenges. Design, strategic, financial and customer-related considerations aside, businesses must give greater consideration to the wider impact of new technologies. As in the case of online distribution, the ramifications have already caused seismic changes to the way in which the music sector operates, as witnessed in cases surrounding file sharing and the rapidly declining sales of traditional CDs (see BBC, 2008; Lam and Tan, 2001; Premkumar, 2003) and in the case of u-commerce, businesses must take great care to inform users about any collection and use of personal information. From a design perspective, EPSS can continue to exert its influence by maintaining its ability to provide increasingly seamless yet effective resources (and where possible, clear performance benefits) to all users. Here, the term 'obvious product' has been coined by Bezanson (2002: pp. 15–6) to emphasise one of EPSS' essential characteristics of delivering intuitive and accessible support tools to end-users – a characteristic reinforced by the majority of the examples presented in this chapter. EPSS designers and practitioners must therefore be cautious not to overlook these issues, as poorly designed applications will, in some cases, actually impede rather than enhance users' performance (Rossett and Schafer, 2007: pp. 201–2).

On an even broader scale, future developments are predicted to blur the boundaries even further between EPSS and general computer-based tools. Although the majority of new applications discussed above (such as RFID, GPS, Web 2.0 and virtual worlds) can deliver clear performance benefits, there remains a relative lack of acknowledgement in the literature that these applications may, in fact, be considered as central figures in the EPSS family. For the most part, these technologies have maintained their status as standalone fields of study, and are rarely referred to as explicit performance support tools. As a result, the greatest potential for EPSS lies in the continued creation of rich, focused content which incorporates features from new and emerging applications, but critically, to emphasise the use and manipulation of information for the achievement of real, tangible benefits for everyone. In doing so, EPSS can not only maintain its distinction from other computer-based tools by helping those seeking to increase profits and/or output, but also expand its reach to provide direction and focus on the use of technology to enable anyone, anywhere to achieve performance benefits outside the confines of specific locations or task domains.

Acknowledgement

I am grateful to Suk Ting Ip for her regular critique on the development of this chapter.

References

Bastiaens, T. (1999). Assessing an electronic performance support system for the analysis of jobs and tasks. *International Journal of Training and Development*, 3(1), 54–61.

Bastiaens, T., Nijhof, W. and Abma, H. (1995). The effectiveness of an electronic performance support system on learning and performance. In E. Holton (ed.), *Academy of Human Resource Development Conference Proceedings*. St, Louis, MO: Academy of Human Resource Development.

BBC. (2007). Hi-tech helps pay penalty charge. *BBC News*. Retrieved April 13, 2008, from *http://news.bbc.co.uk/1/hi/technology/7104022.stm*

BBC. (2008). EMI set to cut up to 2,000 jobs. *BBC News*. Retrieved April 13, 2008, from *http://news.bbc.co.uk/1/hi/business/7188898.stm*

Beatty, R., Huselid, M. and Schneier, C. (2003). New HR metrics: Scoring on the business scorecard. *Organizational Dynamics*, 32(2), 107–121.

Bendavid, Y., Wamba, S. and Lefebvre, L. (2006). Proof of concept of an RFID-enabled supply chain in a B2B e-commerce environment. *ACM International Conference Proceeding Series, Proceedings of the 8th International Conference on Electronic Commerce: The New E-Commerce: Innovations for Conquering Current Barriers, Obstacles and Limitations to Conducting Successful Business on the Internet*, 156, pp. 564–568. New York, NY: ACM.

Benko, S. and Webster, S. (1997). Preparing for EPSS projects. *Communications of the ACM*, 40(7), 60–63.

Bezanson, W. (2002). *Performance Support Solutions – Achieving Business Goals Through Enabling User Performance*. Victoria, BC, Canada: Trafford Publishing.

Bocij, P., Chaffey, D., Greasley, A. and Hickie, S. (1999). *Business Information Systems. Technology Development and Management*. London, UK: Financial Times Pitman Publishing.

Borchers, J., Deussen, O. and Knorzer, C. (1995). Getting it across. Layout issues for kiosk systems. *SIGCHI Bulletin*, 27(4), 68–74.

Boudioni, M. (2003). Availability and use of information touch-screen kiosks (to facilitate social inclusion). *Aslib Proceedings*, 55(5/6), 320–333.

Brusilovsky, P. and Cooper, D. (2002). Domain, task, and user models for an adaptive hypermedia performance support system. *Proceedings of the 7th International Conference on Intelligent User Interfaces*, pp. 23–30, New York, NY: ACM.

Desmarais, M., Leclair, R., Fiset, J-Y. and Talbi, H. (1997). Cost-justifying electronic performance support systems. *Communications of the ACM*, 40(7), 39–48.

Driscoll, M. and Hynes, C. (2002). Back to fundamentals: The business realities of funding for performance support projects. *Technical Communication*, 49(4), 458–466.

Eckfeldt, B. (2005). What does RFID do for the consumer? *Communications of the ACM*, 48(9), 77–79.

Francisco-Revilla, L. and Shipman, F. (2000). Adaptive medical information delivery combining user, task and situation models. *Proceedings of the 5th International Conference on Intelligent User Interfaces*, pp. 94–97, New York, NY: ACM.

Gery, G. (1991). *Electronic Performance Support Systems: How and Why to Remake the Workplace Through the Strategic Application of Technology*. Boston, MA: Weingarten Publications.

Gery, G. (1995). Attributes and behaviors of performance-centered systems. *Performance Improvement Quarterly*, 8(1), 47–93.

Gery, G. (1997). Granting three wishes through performance-centered design. *Communications of the ACM*, 40(7), 54–59.

Gery, G. (2002). Achieving performance and learning through performance-centered systems. *Advances in Developing Human Resources*, 4(4), 464–478.

Goodman, E. (1998). A methodology for the 'user-sensitive implementation' of information systems in the pharmaceutical industry: A case study. *International Journal of Information Management*, 18(2), 121–138.

Greenfield, A. (2006). *Everyware: The Dawning Age of Ubiquitous Computing*. Berkeley, CA: New Riders.

Guinn, C. and Hubal, R. (2004). An evaluation of virtual human technology in information kiosks. *International Conference on Multimodal Interfaces Archive, Proceedings of the 6th International Conference on Multimodal Interfaces*, pp. 297–302. New York, NY: ACM.

Günther, O. and Spiekermann, S. (2005). RFID and the perception of control: The consumer's view. *Communications of the ACM*, 48(9), 73–76.

Hsi, S. and Fait, H. (2005). RFID enhances visitors' museum experience at the Exploratorium. *Communications of the ACM*, 48(9), 60–65.

Johnston, M. and Bangalore, S. (2004). MATCHKiosk: A multimodal interactive city guide. *Annual Meeting of the ACL Archive, Proceedings of the ACL 2004 on Interactive Poster and Demonstration Sessions*, Article Number 33, Morristown, NJ: Association for Computational Linguistics.

Jurishica, C. and Schwieters, R. (2004). Simulation shows savings with RFID implementation. *WSC '04: Proceedings of the 36th Conference on Winter Simulation*, Article Number 3, Washington, DC: Winter Simulation Conference.

Karat, J. (1997). Evolving the scope of user-centered design. *Communications of the ACM*, 40(7), 33–38.

Lam, C. and Tan, B. (2001). The Internet is changing the music industry. *Communications of the ACM*, 44(8), 62–68.

Lee, Y., Cheng, F. and Leung, Y. (2004). Exploring the impact of RFID on supply chain dynamics. *WSC '04: Proceedings of the 36th Conference on Winter Simulation*, pp. 1145–1152. Washington, DC: Winter Simulation Conference.

Lee, S., Park, S-H., Yoon, S-N. and Yeon, S-J. (2007). RFID based ubiquitous commerce and consumer trust. *Industrial Management and Data Systems*, 107(5), 605–617.

Massey, A., Montoya-Weiss, M. and O-Driscoll, T. (2002). Performance-centered design of knowledge-intensive processes. *Journal of Management Information Systems*, 18(4), 37–58.

Miller, M., Ferrin, D., Flynn, T., Ashby, M., White, P. and Mauer, M. (2006). Using RFID technologies to capture simulation data in a hospital emergency department. *WSC '06: Proceedings of the 38th Conference on Winter Simulation*, pp. 1365–1370. Washington, DC: Winter Simulation Conference.

Mudambi, S., Doyle, P. and Wong, V. (1997). An exploration of branding in industrial markets. *Industrial Marketing Management*, 26(5), 433–446.

Narayanasamy, V., Wong, K-W., Fung, C-C. and Rai, S. (2006). Distinguishing games and simulation games from simulators. *ACM Computers in Entertainment*, 4(2), 1–18.

Nicholas, D., Huntington, P. and Williams, P. (2004). The characteristics of users and non-users of a kiosk information system. *Aslib Proceedings*, 56(1), 48–61.

Nicholas, D., Williams, P. and Huntington, P. (2002). An evaluation of the use of NHS touch-screen health kiosks: a national study. *Aslib Proceedings*, 54(6), 372–384.

Niederman, F., Mathieu, R., Morley, R. and Kwon, I-W. (2007). Examining RFID applications in supply chain management. *Communications of the ACM*, 50(7), 92–101.

Ockerman, J., Najjar, L. and Thompson, C. (1999). FAST: Future technology for today's industry. *Computers in Industry*, 38, 53–64.

Ohkubo, M., Suzuki, K. and Kinoshita, S. (2005). RFID privacy issues and technical challenges. *Communications of the ACM*, 48(9), 66–71.

O'Reilly, T. (2005). What is Web 2.0? Design patterns and business models for the next generation of software. Retrieved April 13, 2008, from *http://www.oreillynet.com/pub/a/oreilly/tim/ news/2005/09/30/what-is-web-20.html*

Pace, S. (1996). The global positioning system: Policy issues for an information technology. *Space Policy*, 12(4), 265–275.

Premkumar, G. (2003). Alternate distribution strategies for digital music. *Communications of the ACM*, 46(9), 89–95.

Qiu, L. and Benbasat, I. (2005). An investigation into the effects of text-to-speech voice and 3D avatars on the perception of presence and flow of live help in electronic commerce. *ACM Transactions on Computer-Human Interaction*, 12(4), 329–355.

Raybourn, E. (2007). Applying simulation experience design methods to creating serious game-based adaptive training systems. *Interacting with Computers*, 19(2), 206–214.

Regan, E. and O'Connor, B. (2002). *End-User Information Systems: Implementing Individual and Work Group Technologies* (2nd edn). Upper Saddle River, NJ: Prentice Hall.

Rincon, P. (2005). Navigating future for road charges. *BBC News*. Retrieved April 13, 2008, from *http://news.bbc.co.uk/1/hi/sci/tech/4552132.stm*

Rocha, R., Cunha, A., Varandas, J. and Dias, J. (2007). Towards a new mobility concept for cities: Architecture and programming of semi-autonomous electric vehicles. *Industrial Robot: An International Journal*, 34(2), 142–149.

Rossett, A. and Schafer, L. (2007). *Job Aids and Performance Support. Moving From Knowledge in the Classroom to Knowledge Everywhere*. San Francisco, CA: John Wiley and Sons.

Roussos, G. and Moussouri, T. (2004). Consumer perceptions of privacy, security and trust in ubiquitous commerce. *Personal and Ubiquitous Computing*, 8(6), 416–429.

Rowley, J. and Slack, F. (2007). Information kiosks: A taxonomy. *Journal of Documentation*, 63(6), 879–897.

Ruta, M., Di Noia, T., Di Sciascio, E., Piscitelli, G. and Scioscia, F. (2007). RFID meets bluetooth in a semantic based u-commerce environment. *ICEC '07: Proceedings of the Ninth International Conference on Electronic Commerce*, pp. 107–116. New York, NY: ACM.

Ryan, H. (1995). Multimedia and the data processor. *Information Systems Management*, 12(3), 73–75.

Saha, D., Sahu, S. and Shaikh, A. (2003). A service platform for on-line games. *NetGames '03: Proceedings of the 2nd Workshop on Network and System Support for Games*, pp. 180–184. New York, NY: ACM.

Shaw, M. (2004). Modernization of the global positioning system. *Acta Astronautica*, 54, 943–947.

Simchi-Levi, D., Kaminsky, P. and Simchi-Levi, E. (2004). *Managing the Supply Chain: The Definitive Guide for the Business Professional*. New York, NY: McGraw-Hill.

Slack, F. and Rowley, J. (2002). Online kiosks: The alternative to mobile technologies for mobile users. *Internet Research: Electronic Networking Applications and Policy*, 12(3), 248–257.

Stair, P. and Reynolds, G. (2001). *Principles of Information Systems* (5th edn). Cambridge, MA: Course Technology.

Stockburger, S. and Fernandez, T. (2002). Virtual onsite support: Using Internet chat and remote control to improve customer service. *SIGUCCS '02: Proceedings of the 30th Annual ACM SIGUCCS Conference on User Services*, pp. 143–147. New York, NY: ACM.

Stopher, P., FitzGerald, C. and Zhang, J. (2008). Search for a global positioning system device to measure person travel. *Transportation Research Part C*, 16(3), 350–369.

Taylor, M., Woolley, J. and Zito, R. (2000). Integration of the global positioning system and geographical information systems for traffic congestion studies. *Transportation Research Part C*, 8(1), 257–285.

Theiss, A., Yen, D. and Ku, C-Y. (2005). Global positioning systems: An analysis of applications, current development and future implementations. *Computer Standards and Interfaces*, 27, 89–100.

Totty, P. (2004). CU call centers move to multichannels. *Credit Union Magazine*, May, 84–86.

Van Slyke, C., Belanger, F. and Comunale, C. (2004). Factors influencing the adoption of web-based shopping: The impact of trust. *ACM SIGMIS Database*, 35(2), 32–49.

Watson, R., Pitt, L., Berthon, P. and Zinkhan, G. (2002). U-commerce: Expanding the universe of marketing. *Journal of the Academy of Marketing Science*, 30(4), 333–47.

Winslow, C. and Caldwell, J. (1992). Integrated performance support. *Information Systems Management*, 9(2), 76–78.

Wisener, G. (2002). Overcoming barriers to performance centered design. *Job Performance Aids and EPSS*. Retrieved April 13, 2008, from *http://files.epsscentral.info/gery/pdfarticles/barriers_to_pcd.pdf*

Wu, F., Kuo, F. and Liu, L-W. (2005). The application of RFID on drug safety of inpatient nursing healthcare. *ICEC '05: Proceedings of the 7th International Conference on Electronic Commerce*, pp. 85–92. New York, NY: ACM.

Yoder, R. (2006). Using RFID in the classroom to teach information systems principles. *Journal of Computing Sciences in Colleges*, 21(6), 123–129.

12 *EPSS Applications in a Corporate Setting*

ERAN GAL AND PAUL VAN SCHAIK

Electronic Performance Support Systems (EPSS) are a very powerful tool for reducing training costs while improving productivity. Customer-oriented corporations can benefit from performance support technology during their most important task: customer-enterprise interaction. As a result of frequent changes in the corporate information-technology systems used to interact with customers, workers are continually required to learn and master new procedures and absorb other work-related information. New ways of thinking and a new set of tools to meet an enterprise's competency-demands needs to be adopted to meet this challenge. In this context, new performance support tools are required, in addition to training. This chapter discusses the necessity of using performance support technology and its benefits in contemporary work environments. It also discusses how the deployment of this technology can have significant implications for enterprises.

The Development of Electronic Performance Support in Corporate Settings

The concept of electronic performance support was conceived and nurtured in corporate settings as a result of the serious challenge organisations have been facing over the last two decades, a challenge which Gery (1989) describes as the 'performance crisis'. Barker (1995) confirms that much of the interest and development of EPSS facilities was a consequence of the performance challenge within business and commerce. He lists the following factors leading to the performance challenge: increased competition, more diverse markets, the need for diversity in new fields of endeavour, the need to recognise and restructure organisations, and a growing need to optimise the use of resources – all pointing to the need for information to support workers' performance in organisations. Thus, the concept of electronic performance support in corporate settings has emerged as an important solution to this challenge, promising important benefits all related to solving the performance challenge.

COMPETENCY CHALLENGES OF CORPORATE SETTINGS

The performance challenge is caused by the gap between the level of competency of a workforce and that required in order to meet organisational business goals. As Gery

(1991) states, contemporary organisations need to go beyond competence, proficiency or even mastery. When employees are not sufficiently competent, this has negative consequences in terms of limited business results. Organisations must compensate with costly mechanisms aimed at supporting the workforce. Such mechanisms are considered 'overhead' expenses as they do not contribute directly to production but rather to making sure production is aligned with business goals. Examples include help-desk functions, quality assurance, work supervision, coaching and training. It seems that training is usually responsible for the competency problem as it lacks the tools or methods to produce an effective and efficient solution.

THE INABILITY OF TRAINING TO MEET CURRENT CORPORATE COMPETENCY DEMANDS

Traditional training in organisations plays a major part in the performance challenge, as it is unable to answer modern challenges with old tools and paradigms. Usually an organisation will turn to training to resolve competency issues. Unfortunately, traditional training is not always successful in meeting the competency demands of contemporary business environments. Agility, adoption and change are the main characteristics of current business environments. Hudzina et al. (1996) identify three conditions facing corporate organisations: the need to keep pace with the rapid development of computer technology, an increasing complexity of the workplace and a necessity for continual performance improvement by workers to enable organisations to compete successfully. Maughan (2005) discusses technology's great influence on modern life and the consequent continual changes in the modern workplace. As a result, workers will not only need to use current skills and knowledge to perform their jobs, but they will be required to keep up with the demands of a changing organisation (Bailey, 2004). Business environments call for immediate responses to change. However, traditional solutions – including e-learning – cannot answer this challenge (Racine et al., 2004). Rosenberg et al. (1999) describe the difficulties traditional training departments face nowadays as a result of tremendous amounts of complex information needed to perform job-related tasks.

A fundamental problem is that attempts to apply traditional methods and tools to resolve the situation result in unprecedented overhead expenses. The American Society for Training and Development estimated that in 2005 workers in leading American firms spent an average 40 hours a year in training. The training market was estimated at around 51 billion dollars that year, not including time spent in training (Dolezalek, 2005). Many will agree that new ways of thinking and a new way of acting are required to help organisations deal with the performance challenge. The concept of electronic performance support is one vehicle to enable modern organisations to face this challenge (Gery, 1991; Raybould, 1995; Bayram, 2004; Cagiltay, 2001; Barker, 1995; Maughan, 2005; Rossett and Schafer, 2006).

BENEFITS OF ELECTRONIC PERFORMANCE SUPPORT TO ENTERPRISES

When considering the implementation of an EPSS as a means of dealing with the performance challenge, two major goals are set: first, to increase performance quantity and quality and, second, to reduce training-related costs, or – ideally – to fully eliminate training needs (Chase's, 1998, as cited in Nguyen et al., 2005; Desmerais et al., 1997; Foster, 1997; Nguyen and Klein, 2008; Raybould, 1995).

There are numerous definitions of the concept of electronic performance support. Among those, two approaches stand out, enabling organisations to realise the potential of the concepts involved.

1. The individual-level approach proposed by Gery (1989, 1991, 1995). An EPSS is seen as a means of providing whatever is necessary to support performance and learning at the time of need.
2. The organisational-level approach proposed by Raybould (1995) and supported by others (Barker, 1995; Passmore's, 1996, study as cited in Bill, 1997). An EPSS is seen as an infrastructure that captures, organises and distributes organisational and individual knowledge assets to achieve a required level of performance as fast as possible.

Both approaches target the essence of the performance challenge and offer a new way for organisations to manage a workforce's competencies, leading to great benefits for businesses, including the following: first, tasks can be completed faster (if this benefit is accomplished across a wide range of tasks, it could lead to fewer workers needed to accomplish the specified tasks). Second, the error rate can be reduced. Third, workers can produce better results. Fourth, less training or external support is likely to be needed to accomplish tasks (Liner and Woods, 1999).

Due to the commercial nature of corporate environments, these benefits must be realised to such an extent that they produce meaningful results for the enterprise, that is, results measurable according to an enterprise's main goals. Usually such goals are (linked to) profits, which lead advocates of the use of electronic performance support to adopt the concept of Return on Investment (ROI) in order to measure and verify the contribution that an EPSS makes to an enterprise.

RETURN ON INVESTMENT BY ACHIEVING BUSINESS GOALS DUE TO PERFORMANCE IMPROVEMENTS

A goal of electronic performance support is to reduce training costs while improving productivity (Raybould, 2000). These benefits can be and must be translated to business-related goals in order to be recognised and measured by enterprises. Business-related benefits of electronic performance support have been described in detail through work done regarding the effect of this support on ROI outcomes. ROI measurements allow an organisation to compare the monetary benefits of a certain effort with its costs.

There have been a few significant studies addressing ROI as a function of electronic performance support. Among those are the work by Desmarais et al. (1997), and Hawkins et al. (1998). A review of the factors suggested by Hawkins et al. (1998) relating to the collection of ROI data (following the implementation of an EPSS) reveals a detailed list of benefits to corporate organisations (see Table 12.1). As Phillips (1997) noted, 'other benefits' of electronic performance support are considered 'soft' benefits and are much harder to collect and calculate. In Hawkins et al.'s (1998) case study of the US Department of Veterans Affairs, the soft benefit contribution was negligible.

In theory, electronic performance support can address the challenges of modern corporations and be successful in such a way that few technological solutions have ever done in the past. The review of the practice of electronic performance support presented in this chapter will help further establish its true potential.

Table 12.1   Specific ROI benefits of electronic performance support

Employees' work hours
- Reduced time to perform operations
- Reduced overtime
- Reduced supervision (supervision hours)
- Reduced help from co-workers (work hours)
- Reduced calls to help-line assistance (help-desk personal hours)
- Fewer or no calls from help-line to supervisor about over use of help-service
- Reduced time to learn system/job (work hours)
- Fewer employees needed

Quality improvement benefits
- Fewer mistakes
- Fewer rejects
- Reduced employee turnover
- Reduced grievances
- Reduced absenteeism/tardiness

Source: Hawkins et al., 1998.

THE EFFECTIVENESS OF ELECTRONIC PERFORMANCE SUPPORT

Electronic performance support represents the greatest promise that training departments (in particular) and corporations (in general) have witnessed since the introduction of e-learning in the 1980s. It is a great surprise to learn, in that context, that very little research was done to investigate and demonstrate evidence for most of this promise. The information gathered by the research community can be divided into three categories. First, what an EPSS can and should do. Second, what is known from case studies and success stories. Third, what was tested and demonstrated in empirical studies.

Most literature to date can be categorised as theories detailing the concept of electronic performance support and effects in different areas of life and business. Some of the theoretical background of electronic performance support is described in Chapters 1, 2, 3 and 4 of this book. There are quite a few success stories and case studies, mainly from industrial and corporate environments. However, academic empirical research is scarce.

Empirical research

Empirical research is the smallest category of the three and, disappointingly, only deals with basic assumptions regarding the effectiveness of electronic performance support. Table 12.2 presents a comprehensive list of empirical studies performed to date regarding electronic performance support.

As seen in Table 12.2, research can be categorised as either addressing basic effectiveness of the concept or comparing electronic performance support with other (learning) methods. The findings presented in Table 12.2 confirm the idea that though EPSS technology has been discussed in the literature for about 20 years now, it remains a relatively new concept (Cagiltay, 2001). The type of research and conclusions reached to date resemble the vast amount of research done regarding the effectiveness of e-learning when it was first introduced. Russell's work (1999) titled the *No-Significant-Difference Phenomenon*, concluded that e-learning is as effective as traditional learning – in some

Table 12.2   A summary of empirical research on EPSS technology

Publication	Organisation	Topic	Findings	Limitations	Category
Morrison and Witmer (1983)	American Army	Comparison of supporting media: computer versus paper-based.	No significant differences were found.	Did not deal with important issues such as design and effectiveness.	Comparison of methods
Bastiaens et al. (1997b)	Business	Learning effectiveness when incorporating support tools (computer and paper-based) compared with classroom- and Computer-Based Training (CBT) methods.	Paper-based support was preferred overall. Classroom-based learning was preferred over CBT. No significant differences were found regarding test results, performance or sales level over a year.	Even though CBT was mentioned as an EPSS component in early EPSS literature, it does not meet basic requirements of electronic performance support; thus, findings relate more to e-learning than EPSS.	Comparison of methods
Wild (1998)	Novice students	Effectiveness of support system for classroom-planning tasks with the intent of reaching an experienced user's performance level.	All participants benefited from the support system and showed a high level of task performance.	Self-learning strategies have an effect on success rate of an EPSS; thus, findings are inconclusive.	Effectiveness
Bastiaens (1999)	Business	Comparing two groups of instructional designers on performance and learning achievements. One group received EPSS, the other a traditional learning method.	Performance was significantly better in the EPSS group. Learning achievements were significantly higher in the traditional learning group.		Comparison of methods

Table 12.2 *Continued*

Publication	Organisation	Topic	Findings	Limitations	Category
van Schaik et al. (2002)	Academic	Evaluating effectiveness of learning and performance in quantitative research methods for students using a specially designed EPSS.	Students supported by the system showed significant improvements in performance and self-confidence.		Effectiveness
Nguyen et al. (2005)	Business	Comparison of three EPSS types: external, extrinsic and intrinsic using four outcome measures: performance, attitude, time on task and EPSS use.	All types improved performance. Integrated systems (extrinsic, intrinsic) were better than external on all outcomes.	Tasks and task support offered were designed specifically for the research. Different tasks and support may produce different results.	Effectiveness
Mao and Brown (2005)	Business	Comparison between two groups performing procedural tasks with software (*Microsoft Access*™). One group received traditional training and the other electronic support in addition to training.	EPSS group scored significantly higher than the training-only group. No significant differences were found regarding procedural tasks.	Results can be explained by a poor training program.	Comparison of methods

cases even more effective. This was a significant step in gaining acceptance of e-learning as a proven method of training. The authors of this chapter foresee that the same will apply to electronic performance support. The debate on whether electronic performance support matches or exceeds the results of other learning methods or whether it is able to support both performance and learning is likely to disappear with time and experience.

Table 12.2 *Concluded*

Publication	Organisation	Topic	Findings	Limitations	Category
van Schaik et al. (2007a)	Academic	Assessment of the effectiveness of an EPSS for library tasks. Comparison of performance with and without support.	Aided performance was significantly better than unaided performance.		Effectiveness
Nguyen and Klein (2008)	Business	Comparing three learning methods: a web-based, self-paced learning program; EPSS; and a combined program. Four outcome measures were used: performance, attitude, time-on-task and EPSS use.	The combined method produced best performance and was favoured by participants.	Weak validity outside the research setting.	Comparison of methods
Nguyen (2008)	Business	A similar research method to that used by Nguyen and Klein (2008). The goal was to establish the preferred learning method by participants.	Similar to Nguyen and Klein (2008). The combined method (EPSS and traditional training) was most preferred.	EPSS type, design and training type can influence the outcome of this research. Moreover, the task at hand (tax preparation) may have caused a negative approach to task performance in some participants.	Comparison of methods

Training departments and business managers are likely to embrace electronic performance support as a valuable solution for the performance challenge and as a most efficient method for online learning. Research concerning best practice of the implementation and ROI benefits of EPSS technology is likely to contribute greatly to this change.

Case studies and success stories

Electronic performance support is reported to have great success in all fields of industry, government and education institutes. As early as 1991, Gery reported success stories of enterprises (including Intel, IBM, AT&T and American Express) implementing and gaining significant benefits from electronic performance support. Ip (2010, Chapter 11 of this volume) discusses the implementation of electronic performance support in industry. It is important to note that most academic case studies are supported by empirical data. Laffey and Musser (1996), van Schaik et al. (2002) and Wild (1998) have reported successful implementation in academic institutes.

When examining most case studies it becomes clear that EPSS technology can and is producing important benefits for enterprises. However, as the validity of case studies is limited, the findings need to be supported by results from thorough empirical research. Some typical examples of such success stories are reported by Desmarais et al. (1997), Foster (1997) and Villachica and Stone (1999).

Though the validity of case studies is limited, they do complement the mostly theoretical publications with application data and ROI figures. All researchers who have conducted empirical studies of electronic performance support encourage more scholars to perform further research regarding its capabilities and benefits. A broader and more comprehensive knowledge base is likely to help researchers and practitioners better understand and adopt EPSS technology as the new way of thinking and acting in corporate settings that face the performance challenge.

Very little research appears to exist addressing the implications that the implementation of an EPSS will most likely have on adopting enterprises. However, publications reporting on EPSS (including Gery, 1989, 1991, 1995; Malcolm, 1992, 1998; Raybould, 1995; Bill, 1997; Chase, 1998, as cited in Nguyen et al., 2005; Wild, 1998; Hawkins et al., 1998; Cagiltay, 2001; Altalib (2002); Rupel, 2002; Nguyen, 2005, 2008; Nguyen et al., 2005; Maughan, 2005; Rossett and Schafer, 2006; van Schaik et al., 2007a, 2007b; and Nguyen and Klein, 2008) have done so with a positive attitude and imply that, once implemented, it should produce the expected benefits. Scholars, business people and training practitioners in particular should be aware of possible implications concerning the implementation of EPSS technology when considering a cost-benefit ratio of a future project.

Types of Application of Electronic Performance Support Systems in Corporate Organisations

ELECTRONIC PERFORMANCE SUPPORT SYSTEMS TOOLS

Initially, EPSS applications were developed by enterprises without the use of specialised tools. In recent years, due to technological developments and the growing demand for electronic performance support, several (off-the-shelf) EPSS tools have been introduced to customer-oriented corporations. These tools have been designed to provide performance support for the use of target software applications. They usually contain a performance support editor, which allows practitioners to concentrate their efforts on the design of performance support rather than the design of a framework and the task of establishing connectivity to a target application.

Gery (1995) defined three types of EPSS: external, extrinsic and intrinsic. An *external* EPSS stores the content that is used to support task performance in an external database. This content is not integrated within the end-users' interface to target applications. As a result, users are forced to manually locate relevant information in the external EPSS. Examples include search engines, frequently asked question pages and help indexes (see Figure 12.1). An *extrinsic* EPSS is integrated within a corporation's IT system, but in order to receive support its users must stop their work and turn to the support system to obtain the necessary information. Such systems are often context-sensitive, that is they constantly offer support according to the task at hand. Workers do not have to search for support but only turn to the EPSS when needed. An *intrinsic* EPSS provides users with task support that is incorporated directly within the user-interface to the target applications. Gery noted that this type of support is so well integrated that, to users, it is part of the system. Its ability to merge completely within the target application allows it to offer the following two types of support:

1. *Work-flow support.* The EPSS offers information, data and advice to support a specific task within the target application. For example, a pop-up window containing decision-support data appears when a worker is about to make the designated decision during a particular work procedure.
2. *Adaptation of a target application's user-interface.* Rather than presenting additional information, the EPSS makes changes to the user-interface to facilitate successful completion of the task at hand. For example, the EPSS can make unavailable ('disable') screen options that are not relevant for the current work flow or may cause confusion and lead to mistakes. In other cases, an EPSS can provide automated procedures to assure correct work flow. Integrated support (extrinsic or intrinsic) is considered the best form of support.

In a comparative study, Nguyen et al. (2005) concluded that all EPSS interventions have a positive impact on workers and task-related outcomes (time-on-task and accuracy). Integrated support produced significantly better results than the extrinsic support on all outcomes, including workers' attitude. Furthermore, earlier research (Bailey, 2004; Spool, 2001) concluded that users often had difficulty using search engines to look for support content.

Off-the-shelf EPSS applications can be classified as either extrinsic or intrinsic. External tools exist in the market but are often not referred to as EPSS tools (for example, database search engines and tools with answers to frequently asked questions).

BASIC FUNCTION AND CAPABILITIES OF INTRINSIC ELECTRONIC PERFORMANCE SUPPORT SYSTEMS APPLICATIONS

Raybould (1995) and Bill (1997) have suggested a broader approach to the contribution of electronic performance support to enterprises. They call for a learning-organisation

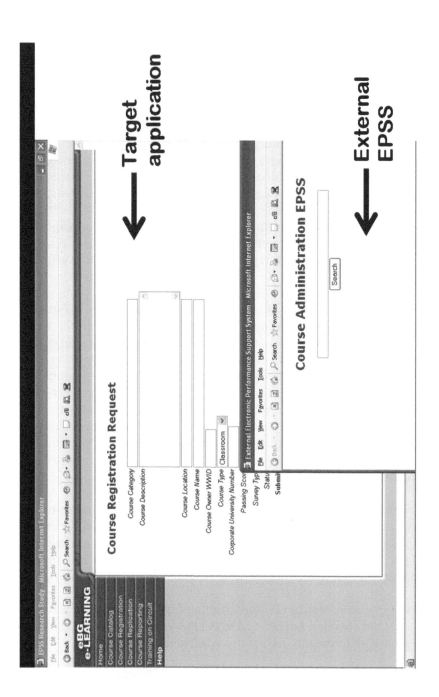

Figure 12.1 A sample screen from eBG e-Learning – an external EPSS

approach – using EPSS technology to capture, organise and distribute individual and organisational knowledge assets. Contemporary intrinsic EPSS tools available on the market as off-the-shelf applications support Raybould's and Bill's vision. The learning cycle (see Figure 12.2), as described by Raybould (1995), begins with performance supported by an EPSS and continues with new knowledge generated at the level of individual workers and gathered by the system itself.

In order for an EPSS to support the cycle it must possess three basic features: (1) connectivity to and awareness of one or more target applications; (2) availability of an EPSS-rule editor ('support design workshop'); and (3) measurement and reports.

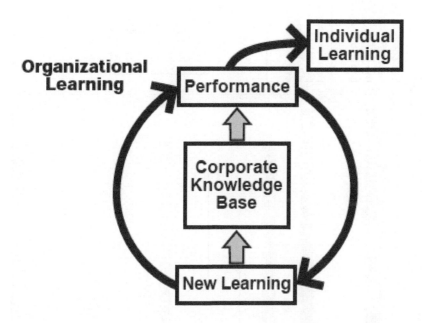

Figure 12.2 Raybould's (1995) organisational performance/learning cycle

Connectivity to and awareness of target applications

An EPSS can be described as an outer layer placed over a target application. This layer of support must interact with the target application in such a way that it identifies all interface elements, including screens, fields, data, buttons and menus, and can sense changes in them. Thus an EPSS application must connect to any standard application and recognise its interface elements. Once connected, the EPSS is constantly 'aware' of the target application's interface. By constantly examining the target, and recording actions and changes, the EPSS becomes a platform for context-sensitive support interventions. The next step is to determine the form of intervention, which depends on the type of EPSS. An extrinsic intervention will usually include a separate window displaying target-application context-related declarative (knowing what) and procedural (knowing how) knowledge, for example a work-flow chart presenting relevant sections of the flow as a worker completes a task (see Figure 12.3).

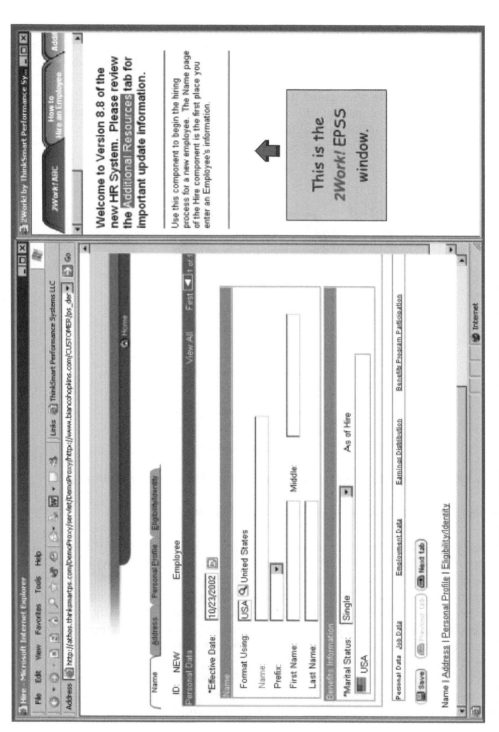

Figure 12.3 A sample screen from 2Work! EPSS – an extrinsic EPSS application

Electronic Performance Support Systems-rule editor ('support design workshop')

EPSS assistance is defined in the form of rules. An EPSS application offers an editor for creating, testing and maintaining support rules. A rule is comprised of two components: a trigger and an action. A trigger is an event in the execution of a target application that signals the need for specific performance support, for example, the initiation of a procedure from an action menu in the target application. An action is an intervention designed to support performance in response to a specific trigger. Actions vary according to the type of EPSS. An intrinsic application can offer a wide range of rules and action settings, such as pop-up windows containing data, information or details collected from other screens or applications, procedural advice and automated calculations using on-screen data (see Figure 12.4 for an example of step-by-step procedural support).

Measurement and reports

Some EPSS facilities maintain their own database, in which they store all data collected during their execution. Raybould's (1995) definition of EPSS requires an active database at the heart of an organisational learning cycle. The data are collected from the target application and are recorded as support rules consisting of triggers and actions. Every time a trigger is met the EPSS records the event in its database along with the action it took and a specific user's response to the action. For example, if a callout message was displayed, the system would record how long it was displayed on screen and whether the user activated any links present in it. The database presents an opportunity to assess not only the EPSS facility's performance, but also the users' competency before and after an EPSS intervention – thus fully completing the learning cycle.

Current EPSS tools comply with Raybould's (1995) and Bill's (1997) vision by offering not only support, but also the collection of data relating to users' behaviour using the target application and the EPSS, and an analysis of competency before and after interventions. Most enterprises using EPSS technology nowadays employ it as individual supports rather than exploring its benefits to the enterprise, although the latter is technically possible. This is mainly due to the relatively new technology and the limited effort invested in implementing the technology.

Implications of the Implementation of an Electronic Performance Support System

As established in the previous section, modern corporate organisations should include electronic performance support as part of their competency management alongside training and other competency-enhancement strategies. The benefits to an enterprise can be significant, including the achievements of reaching business goals and staying competitive.

Before an EPSS is considered as a technical solution for performance problems, the concept of electronic performance support must first be considered more broadly as a new way of thinking and a new way of promoting competency in an enterprise. Implementing

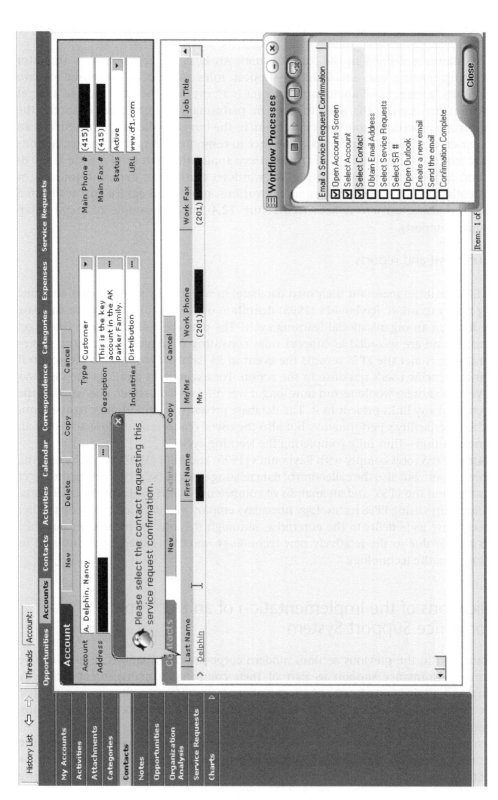

Figure 12.4 A sample screen from e-glue – an intrinsic EPSS application

a new technological solution throughout the enterprise can be a difficult and complex assignment. Implementing a new way of thinking and acting is a much greater task.

Most literature regarding EPSS does not deal with implementation in a business organisation. This can be attributed to two facts. First, electronic performance support is still a relatively new concept (Cagiltay, 2001). Second, EPSS facilities are usually implemented by business organisations that aim for competitive advantage and therefore keep their work strictly confidential (Gustafsun, 2000; Winer et al., 1999). Most reviews of implementation work deal with successful case studies – which focus on results rather than the way to achieve them. A more realistic and accurate review of implementation and challenges is therefore needed to develop a knowledge base of electronic performance support. Potential implications of the implementation of electronic performance support and possible obstacles will now be discussed.

PREREQUISITES FOR ACHIEVING THE POTENTIAL BENEFITS OF AN ELECTRONIC PERFORMANCE SUPPORT SYSTEM

The implementation process of an EPSS will more than likely be long and costly. The process begins long before the first user receives online support. One very important aspect in the preparation for implementation is the justification of costs in relation to expected benefits. The following cultural and other organisational characteristics must be taken into consideration to assess the potential of electronic performance support and preliminary work that may be required to allow an efficient implementation.

Self-directed learning

EPSS facilities, whether extrinsic or intrinsic, rely heavily on users being self-directed learners (Bailey, 2004). If e-learning already takes place on a regular basis and if search engines or organisational-information portals are being used to locate task related-information, then the chance of a successful implementation of an EPSS is enhanced. However, if training consists of paper-based materials and mostly classroom-based events, the transition to an EPSS may be too great. Actions can be taken to help employees become more self-directed but this should be considered a project of its own.

IT infrastructure and architecture

Establishing connectivity between an EPSS and target applications is a basic requirement of any implementation of electronic performance support. However, the IT infrastructure of the target application may influence the extent to which an EPSS can realise its potential. One very distinct example is the ability to access off-screen data: such data are located in tables (often called 'background tables') invisible to employees which populate particular screens according to the design of the target application that is used. For instance, a customer's payment history will populate a 'financial-history' screen only when a worker accesses this specific screen. It is important to note that at all times payment-history data are maintained in a designated (background) table in the target application's 'background'. However, the data infrastructure of the target application may prevent any other application connecting to and drawing data from those tables. In that case, the EPSS could only use data visible to the workers (on-screen data). No background retrieval could be performed so that not all situations concerning data or information allocation in the target application could be addressed by the EPSS. It is recommended, when the implementation of an EPSS is considered, to list all major processes considered for support. This will also be useful when predicting the ROI of the EPSS (discussed earlier in this chapter). Meetings should then be held with IT personnel, and preferably with the intended EPSS vendor, to assess what processes can be implemented, taking into consideration the existing infrastructure of target applications and the capabilities of the EPSS. These meetings can help in deciding whether to proceed with implementation or to attend to IT infrastructure first.

Stakeholders' support

Once introduced, an EPSS will have many stakeholders in an enterprise. Preliminary and ongoing work is required to maintain their support and cooperation in order to improve the chance of success. Stakeholders include top management and major decision makers. Wisener (2002) suggests that a clear financial and strategic case should be made, presenting benefits to overcome management's reluctance to change. Gery (1991) stresses the need to focus on benefits for business which are much more appealing to management than training goals or training-budget control. A recommendation is therefore to create a demonstration application specially designed for an adopting enterprise, demonstrating the potential benefits of the proposed EPSS and its ROI. Such demonstrations are usually created by vendors, but can also be easily created by training and IT personnel. It is important to note that there are many other stakeholders besides management. These include workers, professional management and system experts, training staff and IT personnel, and they should be targeted as part of a campaign to win support from management (Gery, 1991).

Electronic performance support system project team

There appears to be general agreement that electronic performance support is not training and should not be considered as part of the training activity in an enterprise (Rosenberg, 1995; Witt and Wager, 1994; Cole et al., 1997; Milheim, 1997; Northrup, 1999; Cagiltay, 2001). In fact, an EPSS should divert resources away from conventional training to achieve better results in less time. However, an EPSS will usually support the competency of a workforce in relation to performing job-related tasks. Nevertheless, this has always been the primary aim of training departments and will continue to be so after an EPSS has been introduced into the enterprise. Therefore, both training and IT departments may claim responsibility for electronic performance support. The process of implementing an EPSS will require a substantial team comprised of both IT staff and training personnel (Gery 1991: pp. 195–204, 214–30) and the question of who should lead the team and what department should be responsible for its management must be addressed and resolved in advance. The composition and leadership of the team are critical to ensure the success of the implementation of an EPSS and its deliverables.

Preliminary return-on-investment projection

Once all preliminary considerations have been thought through it should be possible to create a preliminary *ROI projection*. This is a powerful tool to win support and collaboration within an organisation for an EPSS. The ROI projection should rely on the benefits discussed in the section entitled 'Return on investment by achieving business goals due to performance improvements' in this chapter with data that are specific to the organisation. The following two precautionary measures are suggested at this stage – in order to prevent impossible future obligations and even stakeholders' disapproval as a result of the ROI projection.

- *Realistic ROI.* When creating a projection, challenges and obstacles to implementation are seldom taken into consideration. This can result in an unrealistically optimistic ROI projection which may create difficulties in the future. It is therefore recommended to create a modest predicted ROI and state clearly the conditions for its achievement.
- *Non-threatening ROI.* When suggesting measures to improve efficiency – such as the implementation of an EPSS to an enterprise – it is important to note that the consequences that subsequently arise could include reduced budget allocation and even a reduction of the workforce for some organisational units. Consequently, an ROI projection with such implications may be rejected. It is therefore recommended to focus the projection on non-threatening and more positive benefits of electronic performance support, such as, productivity improvement, reduced error rate and time spent on training.

COST IMPLICATIONS OF THE APPLICATION OF AN ELECTRONIC PERFORMANCE SUPPORT SYSTEM

Considerations and calculations of ROI focus on the ratio between monetary benefits and costs. Benefits should eventually exceed costs, although it is likely that costs will continue long after initial purchase and set-up of an EPSS (Rossett and Schafer, 2006). Costs can be characterised as direct and indirect ones.

Direct costs

- *Costs related to EPSS project team.* An EPSS project team will consist of IT personnel (those programming, working in quality assurance and integrating the EPSS with target applications), instructional designers and graphic designers. Gery (1991: pp. 195–204, 214–30), Benko and Webster (1997) and Bezanson (2002: pp. 32–5, 113–20) suggest a similar composition of an EPSS project team. They also discuss the role of subject-matter experts. Subject-matter experts and reviewers from all enterprise departments that are considered to be 'EPSS customers' should be included in various stages of the design, development and implementation process. Gery refers to these as 'programme sponsors' and stresses their essential role in both the development and implementation stages (Gery, 1991).
- *Vendor's ongoing support.* Although most of the work should be carried out by the EPSS project team, an ongoing relationship with the EPSS vendor is important. Following the set-up and first versions of an EPSS, the vendor's experience and system know-how can be very useful when encountering problems and when expanding the scope of the EPSS.
- *Ongoing maintenance.* The technical maintenance requirements of an EPSS should not incur unusual costs compared to any standard IT system. Maintenance costs of an EPSS

will be significant due to the urgency of solving intervention-related maintenance issues. Because the EPSS connects to and applies interventions in the most critical systems of an enterprise, all interventions should be monitored constantly and problems should be fixed in as short a timescale as possible. The cost of creating and monitoring an online report system – together with an on-call IT maintenance team – will result in considerably higher maintenance costs then a typical IT system.

Indirect costs

* *Implementation costs*. Depending on an enterprise's culture and experience with self-directed learning and IT system implementation, the development of an EPSS can be a long and costly process. Cultural barriers and non-supportive management of workers who are target users of the EPSS can result in extra effort required from departments working on the implementation of the EPSS. Some of the consequences of this extra effort include: personnel in the implementing business unit having to work with the adopting unit; a wide and ongoing educational campaign to promote the EPSS; and special reports on the speed of and problems with implementation. It is recommended that the implementation budget, schedule and factors affecting the success of an EPSS are estimated from past experiences with this type of technology and training across the organisation. The results, together with an ROI projection, should be communicated to all stakeholders – especially top management.
* *Adjustments to training*. To address cultural issues and promote EPSS use by trainees, it is recommended that EPSS use should be included in official training events – such as existing courses. This is likely to assure that new workers learn and experience the benefits of the EPSS (Nguyen, 2008). At present, many training departments are not ready to adopt electronic performance support. They must therefore adopt considerable changes when an EPSS is implemented – as discussed later in this chapter. When considering the adjustments that need to be made to training materials as a result of the implementation of an EPSS, the time and effort expended by instructional designers and training staff working on the EPSS should be taken in to account.
* *Focal points*. An EPSS team will include focal points (subject-matter experts and reviewers) from all units affected by the EPSS ('programme sponsors'). These focal points play a significant role in identifying procedures that need support and will help in defining and approving specific interventions to answer the performance challenge in a comprehensive way. As the implementation of an EPSS expands, the number of focal points and time invested is likely to increase. Focal points are usually not EPSS-dedicated personnel, but they perform other duties in the enterprise. The issues of ongoing costs and priority of tasks associated with focal points are likely to become critical in later stages of the project.

THE DESIGN OF THE FUNCTIONALITY AND THE USER-INTERFACE OF AN ELECTRONIC PERFORMANCE SUPPORT SYSTEM

The user-interface may be the single-most important element of a successful EPSS (Gery, 1991). Usability and acceptance procedures need to be tested and the system's design needs to be approved with a sample of the target audience before full implementation commences – as discussed by van Schaik (2010, Chapter 2 of this volume). The following few rules are suggested to keep early interventions simple and easy to adopt by users and maintenance teams.

1. Provide visible and simple support to a large body of host application users.
2. Make sure the users as well as management can see clearly the benefits and values of EPSS interventions.
3. Keep the performance support rules as simple and as clear as possible (Rossett and Schafer, 2007: pp. 178–82). Simplicity of design will enhance the efficiency of updates which are bound to be required.
4. Automate individual (task-level) intervention actions (for example, call-outs) rather then ask users to access these when needed.
5. Refrain from automated-procedure interventions consisting of several actions. These may be considered as a threat to workers' independence. Moreover, this kind of intervention requires extra design effort because it is likely to create confusion for older users.

A well-designed EPSS intervention is not enough to ensure effective support. As van Schaik stresses in Chapter 2, people also need to have prerequisite knowledge. Instructional designers should identify and incorporate prerequisite knowledge for each procedure. Neglecting prerequisites may lead to poor results, the source of which might be unclear at first due to the apparently perfect design of an EPSS intervention.

THE MANAGEMENT OF ORGANISATIONAL CHANGE

The competency challenge discussed in the section entitled 'Competency challenges of corporate settings' applies to training departments in organisations that face difficulties in meeting goals related to competencies. An EPSS can be an important measure for dealing with this challenge but it requires a training department to change and adopt new ways of thinking and to produce new deliverables to the enterprise. Online learning, learning-on-demand and even job aids are all methods well within the traditional boundaries of training. Electronic performance support, even though it relates to these methods, is a different concept and will force a change on the entire organisation – starting with the training department.

One of the most widely recognised benefits of electronic performance support is reducing the costs of traditional training. Though this may be perceived as a threat to training managers it is actually one of the most powerful incentives for them as well. If an EPSS is implemented as a competency-enhancement tool and the training department is responsible for its operation, the EPSS will help mainly to reduce older workers' costly training hours – thereby helping the training department to increase a business's productivity and efficiency.

The difficulties that training personnel in general and managers of training departments in particular will face with the implementation of electronic performance support originate from new responsibilities outside the perceived boundaries of traditional training. An EPSS will address major deficiencies in workers' task performance by incorporating interventions in a business's essential IT systems. The influence of a training department on essential IT systems is a considerable change – not only for the training department, but also for IT departments and production/service units. Training departments, which were usually involved in training activities taking place in classrooms before the actual tasks were being performed, are now influencing the performance of tasks as they are being performed. IT departments and production/service units need to allow this to happen, but in particular managers of training departments must accept their new and much more powerful role in competency management.

ASSESSING THE NATURE OF ELECTRONIC PERFORMANCE SUPPORT

As previously discussed in the section entitled 'Implications of the implementation of an EPSS', issues relating to the conceptual changes of certain departments that an enterprise must undergo to achieve successful implementation are project leadership, the construction of an EPSS project team and inter-departmental collaboration. It is recommended that a holistic view be taken of the implementation of electronic performance support from the start in order to overcome these conceptual obstacles. Based on van Schaik's (Chapter 2) distinction of approaches to electronic performance support, it is possible to assess whether an EPSS implemented in an enterprise gives more responsibility to the IT department or to the training department. van Schaik claims that the goal of electronic performance support is to enhance task performance by changing problem-solving-based performance to skill-based performance. He discriminates between two approaches used to achieve this goal.

First, immediate support of task performance without a course of instruction. van Schaik's example of this approach was providing procedural steps. When considering intrinsic EPSS capabilities, the examples can range from automatic data population and changes in the user-interface to data capture from other systems and automated calculations using on-screen data.

Second, providing instruction (or other learning activities) to enhance future task performance. An example is procedural step-by-step support explaining not only the next step, but also, what data should be considered and how certain decisions should be made using it.

These approaches can also be distinguished by their level of influence on target applications. In the first approach, interventions permanently change the target application's interface. The reason is that every time a worker performs a designated task they have to rely on the intervention to achieve the required level of performance. The second approach represents a temporary scaffolding intervention which is likely to become redundant with use and time. Workers learn and incorporate the capabilities of performing the task on their own.

Using the two approaches, it is possible to categorise EPSS solutions in the enterprise and assess whether the nature of the solution is more related to IT or training. Permanent changes to the work environment without learning or enhancements provided by instruction are considered IT in nature, whereas enhancements in learning and capabilities are responsibilities related to training. This distinction can be reduced to the question of 'Which factor in the performance challenge is being targeted: the IT system or human capabilities?' The answer to this question ought to help decide who should lead the implementation of electronic performance support, what personnel should be assigned to an EPSS project team and what benefits and ROI are expected. Another approach could be to allocate interventions to training and IT teams, creating two sub-teams, each responsible for different kinds of solution and benefit using an (off-the-shelf)

EPSS development platform. In conclusion, it is important to note that once the nature of a particular EPSS has been introduced and accepted by management and workers, it is likely to be extremely difficult to change it later.

Conclusions

This chapter has argued and presented evidence for the notion that the concept of electronic performance support needs to be implemented in contemporary corporate settings to allow businesses to better face current performance challenges. When introduced in such settings, an EPSS can enhance the ability of training and IT departments to address human factors and system factors that impact on issues of performance and productivity.

As the potential benefits are great, the ongoing costs of the implementation of electronic performance support are likely to be high. Costs will include monetary expenses claimed by different departments of an enterprise and vendors as well as non-monetary costs concerning mainly the management of change in training and IT departments.

Training departments should welcome this change and the responsibilities that come with it. The long and arduous goal of achieving ROI from training efforts that was difficult to realise before can now finally be accomplished by EPSS interventions.

Further research and information-sharing regarding electronic performance support in corporate settings is essential for achieving a common understanding and standards regarding the role of electronic performance support and effective implementation within business corporations. It is the authors' belief that the concept which was first introduced in corporate settings has not yet reached its potential in the methods and deliverables of present-day training departments. As technology, research methodology and development know-how advance, so will the successful implementation of electronic performance support in corporate and academic institutes. The cooperation of academic research and corporations is an important factor in achieving this goal.

References

Altalib, H. (2002). ROI calculations for electronic performance support systems. *Performance Improvement*, 41(10), 12–22.

Bailey, K.D. (2004). Supporting your learning organization through the integration of a performance support system. *Journal of Instruction Delivery Systems*, 18(2), 34–39.

Barker, P. (1995). *Emerging principles of performance support*. Online Information-International Meeting. University of Teesside, UK: Human-Computer Interaction Laboratory. Last accessed 26/12/2008 from *http://www.scm.tees.ac.uk/users/philip.barker/online95/online95.doc*

Bastiaens, T.J. (1999). Assessing an electronic performance support system for the analysis of job and tasks. *International Journal of Training and Development*, 3(1), 54–61.

Bastiaens, T.J., Nijhof, W.J. and Abma, H.J. (1997a). *Electronic performance support for telephone operators*. In Proceedings of the Conference for Academy of Human Resource Development, Minneapolis, MN. Last accessed 26/12/2008 from *http://eric.ed.gov/ERICWebPortal/custom portlets/recordDetails/*

detailmini.jsp?_nfpb=trueand_andERICExtSearch_SearchValue 0=ED406569andERICExtSearch_Search Type_0=noandaccno=ED406569

Bastiaens, T.J., Nijhof, W.J., Streumer, J.N. and Abma, H.J. (1997b). Working and learning with electronic performance support systems: An effectiveness study. *International Journal of Training and Development*, 1(1), 72–78.

Bayram, S. (2004). Revisioning theoretical framework of electronic performance support systems (EPSS) within the software application examples. *Turkish Online Journal of Distance Education*, 5(2), Article 5. Last accessed 26/12/2008 from *http://tojde.anadolu.edu.tr/tojde14/articles/bayram.htm*

Benko, S. and Webster, S. (1997) Preparing for EPSS projects. *Communications of the ACM*, 40(7), 60–63.

Bezanson, W. (2002). *Performance support solution: Achieving business goals through enabling user performance*. Victoria, BC, Canada: Trafford Publishing.

Bill, D. (1997). Transforming EPSS to support organizational learning. *Journal of Instructional Delivery Systems*, 11(2), 3–11.

Cagiltay, K. (2001). A design and development model for building electronic performance support systems. *Proceedings of the Association for Educational Communications and Technology*, 1–2, 433–440.

Chase, N. (1998). Electronic support cuts training time. *Quality Magazine*. Last accessed 12/1/2005 from *http://openacademy.mindef.gov.sg/OpenAcademy/Learning%20Resources/EPSS/c16.htm*

Cole, K., Fischer, O. and Saltzman, P. (1997). Just-in-time knowledge delivery: A case study of an award-winning support system demonstrates the vital characteristics and primary design goals for generating peak performance. *Communications of the ACM*, (40)7, 49–53.

Desmarais, M.C., Leclair, R., Fiset, J.V. and Talbi, H. (1997). Cost-justifying electronic performance support systems. *Communications of the ACM*, 40(7), 39–48.

Dolezalek, H. (2005). The 2005 industry report. *Training*, 42(12), 14–28.

Foster, E. (1997). Training when you need it. *Info World*. Last accessed 17/11/2004 from *http://openacademy.mindef.gov.sg/OpenAcademy/Learning%20Resources/EPSS/c1.htm*

Gery, G. (1989). *Electronic Performance Support Systems*. Boston, MA: Weingarten Publications.

Gery, G. (1991). *Electronic performance support systems: How and Why to Remake the Workplace through the Strategic Application of Technology*. Tolland, MA: Gery Performance Press.

Gery, G. (1995). Attributes and behaviors of performance-centered systems. *Performance Improvement Quarterly*, 8(1), 47–93.

Gustafson, K. (2000). Designing technology-based performance support. *Educational Technology*, 40(1), 38–44.

Hawkins, C.H., Gustafson, K.L. and Nielson, T. (1998). Return on investment (ROI) for electronic performance support systems: A web-based system. *Educational Technology*, 38(4), 15–22.

Hudzina, M., Rowley, K. and Wagner, W. (1996). Electronic performance support technology: Defining the domain. *Performance Improvement Quarterly*, 9(1), 36–48.

Ip, B. (2010). Business and commerce. In P. Barker and P. van Schaik (eds), *Electronic Performance Support: Using Technology to Enhance Human Ability*. Aldershot, Hants: Gower.

Laffey, M.J. and Musser, D. (1996). *Building Internet-based electronic performance support for teaching and learning*. Last accessed 26/12/2008 from *http://ad.informatik.uni-freiburg.de/bibliothek/proceedings/webnet96/Html/139.htm*

Liner, D. and Woods, H. (1999). *Measuring the impact of performance support systems*. Department of Educational Technology at San Diego State University. Last accessed 26/12/2008 from *http://home.pacbell.net/lwhyman/rwd/eval.html#brief*

Malcolm, S. (1992). Reengineering corporate training. *Training*, 29(8), 57–61.

Malcolm, S. (1998). The 100 percent solution. *Training*, 35(7), 72. Last accessed 1/1/2009 from *http://www.performance-vision.com/articles/art-metrics-viewpoint.htm*

Mao, J. and Brown, B. (2005). The effectiveness of online task support versus instructor-led training. *Journal of Organizational and End User Computing*, 17(3), 27–46.

Maughan, R.G. (2005). Electronic performance support systems and technological literacy. *The Journal of Technology Studies*, 31(1), 49–56.

Milheim, W. (1997). Instructional design issues for electronic performance support systems. *British Journal of Educational Technology*, 28(2), 103–110.

Morrison, J.E. and Witmer, B.G. (1983). A comparative evaluation of computer-based and print-based job performance aids. *Journal of Computer-Based Instruction*, 10(3), 73–75.

Nguyen, F. (2005). EPSS needs assessment: Oops, I forgot how to do that! *Performance Improvement*, 44(9), 33–39.

Nguyen, F. (2008). The effect of performance support and training on performer attitudes. *Performance Improvement*, 21(1), 95–114.

Nguyen, F. and Klein, J.D. (2008). The effect of performance support and training as performance interventions. *Performance Improvement Quarterly*, 21(1), 95–114.

Nguyen, F. Klein, J.D. and Sullivan, H. (2005). A comparative study of electronic performance support systems. *Performance Improvement Quarterly*, 18(4), 71–86.

Northrup, P.T. (1999). *Building the design framework and user interface for an EPSS*. Paper presented in AECT Conference, Houston TX. Last accessed 26/12/2008 from *http://www.uwf.edu/pnorthru/AECT99/considerations_for_designing_eps.htm*

Phillips, J.J. (1997). *Handbook of Training Evaluation and Measurement Methods* (3rd edn). Houston, TX: Gulf Publishing Company.

Racine, S. Kralick, K. andYesuraja, S. (2004). Defining an effective electronic performance support system. *STC Usability SIG newsletter*, 10(3), 1. Last accessed 1/1/2009 from *http://www.stcsig.org/usability/newsletter/0401-epss.html*

Raybould, B. (1995). Performance support engineering: An emerging development methodology for enabling organizational learning. *Performance Improvement Quarterly*, 8(1), 7–22.

Raybould, B. (2000). Performance support engineering: Building performance-cantered web-based systems, information systems and knowledge management systems in the 21st century. *Performance Improvement Journal*, 39(6), 32–39.

Rosenberg, M.J. (1995). Performance technology, performance support, and the future of training: A commentary. *Performance Improvement Quarterly*, 8(1), 94–99.

Rosenberg, M.J., Coscarelli, W.C. and Hutchison, C.S. (1999). The origins and evolution of the field. In H.D. Stolovitch and E.J. Keeps (eds), *Handbook of Human Performance Technology: Improving Individual and Organizational Performance Worldwide* (pp. 24–46). San Francisco, CA: Jossey-Bass, Pfeiffer.

Rossett, A. and Schafer, L. (2006). Job aids and performance support: the convergence of learning and work. *International Journal of Learning Technology*, 2(4), 310–328.

Rupel, R. (2002). Learning from EPSS. *Technical Communication*, 49(2), 328–332.

Russel, T.R. (1999). *The No Significant Difference Phenomenon* (5th edn). Montgomery, AL: International Distance Education Certification Center.

Schaik, P. van (2010). Psychological perspective. In P. Barker and P. van Schaik (eds), *Electronic Performance Support: Using Technology to Enhance Human Ability*. Aldershot, Hants: Gower.

Schaik, P. van, Barker, P. and Famakinwa, O. (2007a). Making a case for using electronic performance support systems in academic libraries. *Journal of Interactive Learning Research*, 18(3), 411–428.

Schaik, P. van, Barker, P. and Famakinwa, O. (2007b). Building electronic performance support systems for first-year university students. *Innovations in Education and Teaching International*, 44(3), 243–255.

Schaik, P. van, Barker, P. and Pearson, R. (2002). Designing electronic performance support systems to facilitate learning. *Innovations in Education and Teaching International*, 39(4), 289–306.

Spool, J.M. (2001). *Users don't learn to search better.* Last accessed 3/4/2005 from *http://www.uie.com/articles/learn_to_search*

Villachica, S.W. and Stone, D.L. (1999). Performance support systems. In H.D. Stolovitch and E.J. Keeps (eds), *Handbook of Human Performance Technology: Improving Individual and Organizational Performance Worldwide* (pp. 442–463). San Francisco, CA: Jossey-Bass, Pfeiffer.

Wild, M. (1998). *Investigating the instructional value of performance support systems.* Internal report. Edith Cowan University, Australia.

Winer, L.R., Rushby, N. and Vazquez-Abad, J. (1999). Emerging trends in instructional interventions. In H.D. Stolovitch and E.J. Keeps (eds), *Handbook of Human Performance Technology: Improving Individual and Organizational Performance Worldwide* (pp. 867–893). San Francisco, CA: Jossey-Bass, Pfeiffer.

Wisener, G. (2002). Overcoming barriers to performance-centered design. *Job Performance Aids and EPSS.* Last accessed 13/4/2008 from *http://files.epsscentral.info/gery/pdfarticles/barriers_to_pcd.pdf*

Witt, C. L. and Wager, W. (1994). A comparison of instructional systems design and electronic performance support systems design. *Educational Technology*, 34(7), 20–2.

13 *Supporting Expert Work Processes*

CHRISTOPHER G. JENNINGS, ARTHUR E. KIRKPATRICK
AND PEYVAND MOHSENI

Although much software exists to support the specific *products* that experts create (for example, tools for writing, computations or graphic design), little, if any, software is designed to support the *processes* typically used by experts to create those products. In this chapter we review research from a range of theoretical perspectives on the work processes of domain experts as they solve problems. From this review, we then derive a list of ten design principles for software to support effective expert processes. We go on to present two prototype performance support systems that we have implemented which incorporate these principles. Both prototypes share the single most important feature, supporting the development of multiple solutions rather than just one. The second prototype, which supports the design of analysis of variance (ANOVA) experiments, includes nearly all the design principles we propose. The strong theoretical basis of the prototype systems suggests that they have the potential to support expert performance differently from product-oriented software. In future work we plan to verify these performance improvements in empirical studies.

Introduction

Contemporary domain experts are supported by a range of powerful applications to help them in their tasks. Databases, spreadsheets and statistical packages support the tasks of managing and analysing data. Web browsers help locate information and opinions from an immense range of available sources. Word processors and presentation packages help present recommendations to others. Decision support systems integrate data from a range of sources and display these informatively. Indeed, support for knowledge work has been a strong trend in human-computer interaction research, dating back to the defining works in the field (Card, Moran, and Newell, 1983; Norman and Draper, 1986). Yet, despite the longevity, breadth and demonstrated power of such software, it may have a significant limitation.

The software currently available focuses on end-products rather than process. While the products are important, expert performance consists of more than executing the detailed steps needed to produce a work product. The most challenging problems appear within the larger processes of choosing and sequencing those steps. Current software provides no overt support for these higher-level processes.

Whether this is a problem depends upon several factors. Perhaps expert processes are so transparent that their performance is effortless or perhaps such processes are so idiosyncratic that there is no common basis to support. In this chapter, we investigate the potential for explicit software support of expert work processes. We begin by selectively reviewing existing research on expert performance, deriving a list of ten software features that are likely to support common expert practices. Current (product-driven) software provides little to no support for them. We then describe two prototype applications that provide explicit support for expert processes. The first, which supports statistical analysis of experimental results, enhances an existing analysis package by adding a minimal subset of the features. The second is a standalone application that supports the design of experiments, implementing nearly all the features for expert practice. These prototypes demonstrate how the principles can inform the design of application software, making it easier for experts to carry out effective problem solving in the overall process of expert work. We conclude the chapter with a discussion of the limitations of the feature set and ways in which their effectiveness may be tested.

Deriving a Theoretical Basis for Supporting Expert Work Processes

Historically, there have been many approaches taken to the study of expertise. We will review some of these perspectives and identify common elements that suggest fruitful areas for software support.

ILL-STRUCTURED PROBLEMS

The problems tackled by many experts in their work are of the so-called *wicked* or *ill-structured* variety. Unlike puzzle-solving problems, ill-structured problems are characterized by incomplete information and ambiguous goals (Hall et al., 1995; Rittel and Webber, 1973). Policy creation, graphic design, story-telling, software development: all are jobs in which expert practitioners create a product which attempts to solve an ill-defined problem. The expert work process can equally well be described as the solving of ill-structured problems. Rittel and Webber (1973) first described ill-structured problems in the context of social planning. They identified the following four general features that all ill-structured problems exhibit.

1. There is no single goal state

Ill-structured problems are defined by both hard (non-negotiable) and soft (negotiable) constraints. While a problem such as a block puzzle has only one solution state, because of soft constraints ill-structured problems have multiple acceptable solutions. Soft constraints cannot be simultaneously optimal (one cannot have maximum freedom and maximum security). The task is therefore not to find *the* solution, but to compare solutions and choose the best compromise.

2. There are no objective, universal metrics for the constraints. Stakeholders do not agree on the relative importance of competing constraints

Comparing solutions is necessary to make a selection, yet the attributes of interest cannot be objectively measured. How can we measure attributes such as happiness, quality, fairness or safety? If we could measure them, how would we agree upon how much is 'enough'? The answer depends not just on objective facts, but on one's social values and the influence of others.

3. Problems cannot be isolated from other problems, and cannot be decomposed into simpler sub-problems

Ill-structured problems are never lonely: each can be considered the symptom of another ill-structured problem. Rather than design an experiment around a small budget, we might instead question the priorities of the budget itself. This problem-symptom duality is a consequence of soft constraints. A problem with only hard constraints has no ambiguity and is therefore well structured: either all of the hard constraints can be met, or they cannot. Soft constraints, on the other hand, are necessarily subjective and ambiguous: choosing the best value for the constraint becomes its own ill-structured problem. The result is a web of problems that form complex feedback loops. Choosing a solution for problem A changes the constraints on its neighbours B and C. Adapting C to meet the new constraints has implications for its neighbours, including A. It also implies that ill-structured problems cannot be broken down into simpler (well-structured) sub-problems. Any decomposition must include at least one ill-structured sub-problem. Problem-solving strategies which rely on recursive decomposition into sub-problems – like those used in classical artificial intelligence – cannot work for ill-structured problems. Even worse, by considering the problem in the context of its neighbours, it is possible to recursively *grow* the problem to include an arbitrary number of related problems.

4. Each problem instance is unique

The resources available to a problem, and therefore the constraints placed upon it, vary with the context in which an ill-structured problem occurs, as do the states of the interconnected problems. Every ill-structured problem is therefore unique. Solutions are not repeatable. One can distinguish general patterns and develop a repertoire of useful strategies (Alexander, 1977), but – unlike for mathematical problems – there is no definitive answer to an ill-structured problem.

PROBLEM-SOLVING STRATEGIES OF PROFESSIONALS

Akin describes some of the strategies employed by human problem-solvers in exploring a problem space. Of particular interest is his study of how the strategies of architects change as they become more experienced (Akin, 2001). Novice architects tend to employ a depth-first search of the design space. They hit on an approach, and then follow through with it as far as they can. It is only when an approach reaches an impasse that they go back to look for alternatives. Over time, expert architects adopt a different strategy, neither breadth-first nor depth-first but rather a mixed strategy that considers alternative approaches and develops each in parallel, borrowing ideas from some to apply to others.

Schön observed expert practitioners from a range of disciplines (Schön, 1983) and identified two key activities. Both are responses to the fluid, experienced work that makes use of tacit knowledge – what Schön calls 'knowledge-in-action' – being interrupted by *surprises*. When practitioners encounter such surprises, they enter one of two *reflective processes*. Schön named these processes *reflection-in-action* and *reflection-on-action*.

During reflection-in-action, the practitioner is thinking about what is being done while actually doing it, with the dual goals of better understanding the surprising phenomenon and influencing the outcome of the process. The practitioner's actions become a cycle of proposing and testing hypotheses about the nature of the phenomenon and how to change it in desired ways. Emerging states 'talk back' to the practitioner, while the practitioner simultaneously talks back by changing to a new state.

During reflection-on-action, practitioners stop and think back over what has been done and how it informs their own understanding of the problem and their practice. Reflection-on-action is a reflection on the already explored paths: unlike reflection-in-action, no new paths are explored. This leaves the practitioner free to explore other questions – for example, to consider their own behaviour and motivations, or to reconsider the nature of the problem being solved.

Schön sees the use of repertoires – collections of examples, actions, images and ideas – as essential to reflective practice. The practitioner's repertoire forms a basis of experience and knowledge through which new phenomena are understood (Schön, 1983: p. 138).

EXPERTISE AS SKILLED PERFORMANCE

The most long-standing approach to expertise considers it as skilled performance, emphasizing the practice of recurrent skills. A leading researcher in this area (Ericsson, n.d.) defines an expert as 'any individual who attained their superior performance by instruction and extended practice'. Typical domains considered are sports and chess (Ericsson, 2002). Sporting skills are analysed in terms of a skilled performer's control of fundamental strokes. Chess is analysed in terms of the player's ability to recognize patterns on the board. Of course, exceptional performance in these domains depends upon non-recurrent skills as well, such as creativity, planning and strategy, but the skilled performance research paradigm focuses on repetitive tasks as the backbone of high performance.

Despite the focus on highly-practised behaviours that have little conscious control in their execution, Ericsson (n.d.) acknowledges the ability of experts to select from amongst several choices, emphasizing that this is achieved by maintaining special representations of appropriate information in working memory, allowing rapid evaluations of alternatives.

Ericsson also emphasizes the importance of representation of knowledge and long-term memory for expert performance. Experts represent their knowledge in domain-specific terms that allow rapid retrieval of information relevant to the current situation. Furthermore, experts have more effective access to long-term memory (Ericsson and Kintsch, 1995), due to the development of memory skills specific to their domain. This increases the range of information available to them when they consider alternatives.

CREATIVITY AND EXPERTISE

Expert work processes rely on the ability to generate and consider alternative approaches when problem solving. The effective generation of such alternatives requires creativity, the ability to produce ideas which are both novel and useful (Sternberg and Lubart, 1988: p. 3). Expert support systems should therefore also be creativity support systems. Csikszentmihalyi and Sawyer (1995) focus on the conditions under which a specific element of creativity – insight – is likely to occur. They specifically argue that the opportunity to test possibilities is necessary for insight.

Candy and Edmonds (1997) argue that a system for support of creative activity should enable users to:

- View the problem holistically. Features such as multiple views with distinct representations and overviews will help.
- Support parallel tracks of exploration. Candy and Edmonds's emphasis on support for multiple representations of knowledge dovetails with Ericsson's evidence that experts represent domain knowledge in ways that allow rapid access from multiple perspectives.
- Temporarily suspend judgement on any matter.
- Make unplanned deviations from a set course.
- Reformulate the problem space.

Shneiderman (2007), another scholar of software support for creativity, recommends the ability to log intermediate steps that led to current situations, to edit history and to replay it with different parameters.

Requirements for Software Support of Expertise and Creativity

The selective summary of problem solving presented above reveals several important commonalities shared across widely differing views and definitions of expertise. There is a common focus on history, considering alternatives and diversity of representations. From these commonalities we have derived the following ten requirements shared by expert workers:

1. The need to represent relevant constraints on the solution, and to determine how well a given solution fulfils those constraints (derived from the sections 'Ill-structured problems' and 'Expertise as skilled performance' above), but also the ability to suspend judgement on an issue (see the section entitled 'Creativity and expertise' above).
2. The need to allow for fluid, subjective metrics for soft constraints (see the section entitled 'Ill-structured problems' above).
3. The need to keep in mind the context of the problem with respect to related problems that it intersects with (see the sections entitled 'Ill-structured problems' and 'Creativity and expertise' above).
4. The need to build internal or external representations of past experiences to aid in understanding new phenomena (see the sections entitled 'Ill-structured problems', 'Problem-solving strategies of professionals' and 'Expertise as skilled performance' above).

5. The need for generality and flexibility in both actions and the representation of solutions, due to the unique nature of problem instances (see the sections entitled 'Ill-structured problems', 'Expertise as skilled performance' and 'Creativity and expertise' above).
6. The need to experiment by forming and testing hypotheses in order to better understand the problem space (see the section entitled 'Problem-solving strategies of professionals' above).
7. The need to review and reflect on the history of actions taken so far ('see the sections entitled 'Problem-solving strategies of professionals' and 'Creativity and expertise' above).
8. The need to explore the breadth and depth of the problem space *in parallel* (see the section entitled 'Problem-solving strategies of professionals' above).
9. The need to take ideas that were discovered while exploring one approach to the problem and reapply these ideas to other approaches (see the sections entitled 'Ill-structured problems', 'Problem-solving strategies of professionals' and 'Creativity and expertise' above).
10. The need to occasionally redefine the problem space itself, in order to accommodate radically new solutions (see the section entitled 'Creativity and expertise' above).

Each requirement in this list is also a potential feature of a performance support system for expert workers. In the next section, we will introduce two projects, *Treesta* and *XDS*, both of which support requirements from this list with the goal of improving expert performance.

Two Prototype Systems Supporting Research Design and Analysis

We present two prototypes that put the principles from the previous section into action. Each prototype supports a different kind of ill-structured problem that occurs during experimental research: statistical analysis (*Treesta*) and experimental design (*XDS*). Although related by a common domain, the projects are quite different. However, both include automatic capturing and structuring of the interaction history to keep previous problem states available for future reuse. Automatic capture allows support for the many requirements that involve previous states, and also prevents the break in attention required to capture and organize history manually. As a result, experts keep their focus on the key task of generating and comparing alternatives.

TREESTA: IMPLEMENTING A CORE SUBSET OF SUPPORT FOR EXPERT PRACTICE

Treesta (Mohseni, 2008), whose name is a portmanteau derived from 'tree' and 'statistics', demonstrates the core set of requirements for supporting expertise and creativity, applied to the domain of analysis of designed experiments. In this domain, an expert analyst has knowledge both of a research area and analysis of variance (ANOVA). Given a set of data from a designed experiment, the analyst searches for the best model of the data, evaluating possible models using ANOVA. Analysts typically use various ANOVA stastistics to assess the quality of a model, including statistical significance (p-values), effect sizes, Bayesian probabilities and model fit. Of these criteria, *Treesta* focuses on p-values, a widely used criterion. A more complete implementation, designed to support the full needs of professional statisticians, could easily incorporate additional criteria.

Treesta is implemented as a front-end to the *MATLAB* statistical computing language (*http://www.mathworks.com*). Most *Treesta* commands are statements in the *MATLAB* language, which *Treesta* records in a history and passes unchanged to the *MATLAB* application. *Treesta* collects the history of *MATLAB* statements and the variables recording their results into *workspaces*. A workspace encapsulates a single ANOVA, together with the variables holding the data for the ANOVA and the history of the statements creating those variables. *Treesta* organizes these workspaces in a tree structure, reflecting the dependencies between data used in the computations. A small set of commands are handled directly by *Treesta* and never passed to *MATLAB*. These commands allow the analyst to name workspaces and select the currently active workspace.

Figure 13.1 illustrates a simple *Treesta* hierarchy of three workspaces. The top workspace, named '*Root*', represents the first analysis of some data. It contains a single variable, named '*data*', the history of two *MATLAB* statements leading to the ANOVA, two figures, and the *p*-value produced by the ANOVA. The analyst next took the log of the original data and performed a second ANOVA. *Treesta* automatically collected the statements and data for this new analysis in a separate workspace, a child of *Root*. The analyst named this new workspace '*Log_analysis*'. The analyst then returned to the original workspace, removed the outliers from the data, and performed a third ANOVA. *Treesta* automatically placed the statements and variables for this analysis in a third workspace, named '*No_outliers*' by the analyst. Because the data for the third analysis was derived directly from the untransformed data in *Root* rather than the logarithmically transformed data in *Log_analysis*, *Treesta* made *No_outliers* a direct child of *Root*.

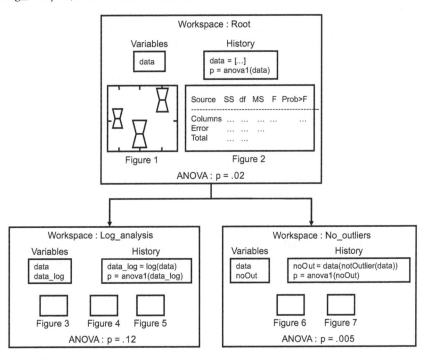

Figure 13.1 A simple *Treesta* hierarchy of three workspaces

Note: The *Root* workspace contains the original analysis, the *Log_analysis* workspace contains an analysis of the log-transformed data, and the *No_outliers* workspace contains an analysis of the data with outliers removed. Each workspace contains the *MATLAB* statements, variables, figures and ANOVA *p*-value comprising each analysis.

By assigning each ANOVA solution to a separate workspace, *Treesta* makes the search for solutions visible, in sharp distinction to the simple linear command history provided by *MATLAB*. The visibility of the search implements Requirement 8 for support of expertise, the ability to explore the breadth and depth of the problem space in parallel, by making it simple for an analyst to maintain multiple concurrent analyses, each with an independent set of variables and analysis. This in turn encourages the analyst to explore multiple solutions.

Requirement 7 for support of expertise is the ability to review and reflect on the history of the search so far. *Treesta* implements this requirement by providing a summary view of all the workspaces, allowing an analyst to compare the *p*-values for each workspace. The hierarchy can assist the analyst's reflection on the analyses to date and identify the next analyses.

Treesta demonstrates that an existing application, providing strong support for specific work products, can be extended to also provide support for expert work processes. Under *Treesta*, the full set of *MATLAB* commands work unchanged. *Treesta* simply adds a higher level of organization to these commands, grouping them around the ANOVA at the heart of each analysis. *Treesta's* design is carefully organized to create this higher level with minimal disruption to an analyst. If the analyst issues no *Treesta* commands, each ANOVA will be assigned its own workspace in a linear sequence. Although simple, this organization provides substantial benefits, separating the variables for each analysis and preserving them. If the analyst wishes to gain the further benefits of organizing the workspaces into a hierarchy, *Treesta* allows this to be done simply and quickly; it is then possible to return to the primary focus, refining the data analysis. Our next sample application, *XDS*, demonstrates how the core support of expert practice shown in *Treesta* can be extended to encompass nearly the full set of requirements listed in the section entitled 'Requirements for software support of expertise and creativity' above.

XDS: IMPLEMENTING FULL SUPPORT FOR EXPERT PRACTICE

XDS (Jennings and Kirkpatrick, 2007) is a design tool for planning experiments that use ANOVA statistical models. The ANOVA computational model is based on Lorenzen and Anderson's (1993) generalized model of ANOVA designs. Design support is based on the technique of *design space exploration* (Woodbury and Burrow, 2006). Recalling Newell and Simon's (1972) work on problem solving, design space explorers model the set of possible designs and the operations that transform one design in the set into another. *XDS* takes the design space representation a step further, using it not just for computation but as an interaction metaphor as well. Designs are represented explicitly as points in a discrete two-dimensional space, and design history is captured by linking explored points with arrows.

Designs in the space can be viewed as a prototype-based object tree: each design recursively inherits its attributes from its parent except for those attributes that it modifies. The arrows connecting designs illustrate these parent-child relations, allowing the user to trace back through the history of an exploration session; for example, to locate a previously considered design in order to expand upon or refine it.

Figure 13.2 shows a small session with *XDS*, and Jennings and Kirkpatrick (2008) provide online videos of *XDS* in use. Sessions begin with a grid (representing unexplored points) surrounding the initial Empty Design. The view is a zooming user interface (Bederson and Meyer, 1998), which can be panned to navigate the space, or zoomed in or out to view the designs at different levels of detail. The zoomed-in view presents designs using traditional statistical notation; the zoomed-out view presents graphical summaries of key soft constraints (such as the design's statistical power and resource cost) and also indicates whether the design satisfies a set of hard constraints defined by the user. We call these summaries *consequences* of the design. Consequences are not easily derived from the problem state by hand but are critical for making informed judgements when comparing designs and when proposing and testing hypotheses about the possible effects of design transformations. Because the interpretation of these metrics can vary from one discipline to another, our consequence computations allow a limited degree of end-user programmability. The difference between the zoomed-in and zoomed-out views is comparable to the difference between considering the particular word choices in a book and wondering whether it tells a satisfying story overall. Both are important, but the story metric is generally more useful when comparing broadly different approaches, while the exact wording is more useful when refining and fine-tuning a specific approach.

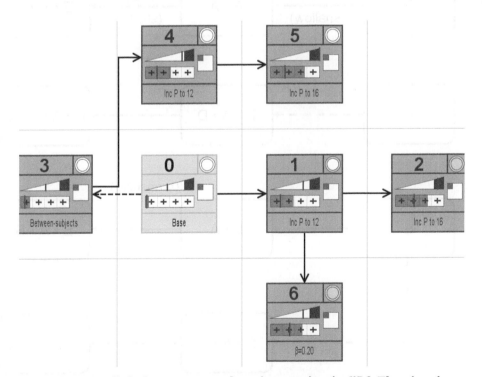

Figure 13.2 A small design-space exploration session in *XDS*. The view is zoomed out, so designs are being shown as summaries of important constraints (consequences)

   Moving the pointer over a design will present the user with the operations that may be applied to that design as a *halo menu*. Like pie menus (Callahan et al., 1988), halo menus lay menu items out in a roughly radial arrangement. However, the principal purpose of halo menus is to encourage users to explore the design space more thoroughly rather than to improve selection efficiency. Each halo menu item is a design-transforming operation, called a *move*, which leads to a new point in the design space. A design's halo menu appears automatically when the pointer moves over it, and disappears when it leaves. Assuming the pointer gives a rough approximation of the user's locus of attention, halo menus continually prompt the user with possible moves for the design the user is considering.

   Using modifier keys, halo menus can apply moves in three different ways, called *shallow*, *deep* and *branching*. Figure 13.3 illustrates the different move types at a conceptual level by representing designs as compositions of moves (indicated by letters).

   Shallow moves are the most common. These create a new design by cloning the target design and then changing the clone's attributes as needed to fulfil the operation. The result is shown as a new point in the space, connected to the target design by an arrow. Shallow moves allow the rapid generation of new designs while keeping related designs ready-to-hand for comparison, reflection and further development.

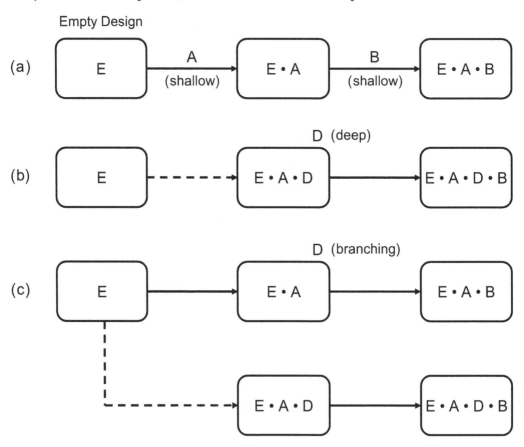

Figure 13.3 **The application of (a) shallow, (b) deep and (c) branch moves in**
            XDS

Deep moves fill two principal roles. The first role is non-destructive error correction. With traditional undo, when a user undoes some actions in order to insert a missing operation, all of the subsequent operations are lost. Deep moves allow the designer to modify the design history and non-destructively insert missing or corrected operations. The target design, and every design directly or indirectly derived from it, will incorporate the correction as if the mistake had never been made. This is illustrated in diagram (b) of Figure 13.3. After creating the state shown in diagram (a), the designer realizes that they should have started with move D instead of move A. Performing D as a deep move on the design $E{\cdot}A$ rectifies this, inserting D into the design history as if it *had* been performed first.

The second role of deep moves is allowing the designer to perform moves without generating visible points in the space, combining two or more moves into a single result. Although these 'combining' deep moves are commonly used at the start of a session to set up a suitable base design, they are uncommon once exploration begins in earnest. There are two reasons for this drop in frequency. First, combining deep moves have low overhead. In *XDS*, shallow and deep moves are performed with equal ease; the choice of which to use is based on appropriateness rather than convenience. Second, the design space model ensures that moves generate complete, valid new designs. This means that moves are more likely to be worth recording than in a traditional tool, since they can be considered as potential solutions. (Contrast this with a word processor, in which the design moves in and out of syntactic correctness as the user types: the invalid states are unlikely to be of future interest.)

Branch moves enable the simultaneous generation of multiple designs. The target design is cloned along with all of its children, and the cloned branch is added as a new sibling of the existing branch. Then, the selected move is applied to the new branch as if it were a deep move. This allows the designer to quickly answer what-if questions that compare entire lines of exploration in a single step, without manually replaying moves.

XDS explicitly supports most of the ten requirements outlined above by using a small set of tightly interwoven techniques. In support of Requirement 1, a designer can define hard constraints and can quickly tell which designs meet them by glancing at a consequence summary; at the same time, this indicator is not so obtrusive as to short-circuit the designer's judgement. The design space model ensures that the set of moves is complete and generalized, and the programmability of the consequence view's metrics allows the designer to consider soft constraints from multiple perspectives (Requirements 2 and 5). Using the design space model as an explicit interface metaphor keeps the entire design history readily available for reflection (Requirement 7) and simplifies the task of building a repertoire (Requirement 4). When combined with shallow or branch moves and the consequence view of designs, the designer can rapidly test hypotheses about the effects of various moves (Requirement 6) and can easily compare or jump between working on designs belonging to different approaches (Requirement 8). All three move types are useful for reapplying ideas across approaches; deep and branch moves were added specifically to support this task (Requirement 9). This leaves Requirements 3 and 10 unaddressed. Requirement 3 (maintaining a global view of the problem) is beyond the scope of *XDS* since it only models the statistical aspects of the problem, while Requirement 10 also involves the broader research question and related problems. This was not an intentional choice: in the next section we will discuss why supporting either Requirement 3 or 10 is problematic for any support tool.

Implications and Next Steps

We began this chapter by considering the process of expert problem solving from several perspectives, leading to a list of ten requirements shared by expert workers. A support system needs not address all of these requirements to be successful. Supporting any of them would be expected to, at the least, reduce a problem-solver's cognitive workload and thus make the process easier for the expert, less prone to error and more likely to improve the quality of solutions.

Treesta illustrates this point well. It focuses on those needs that emphasize generating, recording, comparing, and reflecting on alternatives. By augmenting the command set of existing tools with support for these activities, the interaction paradigm shifts from being product-focused to being process-focused.

While *Treesta* takes a more minimalist approach, *XDS* demonstrates that a support system can embrace more of the principles without a proportional increase in the complexity of the user-interface. A small set of features (the simultaneous view of design space and design history, the ability to perform shallow, deep or branch moves, and the emphasis on important constraints) allow us to provide support for nearly all of our requirements.

Neither *XDS* nor *Treesta* provide significant support for Requirements 3 and 10, because both involve the representation of arbitrary entities that cannot be known at the time the system is designed. Requirement 3 relies on recognizing the other problems that have an impact on the problem of interest. However, because each problem occurs in a unique context, we can only guess at what those problems might be. Nonetheless, if the domain is one in which certain problems are common, and they have a significant impact on the outcome, it is probably worth the effort of at least representing their effect, if not supporting their solution. Requirement 10 refers to those rare times when the problem space itself is transformed to accommodate revolutionary new concepts that cannot be expressed under the existing system. This is problematic for any computerized support system, which will necessarily have internal structures and an external interface that are specialized to represent a particular view. Any attempt to ameliorate this condition must ultimately reduce the support system to an end-user programming environment which is no longer focused on any particular problem domain. This issue is not restricted to performance support systems. Artificial intelligence researchers studying problem-solving encounter the same roadblock (Boden, 1999): a computer can only vary those parameters that were given to it by its programmers.

Our requirements list is derived from a rich tradition of theoretical and empirical work. We are therefore confident that providing computer support for experts' work processes will provide a better fit with the experts' workflow than traditional tools. What remains incomplete is our understanding of *how* and *how much* such an approach can improve expert performance, and how the different requirements interact. The next step is performing empirical studies of systems, including *Treesta* and *XDS*, that implement different subsets of our requirements list. This work has already begun. A preliminary study of *XDS* in which five participants were briefly shown the system and were then allowed to explore freely found that the four participants who worked on experiment designs considered a wider breadth and depth of designs with *XDS* than they had reported doing in their regular practice (Jennings and Kirkpatrick, 2007). Unfortunately, the tightly integrated interaction techniques, along with nontraditional design choices (particularly the zooming user-interface), make it difficult to identify the individual contributions of the 10 requirements. Accordingly, we are moving toward separate studies that consider factors individually, using support systems with more traditional user-interface designs. Early results from the first such study, which focused specifically on the display of consequences, suggest that their presence improves overall design quality and reduces design time.

Solutions do not spring forth from the minds of their creators fully formed, like Athena from the head of Zeus. Yet, traditional knowledge-work applications are geared towards the task of implementing *the* solution instead of the process of discovering *a* solution. This is a carry-over from the early days of computing, when computer time was valuable and users were expected to have worked out the details offline. Today computers are plentiful and the usefulness of this mindset has passed. It is time to recognize it for what it is – a bad habit, and to build performance support systems that emphasize process over product.

Acknowledgements

Funding for the projects in this chapter was provided by the National Sciences and Engineering Research Council of Canada and the Canada Foundation for Innovation.

References

Akin, Ö. (2001). Variants in design cognition. In C.M. Eastman, W.M. McCracken and W.C. Newstetter (eds), *Design Knowing and Learning: Cognition in Design Education* (pp. 105–124). Amsterdam: Elsevier Science.

Alexander, C. (1977). *A Pattern Language: Towns, Buildings, Construction*. New York, NY: Oxford University Press.

Bederson, B. and Meyer, J. (1998). Implementing a zooming user interface: Eexperience building Pad++. *Software-Practice and Experience*, 28(10), 1101–1135.

Boden, M. (1999). Computer Models of Creativity. In R. J. Sternberg (ed.), *Handbook of Creativity* (pp. 351–372). New York, NY: Cambridge University Press.

Callahan, J., Hopkins, D., Weiser, M. and Shneiderman, B. (1988). An empirical comparison of pie vs. linear menus. In *Proceedings of the SIGCHI Conference on Human Factors in Computing Systems* (pp. 95–100). New York: ACM.

Candy, L. and Edmonds, E.A. (1997). Supporting the creative user: A criteria-based approach to interaction design. *Design Studies*, 18(2), 185–194.

Card, S.K., Moran, T.P. and Newell, A. (1983). *The Psychology of Human-computer Interaction*. Hillsdale, NJ: Lawrence Erlbaum.

Csikszentmihalyi, M. and Sawyer, R.K. (1995). Creative insight: The social dimension of a solitary moment. In R. J. Sternberg and J. E. Davidson (eds), *The Nature of Insight* (pp. 329–363). Cambridge, MA: MIT.

Ericsson, K.A. (2002). Attaining excellence through deliberate practice: insights from the study of expert performance. In M. Ferrari (ed.), *The Pursuit of Excellence in Education* (pp. 21–55). Hillsdale, NJ: Erlbaum.

Ericsson, K.A. (n.d.). Expert performance and deliberate practice. Available online at: *http://www.psy.fsu.edu/faculty/ericsson/ericsson.exp.perf.html* [Accessed on 5th February, 2009].

Ericsson, K.A. and Kintsch, W. (1995). Long-term working memory. *Psychological Review,* 102(2), 211–245.

Hall, E.P., Gott, S.P. and Pokorny, R.A. (1995). *A Procedural Guide to Cognitive Task Analysis: The PARI Methodology* (Tech. Rep. AL/HR-TR-1995-0108). Brooks Air Force Base, TX: Human Resources Directorate.

Jennings, C.G. and Kirkpatrick A.E. (2007). Design as traversal and consequences: an exploration tool for experimental designs. In C. G. Healy and E. Lank (eds), *Graphics Interface 2007* (pp. 79–86). Wellesley, MA: A K Peters.

Jennings, C.G. and Kirkpatrick A.E. (2008). *XDS* demonstration videos. Available online at: *http://gruvi.cs.sfu.ca/videos/xds/* [Accessed on 5th February, 2009].

Lorenzen, T. J. and Anderson, V.L. (1993). *Design of Experiments: A No-name Approach.* New York, NY: Marcel Dekker.

Newell, A. and Simon, H.A. (1972). *Human Problem Solving.* Englewood Cliffs, NJ: Prentice-Hall.

Mohseni, P. (2008). *Treesta: A System for Supporting Statistical Analysis Using ANOVA.* Unpublished master's thesis, Simon Fraser University, Burnaby, British Columbia, Canada.

Norman, D.A. and Draper, S.W. (Eds) (1986). *User Centered System Design.* Hillsdale, NJ: Lawrence Erlbaum.

Rittel, H. and Webber, M. (1973). Dilemmas in a general theory of planning. *Policy Sciences,* 4(2), 155–169.

Shneiderman, B. (2007). Creativity support tools. *Communications of the ACM,* 50(12), 20–32.

Schön, D.A. (1983). *The Reflective Practitioner: How Professionals Think in Action.* New York, NY: Basic Books.

Sternberg, R.J. and Lubart, T.I. (1999). The concept of creativity: Prospects and paradigms. In R. J. Sternberg (ed.), *Handbook of Creativity* (pp. 3–15). New York, NY: Cambridge University Press.

Woodbury, R.F. and Burrow, A.L. (2006). Whither design space? *Artificial Intelligence for Engineering Design, Analysis and Manufacturing,* 20(2), 63–82

14 Schooltrack: *An EPSS for Action Research*

SJOERD DE VRIES, PAUL VAN SCHAIK AND DICK
SLETTENHAAR

Schooltrack is an environment for school teachers enabling and supporting them in conducting action research. This provides a practical approach for practitioners to evaluate their own work with reference to criteria set by these practitioners themselves (McNiff and Whitehead, 2002). This chapter describes the fundamentals of action research and the design of *Schooltrack*. It then presents two projects in which *Schooltrack* was used. Finally, the potential for the practical use of *Schooltrack* in the Dutch (and other) educational systems is discussed.

Introduction

This chapter addresses the application of electronic performance support in mainstream education to enable teachers to conduct research as part of their job. The Electronic Performance Support System (EPSS) presented here assists teachers in research, publishing and sharing knowledge, and collaboration – all three types of EPSS assistance introduced by Barker (Chapter 5 of this volume) as typical of educational settings. One of the Information and Communication Technology (ICT) innovation strategies in Dutch education is the stimulation of action research into the design, use and effects of ICT – carried out by teachers in their own professional context. The implementation of ICT services in education can be considered one of the major drivers of educational reforms. Examples of ICT services include a school's web site, an intranet, an electronic-learning environment, digital school-boards and computer-assisted instruction. Furthermore, social Web applications are increasingly being introduced into educational settings. Examples of these applications are *Hyves, Flickr, YouTube, Twitter, Google Earth, MSN* and *Trackr*. From an educational point of view, there is a quest for 'proven innovations', that is, innovations that have been demonstrated to be effective. In this context, action research can play a significant role.

Zuber-Skerritt (1982) defined action research in higher education as a critical collaborative enquiry by reflective practitioners who are accountable in making the results of their enquiry public, being self-evaluative in their practice, and engaged in problem solving and continuing professional development. McNiff and Whitehead (2002) offer a practical approach for practitioners to evaluate their own work with reference to criteria set by these practitioners themselves.

Clearly, practitioners rather than academic researchers conduct action research and therefore it is often referred to as practitioner-based research. Furthermore, because it involves practitioners thinking about and reflecting on their own work, it can be considered as a form of self-reflective practice (McNiff and Whitehead, 2002). Developing these competences is one of the major goals of the Dutch action-research programme *Kennisrotonde* (*Knowledge Roundabout*, *http://www.kennisrotonde.nl*). This programme offers funding for innovative action-research projects to groups of schools.

The major justification for the promotion of action research is that (a) teachers have to plan the use and effects of each of their ICT-based projects, (b) during a project they have to collect data about its use and effects, (c) after the project they have to reflect on this by analysing their data, and (d), by doing so, they bridge their daily educational work with broad academic theory (Magos, 2007). It is expected that, eventually, teachers will disseminate their findings by sharing examples of best practice, presenting their work and, if possible, publishing their research.

Zuber-Skerrit (1996) and McNiff and Whitehead (2002) have discussed the methods, guidelines, techniques and instruments used in action research. More specifically, action research offers a systematic approach to introducing innovations in teaching and learning (Riding, Fowell and Levy, 1995). Usually, action research is iterative and distinct phases include problem identification, action planning, implementation, evaluation and reflection. Based on the results of reflection, a revised plan of work can be developed and an additional action-research cycle begins. However, in practice it is not easy for teachers to carry out action research, especially if an academic-research attitude and corresponding research quality are expected. Teachers have to develop their competences in 'scientifically grounded' action research. In addition, performance support for action research is needed in order to enable teachers to conduct their own action research. For this purpose, we designed *Schooltrack*. In two projects related to *Knowledge Roundabout*, we are using *Schooltrack* as an EPSS, to support teachers in performing action research in their professional context.

In the remainder of this chapter, we describe the design of *Schooltrack* as an EPSS. We then discuss how *Schooltrack* is used in the two projects. We conclude with a discussion of the significance of *Schooltrack* for the support of action research in education.

The Design of *Schooltrack*

The design of *Schooltrack* is based on the action-research method (see Figure 14.1) developed in the *Peat Lab* project (de Vries and Koolschijn, 2007). (The Dutch name is *Veenlab*; see *http://veenlab.konict.nl*.) The method is based on our discussion of action research presented in the existing literature (see the section 'Introduction'). The main research cycle in our method is the action-research programme. The programme consists of four phases. The first phase is called *Exploration*, in which *research themes* are explored; a teacher chooses a specific theme and produces the action plan of a research project. The second phase involves conducting the *Research Project* of which there are four basic stages: *Problem analysis, Data collection, Data analysis* and *Reporting* – these form an additional, nested, research cycle. An action-research programme can include one or more research projects. The third phase in the research programme is *Reflection*. It is expected that in this phase teachers engage in connecting the research project's results with existing knowledge or earlier findings.

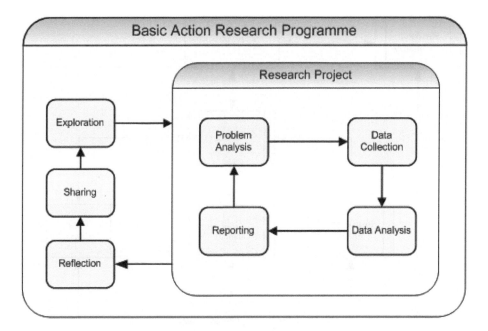

Figure 14.1 The action-research method

For example, it is expected that teachers will produce a description of examples of best practice, based on their findings and experiences. In the fourth phase of *Sharing*, teachers offer the results of their personal reflection – that is, insights, conclusion and products – to other teachers and professionals. For example, teachers may present, discuss and reuse their work. In the action-research method, *Sharing* leads to new interesting research themes to be explored in future projects.

Our distinction between a research programme and a research project as research cycles is based on the professional practice and competences of involved teachers. We consider collaboration between teachers in action-research programmes as one of the requirements for successful action research. Additionally, in general, it is not possible for teachers to carry out full collaborative research project cycles due to practical considerations – such as time issues, curriculum and organisational constraints, planning problems and resources, and teachers' competences. Therefore, it is possible to ask a group of teachers to develop a research programme together for a period of one year, but to give individual teachers the opportunity within such a programme to decide if, when, with whom, and how to carry out their own research projects. After conducting their specific action-research project, teachers reflect together on their work and findings and share their results and insights with others.

Based on this action-research method, we developed the conceptual design of *Schooltrack*. This design is presented in Figure 14.2. The different shapes in this figure represent the various types of process involved in the implementation of the system. *Schooltrack* consists of the *Schooltrack* portal, the *Schooltrack* community and *Schooltrack* projects.

Schooltrack's homepage gives access to projects and, through these projects, *Schooltrack* modules. However, for the purpose of this chapter, it can be conceptualised as an information *Portal* for action research in education and access to the results of this

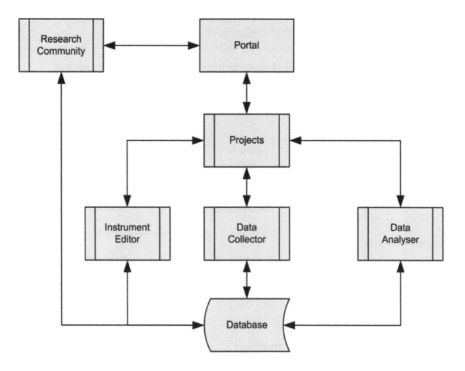

Figure 14.2 Conceptual design of *Schooltrack*

research as carried out by the members of *Schooltrack*. Teachers can become a member of *Schooltrack* and get access to the *Research Community* and *Schooltrack* services.

The *Schooltrack* community is the platform for continuing professional development of teachers through action research. The community offers a range of services through *Schooltrack*. Teachers can set up or join research projects. They can share their experiences and use a forum to help them in solving problems quickly.

Schooltrack's *Projects* is a collection of action-research projects. These provide access to the *Instrument Editor*, the *Data Collector* and the *Data Analyser*. The *Instrument Editor* allows teachers to develop their online or offline instruments for data collection and, if they wish, add these to the collection of available instruments. The *Data Collector* offers functionality for the online gathering of data. The *Data Analyser* offers functionality for online data analysis and data export facilities to, for instance, *SPSS*™.

One of the main features of *Schooltrack* is that it includes a repository of psychometric scales stored in the *Database*. Scales are managed and can be reused in *Projects*. The psychometric properties of scales are monitored and teachers can select a psychometrically validated set of scales. *Schooltrack* records the history of the maintenance and use of items and scales in the *Database*. Teachers can reuse existing scales or items in their projects and, at different project stages, examine, for instance, trends in the motivation of their learners. Teachers can also use scales (for example, a learner-motivation scale) and benchmark their findings with those of other teachers using the same scales. The use of trend analysis and benchmarking add to the quality of action research carried out by teachers. *Schooltrack*'s functionality and *Database* also allow the developers of *Schooltrack*, as academic researchers, to re-analyse data across projects and produce new findings. Figure 14.3 shows the portal of *Schooltrack*. The design is simple and straightforward.

Schooltrack

New(s)   Diary   Search

Logout

Information
- About Schooltrack

ProjectMaker
- In preparation
- ItemBank

My Projects
- Apeldoorn
- Leerplein 055
- ASKO
- IJsselgraaf
- Ivo Rossem
- QLiCTintern
- Stampei

How to?
- Support space
- Benchmarks

Pad: Menu/My Projects/Ivo Rossem/

Ivo Rossem

Schooltrack is a coherent set of instruments for tracking the development of educational organizations. We are developing Schooltrack continuously. We apply Schooltrack in research projects in order to monitor school developments. Based on this, we support innovation and quality deveopment.

Project Maker

Project Maker enables you to develop your own research programmes.

How to use Project Maker?

- Create a **research programme.**
- In a **research programme** you can develop one or more research projects.
- In a **research project** you can develop one or more research questionnaires.
- In a **questionnaire** you can develop one or more measurement items and measurement scales.
- If you do have questionnaires, you can develop one or more **data collections** in a research practice.
- Based on a data collection you can develop one or more **data analyses** in a research practice.
- You can copy/paste your research project to where ever you want.

What more?

- You can copy/paste programmes, projects, questionnaires etc to where you want to store or manage them.
- So, you can re-use each object.
- You can build up your own project base, consisting of programmes, projects, questionnaires, scales, and data.

Figure 14.3 A sample screen of *Schooltrack*

The menu at the top gives access to general services, such as the research community and a research diary. The menu on the left is personalised, based on the role of the *Schooltrack* member/user who is logged in. Therefore, the projects shown are those to which a particular user has access.

Schooltrack serves as an EPSS as the following analysis shows. *Schooltrack* offers support for clusters of non-recurrent skills (see Chapter 2) in the following areas: the design of (questionnaire) instruments, the administration of instruments and the analysis of collected data. By providing existing instruments as templates (in the *Database*), *Schooltrack* supports the task of designing instruments. This allows different teachers to design instruments at varying levels of their own contribution, from complete reuse of existing instruments to reuse with modifications (using the *Instrument Editor*) to new or completely redesigned instruments (using the *Instrument editor*). This is similar to the use of different levels of scaffolding, as in the completion strategy used in instruction for learning computer programming and other subjects (van Merriënboer and Kirschner, 2007). By providing the *Data Collector*, *Schooltrack* supports the task of administering (questionnaire) instruments by automatic means, with some degree of control over the way these instruments are presented. The *Data Analysis* function supports different levels of scaffolding in data analysis. In the current version of *Schooltrack*, there are two levels. First, teachers can analyse data stored in the *Database* by using ready-made analyses, with results in the form of frequency tables, descriptives and graphs. Second, teachers can export data into a format that can be used to conduct their own analysis, using specialist statistical packages (for example, *SPSS*™) and/or general-purpose analysis packages (for example, *Excel*™). In addition, the communication facilities in the *Research Community* allow teachers to share their results and experiences, as a means for collaboration and developing the knowledge of individual teachers and the community at large.

Two Case Studies

We present two case studies (projects) in which *Schooltrack* has been used in practice to support teachers in their action research. Both projects were part of the *Knowledge Roundabout* programme and commenced in 2008. The goal of this programme was to promote action research and to develop and use educational innovations in Dutch primary and secondary education. The first project is called *Peat Lab* (*Veenlab* in Dutch). In this project, primary-education pupils used virtual research labs to carry out research into the historical implications of peat lands and the use of peat in their neighbourhood. The second project is called *History Clip*. In this project, primary-education pupils carried out research into the historical implications of the life and the work of monks in the middle ages within their neighbourhood. In both projects the same support strategy was used.

In these projects, learners had to report the findings of their project work by means of networked media. The role of the developers of *Schooltrack* in both projects was to enable and support teachers in finding answers to the various types of question related to the projects that students were carrying out. Naturally, one question to be answered was, 'What are the effects of students' work on their learning?' Another question was, 'How can I, as a teacher, manage these projects in my school, without external project support and funding?' The task of answering these questions implies action research. This section describes how *Schooltrack* was used to support this research and what the first experiences of teachers have been.

The *Peat Lab* project was conducted in the northern province of Drente. One typical geographic phenomenon in this area is the existence of peat lands. According to the Merriam-Webster online dictionary, peat is 'partially carbonised vegetable tissue formed by partial decomposition in water of various plants' (*http://www.merriam-webster. com*). Peat lands have a great influence on Drente, in particular on its history, transport infrastructure, building infrastructure, and even on the social and political behaviour of its population. In the project, learners and local 'peat professionals' from eight primary schools worked together on research tasks in local teams in order to study these influences and to publish their results. The first research tasks started in April 2008 and subsequent tasks commenced in August 2008.

The *History Clip* project was conducted in the northern province of Friesland. The research theme chosen was the Cistercian monks. The Order of Cistercians, sometimes called the White Monks (from the colour of their habit, over which a black scapular or apron is sometimes worn) is a Roman Catholic religious order of monks. The Cistercians preferred manual labour, and especially field-work, which became a special characteristic of Cistercian life. The Cistercians became the main force of technological diffusion in medieval Europe. The Cistercian monastery Klaarkamp existed from 1165 to 1580 in Friesland. Klaarkamp's Cistercian monks had a great influence on life in the province. Even now, many influences can be found in the geography, and social and cultural life in Friesland. In the *History Clip* project, learners and local professionals studied these influences and published their work in so-called history clips – these are short video clips, telling a specific story about the theme. The main project goal for the teachers was to collaboratively develop a media-based method for local-history research, the *local-history research method*. After completion, this media-based method will be disseminated to other primary schools in the Netherlands. We refer to it as a media-based method because the main output of the research consists of (networked) multimedia. The first research tasks started in September 2008.

In both projects, teachers had to carry out action research. The main goals of this action research were to (a) gain insight in learning processes and effects; (b) improve the *local-history research method* that is being designed and used; and (c) disseminate results to other schools. With *Schooltrack* to support them, teachers conducted their action research using the action-research method presented earlier in this chapter.

One of the major tasks in a *Project* is to put the method into practice and to adapt it to local circumstances. As a first step, the teachers participated in a three-hour workshop, which introduced the *Exploration phase*. In the workshop we discussed 'research questions'. The teachers decided together which research questions to answer. Examples of justifications for choosing questions included personal interest, value for the local school's development and personal competence development. Research groups were then formed, each consisting of two teachers and a research coach (one of two academic researchers). Following the phases of *Problem Analysis*, *Data Collection*, *Data Analysis* and *Reporting*, research groups carried out their own projects. In this context, various types of report were appropriate. Examples included an essay, a video interview, a report, a presentation and contributions to the *local-history research method*. The reports were expected to be of practical use for fellow teachers.

The phases of *Reflection* and *Sharing* are crucial in our action-research method. Therefore, we are planning to organise a 'North-Netherlands Local History Research Tour'. The goal of this tour is to implement the *local-history research method* using presentations, discussions and support. Teachers taking part in *Peat Lab* or *History Clip* will be offered the opportunity to present their findings in this tour, and to discuss their findings and reflections with colleagues in the field.

The role of *Schooltrack* as part of the action-research method is that it offers teachers task support. *Schooltrack* offers online research services, for instance a repository of research scales, support in designing a survey, support in online response collection, support in data analysis and support in reporting findings. *Schooltrack* also offers performance support services. An example of performance support is a growing number of factsheets to aid the use of research scales, research techniques and instruments. These factsheets describe briefly, at an appropriate level, the main aspects of techniques and instruments. Furthermore, teachers have access to an online meeting place, consisting of weblogs and forums about relevant research topics. Here, they can meet colleagues working in the *Peat Lab* or *History Clip* projects and discuss issues or ask questions. During each of the two projects described in this chapter (and, we expect, in forthcoming projects) two academic researchers moderate the forums and contribute to online discussions. In this way, a knowledge base is built that is also available after a project has finished.

Discussion and Conclusions

At the time of writing this chapter, we have not yet carried out formal evaluations of the method and the use of *Schooltrack* as part of the projects. Furthermore, we are constantly working on the improvement and extension of *Schooltrack*'s services. The comments from teachers and learners, the ongoing monitoring of the use of *Schooltrack* and formative evaluations provide us with input for the continuing development work. As an example, a recent development is the realisation of *Schooltrack*'s research support for qualitative research. Based on the first teachers' remarks, however, it appears that *Schooltrack* is greatly assisting teachers in their action research.

The value of action research for the quality and efficiency of education is an important subject of debate. In the Netherlands, there is a strong tendency to shift the responsibility for the design and quality of education from the government towards schools. Therefore, schools have to distinguish themselves from the other schools in the neighbourhood and they have started various kinds of innovation in order to achieve this. The Dijsselbloem Report (Dijsselbloem, 2008) showed that most innovations in education, both initiated by the government and by schools themselves, did not meet the expectations of the initiators, teachers, children and parents. In most cases, the quality of education declined. A response has been a call for evidence-based innovations. One of the outcomes is the birth of the 'academic school'; using this concept, the government encourages schools to develop their innovations in a more evidence-based fashion. Consequently, teachers need to develop (action) research skills and apply them in their own work. Schools, as institutions, have to facilitate this development and add these competences in the working profiles and workloads of teachers.

In conclusion, the use of a flexible EPSS – *Schooltrack* – can empower teachers to conduct action research and thereby innovate in relation to the way in which they work.

If we succeed in the integration of action research in the daily work of teachers, it may contribute to a further quality improvement in education.

References

Dijsselbloem, J.R.V.A. (ed.) (2008). *Tijd voor onderwijs* (Time for education). Den Haag: SDU.

Magos, K. (2007). The contribution of action-research to training teachers in intercultural education: A research in the field of Greek minority education. *Teaching and Teacher Education*, 23, 1102–1112.

McNiff, J. and Whitehead, J. (2002). *Action Research: Principles and Practice* (2nd edn). London: Routledge Falmer.

van Merriënboer, J. and Kirschner, P. (2007). *Ten Steps to Complex Learning: A Systematic Approach to Four-component Instructional Design*. Mahwah, NJ: Erlbaum.

Riding, P., Fowell, S. and Levy, P. (1995). An action research approach to curriculum development. *Information Research*, 1(1), Article number 3. Available at: *http://InformationR.net/ir/1-1/paper2.html* Last accessed 9/12/2008.

Vries, S.A. de and Koolschijn, J. (2007). *Schooltrack: Actie onderzoek als methode voor professionalisering van informeel leren* (Schooltrack: Action research as a method for continual professional development of informal learning). Project report. Enschede: Konict b.v.

Zuber-Skerritt, O. (1982). *Action Research in Higher Education*. London: Kogan Page.

Zuber-Skerrit, O. (1996). *New Directions in Action Research*. London: Falmer Press.

III

Concluding Remarks

CHAPTER 15 *Conclusion*

PHILIP BARKER AND PAUL VAN SCHAIK

As editors of this book, this penultimate chapter is intended to summarise our views, and those of our contributors, in relation to the rationale for and utility of Electronic Performance Support Systems (EPSS). The discussion that is presented below follows three broad strands. First, some thoughts on where we may be going in terms of the use of human-performance technology; second, the important role that technology is likely to play in the future; and third, some reflections on the ideas that have been presented in this book.

Where Are We Going?

In order to set the scene for the conclusion to this book it is necessary to emphasise an important point that was made both in Chapter 1 and in numerous other places elsewhere within the book. Namely, that *human memory* constrains virtually everything that people do. For example, if I (PGB – as an author of this book) cannot remember the answer to a question that someone asks me, then I will probably not be able to answer it correctly – unless I make a 'lucky' guess. But then, it could be that I never knew the answer in the first place. Similarly, if I cannot remember how to do something then I will not be able to do it – unless I relearn the skills and knowledge needed to perform the tasks involved (I could, of course, use a trial and error strategy). The importance of learning and its impact on the development of skills and knowledge to facilitate problem solving has been discussed in Chapters 2, 4, 5 and 14. Bearing in mind the simple examples given above, it is easy to see the importance of human memory and the value of performance support tools to support its storage, retention and recall activities. The importance of technology in relation to this has been considered in Chapter 3 and is a topic which is further discussed later in this chapter (see the next section entitled 'A Technological Future?').

Some time ago I (PGB) listened to a radio programme entitled *'Remember, Remember'*.[1] Essentially, this programme dealt with some of the shortcomings of human memory and how appropriate digital technology may be used to overcome these. The programme suggested that 'now' is a very short (instantaneous) time frame and that everything we have in our minds relating to our experiences is a memory of them – if indeed, those memories actually exist. Of course, it is possible to use external 'iconic' representations of

---

1   This programme was broadcast on BBC Radio 3 on the 22nd September, 2008.

memories – such as a photograph of someone once met or a souvenir that was purchased at some previously visited place. These iconic representations can serve as a stimulus to recall memories of past events. Of course, if people have no recollection of an event, then that event might not have happened. Some events will have happened because of the very nature of an individual's existence. For example, someone who is aged 36 years will have experienced being 25 years old. However, how many people can remember what they did on their 25th birthday? How many presents were received? What were they? How many birthday cards were received? Who were they from? Few readers of this book (if they are older than 25) could recall the details of this event.

One way of overcoming the above problem would be through a process of 'life-logging'. That is, keeping a detailed account of everything that happens to one during one's lifetime. In the past, this function was (and to a large extent still is) often facilitated by a 'memory' performance-support aid called a diary. This diary could be a paper-based edition or it could be of an electronic form. Entries made in a diary help us to recall details of events and happenings that have some personal significance for the person that 'keeps' the diary. Of course, keeping a diary requires, on the part of the person involved, devotion to the task and much time and effort. Also, suppose for some reason a day or two is missed or that the diary gets lost. Because of the effort involved in keeping a diary, it would be nice if some mechanism could be found which would enable the whole process to be automated. One approach to achieving this is being explored by *Microsoft Research*.

The researchers at Microsoft have been using a device called a 'sense-cam'[2] to capture (automatically) some of the details of the events that its wearer becomes involved in – walking down a road, playing a game of chess, cooking a meal, and so on. Essentially, the sense-cam is a 'wearable' digital camera that takes a picture at regular periods of time and then archives the images that it takes in an electronic memory system. In other words, it produces a visual record of a person's minute-by-minute activities. If a picture is taken every ten seconds for 12 hours per day, this would result in the creation of an image archive of over nine million photographs each year of a person's life. So while a visual record is now easy to produce, further performance aids would be needed in order to analyse these images and (if necessary) index them in a way that would facilitate retrieving them as and when they are needed. Of course, it may also be necessary to build suitable knowledge structures that represent the content of these images and the relationships that exist between them. From a performance-support perspective, there is still a significant amount of research needed to develop the tools that people would need to achieve this goal – thereby making sense of such a vast image collection.

Naturally, human memory is just one important factor that influences human performance. Perceptual, cognitive and motor skills are also of vital importance. The point has been well made (in Chapters 7, 8 and 9) regarding how problems with the functioning of these areas of human performance can often be overcome through the design and introduction of suitable interventions. As has been mentioned earlier in this book (Chapter 2 and elsewhere), people use their senses, knowledge and skills to solve problems. This process is greatly enriched by the availability of stored collections of appropriate data and information (as described in Chapter 6). These are frequently derived

---

2   Details of the sense-cam can be obtained from the Microsoft Research website at: *http://www.micosoft.co.uk/research/*. (Accessed on 12th December, 2008).

from scientific observations that are often made using powerful research equipment that has been built using appropriate engineering skills (Chapter 10) and processed with tools that help experts to derive meaning from them and an understanding of their implications (Chapter 13).

A natural tendency of people is to organise themselves into groups in order to form organisational structures for undertaking collaborative research and solving business and commercial problems – as discussed and described in Chapters 11, 12 and 14. There are many (including Broers – see below) who believe that collaboration is another important aspect of the successful development of human kind. There is therefore an urgent need to produce performance support tools to facilitate this aspect of human endeavour (see also Chapter 14).

A Technological Future?

As has been discussed in Chapter 3 and subsequent chapters of the book, technology is a very powerful 'enabler'. As an example of this power, consider the tremendous uptake in people's use of mobile phones. This brings a form of empowerment that enables them to project the human voice far beyond close proximal extents to distances involving thousands and thousands of miles. What a powerful performance enhancer this device is! Such devices also enable the transmission of textual and pictorial messages to an individual (or a group of people) located anywhere where a 'signal' can be received. Ultimately, this is likely to be anywhere on the Earth's surface and beyond into outer space.

The importance of technology as an aid to human existence and performance was discussed some 40 years ago by Leon Bagrit – both in his BBC *Reith Lectures*[3] *and in his subsequent book called The Age of Automation* (Bagrit, 1965). More recently, in his 2005 BBC *Reith Lectures,*[4] Alec Broers has also paid significant attention to the role of technology in relation to the future development of the human species. It is his contention that, 'Technology will determine the future of the human race.' Indeed, in the transcript of his first lecture he writes, 'I am convinced that it is technology that shapes our lives and that its influence is paramount and is only going to increase as time passes.' Bearing this in mind and from the perspective of this book, I think it is important to pose the following important question: '*How should we use technology to build new performance-support tools to help humankind solve the problems it will face in the future?*'

Reflections

In a technological future, the paradox of technological complexity and its effects become increasingly important: the more complex technology becomes (presumably aimed at enhancing human performance), the more performance support is required. However, there are three, not mutually exclusive, approaches to tackling the paradox of technological

---

3   Sir Leon Bagrit was Chairman of one of the most well-known British computer manufacturers (Ferranti). He gave the 1965 BBC *Reith Lecture* which was subsequently published as a book (Bagrit, 1965).

4   Lord Alec Broers, a distinguished engineer and President of the Royal Academy of Engineering, gave the BBC 2005 *Reith Lectures* entitled *The Triumph of Technology*. These lectures are available for download (as spoken narratives and in printed form) at: *http://www.bbc.co.uk/radio4/reith2005/lectures.shtml/*. (Accessed on 12th December, 2008).

complexity. In order of preference they are (1) human-centred (system) design (Noyes and Baber, 1999); (2) the use of performance support; and (3) the application of instructional design. The reason for this order of preference is that options (1) and (2) require less effort from technology users. Human-centred design requires the least effort while instruction involves the most effort – with performance support taking an intermediate position. Human-centred design shifts the effort to the designers of technology – this involves making technology as useful and as usable as possible with a minimal requirement for performance support and/or instruction. Performance support takes designed technology as 'axiomatic' and shifts the effort to the designers of 'value-added' performance-support interventions that will aid human performance (using the underlying technological system) through the use of an associated performance-support system. Instructional design takes designed technology (and any performance support) as axiomatic and so shifts the effort to both the designers of instructional interventions (that will aid users' learning) and to the users themselves. These users will first have to learn from instruction how to use the actual technology and then, once they have successfully learned to do this, they will have to use the technology without any further support.

Obviously, if the paradox of technological complexity is not tackled by one of the approaches described above then users will still try to 'do the best they can' – consistent with the *paradox of the active user* (Carroll and Rosson, 1987). This consists of two parts. According to the first part (called the *production paradox*), when performing a task with a piece of technology, humans will tend to focus on using that technology at the expense of any learning that is required to use it successfully, effectively or efficiently. According to the second part (called the *assimilation paradox*), humans will tend to apply their existing knowledge when using new technology – even when that knowledge may be incorrect or irrelevant for successful, effective or efficient task performance.

In addition, especially in domains where humans perform tasks under time constraints (for example, in the process industry), performance may suffer as a result of *ironies of automation* (Bainbridge, 1983) when using technological systems. Bainbridge's main contention is that humans are less effective in solving problems (or, more generally, performing tasks) when under time pressure. However, technological systems that are intended to aid human task performance under time pressure – ironically – create further problems in human performance. These problems include a deterioration of cognitive skills, control skills and monitoring, and an increase in stress, workload and ill health.

Furthermore, increased complexity of technology (or an artefact that is based upon it), is likely to affect (in a significant way) tasks and the nature of the relationship between the main components of human-technology interaction. These main components are person, task and artefact (Finneran and Zhang, 2003). A problem here is that electronic performance support focuses on task and technology (artefact) while usually ignoring individual differences between human users.

In the context of increasing technological complexity, there are several problems (posed by the *paradox of the active user, ironies of automation* and the nature of human-technology interaction) to bear in mind. For new users it may become increasingly hard to learn how to use new systems – because of more complex functionality and consequently a user interface that is usually more complex. Similarly, for experienced users it may become increasingly unlikely that they will use efficient methods to complete their tasks – relying instead on familiar, less efficient methods. In domains where humans work under time pressure, automation by more complex technological systems is likely to result in the requirement of more complex skills to diagnose faults and more complex monitoring of the automated system as well as increased stress, workload and ill health. When human-interaction technology becomes more complex, individual differences in users' abilities to cope with complexity are expected to make task performance more difficult for less-able users.

At the same time, a number of implications of increasing technological complexity for human-centred design, performance support and instructional design need to be considered. Given the aim of maximising ease-of-use (while minimising the need for instruction and performance support), human-centred design is expected to become more demanding in order to ensure that people with different abilities can effectively and efficiently use the technology. As Carroll and Rosson (1987) suggest, instructional design can be effective by controlling the consequences[5] of any given action by users (to reduce or avoid the impact of negative outcomes of users' erroneous actions) and the actions available to users (to reduce the number of actions that users need to consider). With more complex functionality, these strategies can still be applied, but the analysis of consequences and actions will take more effort and, in order to promote learning, a smaller proportion of the total actions available may have to be offered to novice users. However, given the increased challenges of designing easy-to-use systems and instructional interventions to facilitate learning about complex technology, it is likely that neither human-centred design nor instructional design will be sufficient. Instead, performance support may become even more important to ensure effective and efficient task performance. The effort required to design performance support will increase with the functionality offered by the technical system to ensure support for each function. In addition, given the large volume of work required to support all functions it may be necessary to restrict performance support to some of the functions, for example those required by most users or those found to be most difficult for users. Individual differences in users' abilities may have to be accommodated to a larger extent when they use more complex systems by offering different levels of performance support, depending on ability or experience.

Future Possibilities – the Last Word

There are many possible ways in which the future of EPSS could unfold. One of these could involve a future in which people have much greater dependence on digital technologies, both for individual and collaborative ventures – as has been predicted by Broers (above) and by many of the contributions to this book. However, because of the highly specialised knowledge that the contributors to this book possess, we thought it would be appropriate to leave the 'last word' with them. The final short chapter in the book (Chapter 16 – Future Directions for EPSS) has therefore been used to let them express what they feel is likely to be the future role of EPSS (in general) and performance support tools (in particular) within their particular specialist areas of expertise.

---

5   For example, the consequences of deleting a computer file are removing access to the data and information stored in the file and freeing up memory space on the computer's storage device.

References

Bagrit, L. (1965). *The Age of Automation*, The BBC Reith Lectures 1964. London, UK: Weidenfeld and Nicholson.

Bainbridge, L. (1983). Ironies of automation. *Automatica*, 19, 775—779.

Carroll, J. and Rosson, M.B. (1987). The paradox of the active user. In J. Carroll, (ed.) *Interfacing Thought: Cognitive Aspects of Human-Computer Interaction* (pp. 80–111). Cambridge, MA: MIT Press.

Finneran, C.M., and Zhang, P. (2003). A person-artefact-task (PAT) model of flow antecedents in computer-mediated environments. *International Journal of Human-Computer Studies*, 59, 475–496.

Noyes, J. and Baber, C. (1999). *User-centred Design of Systems*. Berlin: Springer.

16 *Future Directions for EPSS*

THE CONTRIBUTORS

For this final chapter of the book, we asked all of the contributors to think about what 'lies ahead' in relation to the future directions of progress we may see within the context of developments in the design, production and utilisation of Electronic Performance Support Systems (EPSS). The subsequent sections of this chapter summarise the views that were expressed.

Education

PHILIP BARKER

Laurillard (2008) has described the importance of digital technologies in relation to the realisation of educational objectives within nations, societies and individuals. Within this context, my own particular specialism is the application of electronic performance support concepts for educational activities. This involves two major initiatives based on the techniques and technologies that have been described earlier in this book. First, their application for the support of teaching and learning processes; and second, their use for the creation of effective infrastructures to facilitate the activities that are involved in these processes. From an individual's perspective, education is primarily concerned with acquiring knowledge and skills – and using these to solve problems of various sorts. Inherent in this is the need to communicate and to share ideas and resources that facilitate learning. Increasingly, people will also need to remember more; they will need to collect, archive, organise and manage collections of digital objects that facilitate what they do and how they learn. Because learning never ends and never stops, my vision of the future for electronic performance support in education will be its use for the provision of electronic tools that will enable individuals to overcome the limitations of the human mind in relation to coping with increasing knowledge demands for solving different types of problem – either on a day-to-day or a long-term basis. As I have discussed elsewhere (Barker, 2008a, 2008b, 2009), this will involve the development of performance support and enhancement aids that will enable people to organise, manage, share and use their own personal digital object repositories in flexible ways to build knowledge structures that reflect the activities in which they are involved and in which they wish to participate.

Information Access

OLADEJI FAMAKINWA

As discussed in Chapter 6, information access is dependent upon the successful integration of a number of different cooperating systems. These include the underlying *storage infrastructure* (where resources are stored), the *communication networks and facilities* (that provide access to these resources), the *interface sub-system* (that links everything together) and, of course, *the users* of the stored information. Users can be either people or automated systems and services.

The creation of new information and knowledge is growing at an exponential rate. Fortunately, the mechanisms used for storing this information and manipulating it are also showing significant improvement but, unintentionally, they are becoming more complex and more demanding for users (Lyman and Varian, 2003; Rosenfeld and Morville, 2002). Despite this technological progress, the cognitive ability of people in relation to handling and coping with large volumes of information has remained relatively unchanged, while more knowledge and skill is required to use the newly emerging information systems in effective ways. Consequently, the EPSS tools that are likely to be needed in the future will need to be much more sophisticated than those presently available – in order to ensure that they continue to meet the end-users' needs and the requirements placed on them.

As has been discussed in Chapter 3, performance tools in the form of mobile devices already exist to overcome some human cognitive limitations and memory shortcomings. Typical examples include calculators (to support computational tasks) and Personal Digital Assistants (PDAs) (to aid memory functions). However, in the future it is likely that many of these EPSS tools will go far beyond external mobile devices – and could involve technology that is actually embedded within people. Already, it is possible for a person to control external devices through the use of a brain implant (Lebedev and Nicolelis, 2006). Such brain implants have found applications in many areas including helping disabled individuals to recover some or all of their lost abilities. Consequently, it is conceivable that such implants could one day provide direct interfaces to communication networks and various forms of human-memory extension. Of course, any major progress in this area (in relation to the end-user interface to information systems) is unlikely to overcome many of the problems currently associated with finding the correct 'sought-after' information from a given corpus of knowledge. However, it is feasible that special types of performance support tool – not requiring implantation in the human body – may be made available to cope with this situation. A typical example of such a tool is an 'autonomous software agent'.

In the future, it is likely that autonomous information-seeking agents could serve as performance support tools. These would be able to find different types of information for their users based upon simple machine-learning processes. Users of these agents would only need to 'show examples' of what type of information is required or examples of what is not required. Through this process of selecting or removing results, the autonomous agent would be able to learn what is required. Furthermore, depending upon a particular individual's information requirements, that person's agents would be able to communicate with other agents. These could be freely available agents (Open Source), personal agents from other more experienced users or agents that are available for a fee from some 'service provider'. This would allow powerful information sub-networks to be formed (within the overall information infrastructure) that are able to cater for the specific information needs of a particular end-user.

Through these sub-networks, relevant information could then be more effectively exchanged and the overall quality of search results could be substantially improved.

Naturally, the overall objective of these advances in electronic performance support is to provide toolsets that are able to handle the ever-expanding collection of information and knowledge resources that are now becoming available – through quicker and more efficient means. These advances would also make it much easier for less-experienced information workers to very quickly benefit from all the knowledge that is available to them on any given topic.

Human Communication

NIGEL BEACHAM

In the future, there are likely to be a number of important developments relating to using EPSS to facilitate human communication.

As the cost of communication becomes more affordable, more advanced forms of communication will become the norm for most people worldwide. What are currently expensive integrated conferencing systems will become more common, not only in education institutions, but also in the home. In future, these systems will become the norm for most people to use and enable learners to communicate and share ideas remotely from home as if they were receiving face-to-face tuition.

People will need ways of summarising information being communicated and tools to convert information into other representations. Such capabilities will enable people, for example, to convert spoken numerical information into a graphical representation or convert images and photographs into textual descriptions. Such tools and aids will improve people's ability to communicate and share ideas with others who, for whatever reason, are currently excluded from particular situations.

Finally, people will need to be able to communicate and share their ideas more effectively regardless of their location and the types of communication device they have to hand. More advanced forms of communication tools and aids will be needed, which can be mixed and matched to enable, for example, someone with a mobile phone to share ideas with a colleague through an integrated conferencing system.

What is inevitable in the future, regarding communication, is that people will want to communicate more to greater numbers of other people – using a greater variety of communication devices. People will require help choosing appropriate ways of communicating and, where necessary, require support in cases where new forms of communication are being used. EPSS will feature evermore prominently at the heart of many forms of human communication.

Disability and Special Needs

STEVE GREEN AND ELAINE PEARSON

We have already said (in Chapter 8), 'In the future, the advent of truly adaptive electronic environments and personalised technologies is likely to produce significant benefits both for able and disabled people.' With ever-increasing advances in technologies, the barriers between the 'abled' and 'disabled', between 'included' and 'excluded' and between 'accessible' and 'inaccessible' will melt away. We will find that devices, systems and environments are designed for the many or the few but adaptable and adapted for all. The distinctions between mainstream and assistive technologies will blur and we will find people of all capabilities using EPSS which will aid them as an individual undertaking their everyday tasks. Perhaps our PDA, phone or a specialised heads-up-device in our glasses will remind us that we need to pick up the pasta from the supermarket. Our PDA, phone and glasses will have access to our position (through GPS), our diary (through wireless technology) and our proximity to the pasta (through Bluetooth). Our devices will be intelligent, know our habits and preferences and could make useful suggestions as to our dietary requirements and lifestyle choices. They will also know what is in the fridge and cupboard at home, what is on offer at the supermarket and what our capabilities and limitations are as a cook. We will also expect support with our physical activities, including electronic walking aids which can prevent fatigue or help the (frail) older adults walk further, perhaps only taking over to steady us or when we need that extra boost. The future, like the past, is another country, but potentially a brighter country for all with no artificial barriers between communities or concept of exclusion.

Medical Applications

JEAN ROBERTS

Developments in this area may happen on a number of fronts. Assistive technologies will become pervasive in clinical situations that require long-term monitoring or where the activities of daily living can be enhanced by using appropriate technologies. Many health-related tests will be automated to the point where 'near-patient' testing by patients themselves will be the norm.

Many developments are likely to involve greater participation by lay end-users who would help in design and developmental testing in order to maximise the likelihood of 'fit-for-purpose' health solutions. These could increase the life span or quality of life (that is, by adding both 'years to life' and 'life to years'). Citizens will also exert their right to choose with whom they share information relating to their complex clinical history. People will carry personal smart cards populated with readable data (or indexes to the sources of data) which they selectively permit clinicians to use to inform clinical decisions made about their own care and treatment.

Increasingly, standards will facilitate enhanced convergence and collation of patient/client records containing health, social care and lifestyle management information from multiple sources – making the possibility of 'whole-life' personal health records a reality. Content will range from personal reflections and self-test results to the detailed genetic and genomic features that uniquely define an individual. Agreement will (eventually) be reached to manage these comprehensive data for secondary analysis at clinical cohort and population levels in a manner that is trusted by the public.

Using health technologies innovatively has no predictable end point. Technology is, however, only one element in the equation of 'effective, efficient and efficacious' care and treatment. In the mid-term, clinical decision making will still require a trusted clinical professional to be able to respond rapidly to unexpected circumstances that could have life or death consequences.

Science and Engineering

ASHOK BANERJI

In 1983, *Time* magazine featured the computer as *Machine of the Year*. In my opinion this was an understatement, judging by the extraordinary progress of computing that is currently being witnessed. Obviously, trying to envision the future of performance support and the role of computers in science and engineering is a very complicated task. I will therefore first refer to the 'tire tracks' diagram of different strands of computing research that illustrates time from concept to billion-dollar industry (Lazowska, 2008). Data management, graphics, processing power and networked applications are emerging as the four major strands. These will engineer the tools of scientific discovery amongst which computer simulation has proved one of the most important. Oliver Smithies (2008) – co-recipient of the 2007 Nobel Prize for Medicine – told an absorbing story of his research path and illustrated this with his lab notes. It highlights how the scientific enquiry flourished as a result of organised documentation, thoughtful reflections, collaborative interactions and computer simulations. Acknowledging the utility of computers, he stresses: 'Devising these and other simulations has helped me to uncover unexpected relationships and has stimulated ideas that I might not have had without this work.' (p. 226). Similarly, in the sphere of engineering applications, networked smart instrumentation with embedded intelligence is likely to lead to the solution of many performance problems. Self-diagnostic instruments and controls can take over monitoring functions, freeing engineers from lower-level activities and allowing them to give more attention to higher-order tasks. Indeed, in many areas of science and engineering, a transformation is now underway. This involves a movement away from the conventional 'manual' approach to knowledge creation towards its semi-automated discovery – by applying techniques such as data mining and machine learning to enormous volumes of experimental data. This often involves computationally intensive processes that usually require the application of grid computing methods (for further details, see *http://en.wikipedia.org/wiki/E-Science*). Undoubtedly, in many areas of human endeavour (in science and engineering, in particular) the role of computers will become that of a cognitive amplifier. This is likely to lead to an increasing cognitive bandwidth in relation to human performance. However, realising these innovations will depend on new system-development methodologies, based on a soft-computing approach incorporating the cognitive aspects of human decision making.

Business and Commerce

BARRY IP

Future developments in EPSS and Performance-Centred Systems (PCS) are predicted to play increasingly important and dynamic roles for the benefit of both businesses and their customers. The growing adoption of ubiquitous and mobile technologies opens up new ways for businesses to communicate, market and sell products to consumers. Concomitantly, consumers will benefit via the availability of new devices and tools with which information may be retrieved and used for a wide range of performance benefits which extend beyond traditional boundaries and expectations. In so doing, businesses will need to develop new strategies and approaches towards the effective use of new technologies such that users may obtain performance enhancements while also being protected against concerns surrounding personal privacy and security. These issues aside, EPSS or PCS may become an even more powerful facilitator, helping business and commerce to build increasingly accessible and user-centred applications which truly expand into the everyday lives of the public.

The Future of Electronic Performance Support in Corporate Settings

ERAN GAL AND PAUL VAN SCHAIK

In order to gaze into the future of electronic performance support in corporate settings it is first necessary to examine the past and address a simple question: what is electronic performance support? Humans have always trained to perform particular jobs. Nowadays many people consider classroom training as 'traditional training' due to the e-learning revolution that occurred in the 1980s. We were all astonished at the idea that learning can be just as effective when students and teachers are separated in time and place. This was the 'New Age' of learning, thus rendering the former method 'traditional'. However, learning a trade or a craft has a long history, long before classroom training became the most common method of learning in corporate settings. In earlier times, people would acquire job-related knowledge and skills by imitating experts and learning directly from them while performing the job-related tasks in an authentic work environment (see, for example, the MAPARI model that was described in Chapter 4). Nowadays this method is called on-the-job training or apprenticeship learning. This is perhaps the most natural learning method as far as job training is concerned.

From a historical perspective, electronic performance support can be seen as a learning method (that has evolved out of e-learning) and which offers the most natural method of acquiring a trade – similar to apprenticeship. In contemporary settings, apprenticeship is usually not performed directly through experts, as most organisations lack experts and an expert's available time is limited. Instead, technology allows an organisation to capture experts' knowledge and experience and then disseminate this across the enterprise. This expertise can be used to provide novice workers with what they need, when they most need it, in order to perform tasks at expert level. Small chunks of knowledge at the appropriate time can allow learning by doing.

From another perspective, when reading the EPSS literature and talking to its practitioners and scholars, a different vision of electronic performance support emerges. There are those who claim that electronic performance support is not a training method and – in fact – was never intended to be one. Electronic performance support is a performance support method that is aimed at productivity enhancement with as little training as possible. Some will even refer to it as 'anti-training'. Indeed, scholars and practitioners generally seem to agree that electronic performance support should cut training time, thus making electronic performance support an oxymoron as a training method: a training method that is aimed at eliminating training as much as possible.

In order to learn about the future of electronic performance support from this intriguing debate, it is first necessary to address another much broader issue: the relationship between training departments and Information Technology (IT) departments within corporations. As e-learning develops and expands in corporate learning settings, the relationship between IT departments and training departments is likely to become stronger and the differences between the two may become blurred. Currently, training departments rely heavily on learning-management systems, e-learning content development software, knowledge management systems and performance support applications – all created, maintained and further developed by IT departments. The future of this relationship may determine the future of electronic performance support in corporations. Training departments and IT departments are most likely to merge when training consists mostly of technology based-applications. Such new organisational departments will not be referred to as Training or IT but rather Human Performance, Workforce Readiness or Usability departments. In some enterprises, this change has all ready commenced but in most the process is in its early stages.

Electronic performance support is a current example of the change we are referring to in the future of corporations. An EPSS project is a co-production of training and IT departments and it blurs the responsibilities of each department in a particular enterprise. Thus we claim that electronic performance support will become an important and major part of learning and working programmes in corporations. In future, new electronic performance support technologies may not be called electronic performance support, but their purpose will remain the same: providing electronic performance support.

Arguably, the most natural way of learning occurs through the use of EPSS facilities. At the same time, the most natural combination of training and IT is found in EPSS facilities. The term EPSS, as coined by Gery (1989) about 20 years ago, used to refer to a learning method that allows working while learning. The future (and much of the present) of this method is better seen as a performance support method that allows better and faster task performance while enabling skill- and knowledge-acquisition. As long as technology is a part of most areas of our lives, organisations compete over market shares and people comprise their workforce, electronic performance support will remain relevant and important, no matter what name or form it may take.

Expert-Work Processes

CHRISTOPHER G. JENNINGS, ARTHUR E. KIRKPATRICK AND PEYVAND MOHSENI

Supporting expert work has always been the primary aim of computer technology. Early systems targeted a limited set of domains (primarily science, mathematics and military applications) and were concerned mainly with the direct computation of specific results that form part of a larger product. Still, Licklider (1960) already envisioned an expanded role for electronic support of expert work. He saw humans and computers combining their strengths in a symbiotic partnership that would involve computers in every stage of expert work, not just data processing. A revolutionary step towards this vision was marked by the Star Information System (Johnson et al., 1989): it aimed squarely at the domain of knowledge workers and expanded the scope of computer support to include the construction of the artefacts that present the product of expert work. Taking the next step – widening the scope of electronic support to include the entire process of expert work – may require a revolution as great as the one embodied in the Star.

A useful taxonomy of the wider expert work process is provided by Jones (1981), who divides it into three types of activities: divergence (the generation of possibilities), transformation (the reuse of solutions), and convergence (refining a solution into its final form). While typical contemporary applications support convergence well, they mostly ignore the other two processes. One focus of our work has been to provide a more equal balance of support for all three activities, while minimising, or even reducing, complexity in the user-interface. This focus is motivated in part by the precedent of the Star, which demonstrated how powerful the combination of a widened scope of activity and a carefully streamlined interface design can be.

When we consider the kinds of expert-support system that we would like to see in the future, the main feature that differentiates them from typical contemporary commercial applications is the future systems' greater support for alternatives. Although Jones's convergence can be modelled effectively in current systems as a sequence of edits performed on a single entity, systems that support divergence and transformation must model multiple, simultaneous alternative solutions. A defining feature of these future systems must therefore be support for alternatives. Currently, the research on providing this support is being pursued in many directions: finding ways to generate or discover new alternatives (for example, Kules, 2005; Stump et al., 2003), managing and navigating sets of alternatives (for example, Klemmer et al., 2002), finding effective computational models (for example, Woodbury et al., 1999) and presentational forms (for example, Jennings and Kirkpatrick, 2007) for alternatives, and providing ways to compare, select and combine alternatives (for example, Terry et al., 2004). Future electronic support systems for expert work will need to integrate many of these strands if they are to reach their full potential.

A Technical Perspective on the Future of Electronic Performance Support Systems

SJOERD DE VRIES

This contribution considers the future of electronic performance support from a more technical perspective. Bearing this in mind, I think that EPSS facilities will become more and more integrated into personal, social, mobile, networked, ambient, adaptive and service platforms. Some of the issues to consider are listed below:

- *Platforms.* The development of performance support services will become based on service-oriented architectures. This means that services can be placed as functions in existing systems or applications and still be maintained as stand-alone applications.
- *Adaptive.* The support is going to be there when needed, in a form that matches the context and devices and in a quality we consider at least as acceptable.
- *Services.* People will talk about embedded services instead of systems.

- *Personal and social.* These services will be characterised more and more as social media that support social networks, with users placed in the centre of this network. Therefore, aspects like social cues, social tagging and personal communication will be considered as basic features of these services.
- *Ambience.* EPS-services will be delivered more and more as embedded in other devices, such as mobile smartphones, e-books, touch-screen devices and laptops. An example is the approach taken by the designers of the *iPhone*, which enables the use of mobile Internet services as a stand-alone facility instead of being enabled by web browsers.
- *Mobile and networked.* Services will be delivered as mobile Internet services. An example is the help functionality available in current software programs. The help file itself is already a web site and that includes a help forum as an added support for finding answers to users' questions.

These technical developments are driven by the needs of both users and service deliverers. Users are becoming used to mobile environments and their social networks in order to find immediate answers to questions and to solve problems fast and reliably. Service deliverers need low-cost platforms that enable them to continuously improve the innovativeness and quality of their services. The perspective described here meets both needs.

New Approaches to Electronic Performance Support Systems Development and Use

PAUL VAN SCHAIK

One potential development is the use of Web 2.0 technology to produce electronic performance support in not-for-profit domains, in particular voluntary-sector organisations. Currently, support may not exist on the World Wide Web, may be difficult to find and/or use, or may not have been designed to ensure effective and efficient task performance. However, a structured approach, in particular the use of a Matrix-Aided Performance System (MAPS) (Hung and Chao, 2007), seems to hold great promise for EPSS facilities in these domains. As an example, consider Hung and Chao's *Behaviour Matrix*, a behaviour-management tool for school-age children with behavioural problems. Important features of this system are that it models a systematic process used by experts to solve various behavioural problems and that it provides a unified user-interface. One of the strengths of the MAPS concept is that it is based on Ausubel's (2000) instructional-design theoretical framework of advance organisers to produce an effective performance support tool, representing both non-recurrent skills and supporting knowledge. The same approach could be applied by voluntary-sector organisations in a range of domains, for example domestic violence, but enhanced by the use of Web 2.0 technology, in particular by making content editable by a community of domain experts. In this way, the knowledge to support people solving problems in a particular domain can be updated and enhanced continually, to the benefit of its users, for instance, police and other professionals, actual survivors, potential victims of domestic violence and other potential users of Internet sites with domestic-violence information (van Schaik, Radford and Hogg, under review).

An obstacle in the large-scale application of the MAPS approach in not-for-profit domains appears to be a lack of tools available to domain experts for building their own MAPS. The availability of Open Source Web 2.0 tools for this purpose would make the promise of MAPS possible. However, an editable Web-based EPSS requires a mechanism for editorial control to ensure, or at least promote, some degree of quality. Quality control should cover not only the accuracy of content, but also instructional design. The latter requires specialist skills in instructional design, but – where instructional designers are not available – support for this could be offered by an instructional-design EPSS within the theoretical framework (for example, Ausubel's advance organisers) on which the tools are based. There is no guarantee that one theoretical framework will suit all domains, but the use of advance organisers has produced at least two promising examples of a MAPS (Hung and Chao, 2007), although not (yet) deployed using Web 2.0 technology, and the applicability of frameworks to domains remains a matter for future research.

References

Ausubel, D.P. (2000). *The Acquisition and Retention of Knowledge: A Cognitive View*. Boston, MA: Kluwer.

Barker, P.G. (2008a). Using Weblogs and Wikis to Enhance Human Performance. In C.J. Bonk, M.M. Lee and T. Reynolds (eds), *Proceedings of the E-Learn 2008 World Conference on E-Learning in Corporate, Government, Healthcare and Higher Education* (pp. 581–588). Chesapeake, VA: Association for the Advancement of Computing in Education.

Barker, P.G. (2008b). *Using Technology to Augment Human Ability*. Keynote Lecture presented at the TELearn 2008 International Conference, Hanoi City, Vietnam. Available online at: *http://www. scm.tees.ac.uk/users/u0000499/TELearn%202008/*.

Barker, P.G. (2009). *Digital Knowledge Management for All*. Keynote presented at the Silesian Moodle Moot Conference, Celadna, Czech Republic, November 2009. Available online at: *http://www. scm.tees.ac.uk/users/u0000499/DKM2009/DKMForAll.pdf/* [Accessed on 11th February, 2009].

Gery, G. (1989). *Electronic Performance Support Systems. How and Why to Remake the Workplace Through the Strategic Application of Technology*. Boston, MA: Weingarten Publications.

Hung, W.-C. and Chao, C.-A. (2007). Integrating Advance Organizers and Multidimensional Information Display in Electronic Performance Support Systems. *Innovations in Education and Teaching International*, 44(2), 181–198.

Jennings, C.G. and Kirkpatrick A.E. (2007). Design as Traversal and Consequences: An Exploration Tool for Experimental Designs. In C.G. Healy and E. Lank (eds), *Graphics Interface 2007* (pp. 79–86). Wellesley, MA: A K Peters.

Johnson, J., Roberts, T.L., Verplank, W., Smith, D.C., Irby, C.H., Beard, M. and Mackey, K. (1989). The Xerox Star: A Retrospective. *IEEE Computer*, 22(9), 11–29.

Jones, C.J. (1981). *Design Methods: Seeds of Human Futures* (2nd edn). Hoboken, NJ: John Wiley.

Klemmer, S., Thomsen, M., Phelps-Goodman, E., Lee, R. and Landay, J.A. (2002). Where do Web Sites Come From? Capturing and Interacting with Design History. In *Proceedings of the SIGCHI Conference on Human Factors in Computing Systems* (pp. 1–8). New York, NY: ACM Press.

Kules, B. (2005). Supporting Creativity with Search Tools. In *NSF Workshop Report on Creativity Support Tools*. Washington, DC. Retrieved December 14, 2006, from *http://www.cs.umd.edu/hcil/CST*.

Laurillard, D. (2008). *Digital Technologies and Their Role in Achieving Our Ambitions for Education.* Inaugural Lecture, 26th February, 2008. London, UK: Institute of Education, University of London.

Lazowska, E. (2008). Viewpoint: Envisioning the Future of Computing Research. *Communications of the ACM*, 51(8), 28–30.

Lebedev, M.A. and Nicolelis, M.A. (2006). Brain-machine Interfaces: Past, Present and Future. *Trends in Neuroscience*, 29(9), 536–546.

Licklider, J. (1960). Man-computer Symbiosis. *IRE Transactions of Human Factors in Electronics*, HFE-1(1), 4–11.

Lyman, P. and Varian, H.R. (2003). *How Much Information?* Available online at: *http://www2.sims.berkeley.edu/research/projects/how-much-info-2003/*. [Accessed on 9th February, 2009].

Rosenfeld, L. and Morville, P. (2002). *Information Architecture for the World Wide Web* (2nd edn). Sebastopol, CA: O'Reilly.

Schaik, P. van, Radford, J. and Hogg, L. (under review). The Acceptance of Internet Sites with Domestic-violence Information.

Smithies, O. (2008). Turning Pages. Nobel Lecture, December 7, 2007. In: K. Grandin (ed.), *The Nobel Prizes 2007* (pp, 209–230). Stockholm: The Nobel Foundation. Available online at: *http://nobelprize.org/nobel_prizes/medicine/laureates/2007/smithies_lecture.pdf*. [Accessed on: 3rd February, 2009].

Stump, G.M., Yukish, M., Simpson, T.W. and Harris, E.N. (2003). Design Space Visualization and its Application to a Design by Shopping Paradigm. In *Proceedings of ASME 2002 Design Engineering Technical Conferences*, Vol. 2, pp. 795–804.

Terry, M., Mynatt, E.D., Nakakoji, K. and Yamamoto, Y. (2004). Variation in Element and Action: Simultaneous Development of Alternative Solutions. In: *CHI 2004* (pp. 711–718). New York: ACM Press.

Woodbury, R.F., Burrow, A.L., Datta, S. and Chang, T.W. (1999). Typed Feature Structures in Design Space Exploration. *Artificial Intelligence in Engineering Design, Analysis and Manufacturing*, 13(4), 287–302.

Index

If you have found this resource useful you may be interested in other titles from Gower

Developing Student Support Groups
Rosie Bingham and Jaquie Daniels
A4 Paperback: 978-0-566-08117-0

70 Activities for Tutor Groups
Peter Davies
A4 Paperback: 978-0-566-08000-5

The Management of a Student Research Project
John A Sharp, John Peters and Keith Howard
Paperback: 978-0-566-08490-4

Winning Research Funding
Abby Day Peters
Paperback: 978-0-566-08459-1

How to Get Research Published in Journals
Abby Day
Paperback: 978-0-566-08815-5

Blended Learning and Online Tutoring 2nd Edition
Janet Macdonald
Paperback: 978-0-566-08841-4

Teaching and Learning at Business Schools
Pär Mårtensson, Magnus Bild and Kristina Nilsson
Hardback: 978-0-566-08820-9

Visit **www.gowerpublishing.com** and

- search the entire catalogue of Gower books in print
- order titles online at 10% discount
- take advantage of special offers
- sign up for our monthly e-mail update service
- download free sample chapters from all recent titles
- download or order our catalogue

If you have found this resource useful you may be interested in other titles from Gower

Cultural Differences and Improving Performance
Bryan Hopkins
Hardback: 978-0-566-08907-7

Handbook of Work-based Learning
Ian Cunningham, Graham Dawes and Ben Bennett
Hardback: 978-0-566-08634-2

Informal Learning:
A New Model for Making Sense of Experience
Lloyd Davies
Hardback: 978-0-566-08857-5

Improving Learning Transfer:
A Guide to Getting More Out of What You Put Into Your Training
Cyril Kirwan
Hardback: 978-0-566-08844-5

An Adventure in Service-Learning:
Developing Knowledge, Values and Responsibility
Anto T. Kerins
Hardback: 978-0-566-08894-0

The Transfer of Learning:
Participants' Perspectives of Adult Education and Training
Sarah Leberman, Lex McDonald and Stephanie Doyle
Hardback: 978-0-566-08734-9

Visit **www.gowerpublishing.com** and

- search the entire catalogue of Gower books in print
- order titles online at 10% discount
- take advantage of special offers
- sign up for our monthly e-mail update service
- download free sample chapters from all recent titles
- download or order our catalogue

For Product Safety Concerns and Information please contact our
EU representative GPSR@taylorandfrancis.com, Taylor & Francis
Verlag GmbH, Kaufmannstraße 31, 60327 Mannheim, Germany